THE SHEER *VERISIMILITUDE* OF IT... WHEN DID THEY GET SO *GOOD*?!
WHY, THE *HAIR ALONE* IS?!!
HMMM~
IT *SO-O-O* IS OVER FOR HIM.
NINGEN SHIKKAKU... "GOING THRU THE MOTIONS."

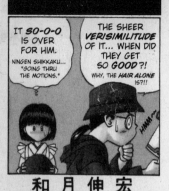

和月伸宏

NOBUHIRO WATSUKI

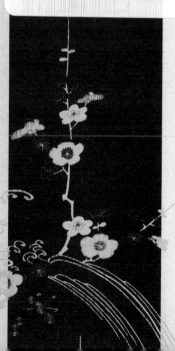

ACTION DOLL

I DID IT, I FINALLY DID IT—A SHÔJO (FEMALE-BODY) ACTION FIGURE! THO' I SWORE I NEVER WOULD, NAKORURU—RIMURURU—POSABLE JOINTS—O, THE POSABLE JOINTS!! "NOBUHIRO WATSUKI" HAS FOUND HIMSELF HAVING TO CATCH 'EM ALL, OLD SCHOOL POKEMON-STYLE! IF THEY WERE TO RELEASE A "TWO-PLAYER" VERSION OF NAKO/RIMU, NOW...OH, MAN. OHMANOHMANOHMAN!!

ACTION DOLLS, THOUGH... WAIT!! THIS ISN'T THE "NEW DIRECTION" I TALKED ABOUT LAST TIME, IS IT?! BECAUSE, IF IT WERE, THAT WOULD BE JUST TOO SAD....

Rurouni Kenshin, which has found fans not only in Japan but around the world, first made its appearance in 1992, as an original short story in ***Weekly Shonen Jump Special***. Later rewritten and published as a regular, continuing ***Jump*** series in 1994, ***Rurouni Kenshin*** ended serialization in 1999 but continued in popularity, as evidenced by the 2000 publication of ***Yahiko no Sakabatô*** ("Yahiko's Reversed-Edge Sword") in ***Weekly Shonen Jump***. His most current work, ***Busô Renkin*** ("Armored Alchemist"), began publication in June 2003, also in ***Jump***.

RUROUNI KENSHIN
VOL. 18: DO YOU STILL BEAR THE SCAR?
The SHONEN JUMP Graphic Novel Edition

STORY AND ART BY
NOBUHIRO WATSUKI

English Adaptation/Gerard Jones
Translation/Kenichiro Yagi
Touch-Up Art & Lettering/Steve Dutro
Design/Matt Hinrichs
Editor/G2 Pro

Supervising Editor/Kit Fox
Managing Editor/Elizabeth Kawasaki
Director of Production/Noboru Watanabe
Vice President of Publishing/Alvin Lu
Executive Vice President & Editor in Chief/Yumi Hoashi
Sr. Director of Acquisitions/Rika Inouye
Vice President of Sales & Marketing/Liza Coppola
Publisher/Hyoe Narita

Printed in the U.S.A.

Published by VIZ Media, LLC
P.O. Box 77010
San Francisco, CA 94107

SHONEN JUMP Graphic Novel Edition
10 9 8 7 6 5 4 3 2 1
First printing, August 2005

www.viz.com

THE WORLD'S
MOST POPULAR MANGA

SHONEN JUMP
GRAPHIC NOVEL
www.shonenjump.com

SHONEN JUMP GRAPHIC NOVEL

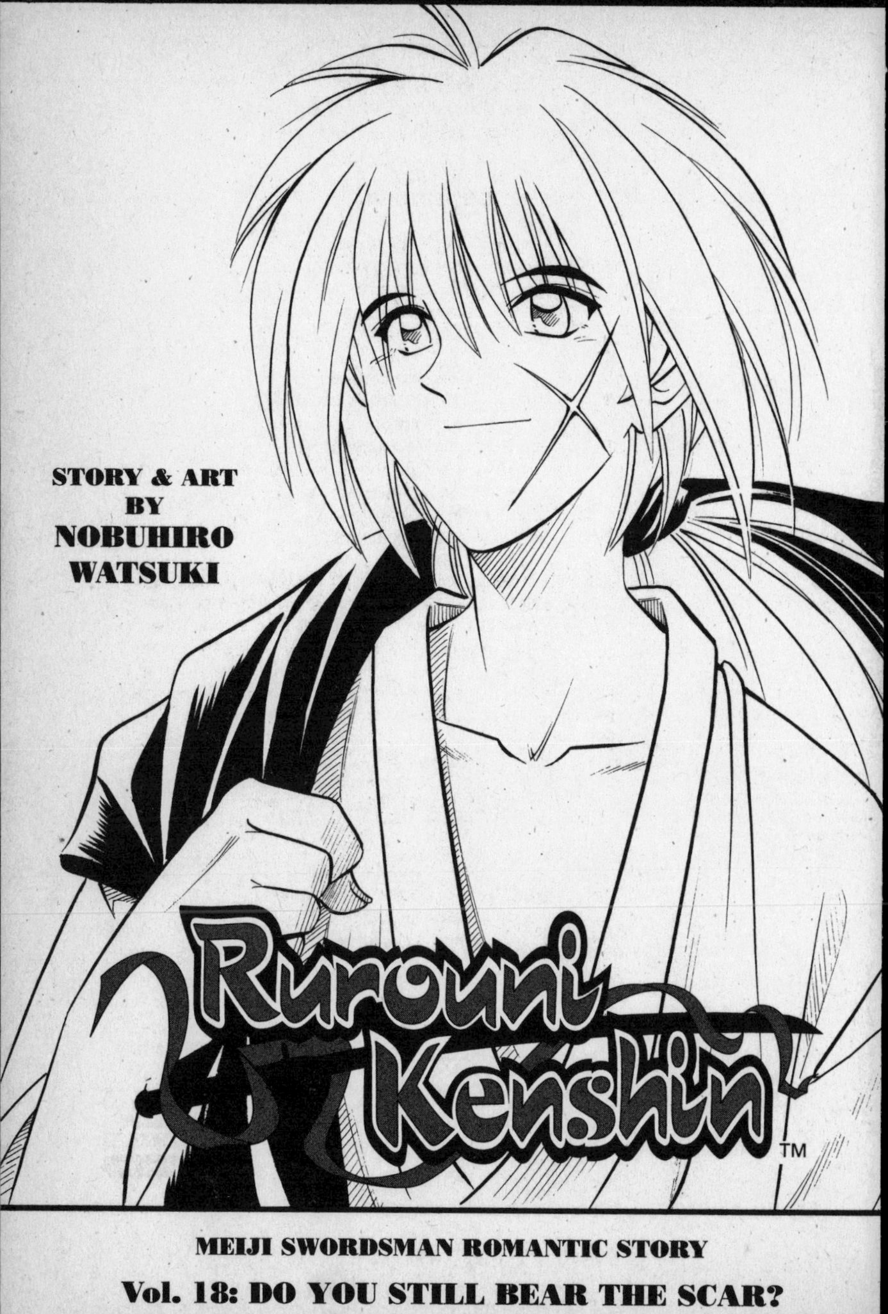

STORY & ART
BY
NOBUHIRO
WATSUKI

Rurouni Kenshin™

MEIJI SWORDSMAN ROMANTIC STORY

Vol. 18: DO YOU STILL BEAR THE SCAR?

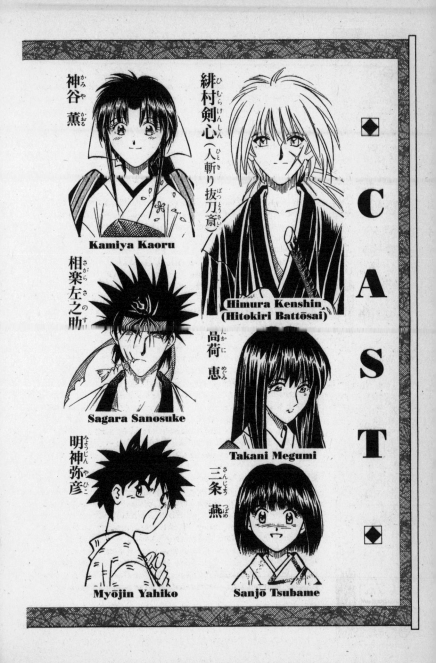

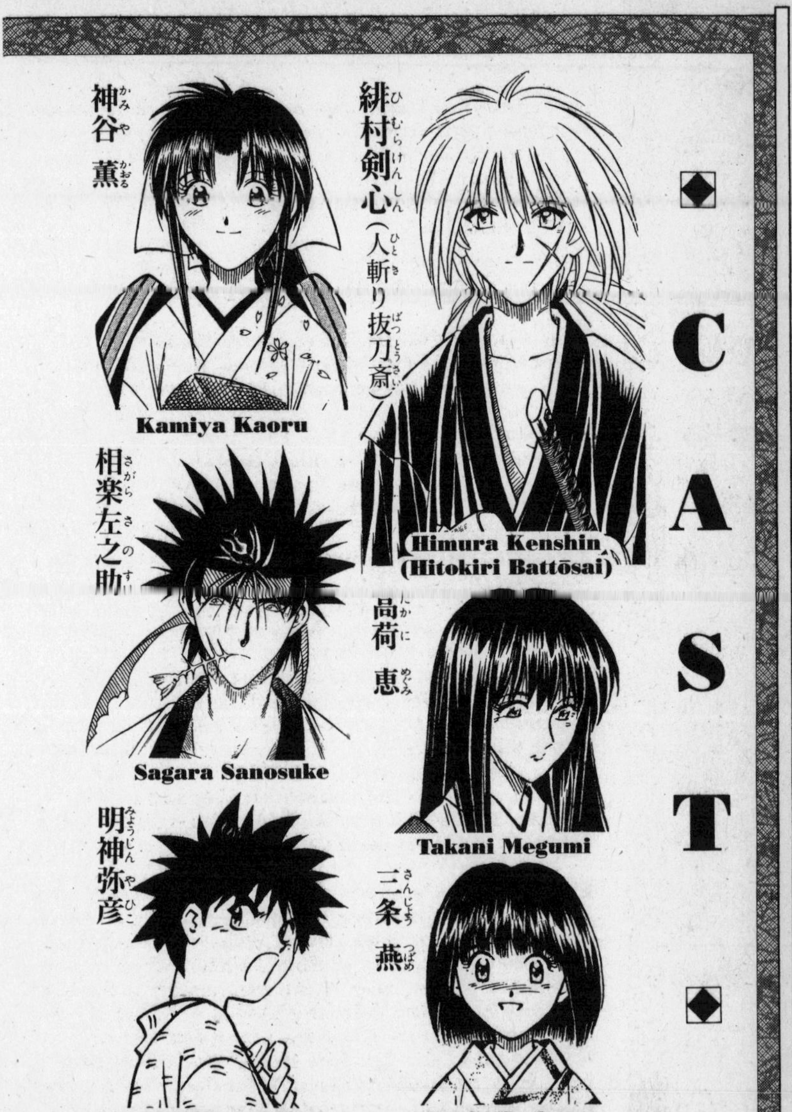
CAST
緋村剣心（人斬り抜刀斎）
Himura Kenshin (Hitokiri Battōsai)
高荷 恵
Takani Megumi
三条 燕
Sanjō Tsubame
神谷 薫
Kamiya Kaoru
相楽左之助
Sagara Sanosuke
明神弥彦
Myōjin Yahiko

Once he was *hitokiri*, an assassin, called Battōsai. His name was legend among the pro-Imperialist or "patriot" warriors who launched the Meiji Era. Now, Himura Kenshin is *rurouni*, a wanderer, and carries a reversed-edge *sakabatō* to prohibit himself from killing.

THUS FAR

Kenshin has journeyed to Kyoto to block the machinations of Shishio Makoto, the man who took Kenshin's place as *hitokiri*, a government-sanctioned slayer of men. In a duel with Sōjirō, one of the madman Shishio's *Juppongatana* "Ten Sword" assassins, Kenshin's former blade is broken and a new one is acquired—"Shin'uchi," a *sakabatō* like the first.

Newly armed (and after an edge-of-death battle with his former *Hiten Mitsurugi* master, Hiko Seijūrō), Kenshin joins up with Sanosuke and Saitō so that they may foil the plans of Shishio to burn down Kyoto and attack Tokyo by cannon. Arriving at Shishio's lair at last, the three are met by Shishio's three best: "Bright King" Anji, "Blind Sword" Usui, and the ever-smiling Sōjirō. After fierce battles, Anji is defeated by Sanosuke, and Usui dies against Saitō. Sōjirō, defeated by Kenshin despite the latter's vow never to kill, decides he must leave Shishio's side and seek the truth on his own terms.

Finally Kenshin reaches the "Infernal Hall" and challenges its madman owner, beginning a terrible battle in which Yumi dies at Shishio's hand, and the overheated body of Shishio himself ignites and disappears into flame. A month goes by, Kenshin's wounds heal, and drinking binges occur daily at Shirobeko, where everyone stays during the rebuilding of Aoi-Ya. Just then, "Sword Hunter" Chō, now an intelligence officer, drops by and tells of the fates of the remaining *Juppongatana*....

CONTENTS

RUROUNI KENSHIN
Meiji Swordsman Romantic Story
BOOK EIGHTEEN: DO YOU STILL BEAR THE SCAR?

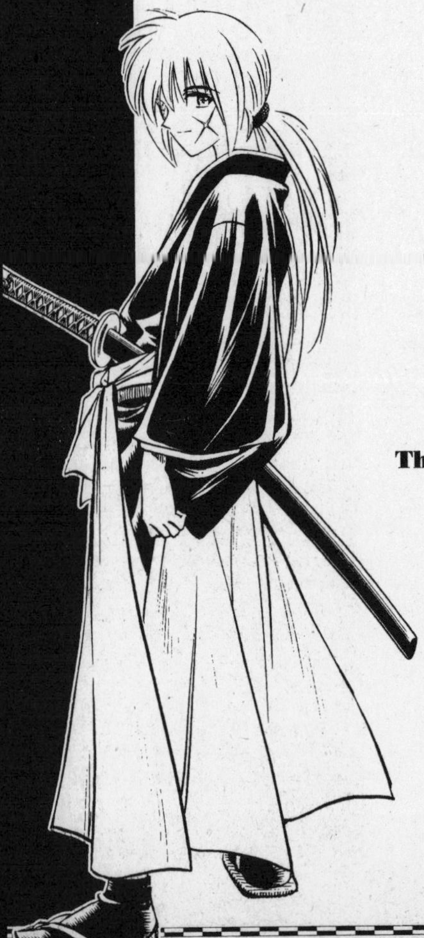

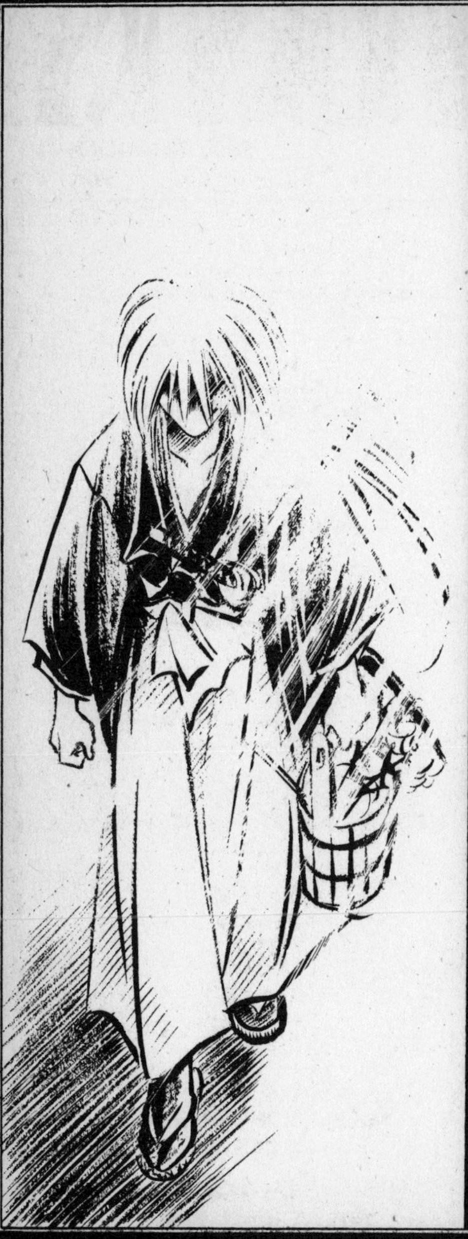

ACT 149
Kyoto Epilogue
Early Summer Morning

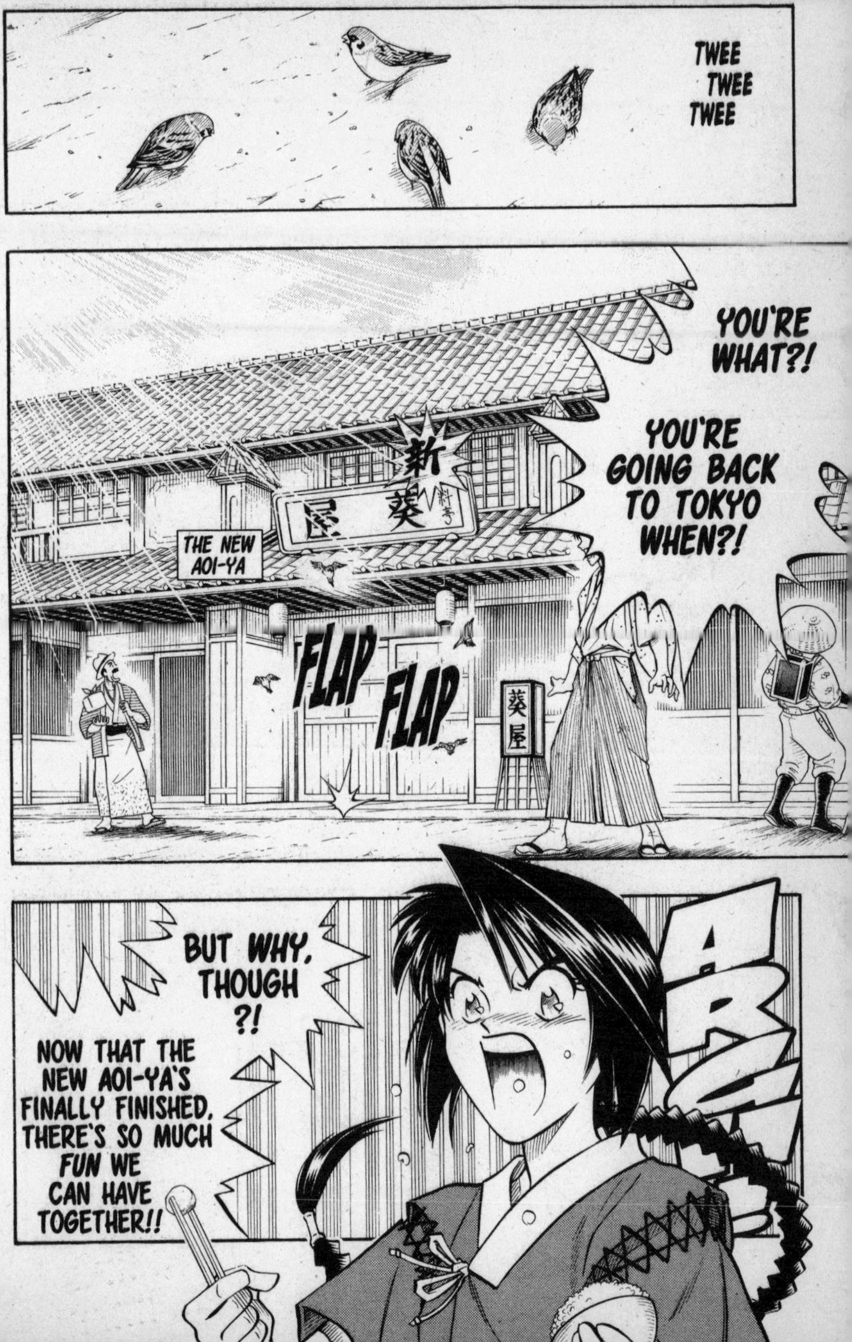

TWEE TWEE TWEE
YOU'RE WHAT?!
YOU'RE GOING BACK TO TOKYO WHEN?!
新
葵屋
料亭
THE NEW AOI-YA
FLAP FLAP
葵屋
BUT WHY, THOUGH?!
NOW THAT THE NEW AOI-YA'S FINALLY FINISHED, THERE'S SO MUCH FUN WE CAN HAVE TOGETHER!!

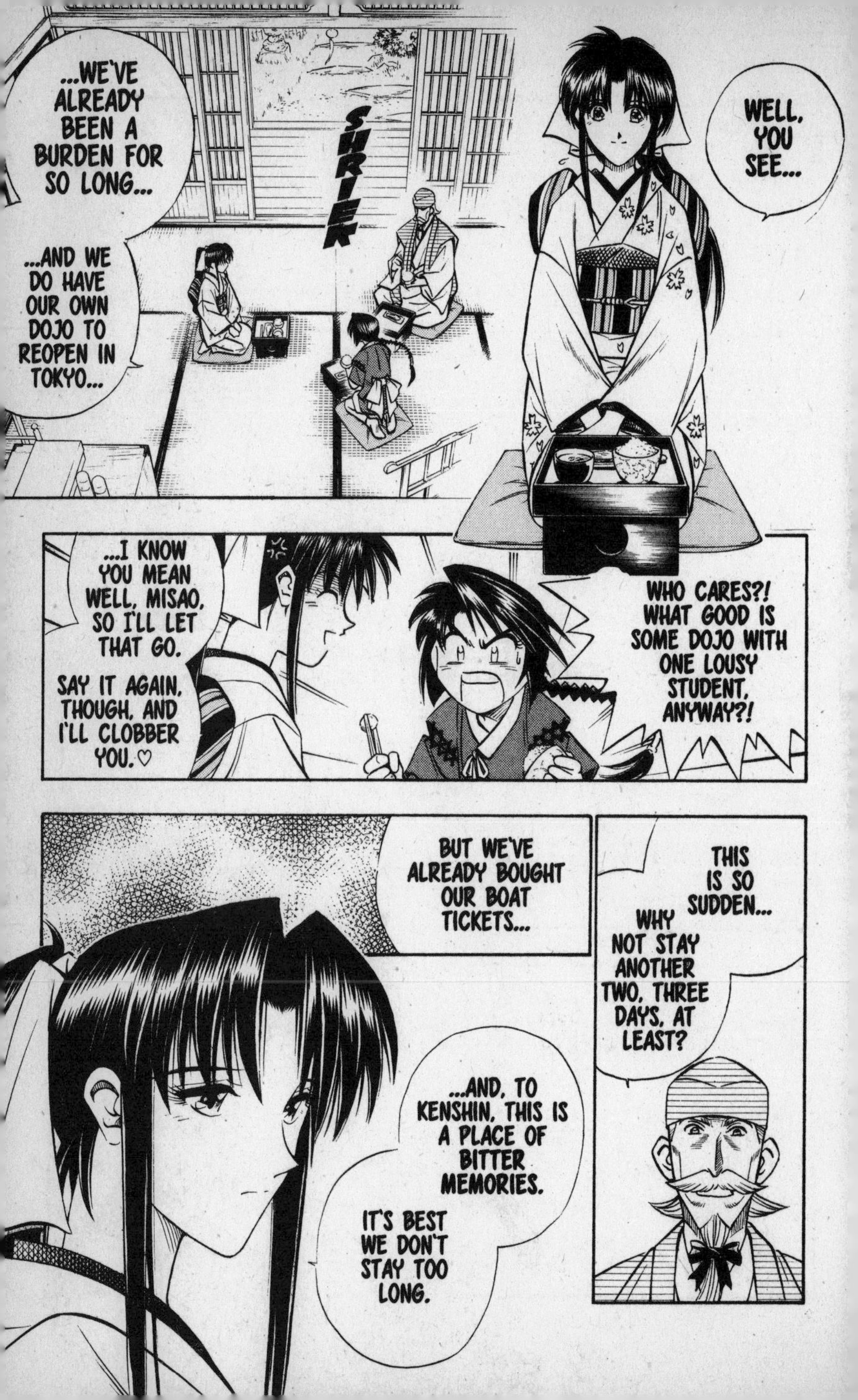
WELL, YOU SEE...
...WE'VE ALREADY BEEN A BURDEN FOR SO LONG...
SHRIEK
...AND WE DO HAVE OUR OWN DOJO TO REOPEN IN TOKYO...
WHO CARES?! WHAT GOOD IS SOME DOJO WITH ONE LOUSY STUDENT, ANYWAY?!
...I KNOW YOU MEAN WELL, MISAO, SO I'LL LET THAT GO.
SAY IT AGAIN, THOUGH, AND I'LL CLOBBER YOU.♡
THIS IS SO SUDDEN...
WHY NOT STAY ANOTHER TWO, THREE DAYS, AT LEAST?
BUT WE'VE ALREADY BOUGHT OUR BOAT TICKETS...
...AND, TO KENSHIN, THIS IS A PLACE OF BITTER MEMORIES.
IT'S BEST WE DON'T STAY TOO LONG.

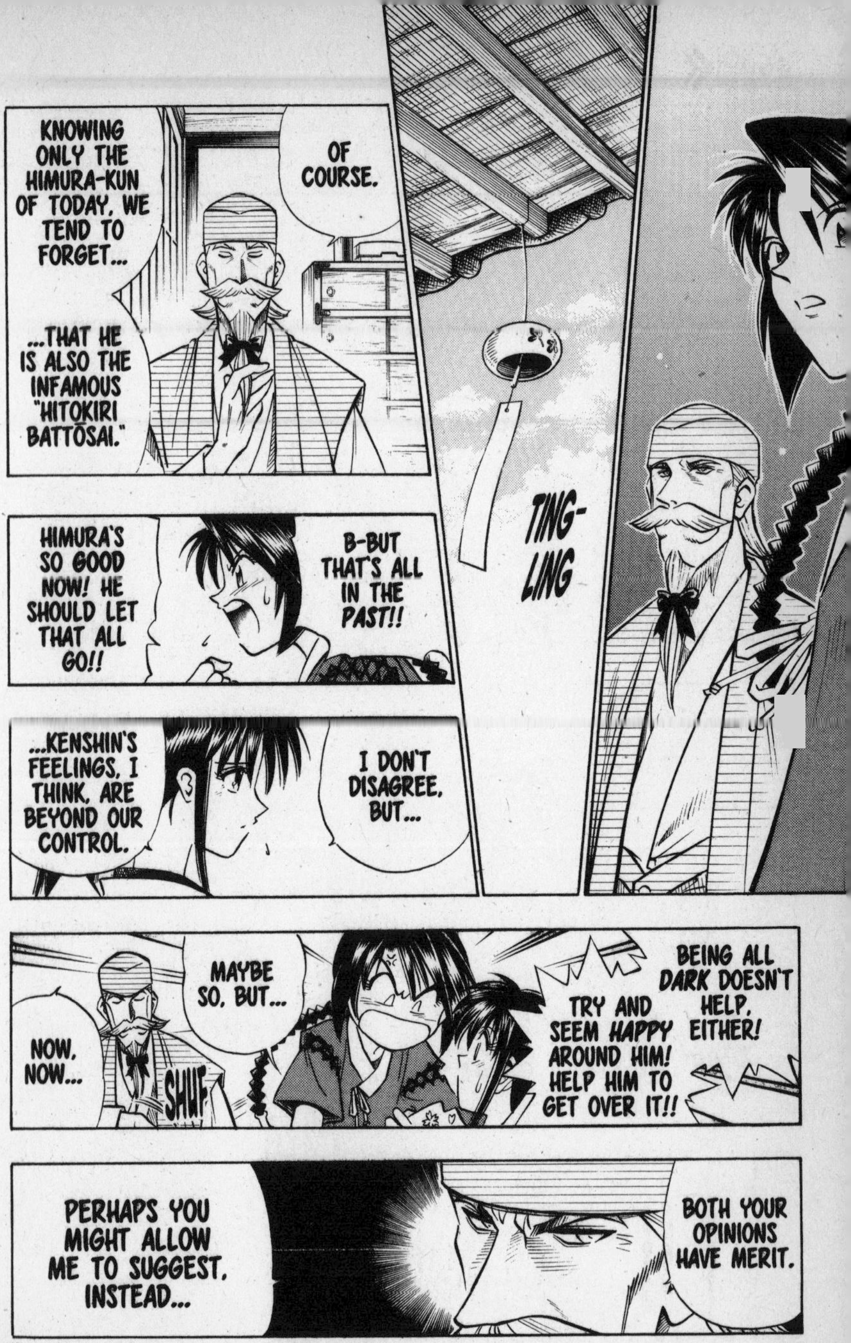
TING-LING
OF COURSE.
KNOWING ONLY THE HIMURA-KUN OF TODAY, WE TEND TO FORGET...
...THAT HE IS ALSO THE INFAMOUS "HITOKIRI BATTŌSAI."
B-BUT THAT'S ALL IN THE PAST!!
HIMURA'S SO GOOD NOW! HE SHOULD LET THAT ALL GO!!
I DON'T DISAGREE, BUT...
...KENSHIN'S FEELINGS, I THINK, ARE BEYOND OUR CONTROL.
BEING ALL DARK DOESN'T HELP, EITHER!
TRY AND SEEM HAPPY AROUND HIM! HELP HIM TO GET OVER IT!!
MAYBE SO, BUT...
SHUF
NOW, NOW...
BOTH YOUR OPINIONS HAVE MERIT.
PERHAPS YOU MIGHT ALLOW ME TO SUGGEST, INSTEAD...

READ THIS WAY

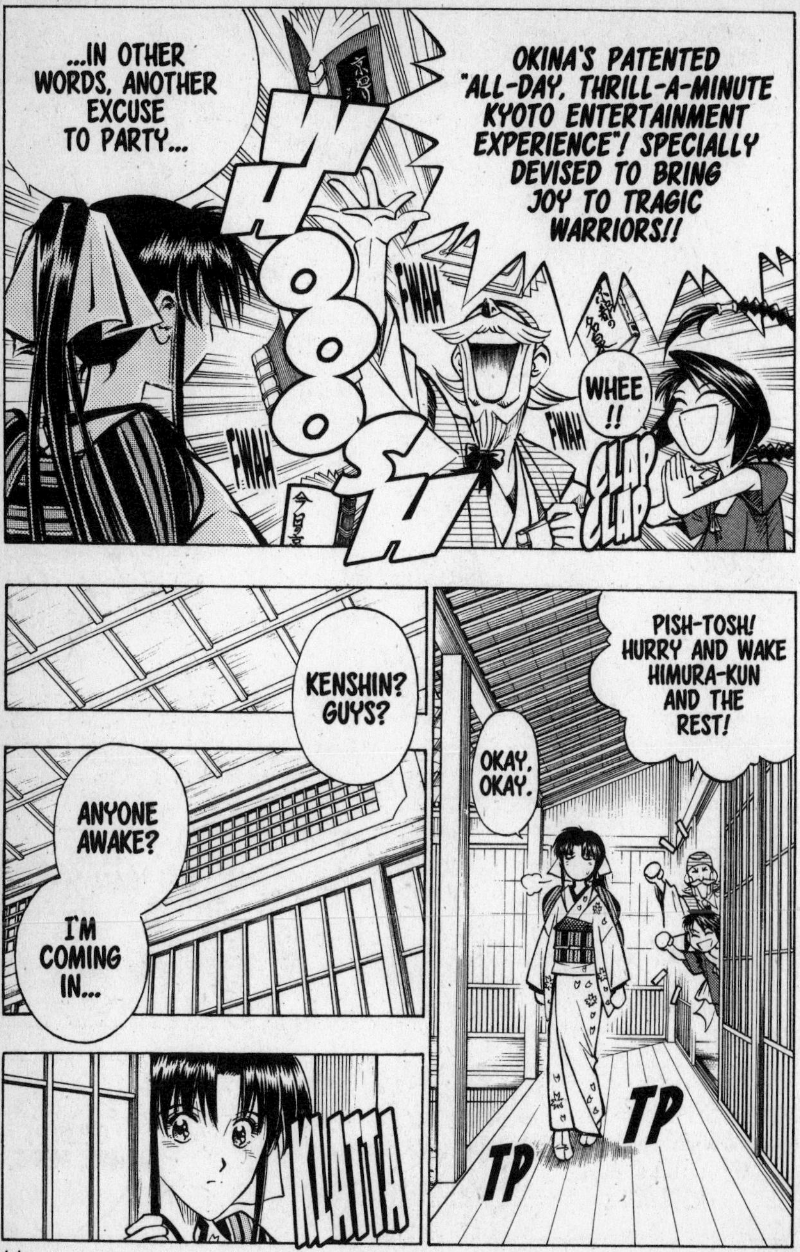
OKINA'S PATENTED "ALL-DAY, THRILL-A-MINUTE KYOTO ENTERTAINMENT EXPERIENCE"! SPECIALLY DEVISED TO BRING JOY TO TRAGIC WARRIORS!!
WHOOSH
FWAH
WHEE !!
FWAH
CLAP CLAP
FWAH
...IN OTHER WORDS, ANOTHER EXCUSE TO PARTY...
PISH-TOSH! HURRY AND WAKE HIMURA-KUN AND THE REST!
OKAY, OKAY.
TP
TP
KENSHIN? GUYS?
ANYONE AWAKE?
I'M COMING IN...
KLATTA

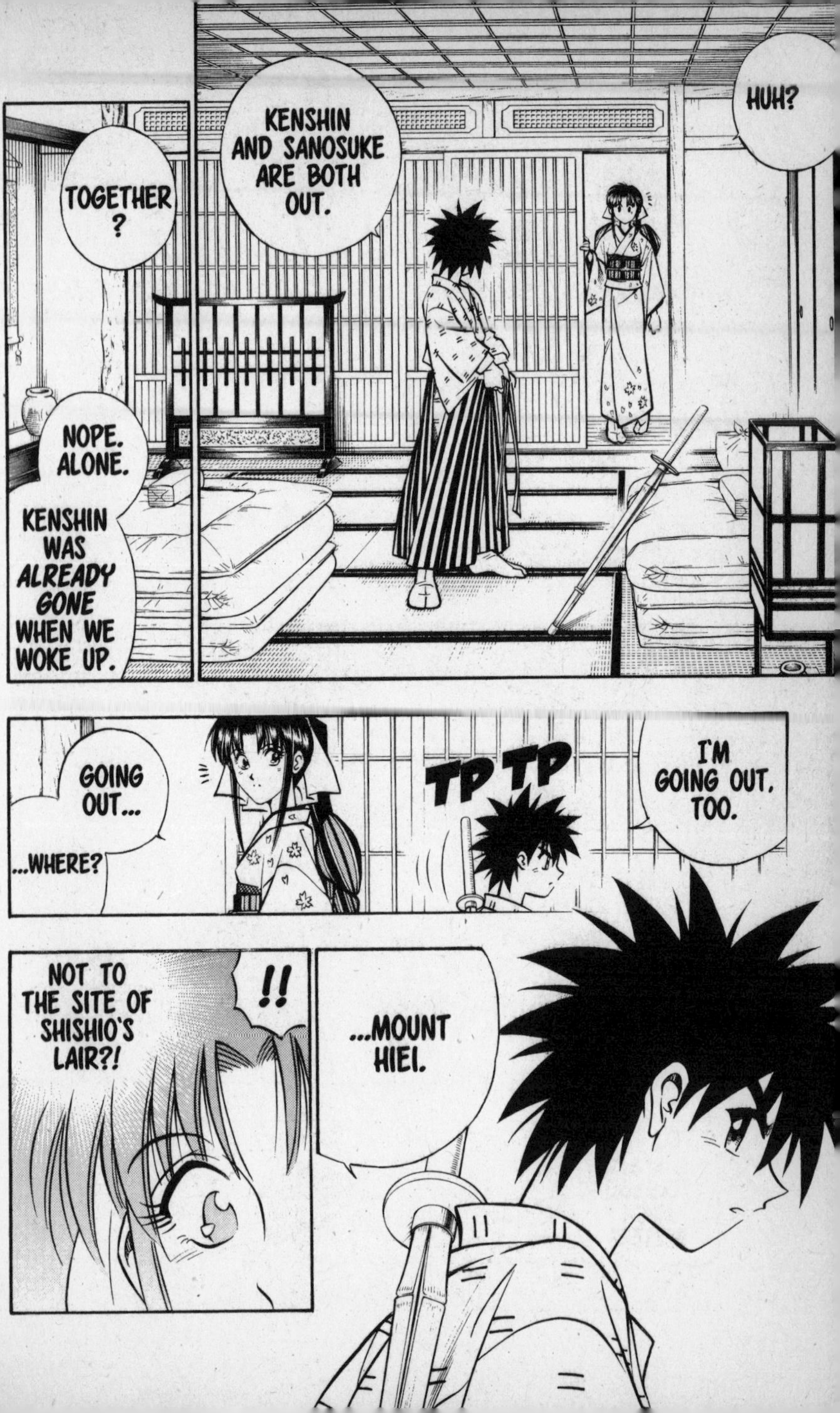
HUH?
KENSHIN AND SANOSUKE ARE BOTH OUT.
TOGETHER?
NOPE. ALONE.
KENSHIN WAS ALREADY GONE WHEN WE WOKE UP.
I'M GOING OUT, TOO.
TP TP
GOING OUT...
...WHERE?
...MOUNT HIEI.
!!
NOT TO THE SITE OF SHISHIO'S LAIR?!

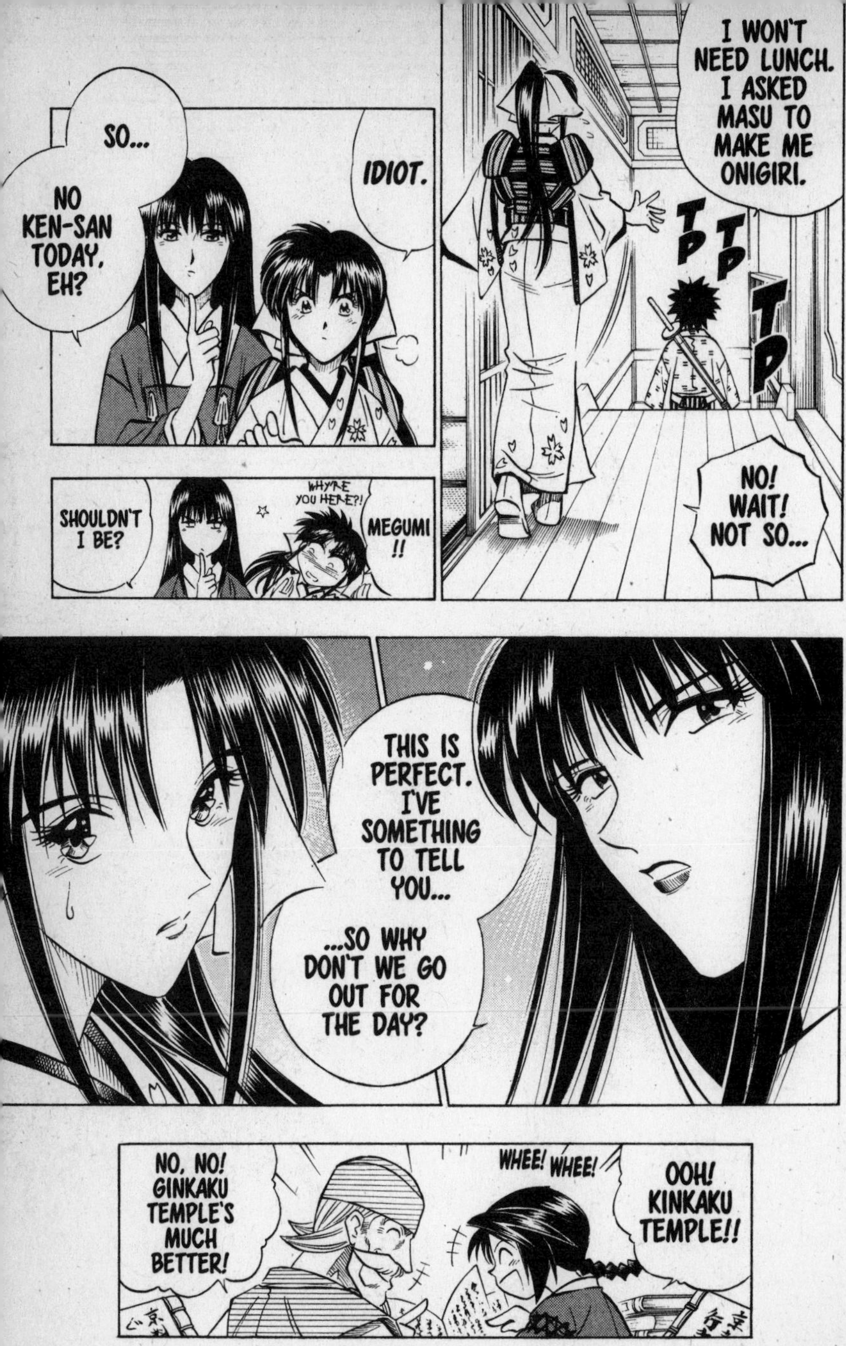
I WON'T NEED LUNCH. I ASKED MASU TO MAKE ME ONIGIRI.
TP TP TP
NO! WAIT! NOT SO...
IDIOT.
SO... NO KEN-SAN TODAY, EH?
MEGUMI!!
WHY'RE YOU HERE?!
SHOULDN'T I BE?
THIS IS PERFECT. I'VE SOMETHING TO TELL YOU...
...SO WHY DON'T WE GO OUT FOR THE DAY?
OOH! KINKAKU TEMPLE!!
WHEE! WHEE!
NO, NO! GINKAKU TEMPLE'S MUCH BETTER!

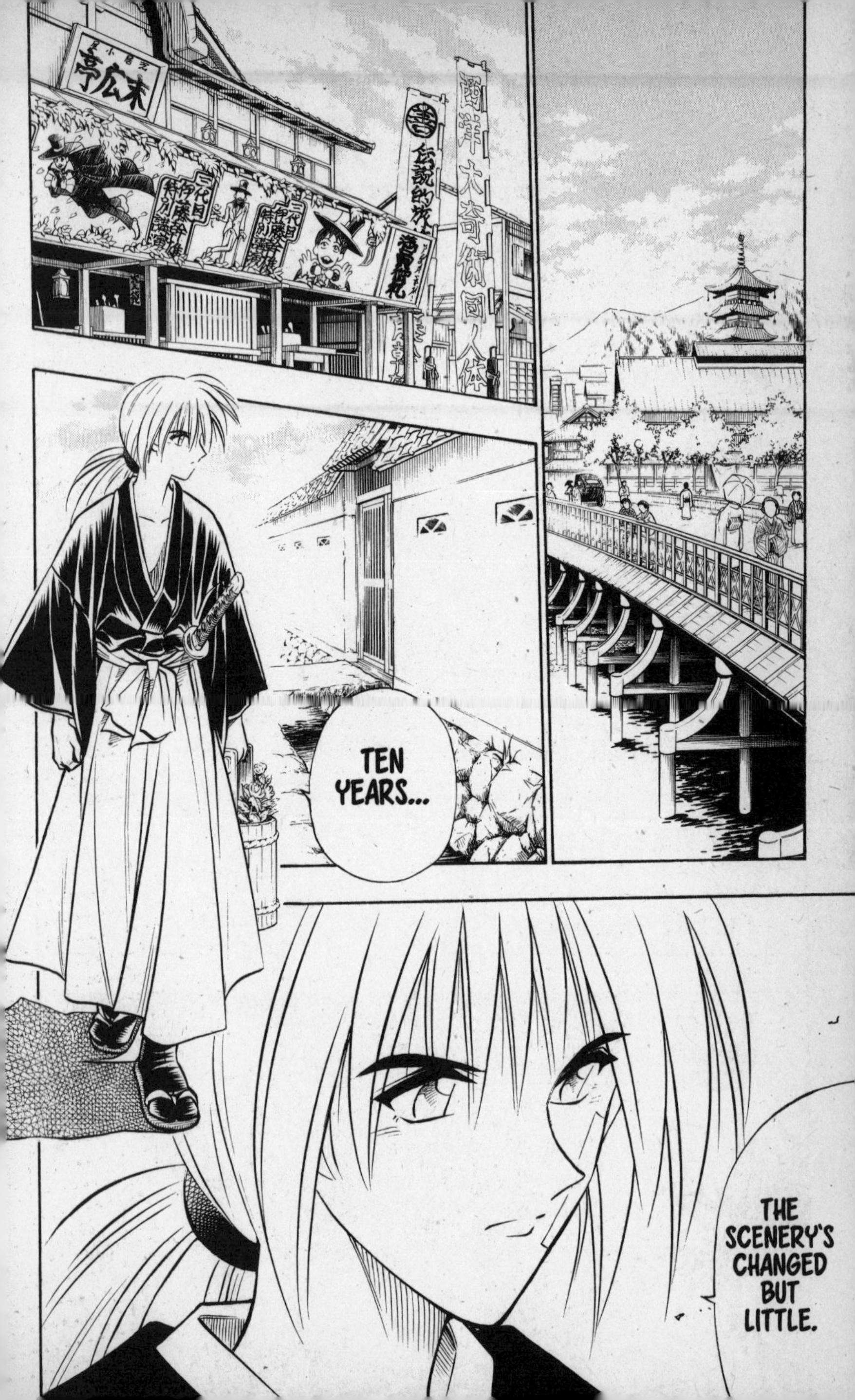
TEN YEARS...
THE SCENERY'S CHANGED BUT LITTLE.

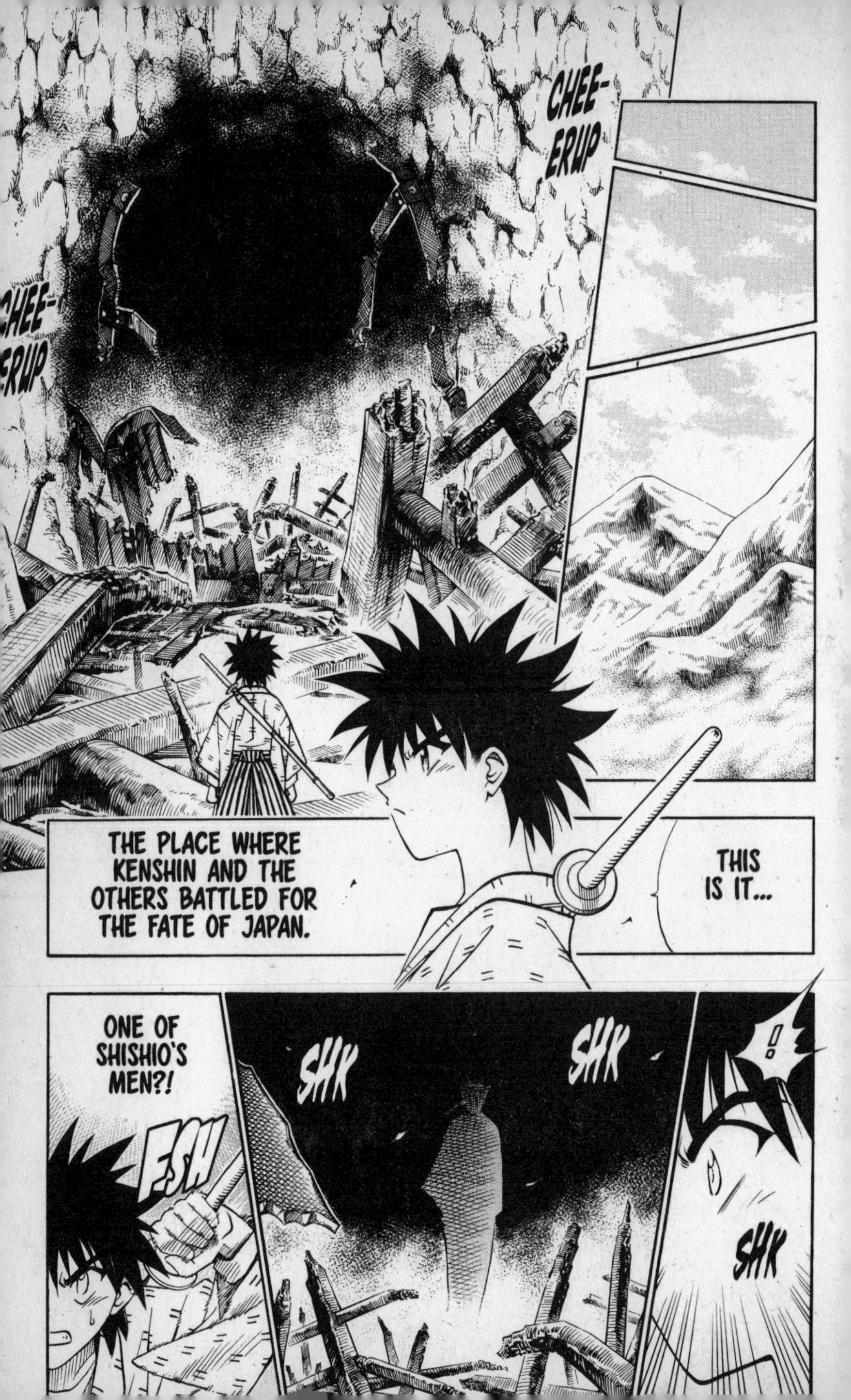
CHEE-ERUP
CHEE-ERUP
THIS IS IT...
THE PLACE WHERE KENSHIN AND THE OTHERS BATTLED FOR THE FATE OF JAPAN.
!
SHK
SHK
SHK
ONE OF SHISHIO'S MEN?!
F-SH

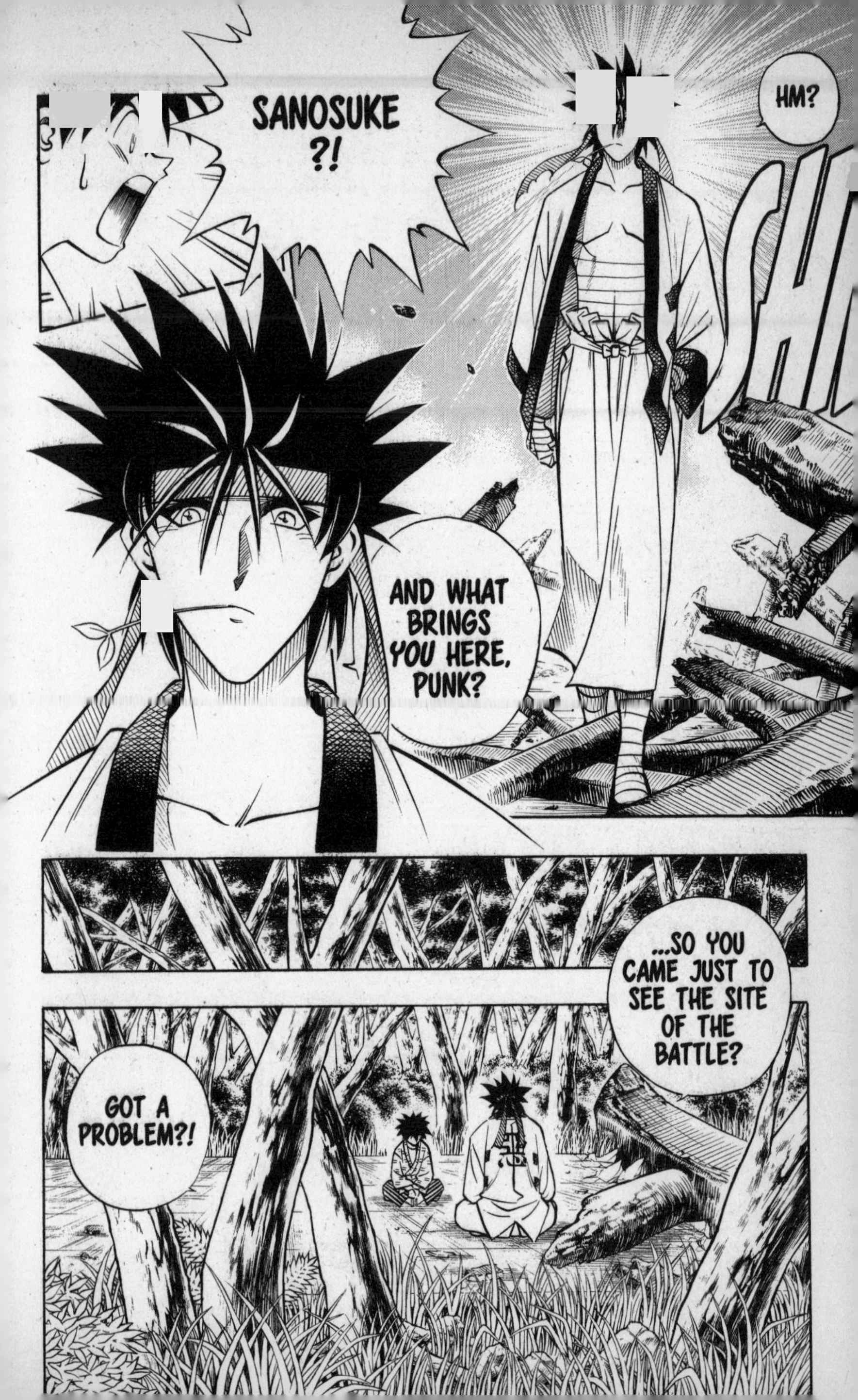
HM?
SANOSUKE ?!
AND WHAT BRINGS YOU HERE, PUNK?
...SO YOU CAME JUST TO SEE THE SITE OF THE BATTLE?
GOT A PROBLEM?!

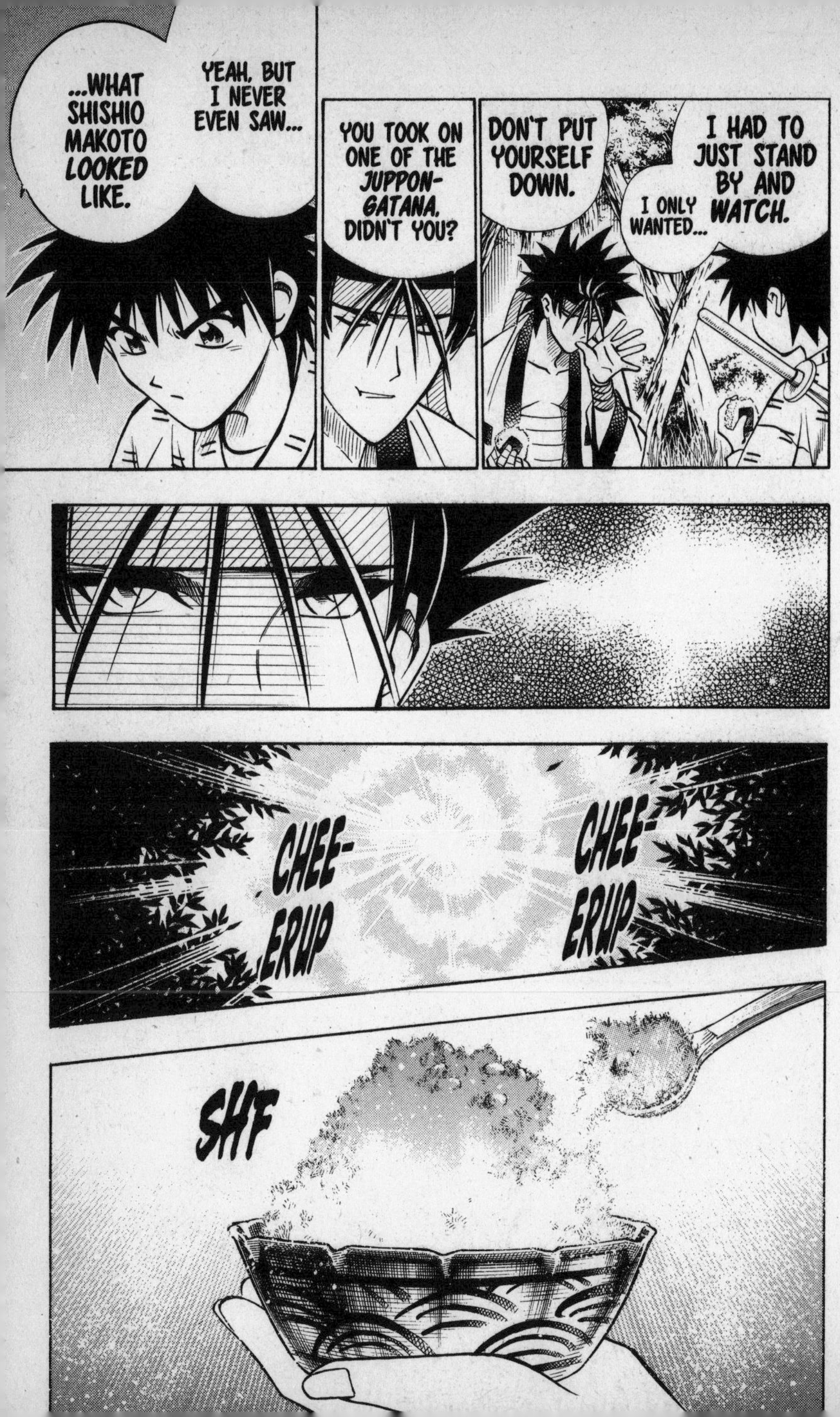
I HAD TO JUST STAND BY AND WATCH.
I ONLY WANTED...
DON'T PUT YOURSELF DOWN.
YOU TOOK ON ONE OF THE JUPPON-GATANA, DIDN'T YOU?
YEAH, BUT I NEVER EVEN SAW...
...WHAT SHISHIO MAKOTO LOOKED LIKE.
CHEE-ERUP
CHEE-ERUP
SHF

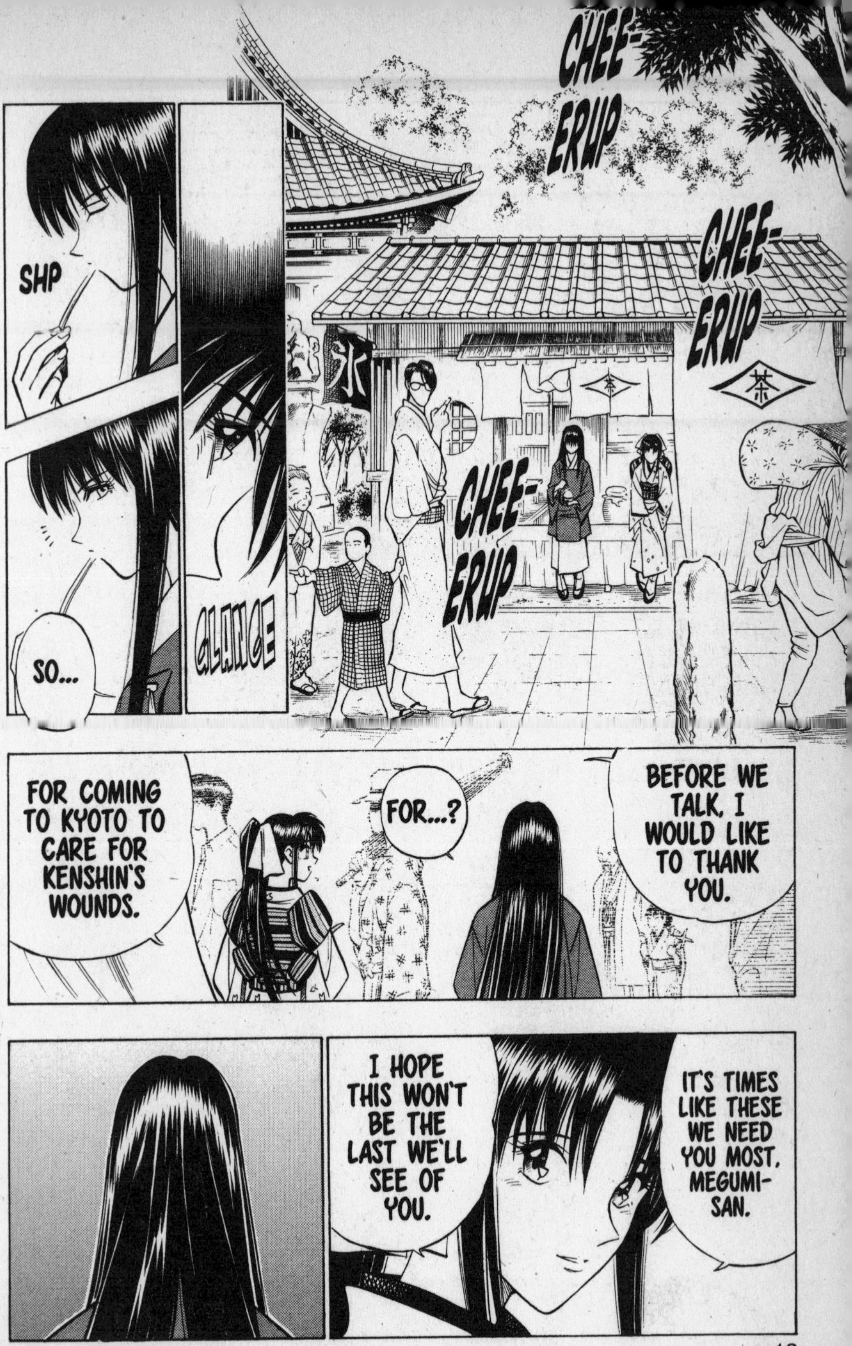
CHEE-ERUP
CHEE-ERUP
CHEE-ERUP
GLANCE
SHP
SO...
BEFORE WE TALK, I WOULD LIKE TO THANK YOU.
FOR...?
FOR COMING TO KYOTO TO CARE FOR KENSHIN'S WOUNDS.
IT'S TIMES LIKE THESE WE NEED YOU MOST, MEGUMI-SAN.
I HOPE THIS WON'T BE THE LAST WE'LL SEE OF YOU.

READ THIS WAY

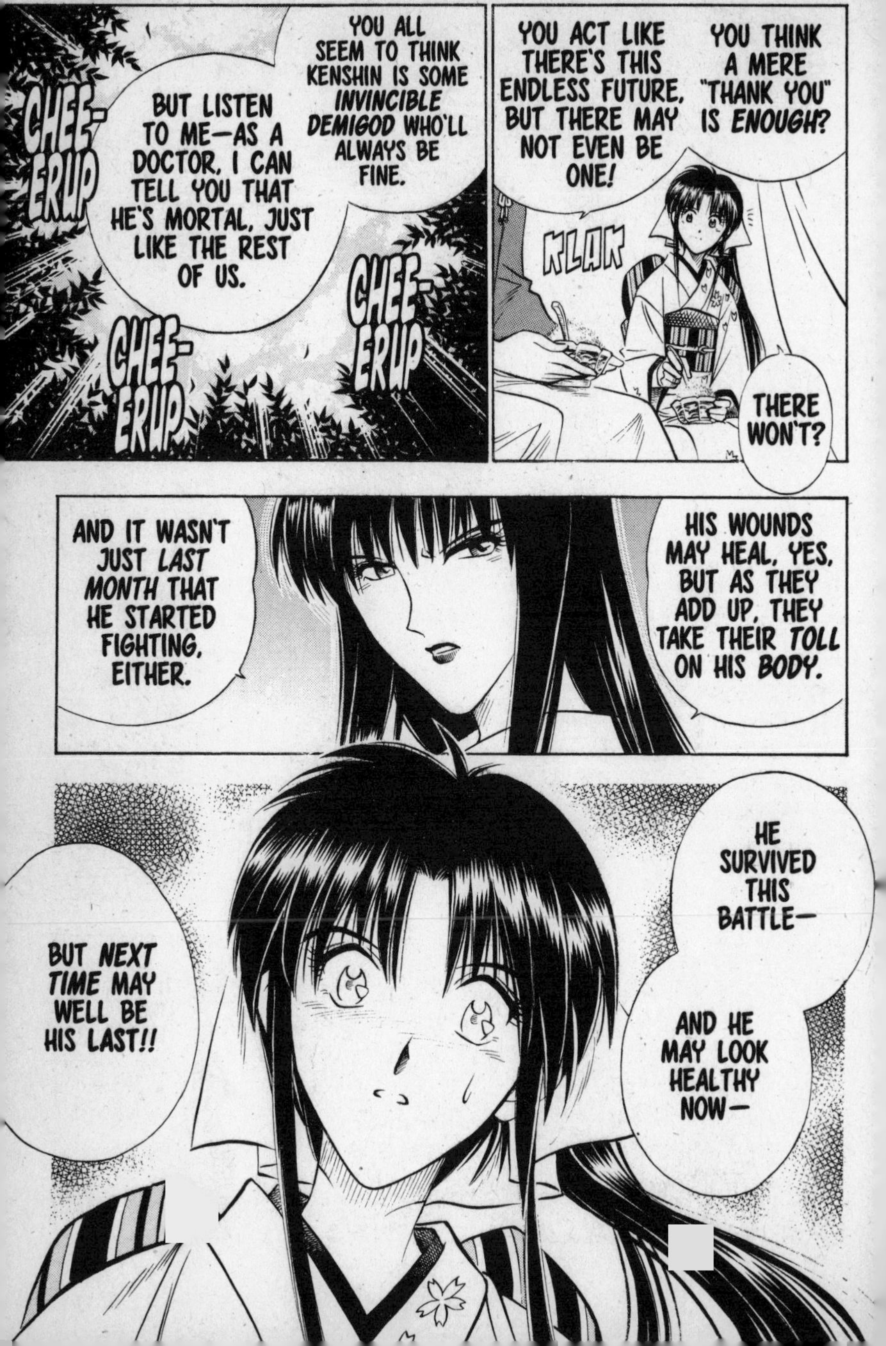
YOU THINK A MERE "THANK YOU" IS *ENOUGH?*
YOU ACT LIKE THERE'S THIS ENDLESS FUTURE, BUT THERE MAY NOT EVEN BE ONE!
KLAK
THERE WON'T?
YOU ALL SEEM TO THINK KENSHIN IS SOME *INVINCIBLE DEMIGOD* WHO'LL ALWAYS BE FINE.
BUT LISTEN TO ME—AS A DOCTOR, I CAN TELL YOU THAT HE'S MORTAL, JUST LIKE THE REST OF US.
CHEE-ERUP
CHEE-ERUP
CHEE-ERUP
HIS WOUNDS MAY HEAL, YES, BUT AS THEY ADD UP, THEY TAKE THEIR *TOLL* ON HIS *BODY.*
AND IT WASN'T JUST *LAST MONTH* THAT HE STARTED FIGHTING, EITHER.
HE SURVIVED THIS BATTLE—
AND HE MAY LOOK HEALTHY NOW—
BUT *NEXT TIME* MAY WELL BE HIS LAST!!

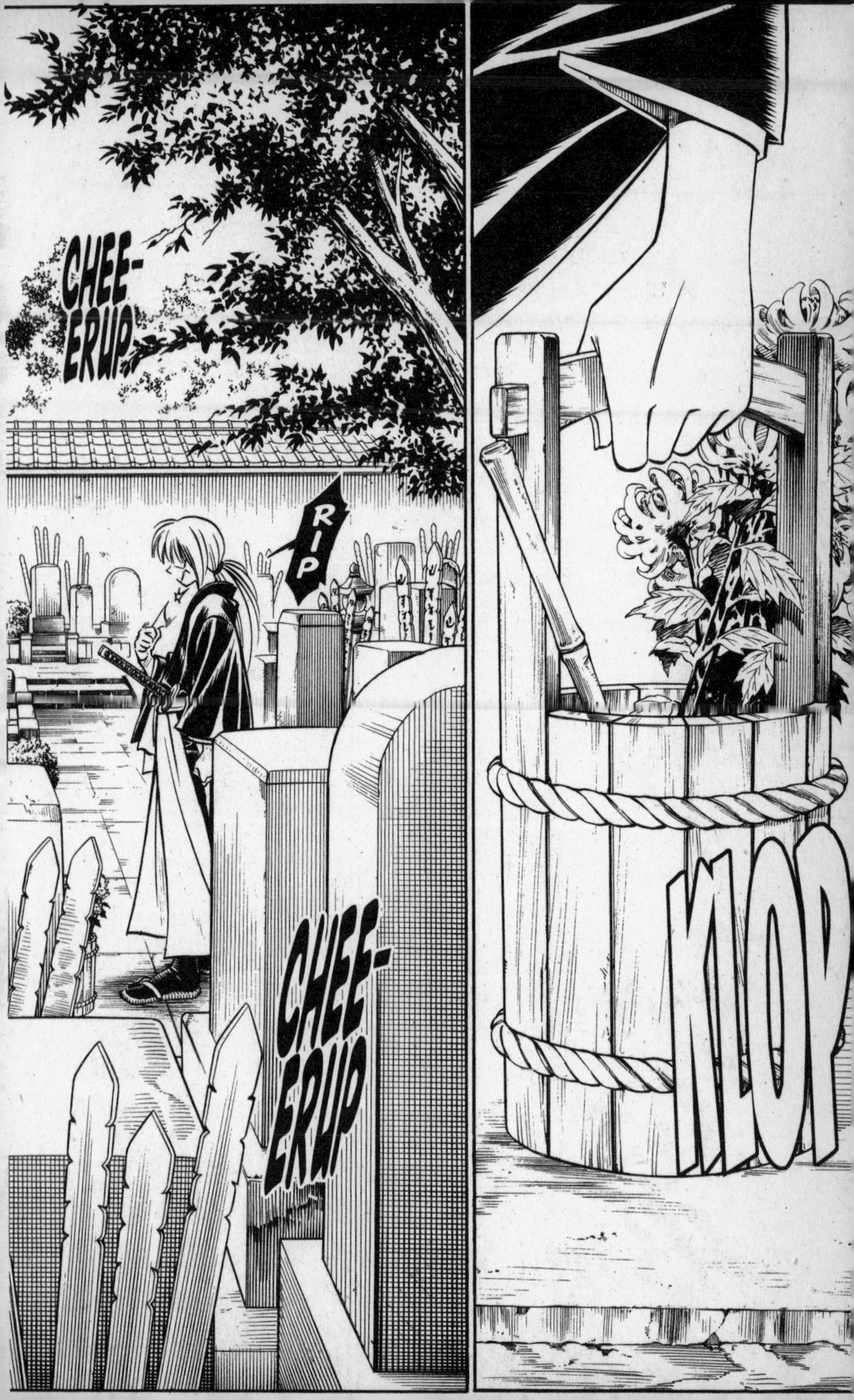
KLOP
CHEE-ERUP
RIP
CHEE-ERUP

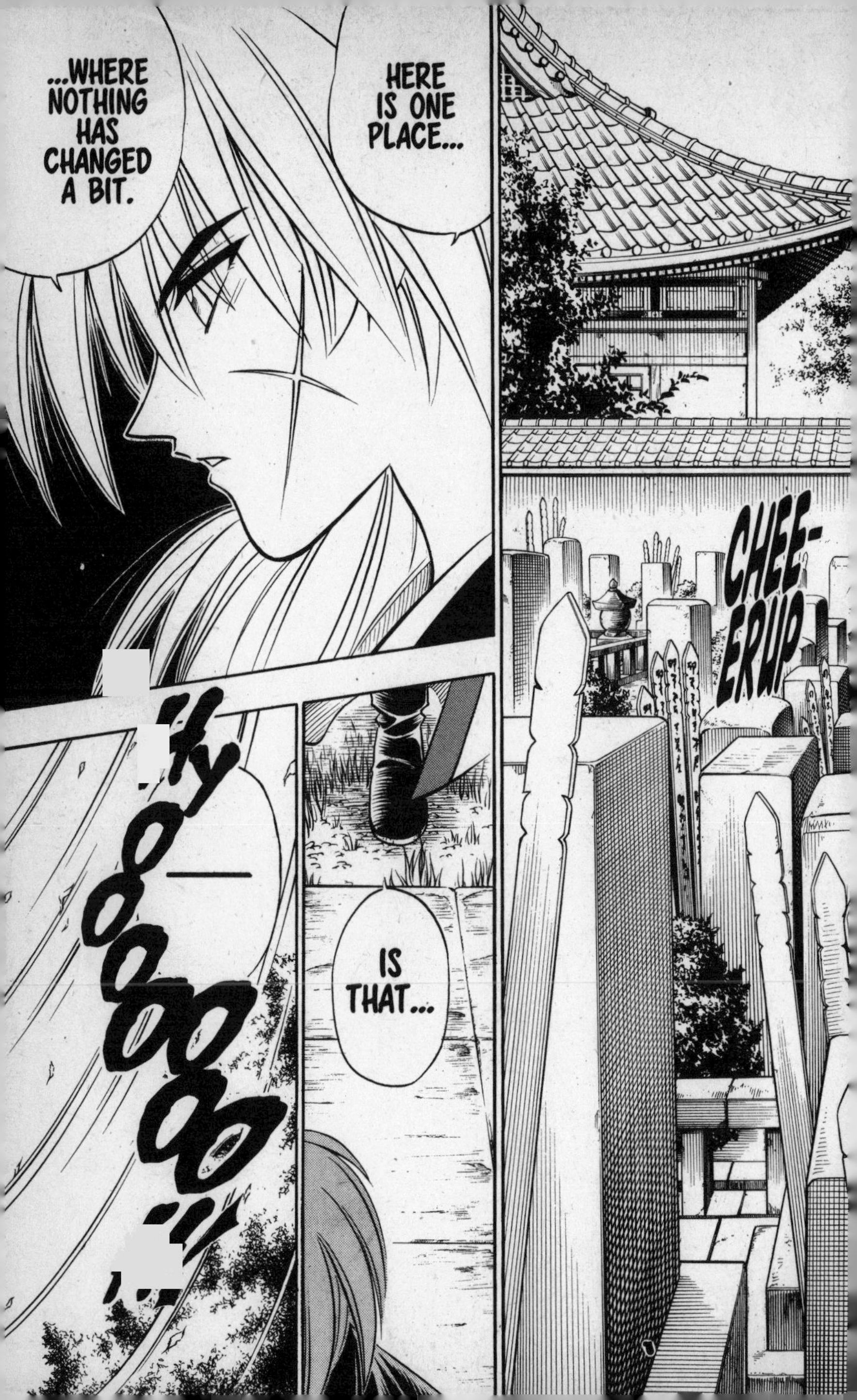
CHEE-ERUP
HERE IS ONE PLACE...
...WHERE NOTHING HAS CHANGED A BIT.
IS THAT...

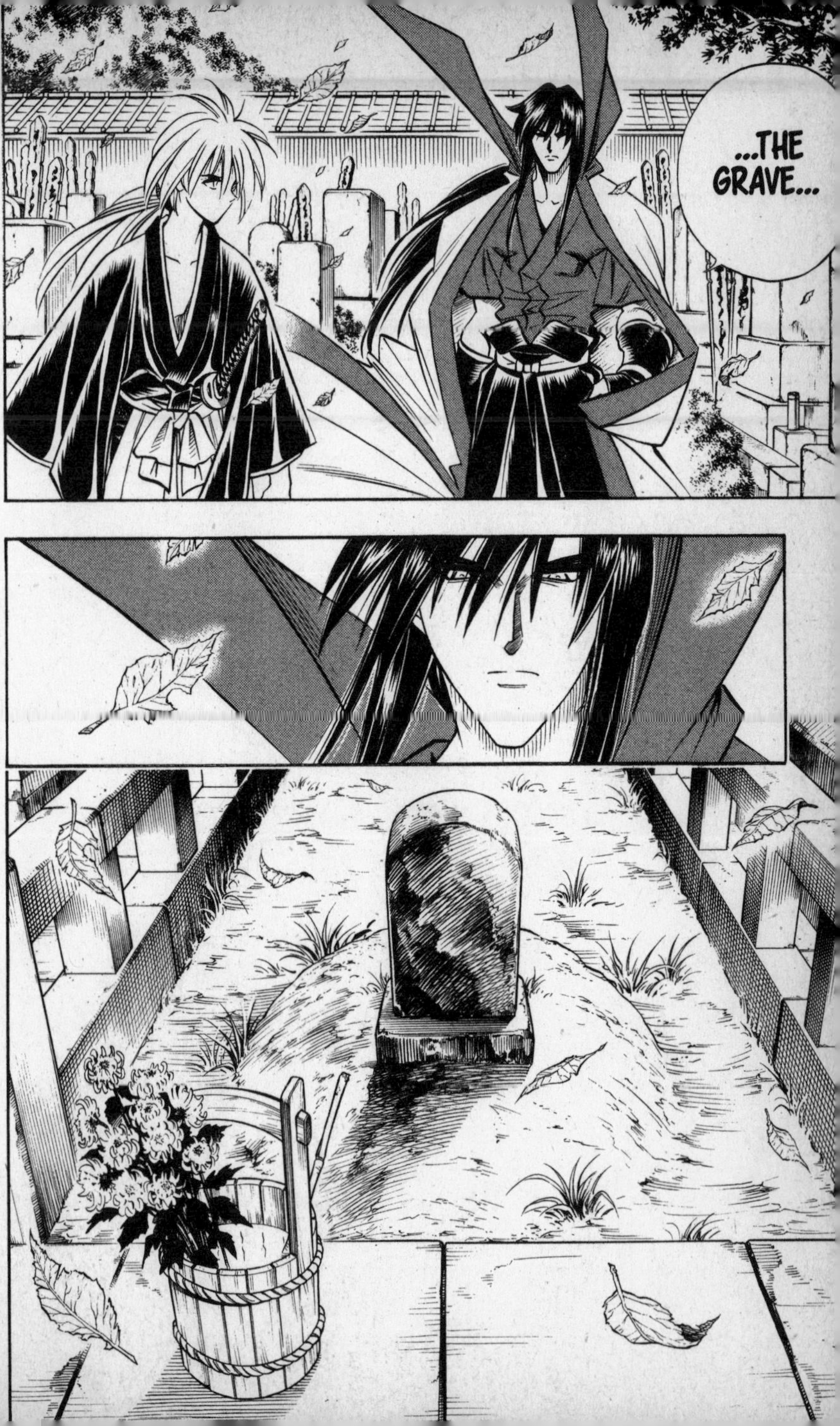
...THE GRAVE...

READ THIS WAY

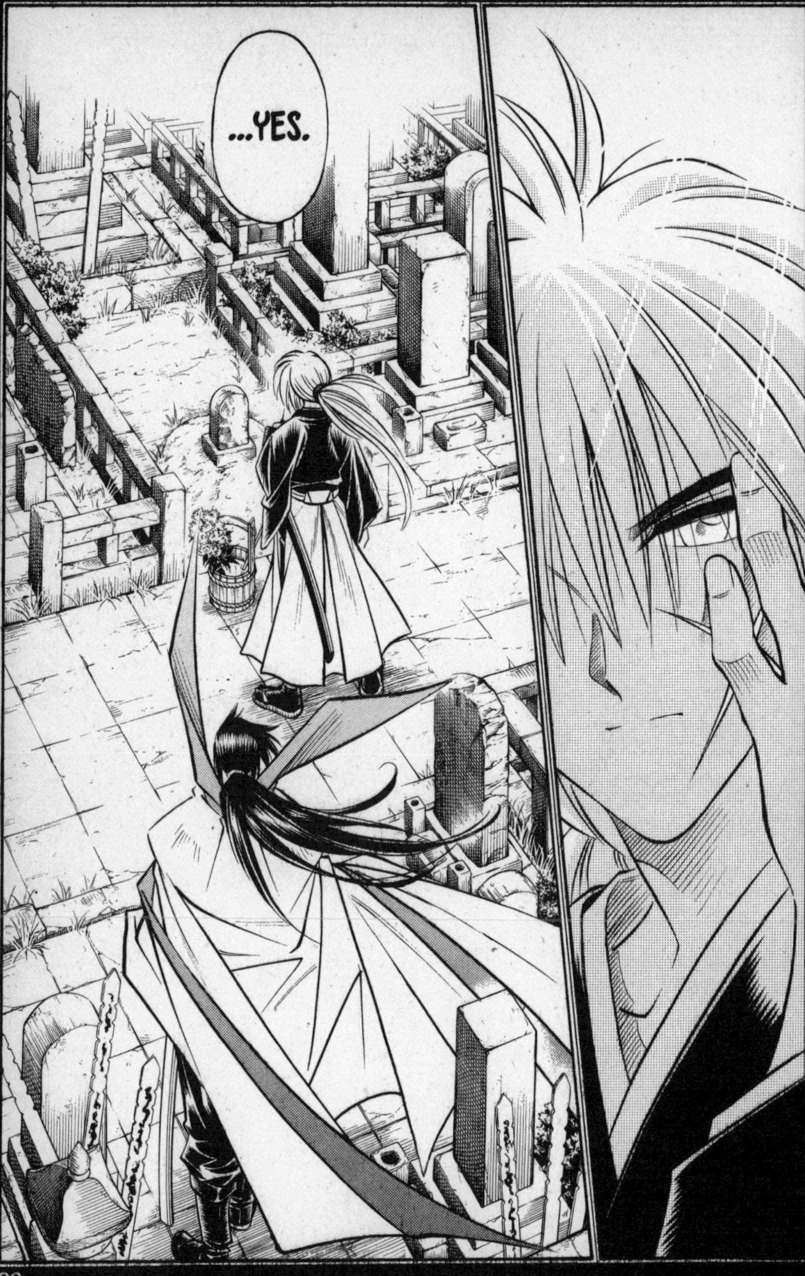
...YES.

Rurouni Kenshin

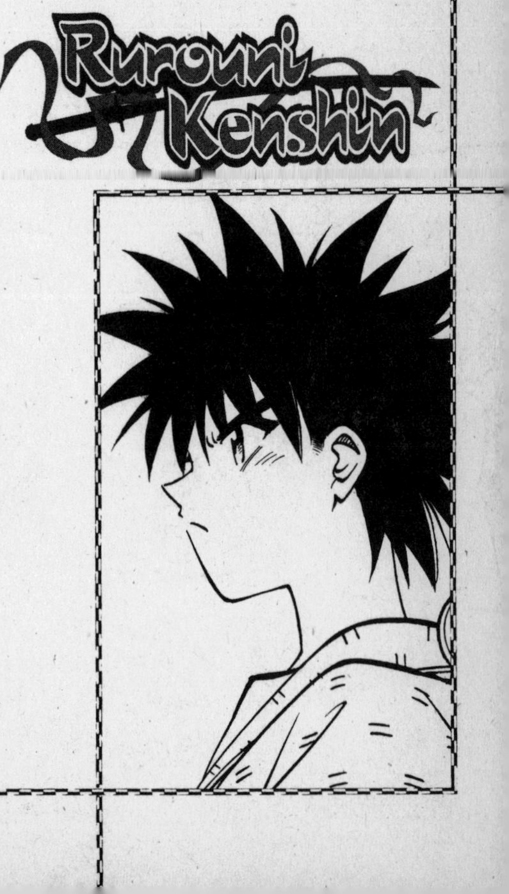

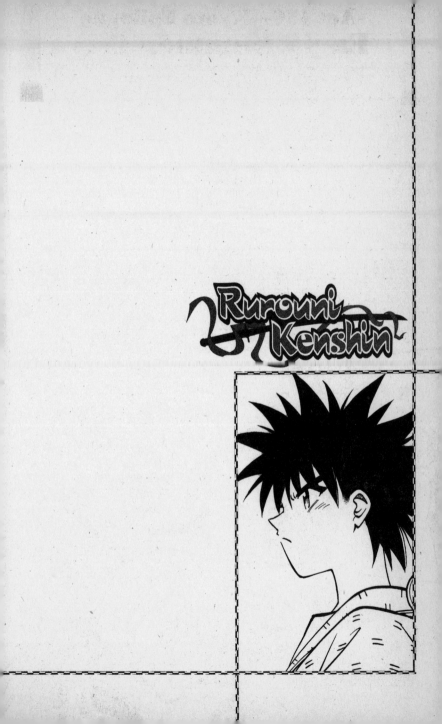

Act 150—Kyoto Epilogue
Early Summer Day

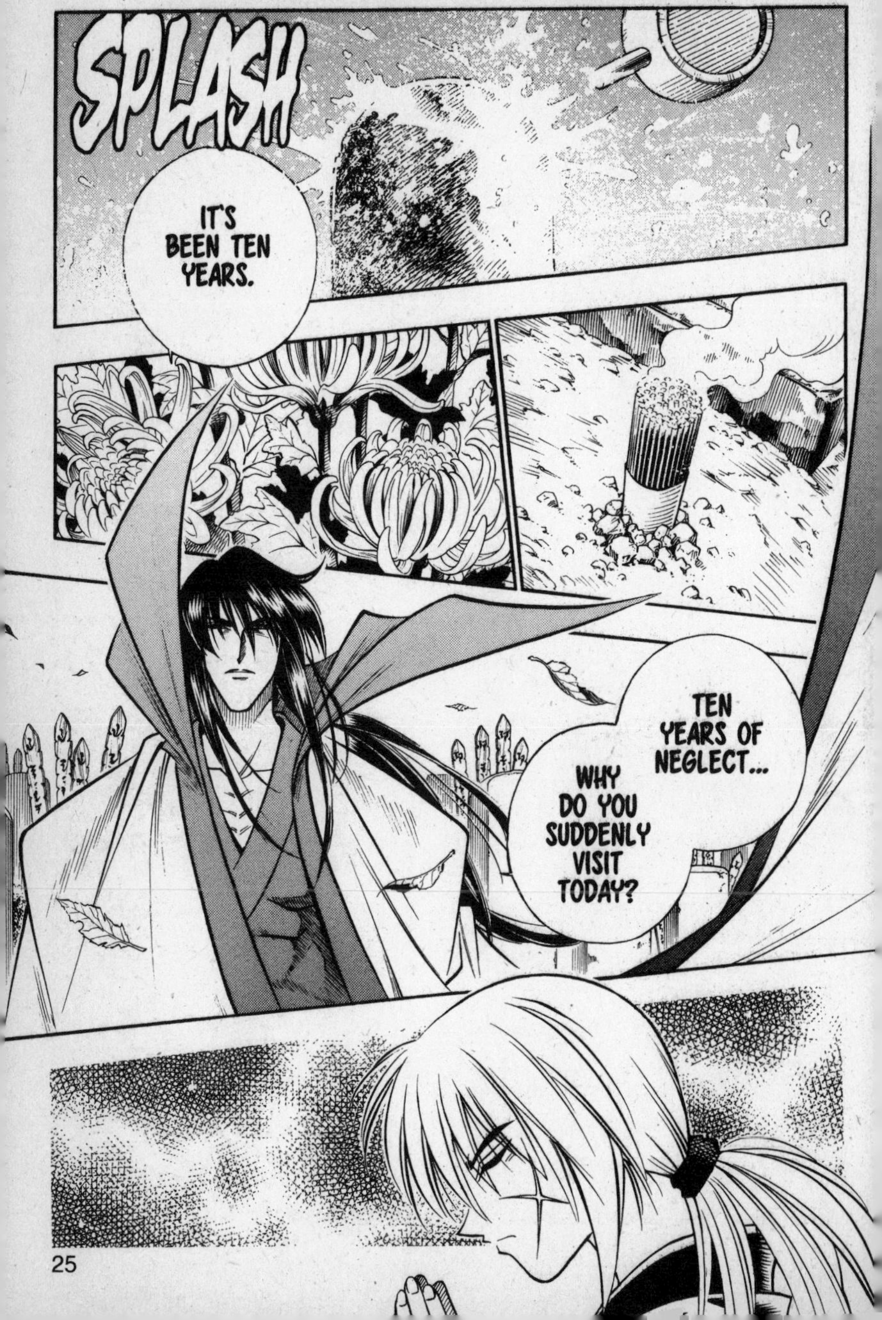
SPLASH
IT'S BEEN TEN YEARS.
TEN YEARS OF NEGLECT...
WHY DO YOU SUDDENLY VISIT TODAY?

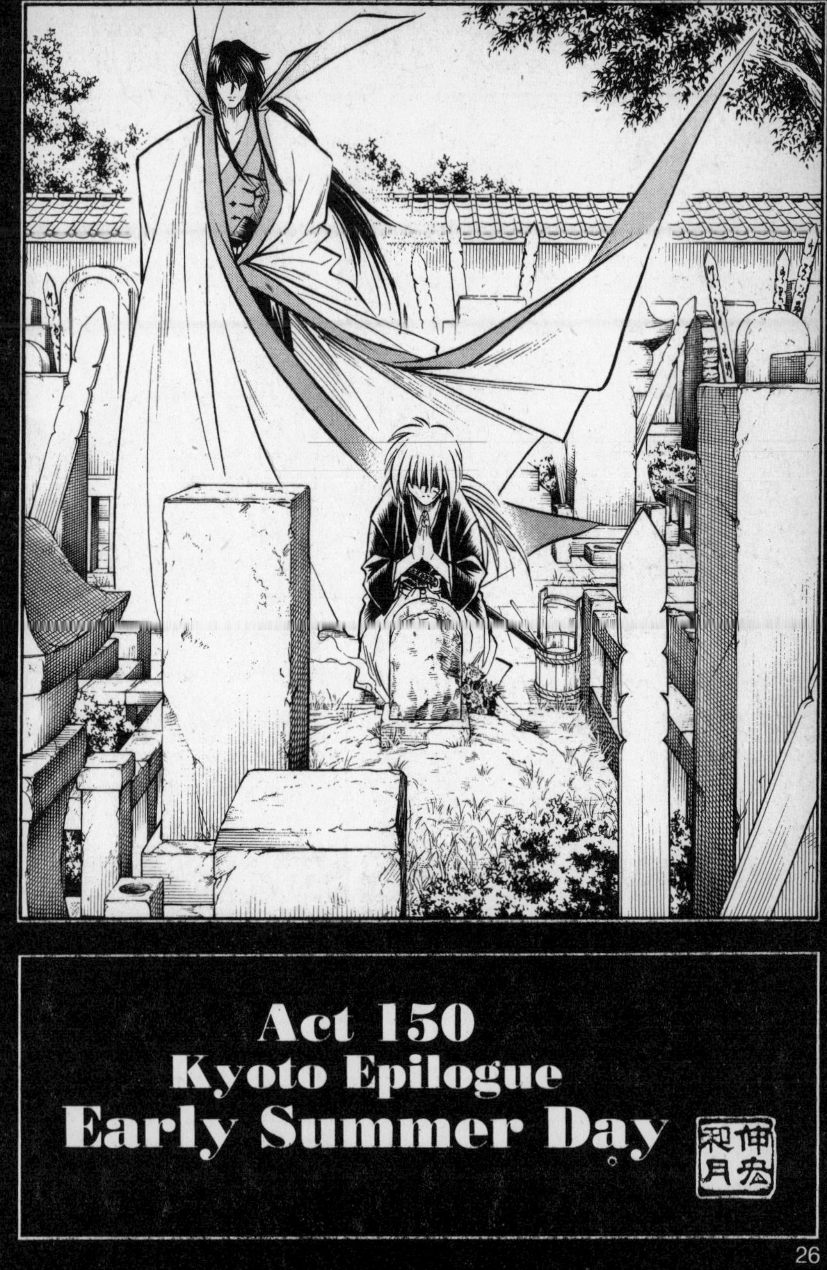

Act 150
Kyoto Epilogue
Early Summer Day

伸宏和月

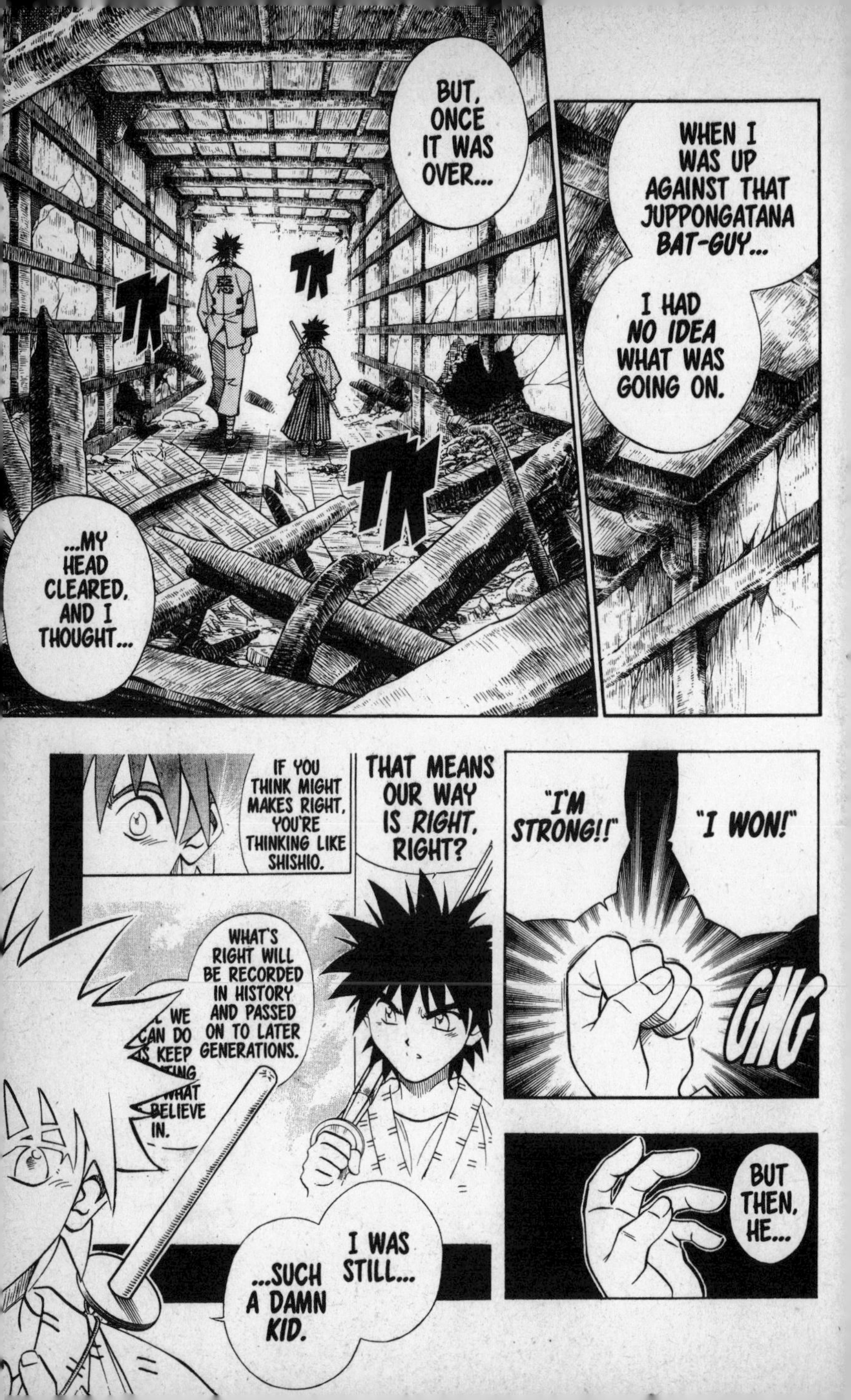
WHEN I WAS UP AGAINST THAT JUPPONGATANA BAT-GUY...
I HAD NO IDEA WHAT WAS GOING ON.
BUT, ONCE IT WAS OVER...
TK
TK
TK
...MY HEAD CLEARED, AND I THOUGHT...
"I'M STRONG!!"
"I WON!"
GNG
BUT THEN, HE...
THAT MEANS OUR WAY IS RIGHT, RIGHT?
IF YOU THINK MIGHT MAKES RIGHT, YOU'RE THINKING LIKE SHISHIO.
WHAT'S RIGHT WILL BE RECORDED IN HISTORY AND PASSED ON TO LATER GENERATIONS.
I WAS STILL...
...SUCH A DAMN KID.

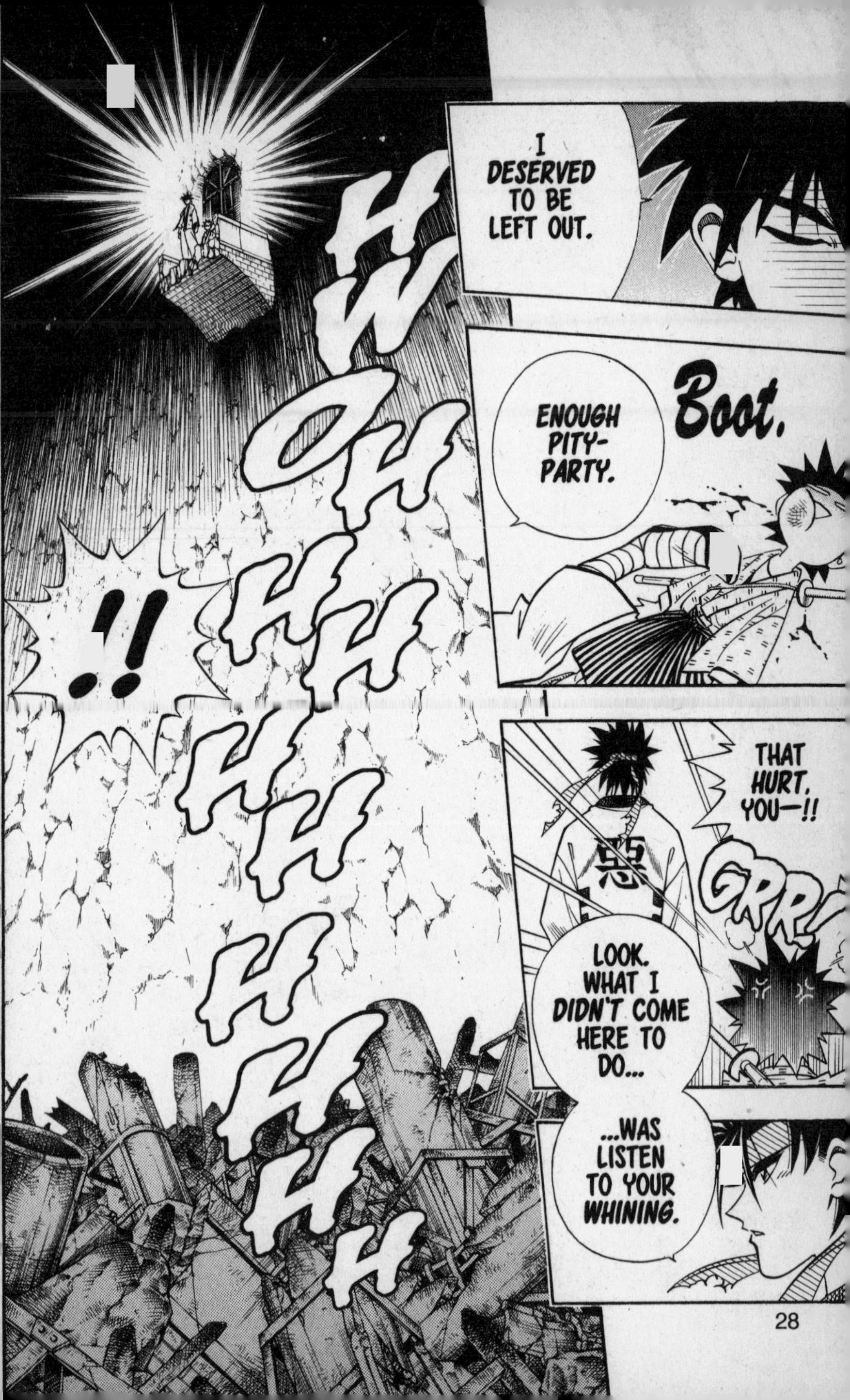
I DESERVED TO BE LEFT OUT.
Boot.
ENOUGH PITY-PARTY.
THAT HURT, YOU—!!
GRR
LOOK. WHAT I DIDN'T COME HERE TO DO...
...WAS LISTEN TO YOUR WHINING.
!!

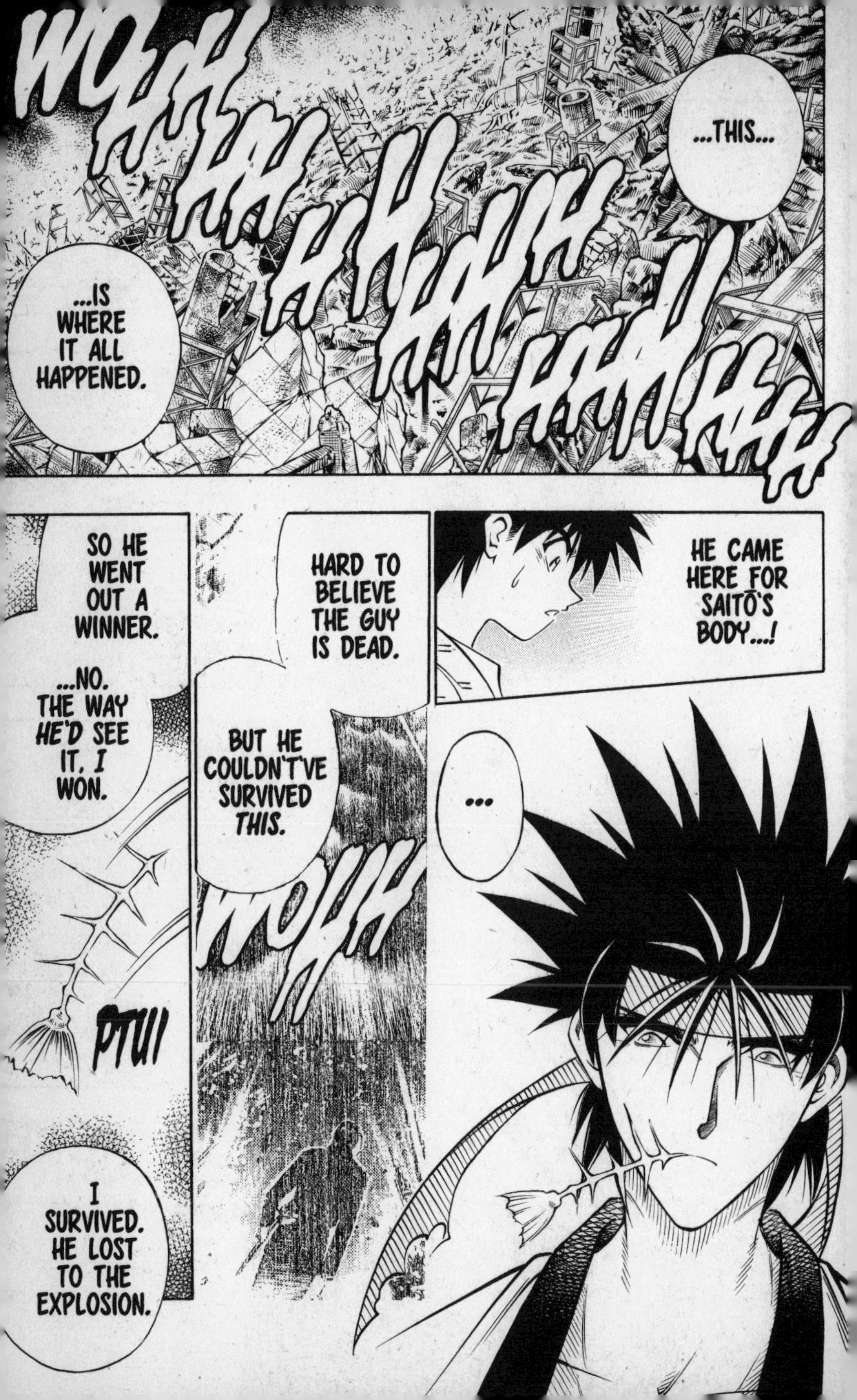
...THIS...
...IS WHERE IT ALL HAPPENED.
HE CAME HERE FOR SAITŌ'S BODY...!
...
HARD TO BELIEVE THE GUY IS DEAD.
BUT HE COULDN'T'VE SURVIVED *THIS.*
SO HE WENT OUT A WINNER.
...NO. THE WAY *HE'D* SEE IT, *I* WON.
PTUI
I SURVIVED. HE LOST TO THE EXPLOSION.

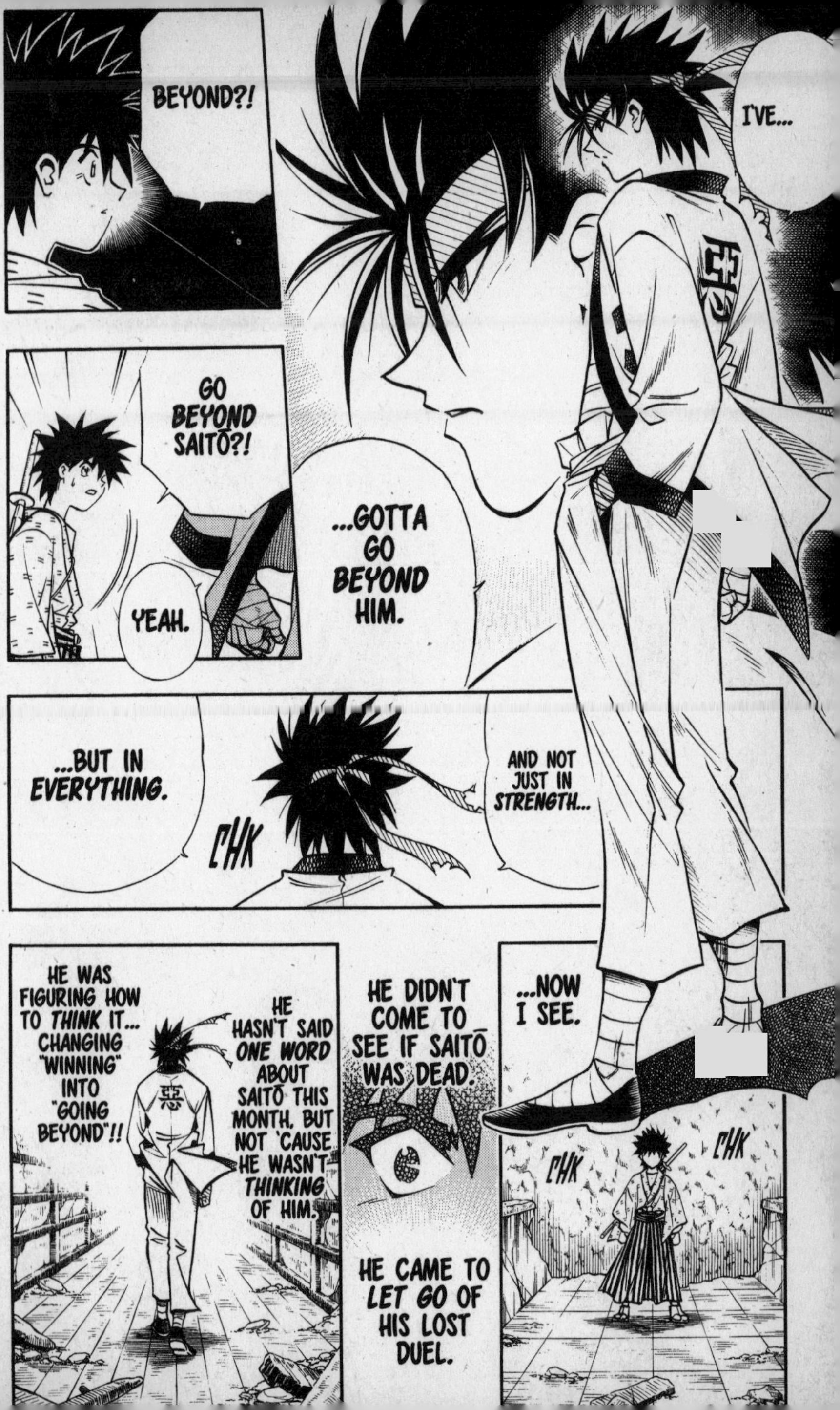
I'VE...
...GOTTA GO BEYOND HIM.
BEYOND?!
GO BEYOND SAITŌ?!
YEAH.
AND NOT JUST IN STRENGTH...
...BUT IN EVERYTHING.
CHK
...NOW I SEE.
CHK
CHK
HE DIDN'T COME TO SEE IF SAITŌ WAS DEAD.
HE CAME TO LET GO OF HIS LOST DUEL.
HE HASN'T SAID ONE WORD ABOUT SAITŌ THIS MONTH, BUT NOT 'CAUSE HE WASN'T THINKING OF HIM.
HE WAS FIGURING HOW TO THINK IT... CHANGING "WINNING" INTO "GOING BEYOND"!!

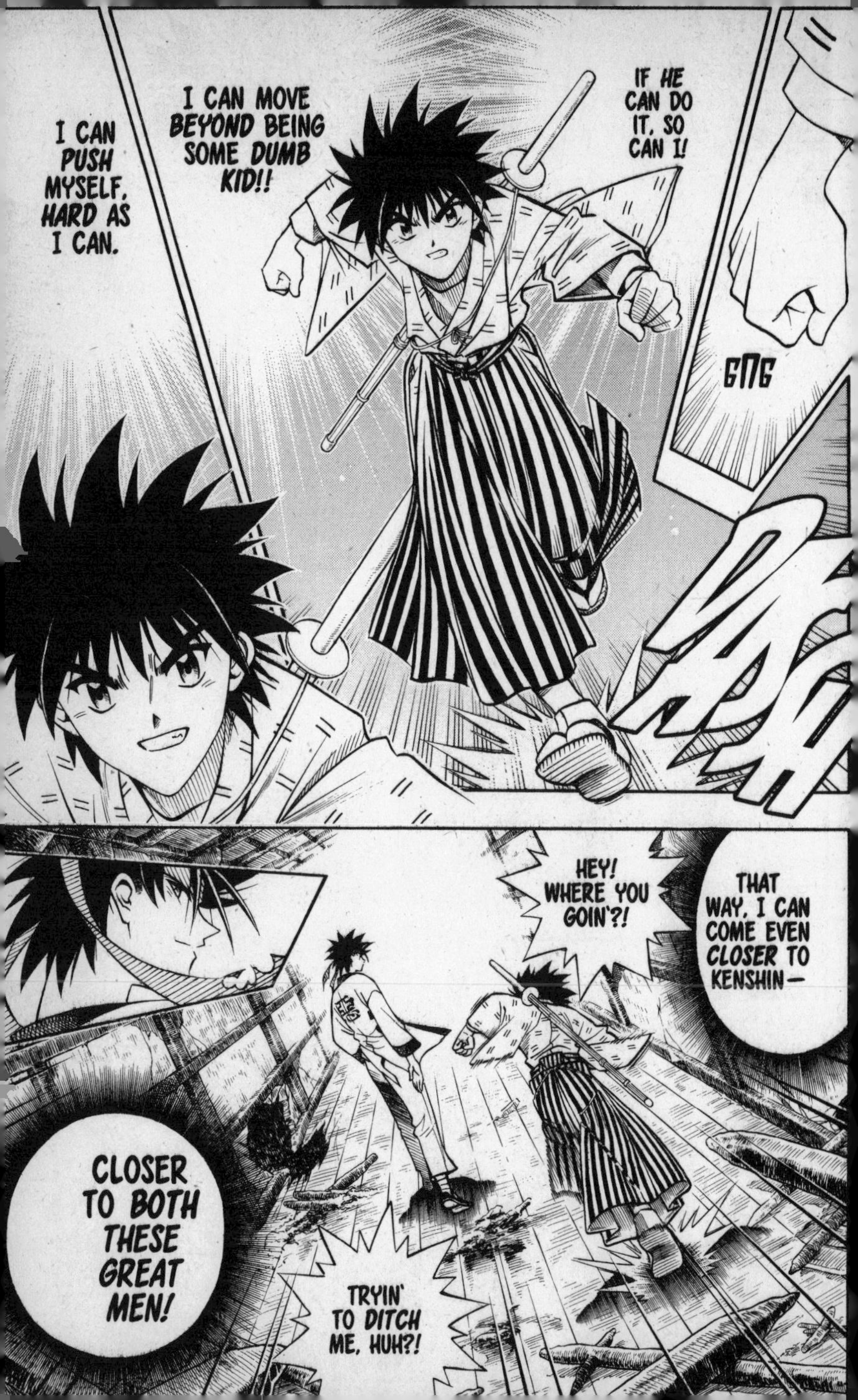
IF HE CAN DO IT, SO CAN I!
I CAN MOVE BEYOND BEING SOME DUMB KID!!
I CAN PUSH MYSELF, HARD AS I CAN.
GNG
THAT WAY, I CAN COME EVEN CLOSER TO KENSHIN—
HEY! WHERE YOU GOIN'?!
CLOSER TO BOTH THESE GREAT MEN!
TRYIN' TO DITCH ME, HUH?!

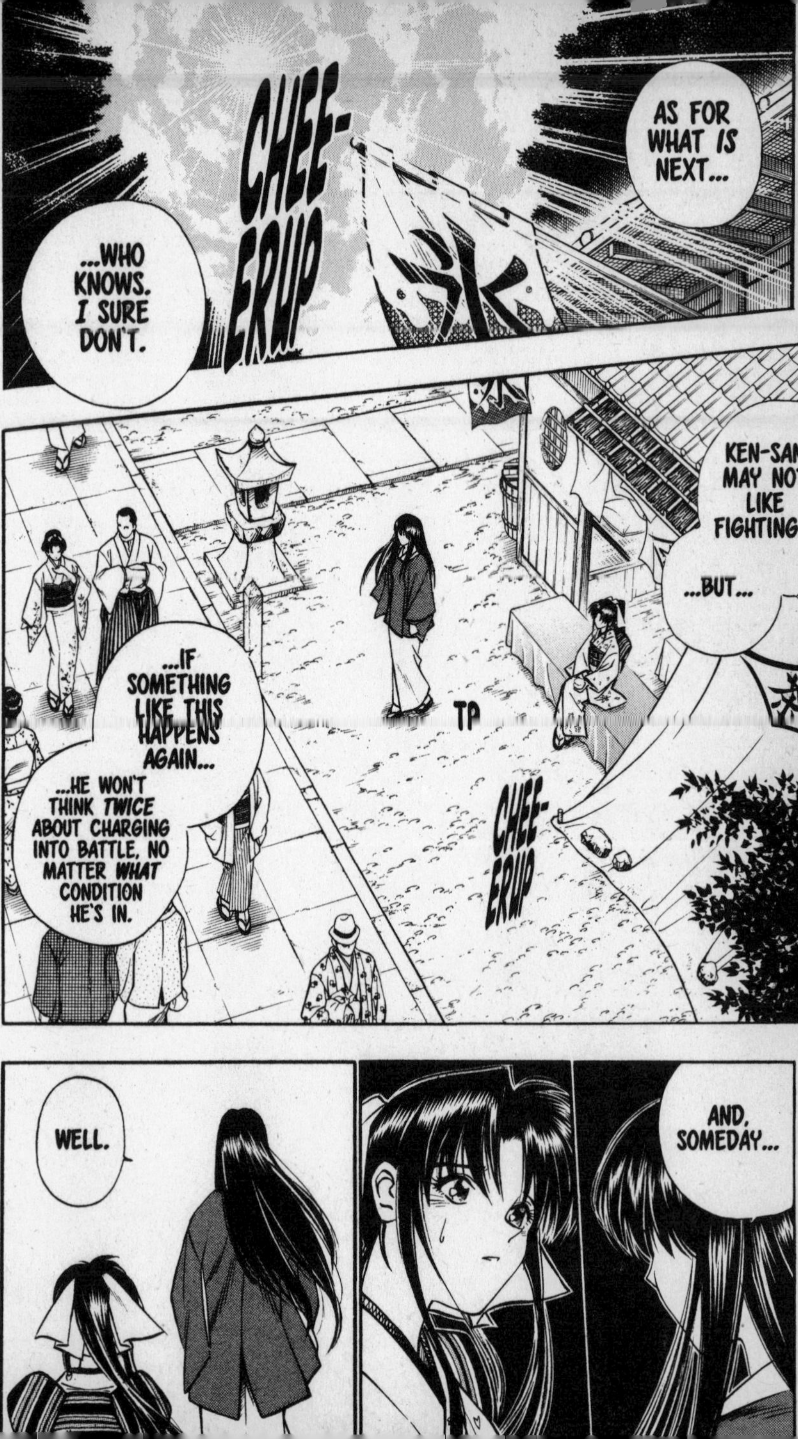
AS FOR WHAT IS NEXT...
CHEE-ERUP
...WHO KNOWS. I SURE DON'T.
KEN-SAN MAY NOT LIKE FIGHTING...
...BUT...
CHEE-ERUP
TP
...IF SOMETHING LIKE THIS HAPPENS AGAIN...
...HE WON'T THINK TWICE ABOUT CHARGING INTO BATTLE, NO MATTER WHAT CONDITION HE'S IN.
AND, SOMEDAY...
WELL.

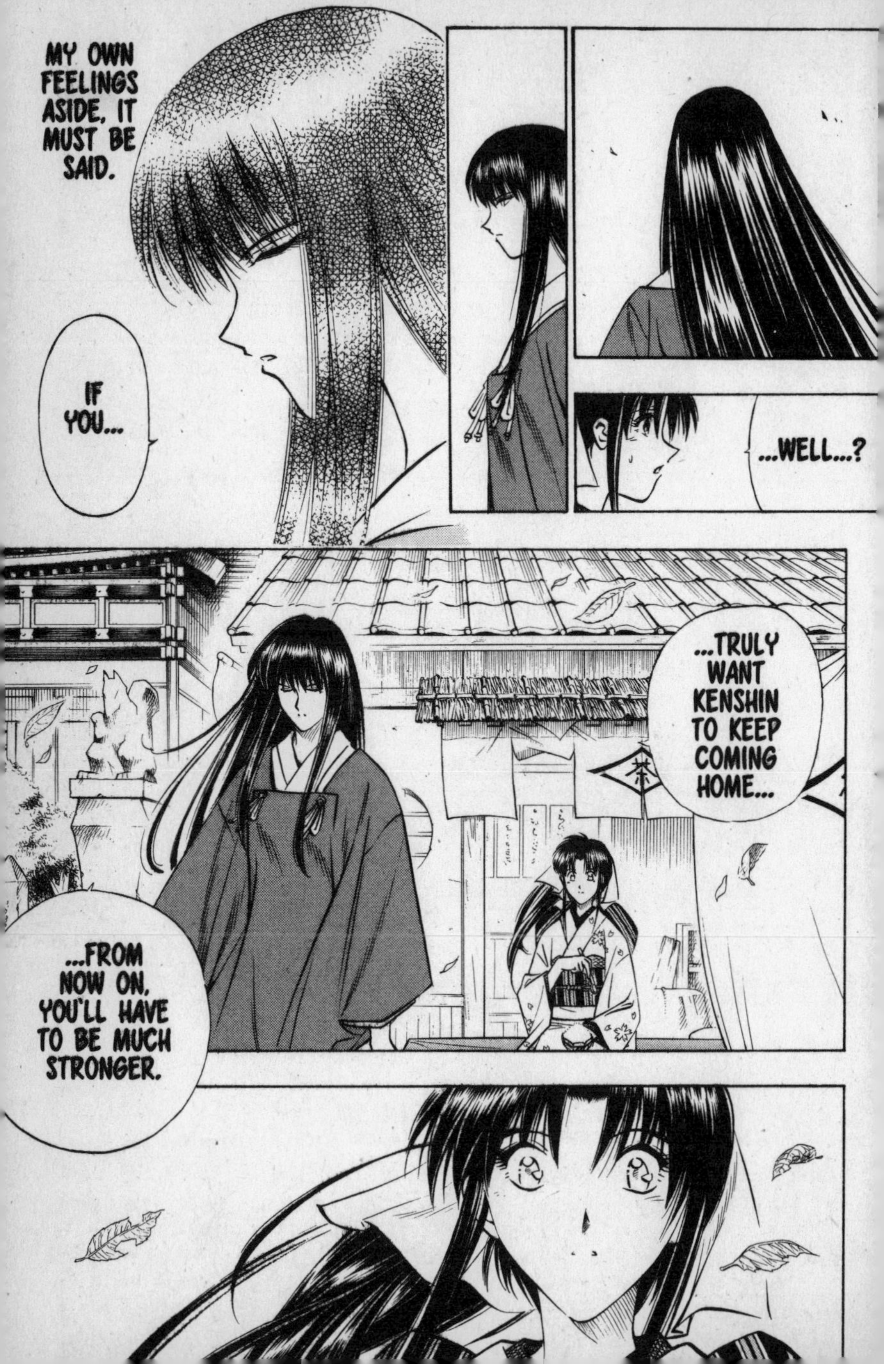
...WELL...?
MY OWN FEELINGS ASIDE, IT MUST BE SAID.
IF YOU...
...TRULY WANT KENSHIN TO KEEP COMING HOME...
...FROM NOW ON, YOU'LL HAVE TO BE MUCH STRONGER.

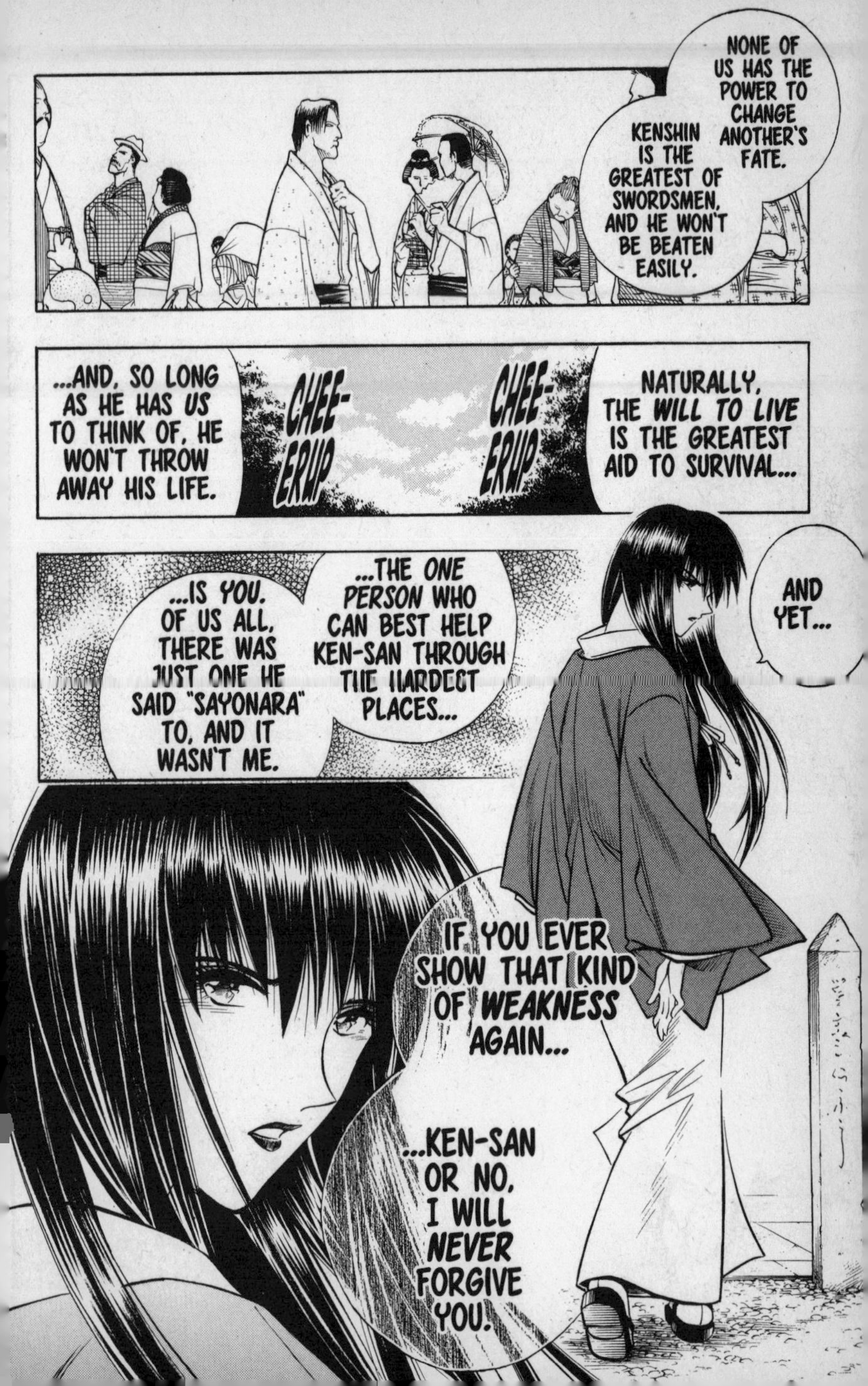
NONE OF US HAS THE POWER TO CHANGE ANOTHER'S FATE.
KENSHIN IS THE GREATEST OF SWORDSMEN, AND HE WON'T BE BEATEN EASILY.
NATURALLY, THE WILL TO LIVE IS THE GREATEST AID TO SURVIVAL...
CHEE-ERUP
CHEE-ERUP
...AND, SO LONG AS HE HAS US TO THINK OF, HE WON'T THROW AWAY HIS LIFE.
AND YET...
...THE ONE PERSON WHO CAN BEST HELP KEN-SAN THROUGH THE HARDEST PLACES...
...IS YOU. OF US ALL, THERE WAS JUST ONE HE SAID "SAYONARA" TO, AND IT WASN'T ME.
IF YOU EVER SHOW THAT KIND OF WEAKNESS AGAIN...
...KEN-SAN OR NO, I WILL NEVER FORGIVE YOU.

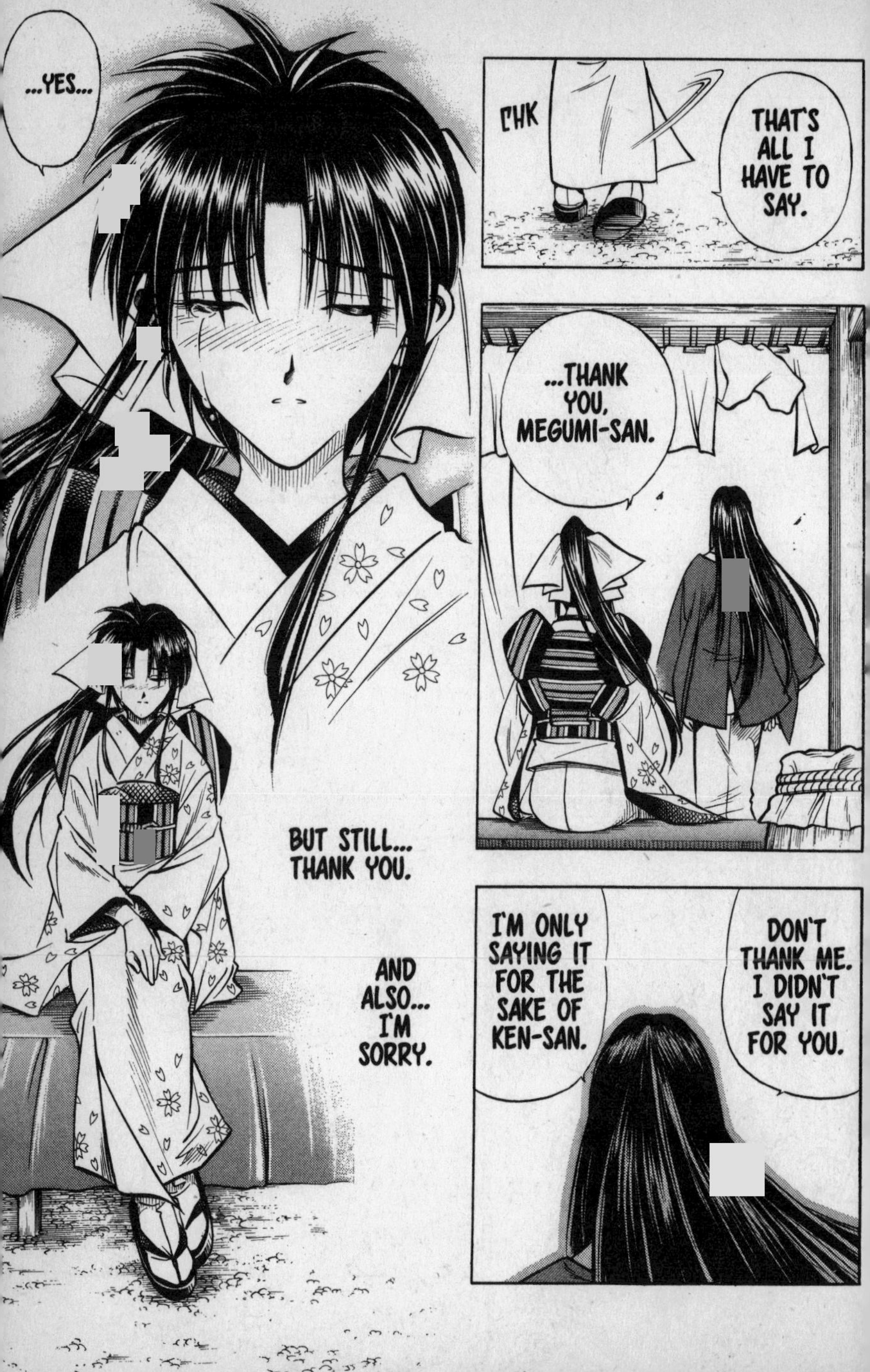

THAT'S ALL I HAVE TO SAY.
CHK
...THANK YOU, MEGUMI-SAN.
DON'T THANK ME. I DIDN'T SAY IT FOR YOU.
I'M ONLY SAYING IT FOR THE SAKE OF KEN-SAN.
...YES...
BUT STILL... THANK YOU.
AND ALSO... I'M SORRY.

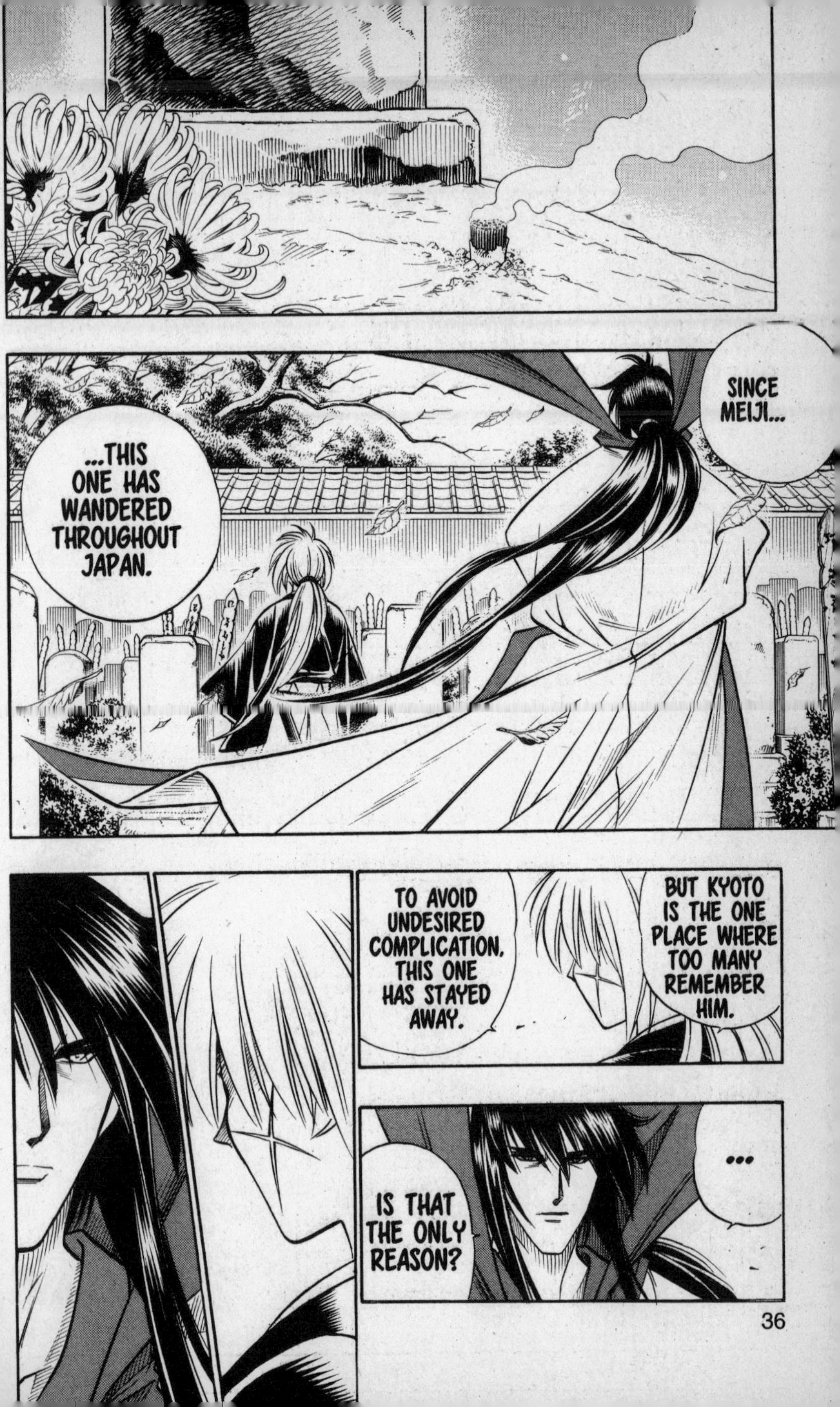
SINCE MEIJI...
...THIS ONE HAS WANDERED THROUGHOUT JAPAN.
BUT KYOTO IS THE ONE PLACE WHERE TOO MANY REMEMBER HIM.
TO AVOID UNDESIRED COMPLICATION, THIS ONE HAS STAYED AWAY.
...
IS THAT THE ONLY REASON?

READ THIS WAY

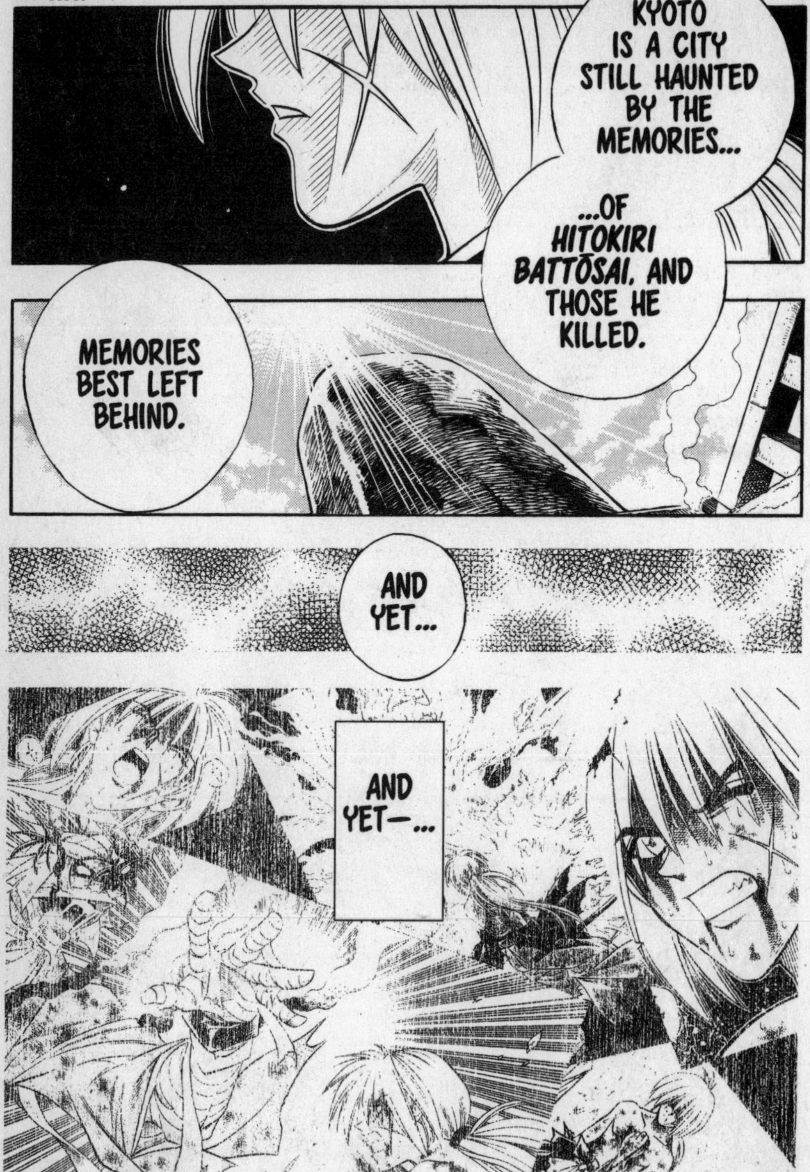

KYOTO IS A CITY STILL HAUNTED BY THE MEMORIES...
...OF HITOKIRI BATTŌSAI, AND THOSE HE KILLED.
MEMORIES BEST LEFT BEHIND.
AND YET...
AND YET—...

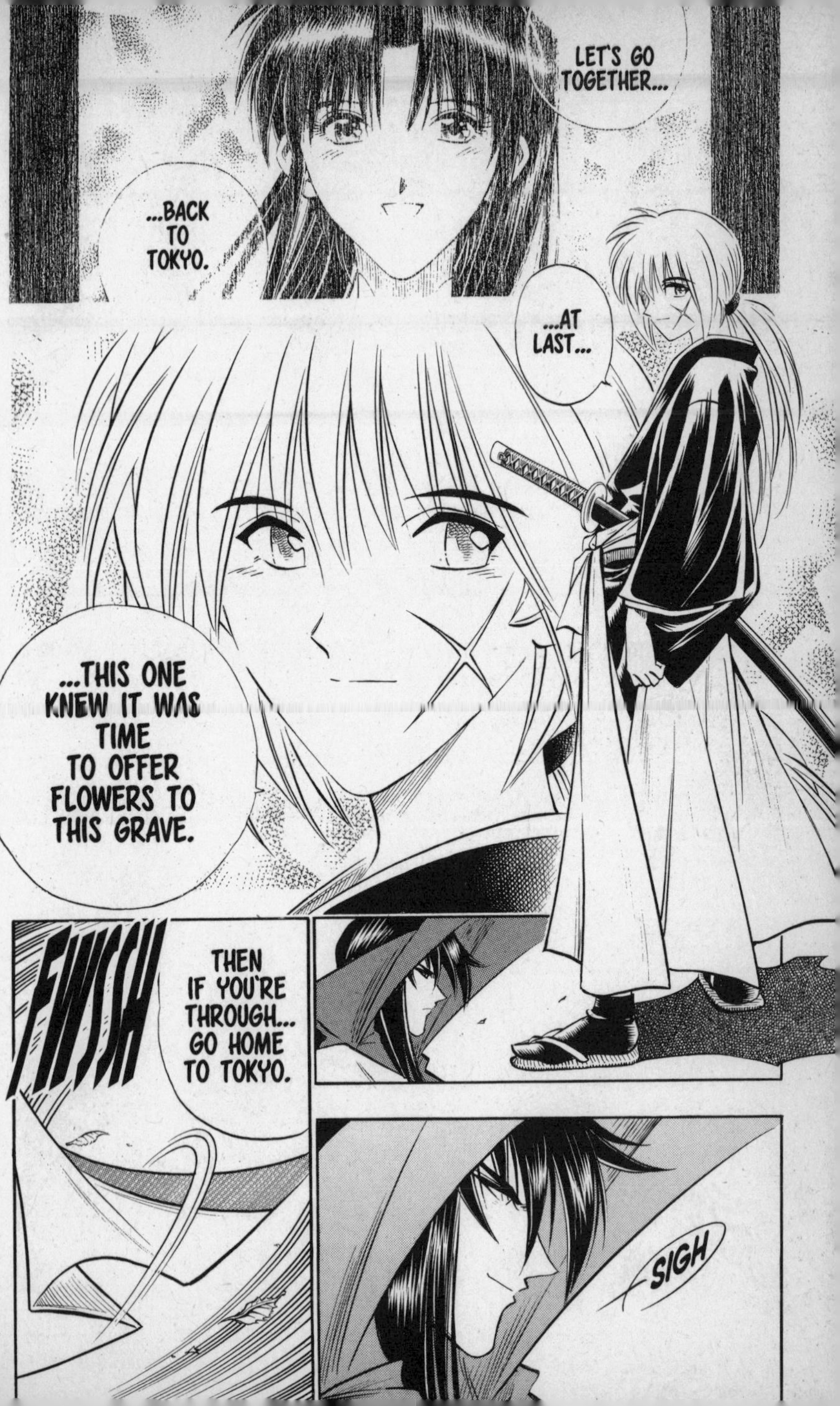
LET'S GO TOGETHER...
...BACK TO TOKYO.
...AT LAST...
...THIS ONE KNEW IT WAS TIME TO OFFER FLOWERS TO THIS GRAVE.
SIGH
FWISH
THEN IF YOU'RE THROUGH... GO HOME TO TOKYO.

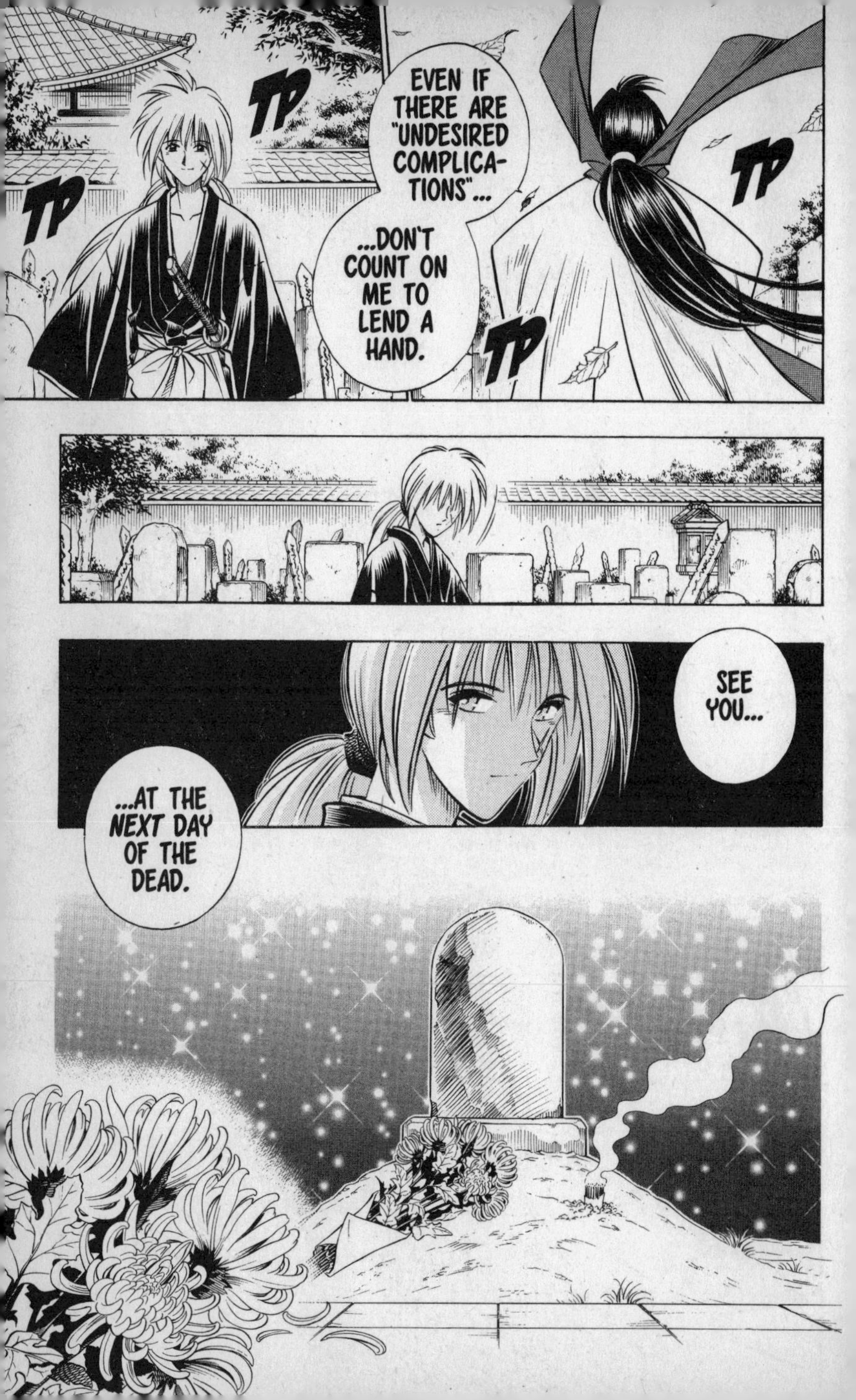
TP
TP
EVEN IF THERE ARE "UNDESIRED COMPLICA-TIONS"...
...DON'T COUNT ON ME TO LEND A HAND.
TP
TP
SEE YOU...
...AT THE NEXT DAY OF THE DEAD.

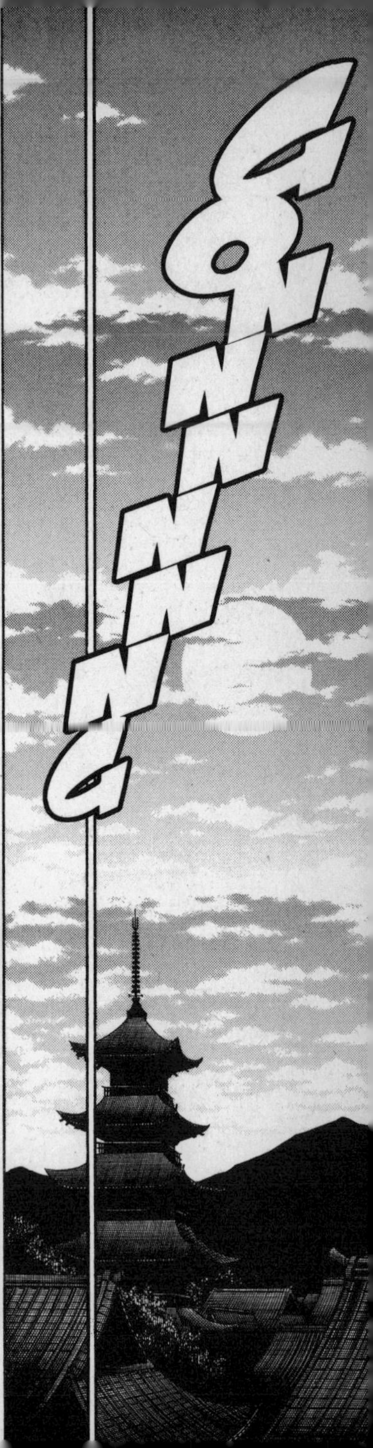
GONNNNNG

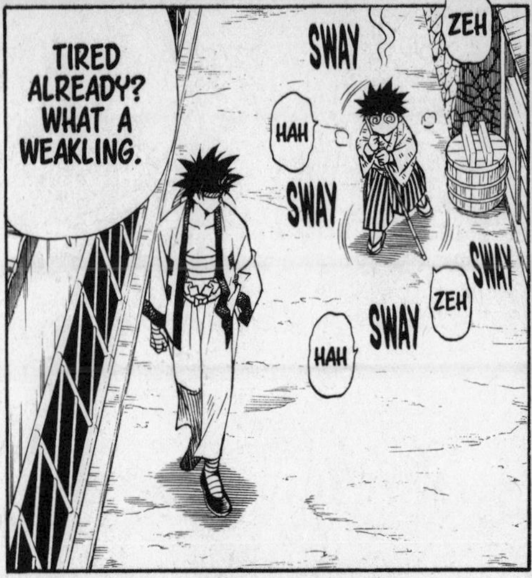
ZEH
SWAY
HAH
TIRED ALREADY? WHAT A WEAKLING.
SWAY
SWAY
ZEH
SWAY
HAH

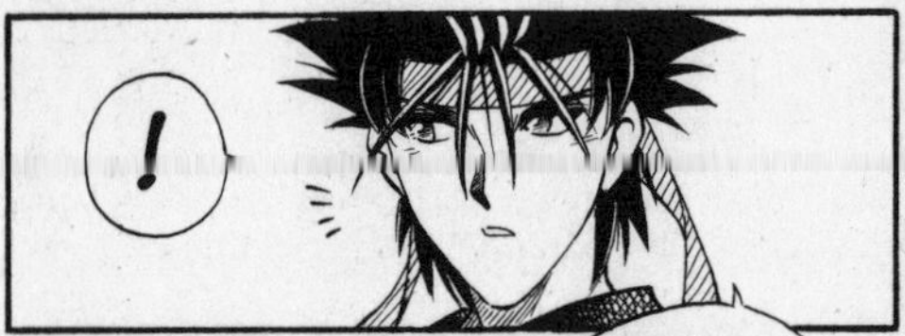
!

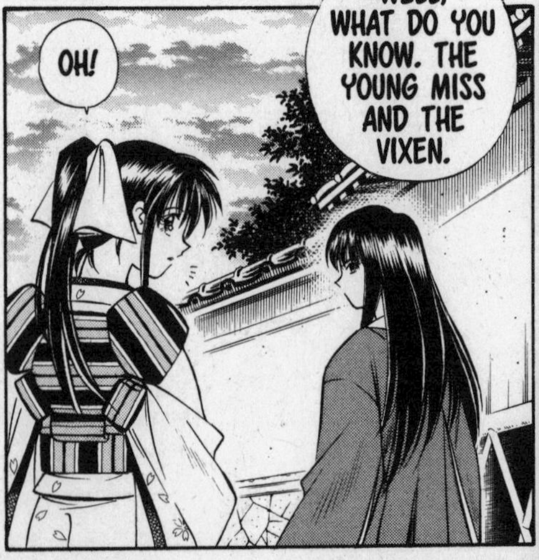
WELL, WHAT DO YOU KNOW. THE YOUNG MISS AND THE VIXEN.
OH!

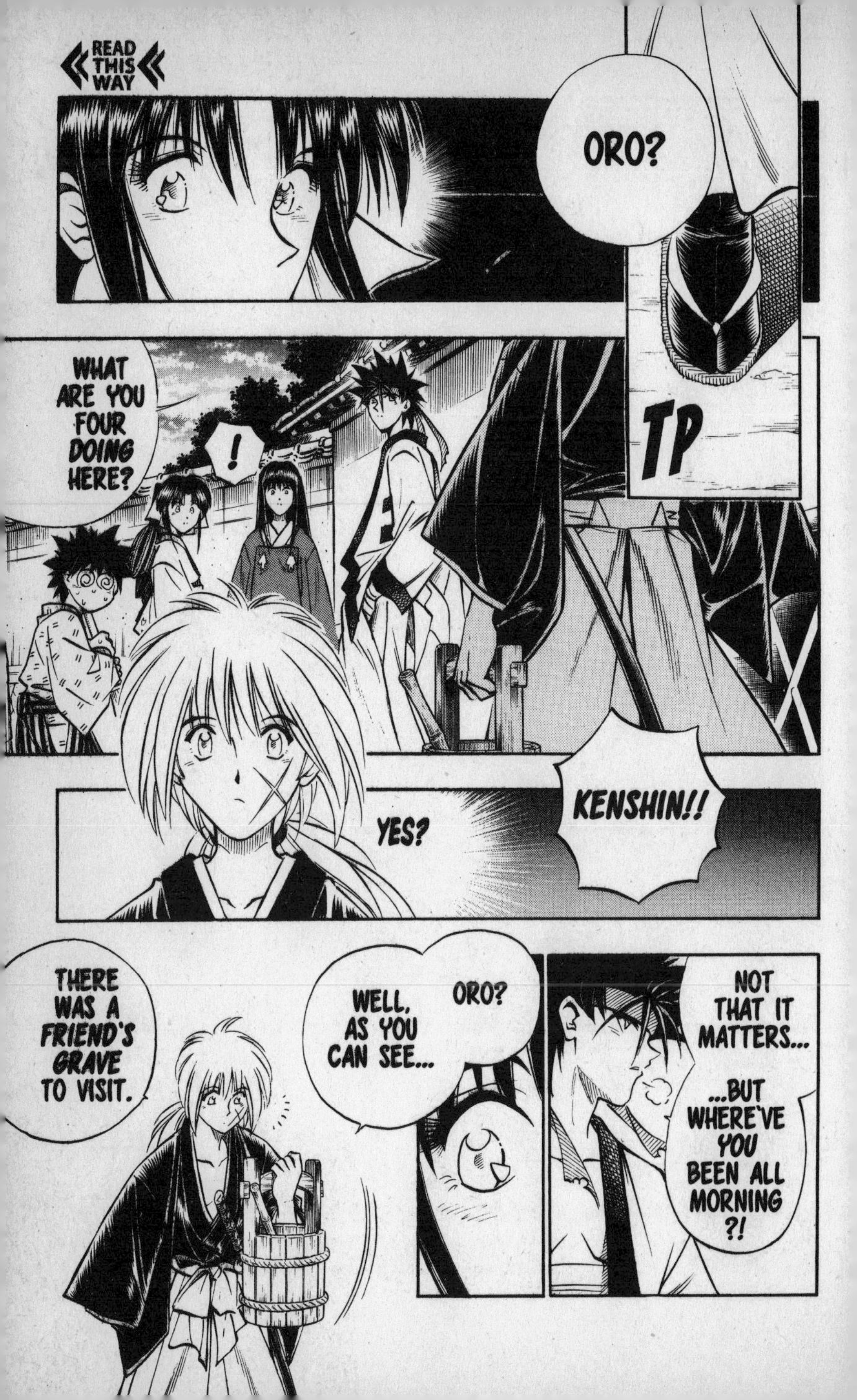
READ THIS WAY
ORO?
TP
!
WHAT ARE YOU FOUR DOING HERE?
KENSHIN!!
YES?
NOT THAT IT MATTERS...
...BUT WHERE'VE YOU BEEN ALL MORNING ?!
ORO?
WELL, AS YOU CAN SEE...
THERE WAS A FRIEND'S GRAVE TO VISIT.

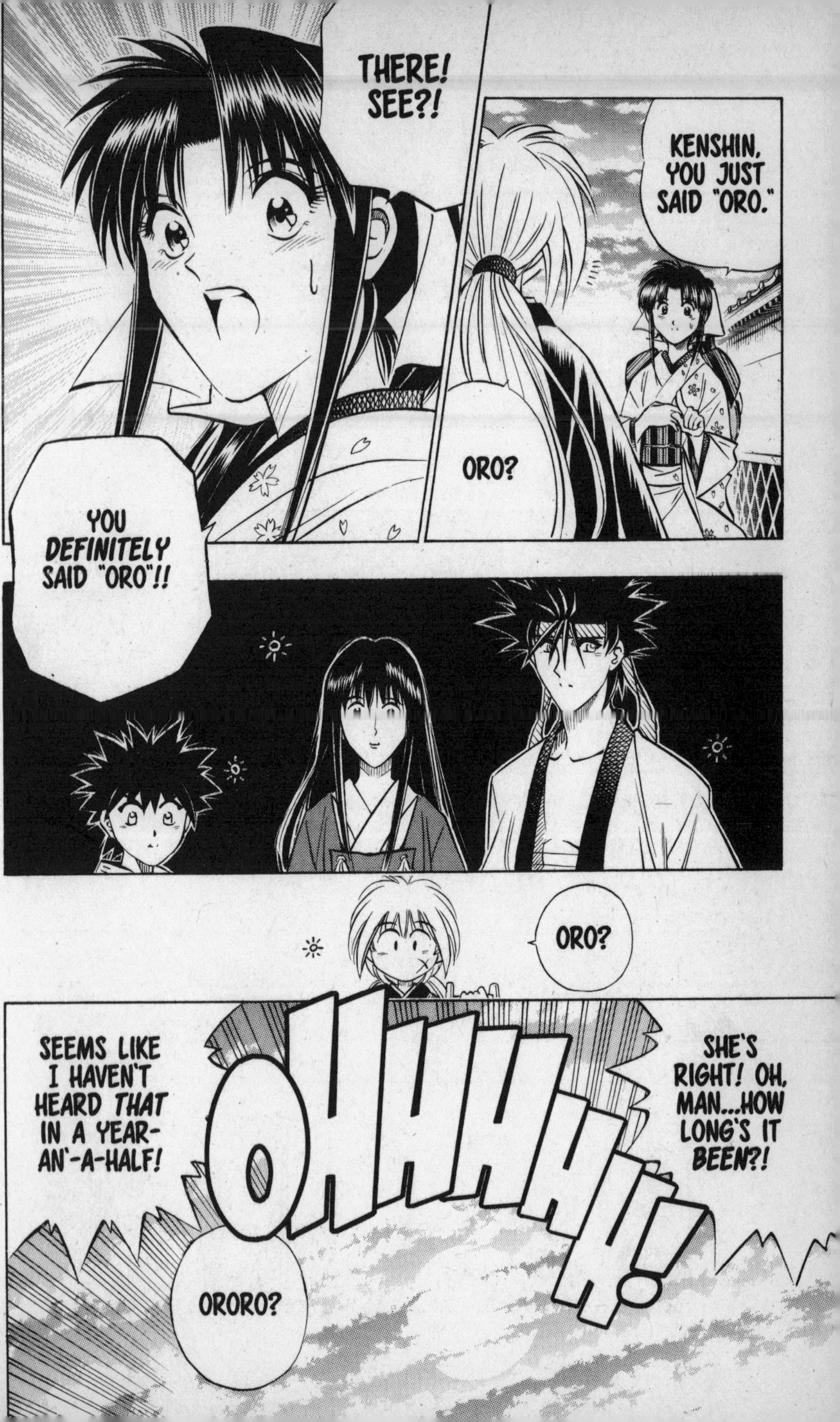
KENSHIN, YOU JUST SAID "ORO."
ORO?
THERE! SEE?!
YOU DEFINITELY SAID "ORO"!!
ORO?
SHE'S RIGHT! OH, MAN...HOW LONG'S IT BEEN?!
OHHHHH!
SEEMS LIKE I HAVEN'T HEARD *THAT* IN A YEAR-AN'-A-HALF!
ORORO?

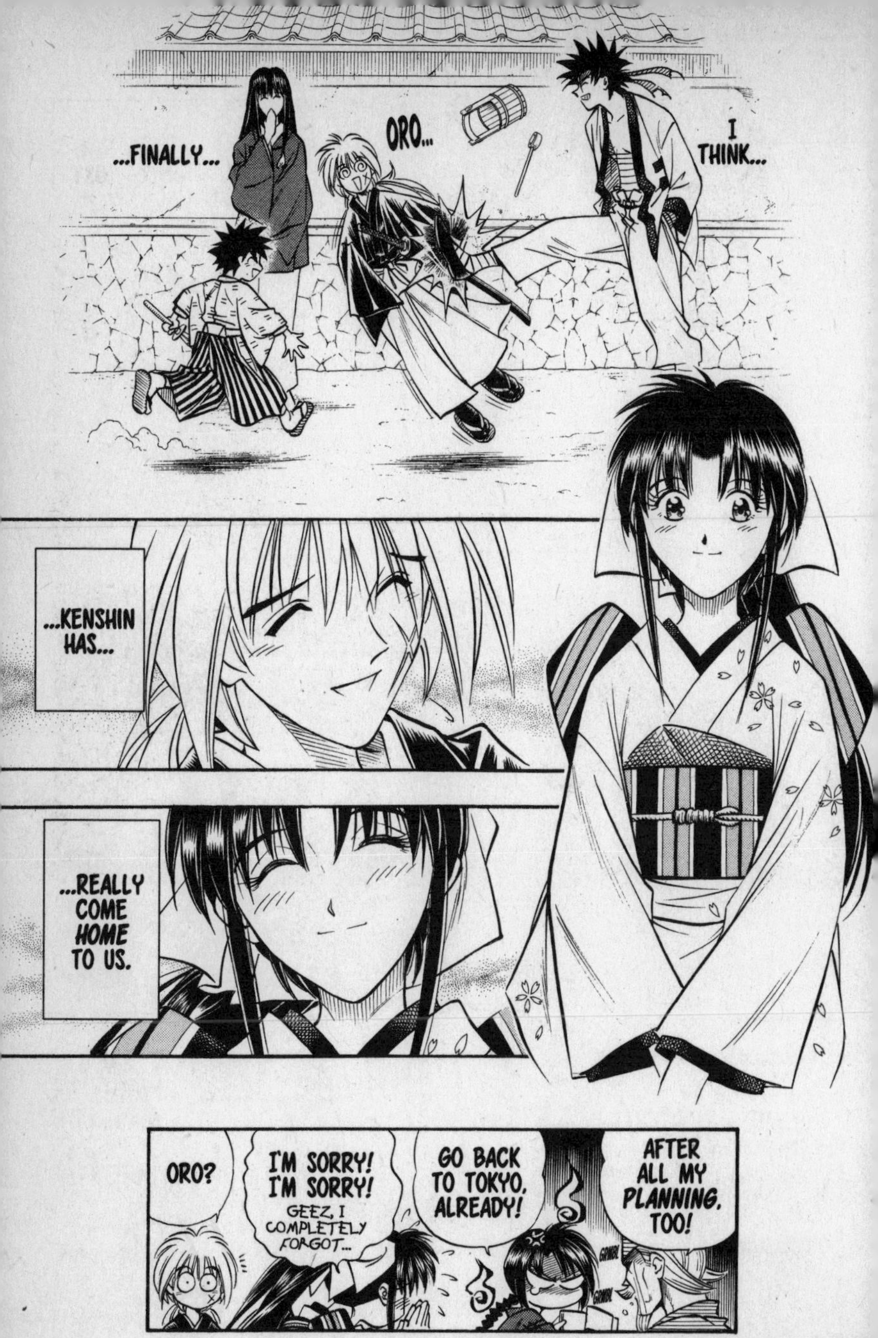

I THINK...
ORO...
...FINALLY...
...KENSHIN HAS...
...REALLY COME HOME TO US.
AFTER ALL MY PLANNING, TOO!
GRMBL
GRMBL
GO BACK TO TOKYO, ALREADY!
I'M SORRY! I'M SORRY!
GEEZ, I COMPLETELY FORGOT...
ORO?

Rurouni Kenshin

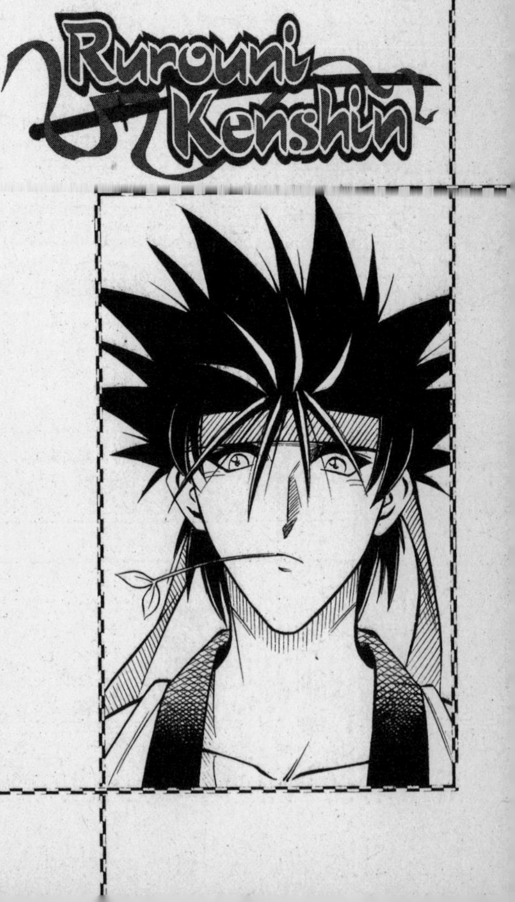

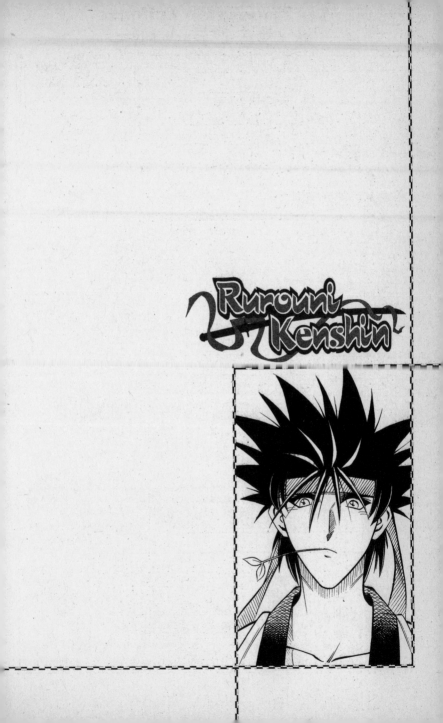

Act 151—Kyoto Epilogue

In the Blue Sky

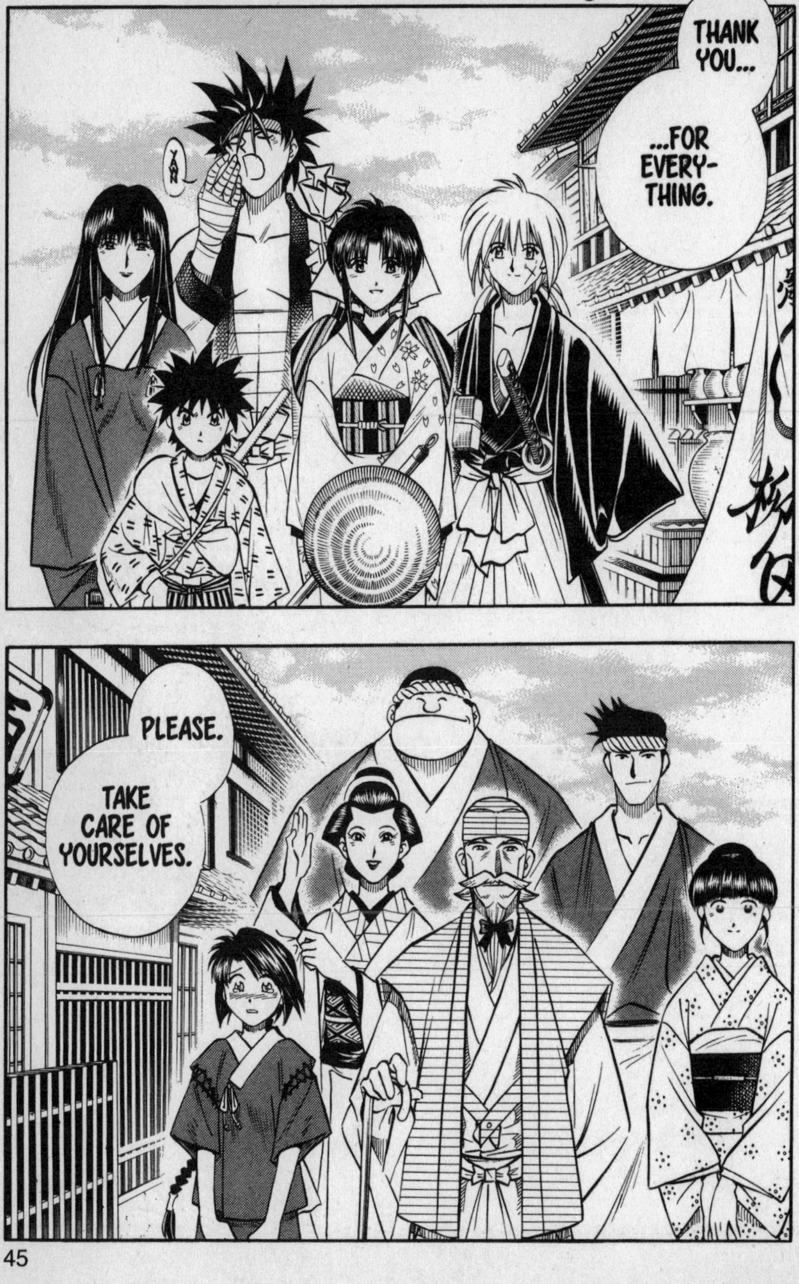
THANK YOU...
...FOR EVERY-THING.
YAWN
PLEASE.
TAKE CARE OF YOURSELVES.

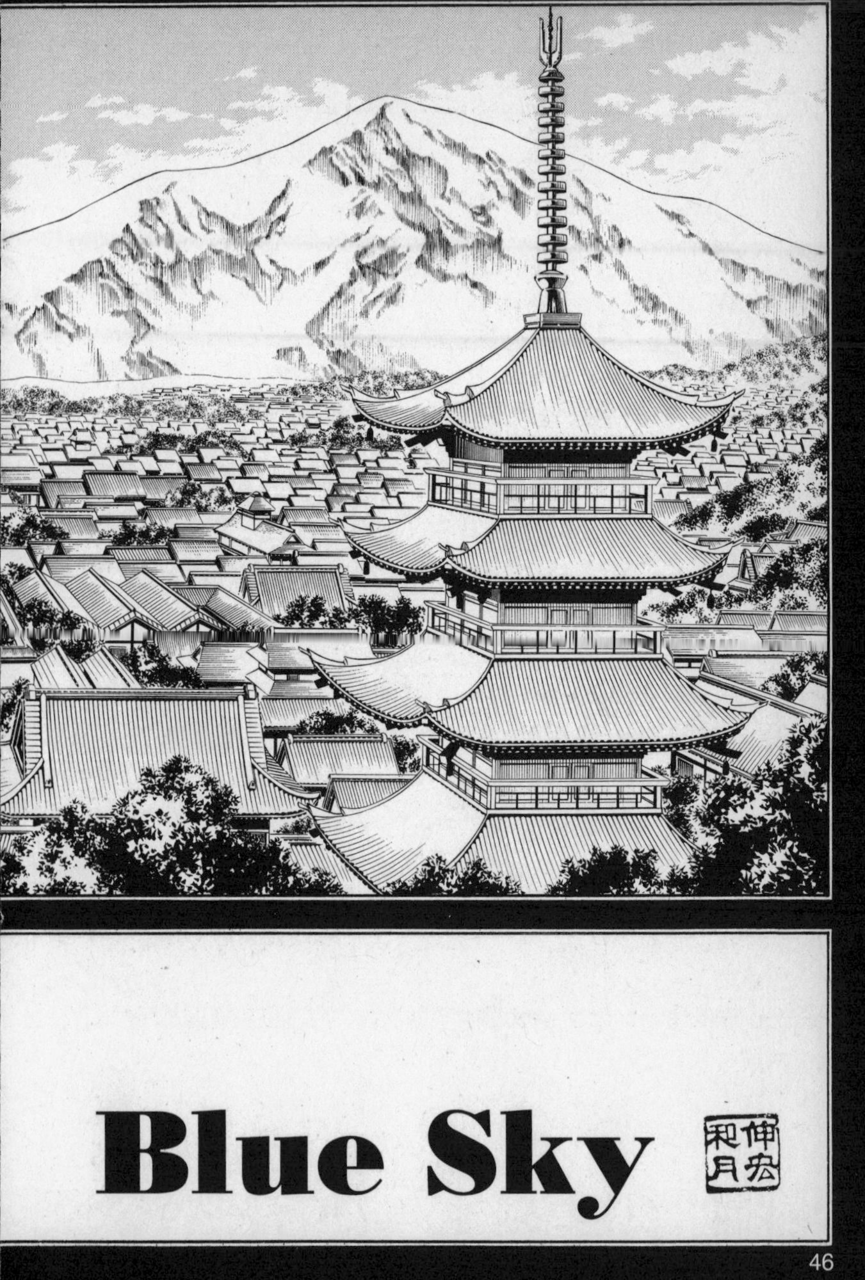

Blue Sky

和月伸宏

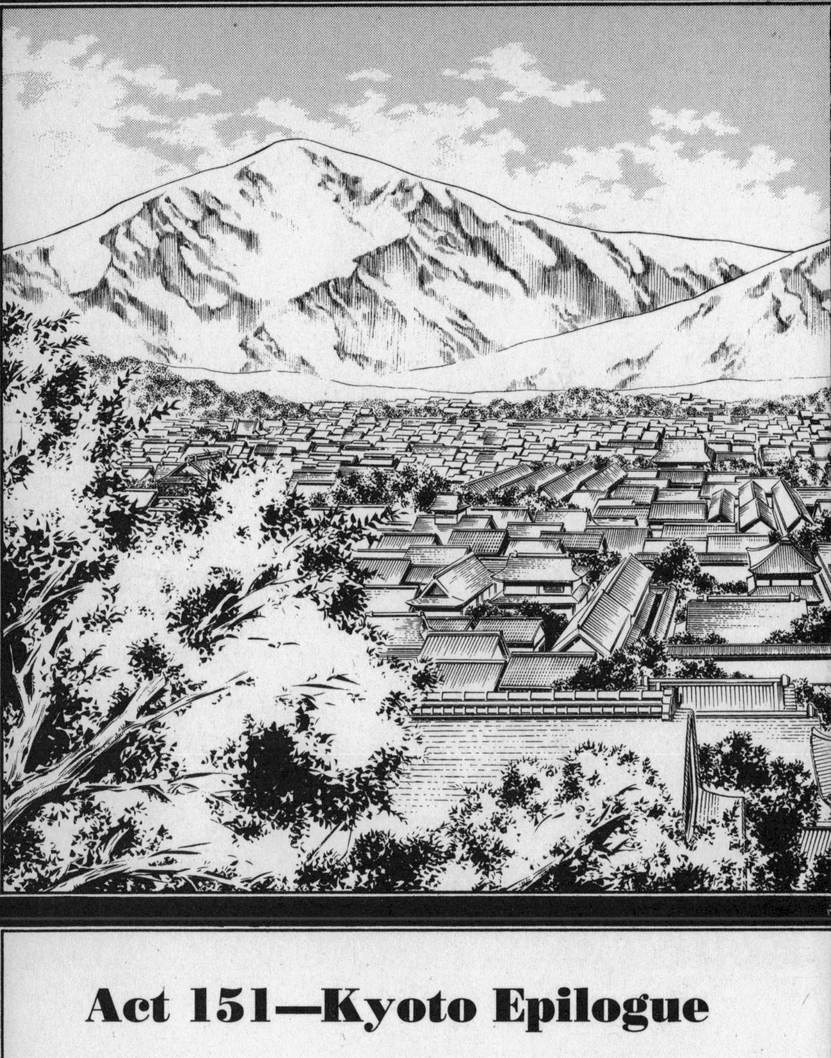

Act 151—Kyoto Epilogue

In the

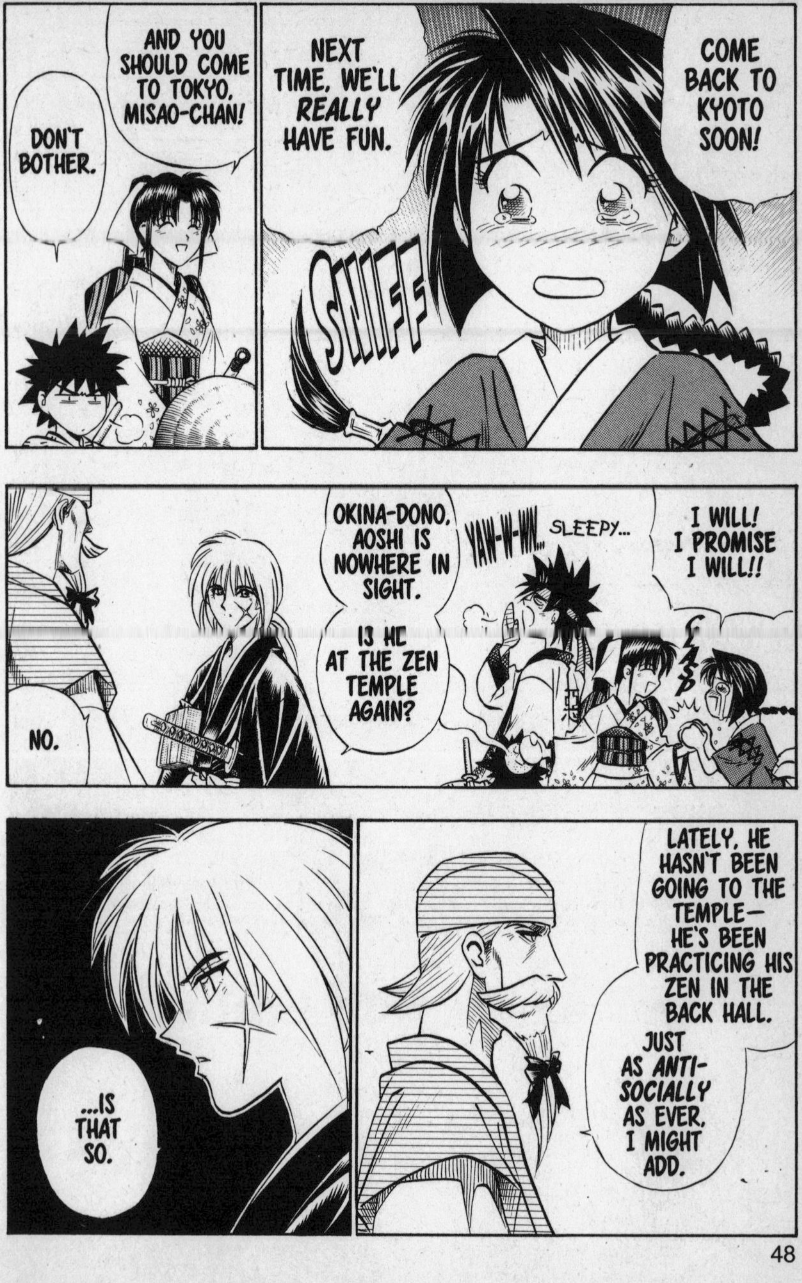
COME BACK TO KYOTO SOON!
NEXT TIME, WE'LL *REALLY* HAVE FUN.
SNIFF
AND YOU SHOULD COME TO TOKYO, MISAO-CHAN!
DON'T BOTHER.
I WILL! I PROMISE I WILL!!
SLEEPY...
YAW-W-WN...
OKINA-DONO, AOSHI IS NOWHERE IN SIGHT.
IS HE AT THE ZEN TEMPLE AGAIN?
NO.
LATELY, HE HASN'T BEEN GOING TO THE TEMPLE— HE'S BEEN PRACTICING HIS ZEN IN THE BACK HALL.
JUST AS *ANTI-SOCIALLY* AS EVER, I MIGHT ADD.
...IS THAT SO.

READ THIS WAY

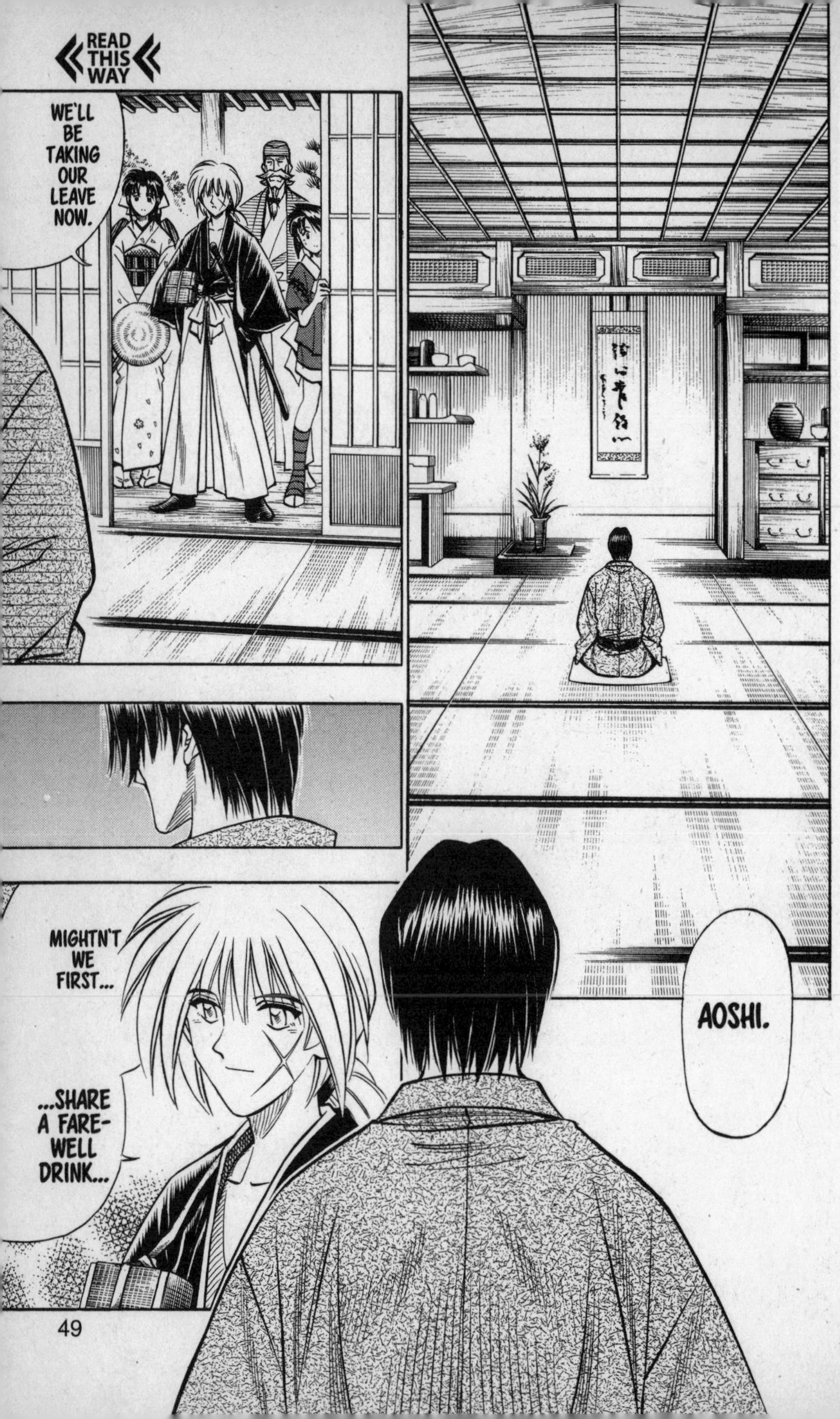
WE'LL BE TAKING OUR LEAVE NOW.
AOSHI.
MIGHTN'T WE FIRST...
...SHARE A FARE-WELL DRINK...

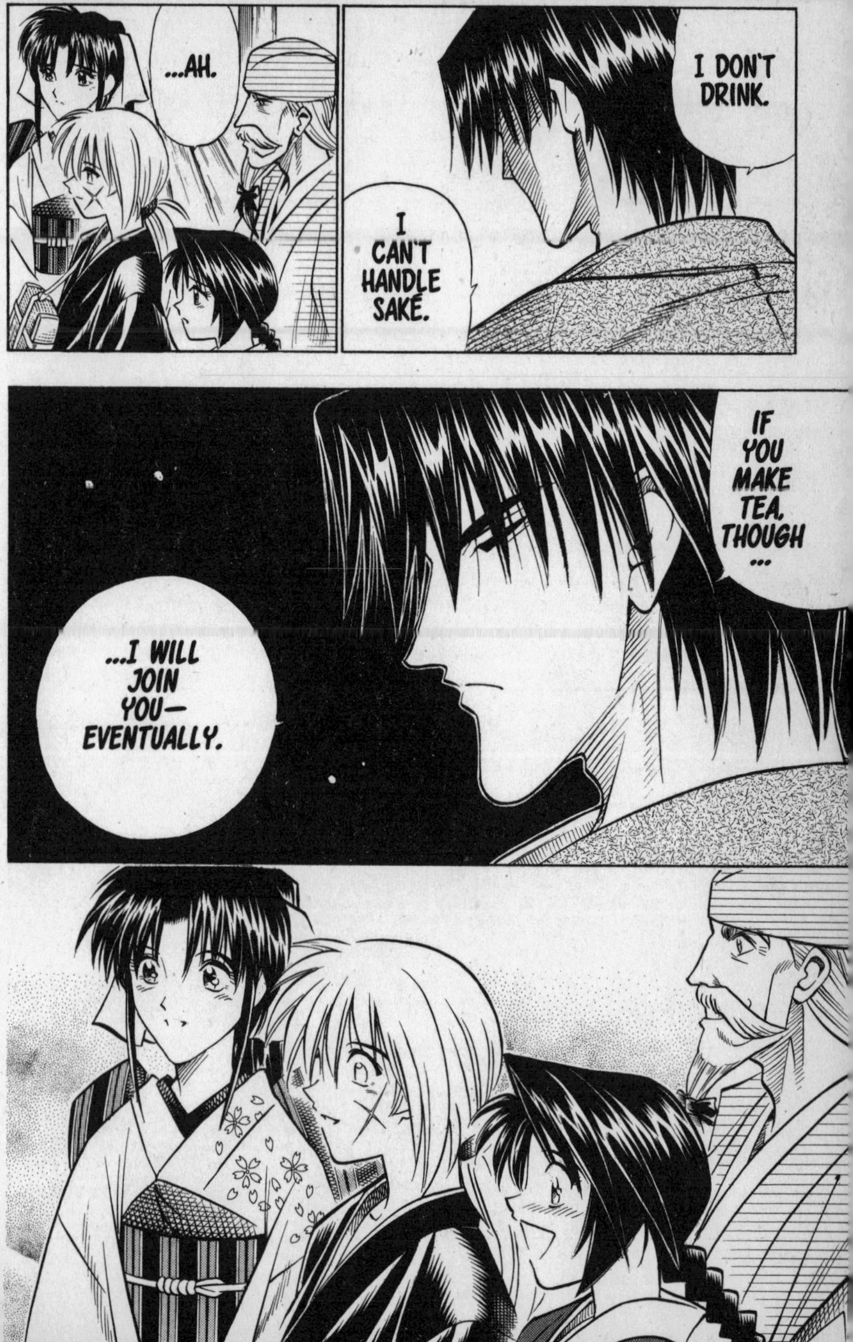
I DON'T DRINK.
I CAN'T HANDLE SAKÉ.
...AH.
IF YOU MAKE TEA, THOUGH...
...I WILL JOIN YOU—EVENTUALLY.

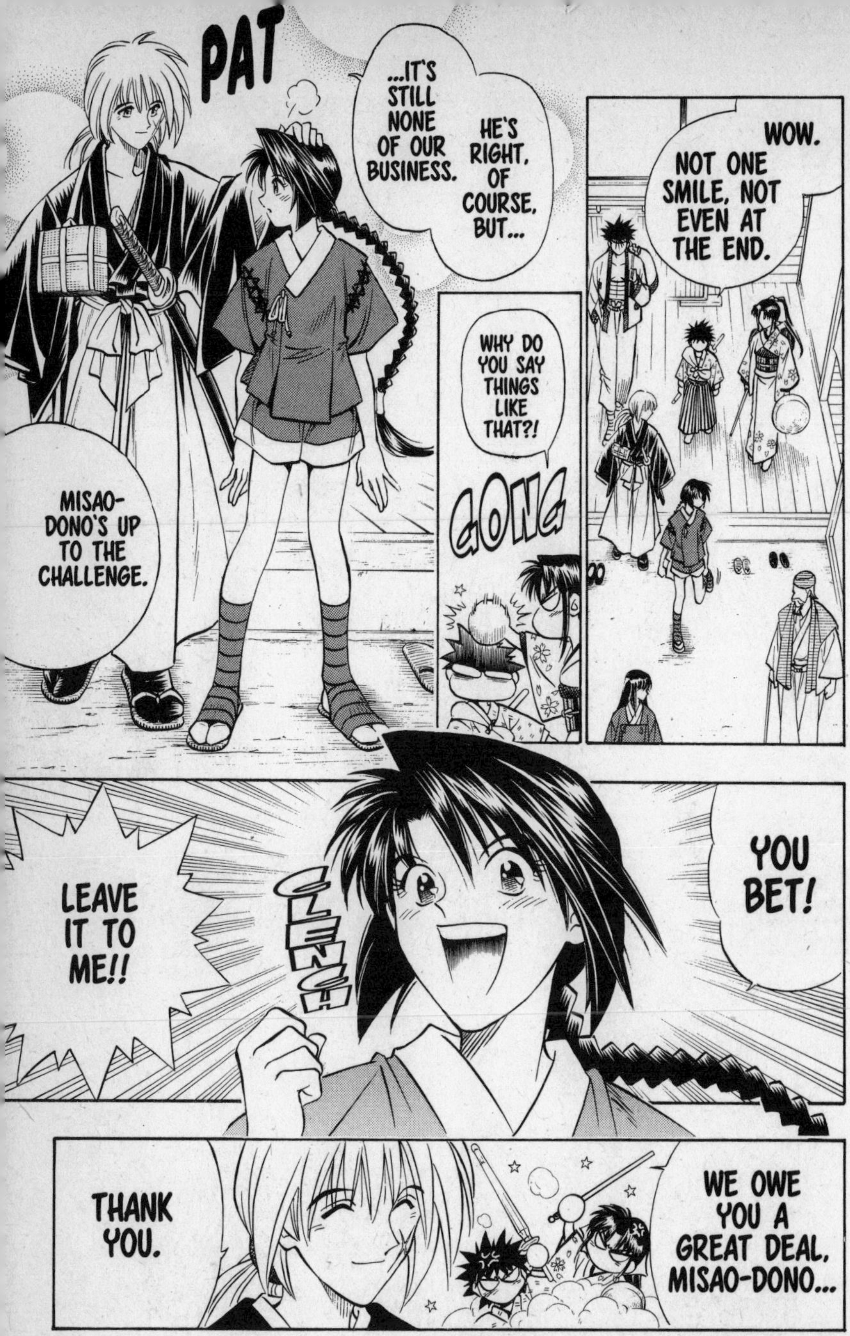
WOW.
NOT ONE SMILE, NOT EVEN AT THE END.
WHY DO YOU SAY THINGS LIKE THAT?!
GONG
PAT
HE'S RIGHT, OF COURSE, BUT...
...IT'S STILL NONE OF OUR BUSINESS.
MISAO-DONO'S UP TO THE CHALLENGE.
YOU BET!
CLENCH
LEAVE IT TO ME!!
WE OWE YOU A GREAT DEAL, MISAO-DONO...
THANK YOU.

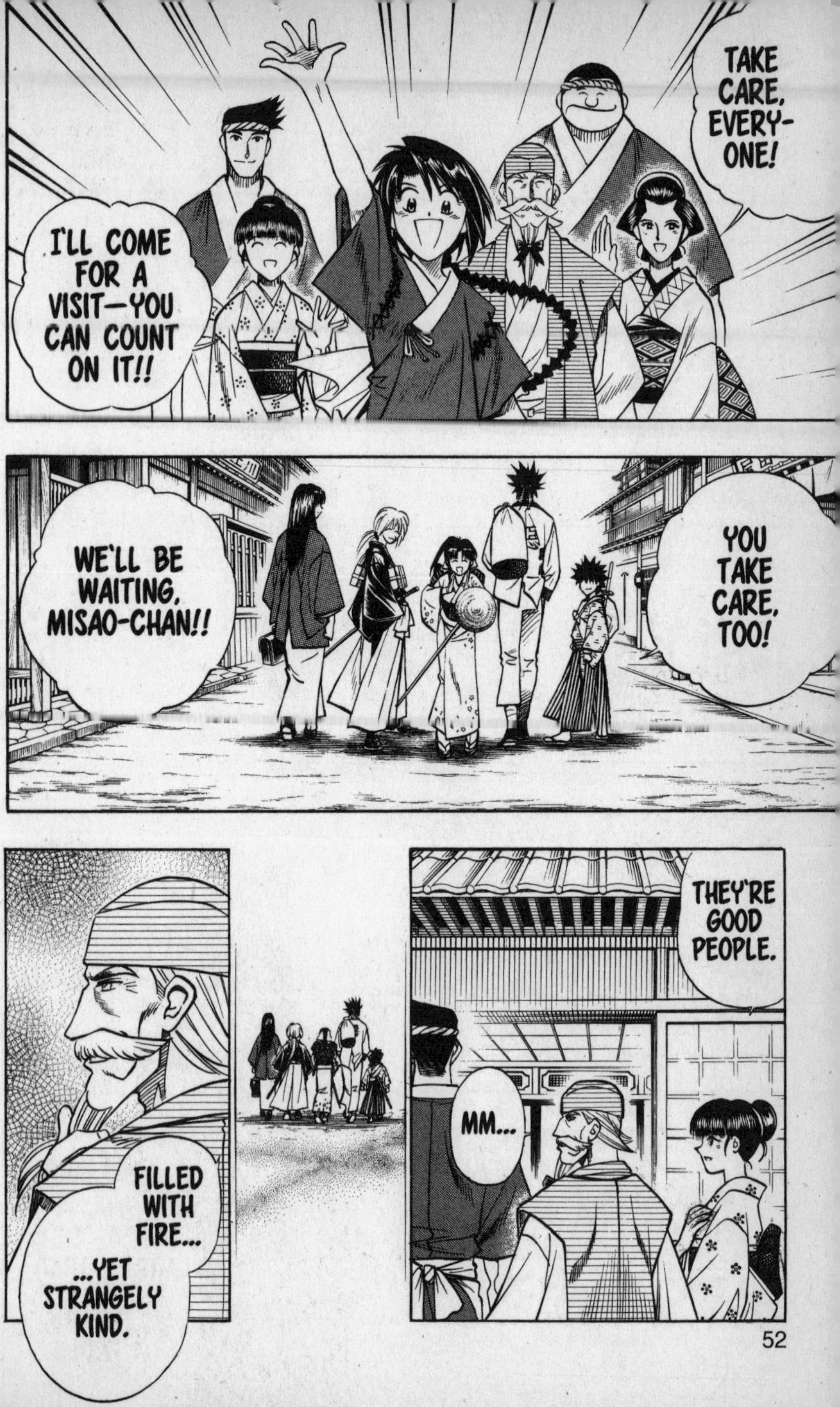
TAKE CARE, EVERY-ONE!
I'LL COME FOR A VISIT—YOU CAN COUNT ON IT!!
YOU TAKE CARE, TOO!
WE'LL BE WAITING, MISAO-CHAN!!
THEY'RE GOOD PEOPLE.
MM...
FILLED WITH FIRE...
...YET STRANGELY KIND.

READ THIS WAY

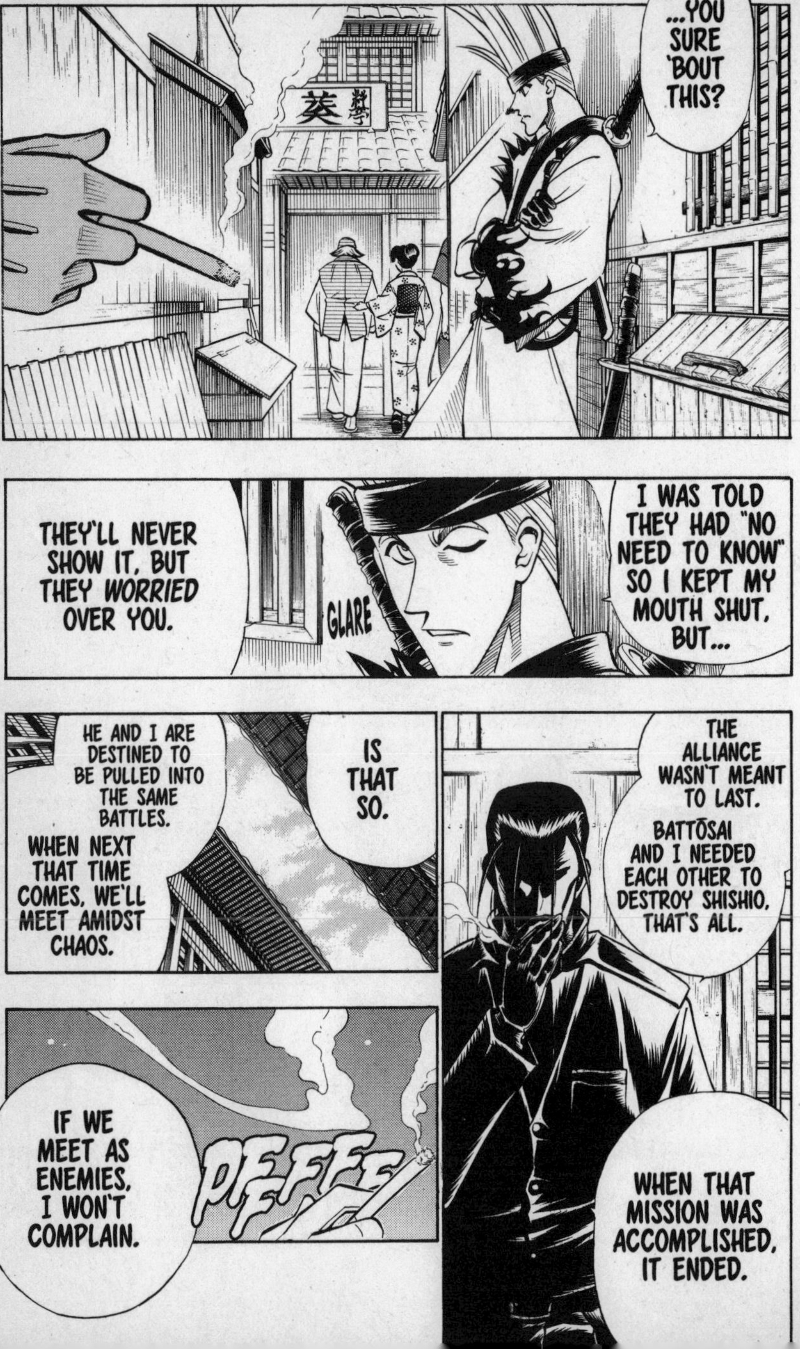
...YOU SURE 'BOUT THIS?
I WAS TOLD THEY HAD "NO NEED TO KNOW" SO I KEPT MY MOUTH SHUT, BUT...
GLARE
THEY'LL NEVER SHOW IT, BUT THEY WORRIED OVER YOU.
THE ALLIANCE WASN'T MEANT TO LAST.
BATTŌSAI AND I NEEDED EACH OTHER TO DESTROY SHISHIO, THAT'S ALL.
WHEN THAT MISSION WAS ACCOMPLISHED, IT ENDED.
IS THAT SO.
HE AND I ARE DESTINED TO BE PULLED INTO THE SAME BATTLES.
WHEN NEXT THAT TIME COMES, WE'LL MEET AMIDST CHAOS.
PFFF
IF WE MEET AS ENEMIES, I WON'T COMPLAIN.

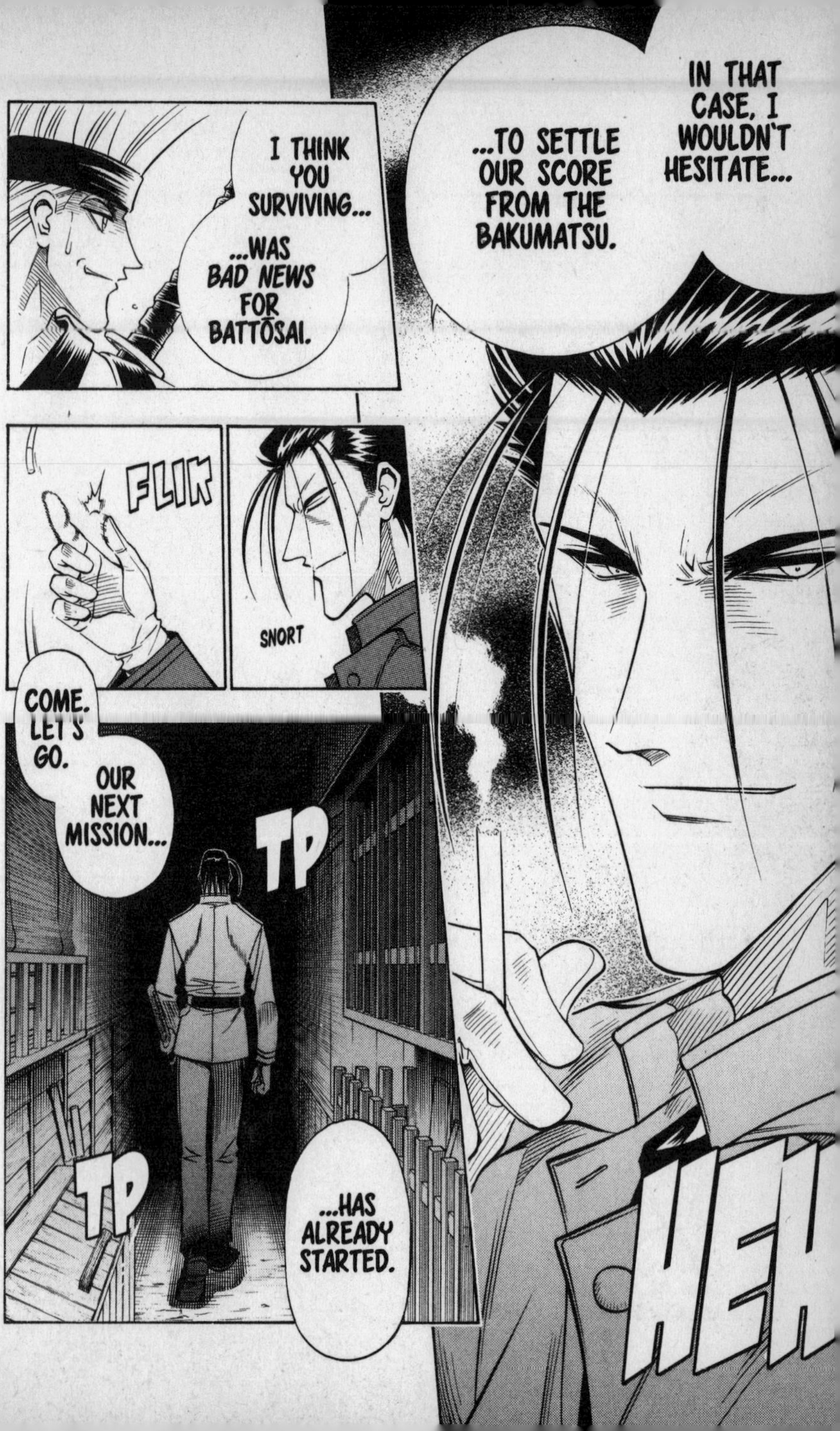
IN THAT CASE, I WOULDN'T HESITATE...
...TO SETTLE OUR SCORE FROM THE BAKUMATSU.
HEH
I THINK YOU SURVIVING...
...WAS BAD NEWS FOR BATTŌSAI.
SNORT
FLIK
COME. LET'S GO.
OUR NEXT MISSION...
TP
TP
...HAS ALREADY STARTED.

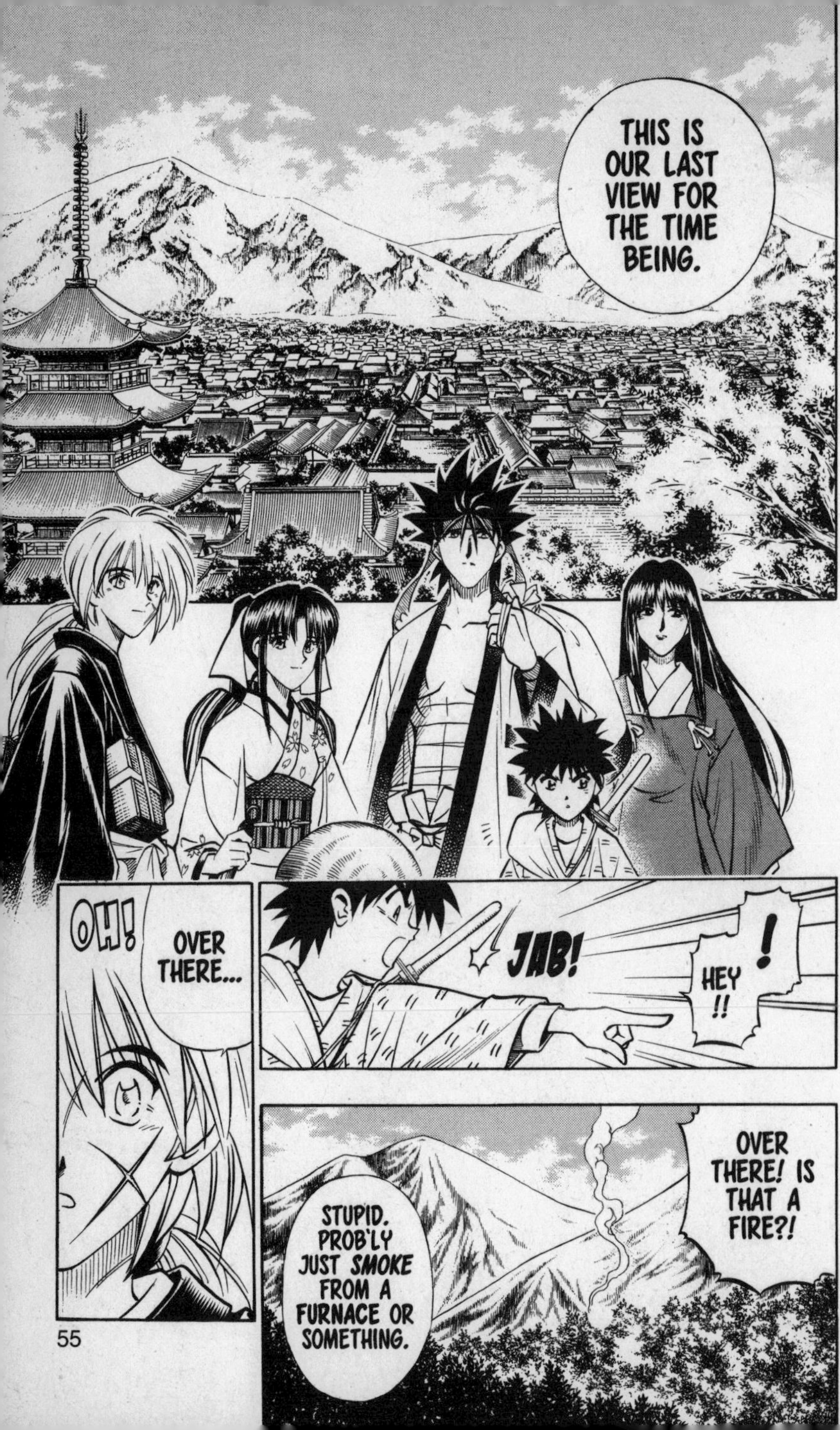
THIS IS OUR LAST VIEW FOR THE TIME BEING.
HEY !!
!
JAB!
OVER THERE! IS THAT A FIRE?!
STUPID. PROB'LY JUST SMOKE FROM A FURNACE OR SOMETHING.
OH!
OVER THERE...

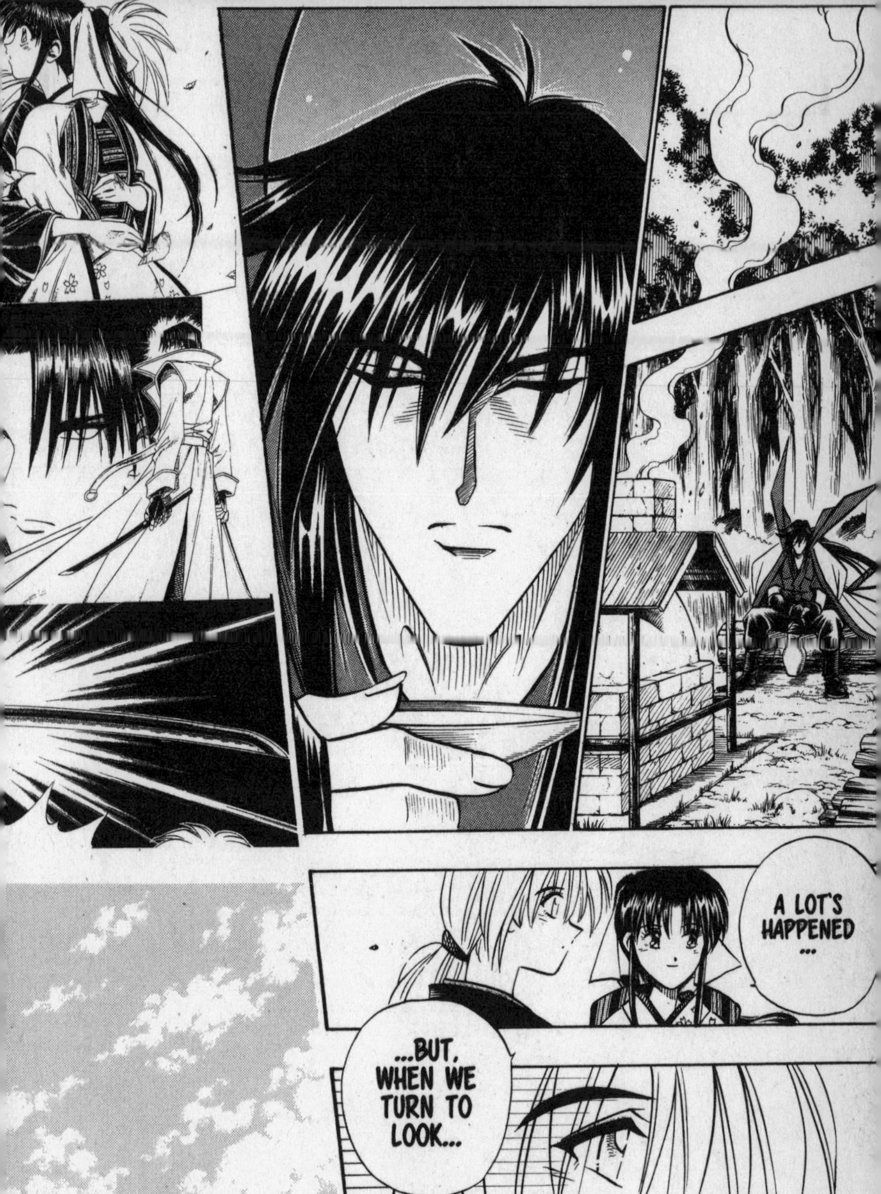
A LOT'S HAPPENED ...
...BUT, WHEN WE TURN TO LOOK...

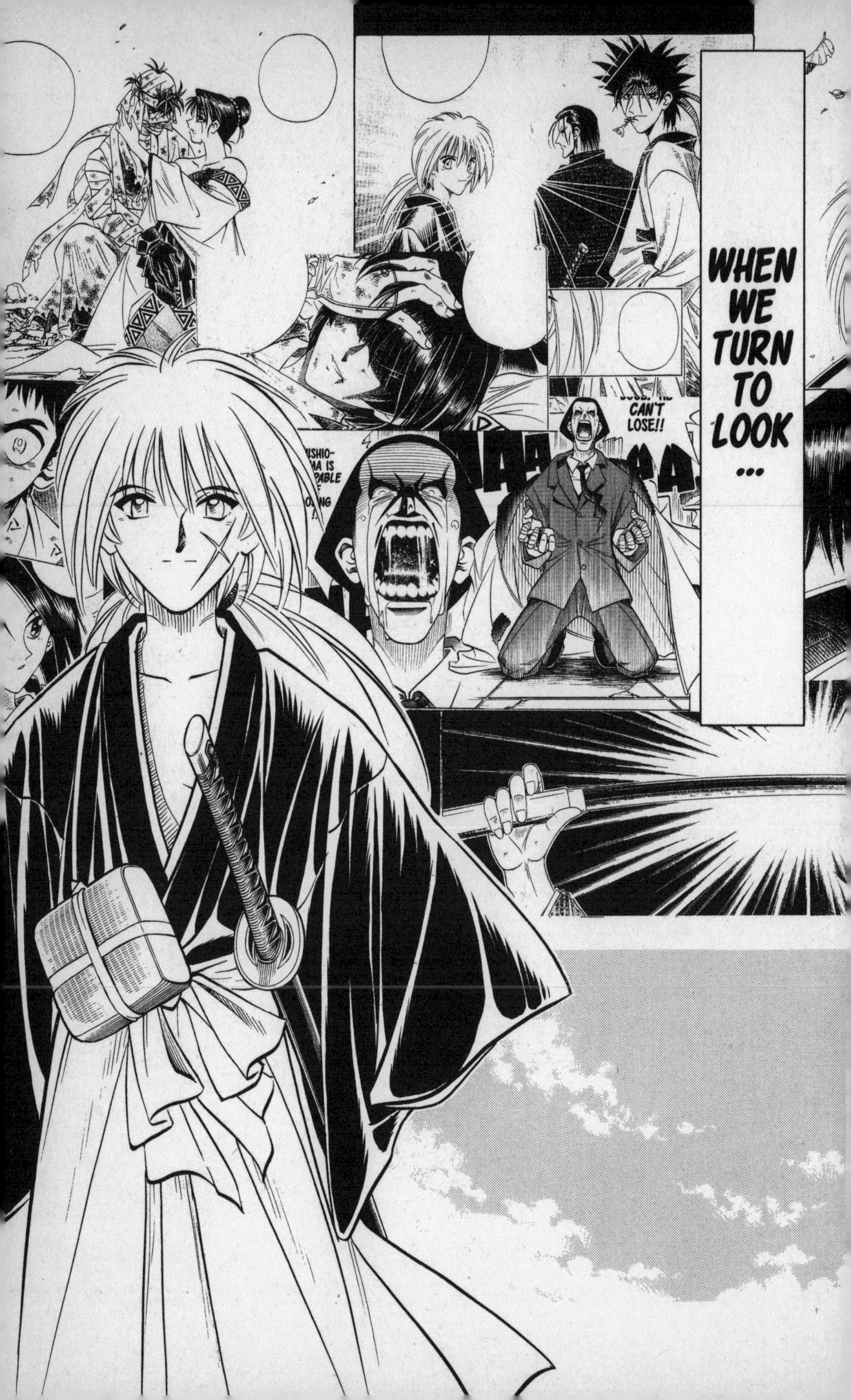

WHEN WE TURN TO LOOK ...
CAN'T LOSE!!

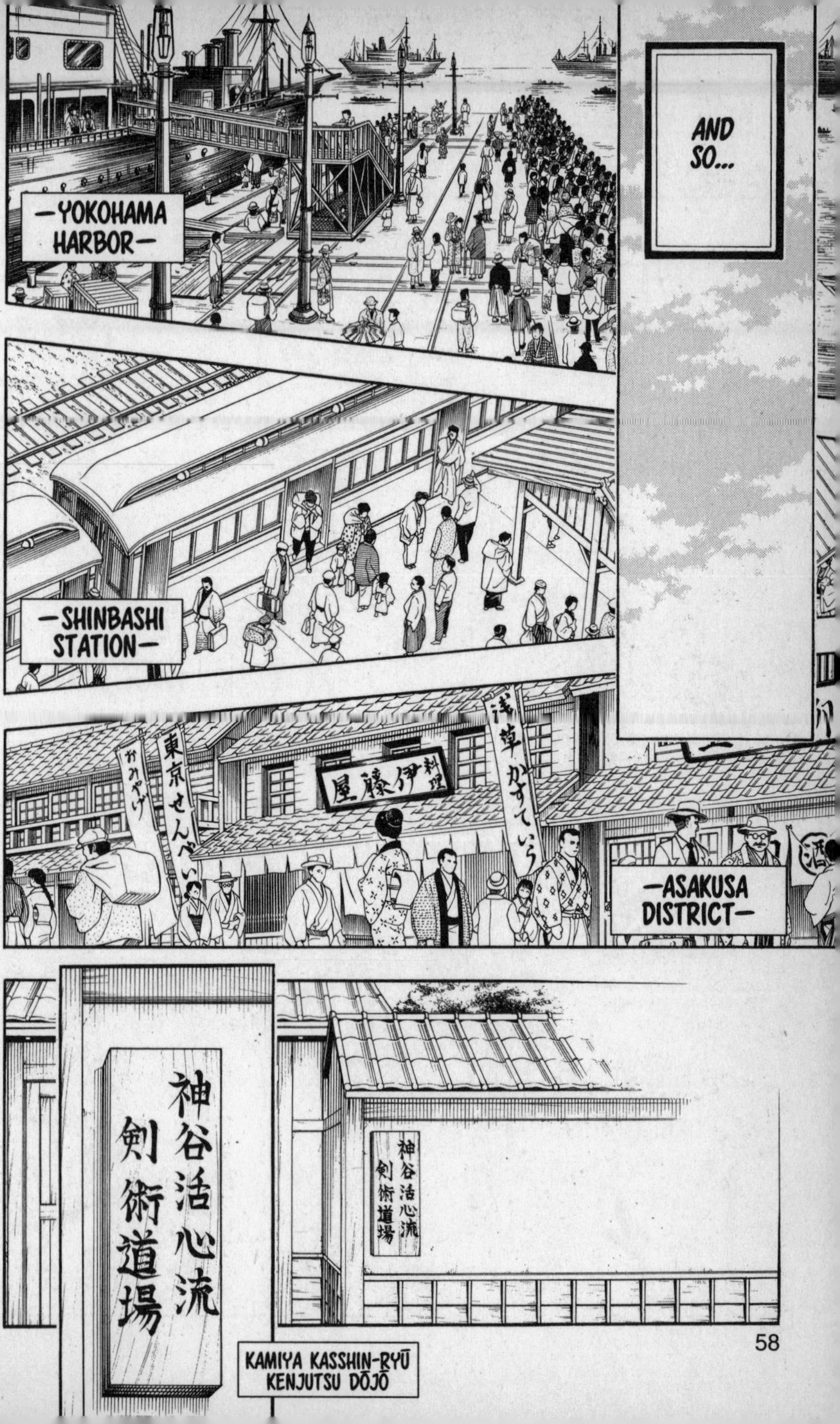
AND SO...
—YOKOHAMA HARBOR—
—SHINBASHI STATION—
浅草かすていら
料理 伊藤屋
東京せんべい
おみやげ
—ASAKUSA DISTRICT—
神谷活心流剣術道場
神谷活心流剣術道場
KAMIYA KASSHIN-RYŪ KENJUTSU DŌJŌ

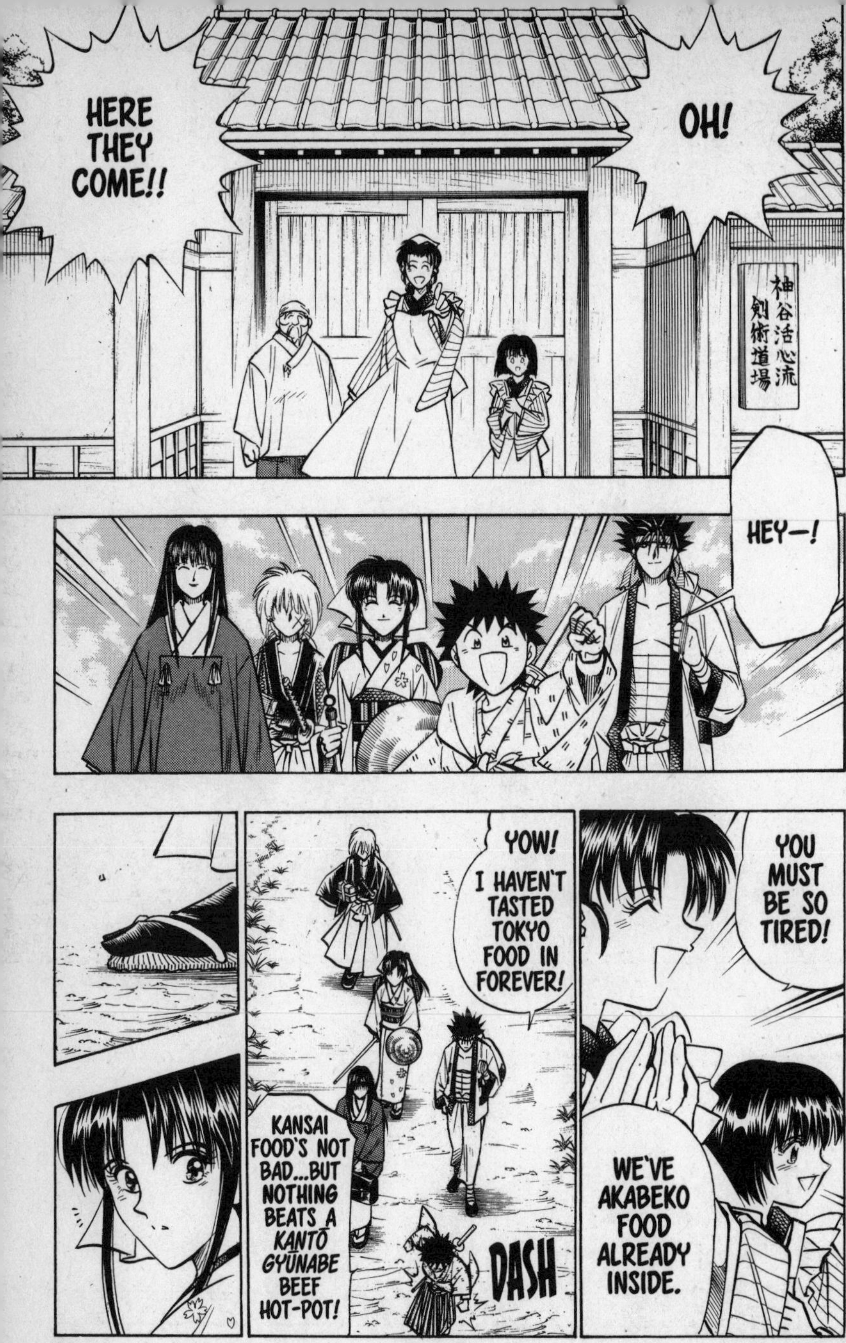
OH!
HERE THEY COME!!
神谷活心流
剣術道場
HEY—!
YOU MUST BE SO TIRED!
WE'VE AKABEKO FOOD ALREADY INSIDE.
YOW! I HAVEN'T TASTED TOKYO FOOD IN FOREVER!
DASH
KANSAI FOOD'S NOT BAD...BUT NOTHING BEATS A KANTŌ GYŪNABE BEEF HOT-POT!

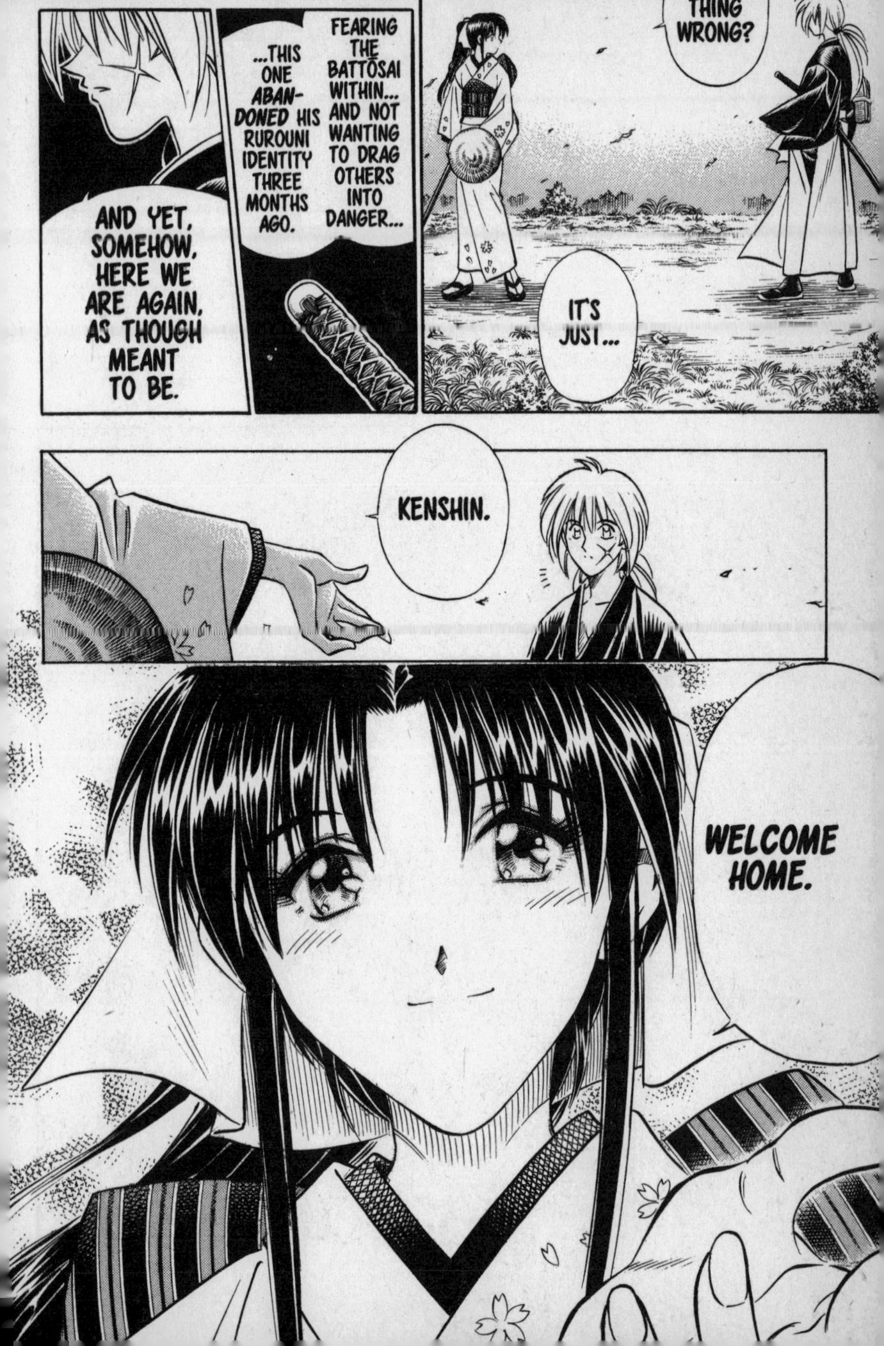
...SOME-THING WRONG?
IT'S JUST...
FEARING THE BATTOSAI WITHIN... AND NOT WANTING TO DRAG OTHERS INTO DANGER...
...THIS ONE *ABANDONED* HIS RUROUNI IDENTITY THREE MONTHS AGO.
AND YET, SOMEHOW, HERE WE ARE AGAIN, AS THOUGH MEANT TO BE.
KENSHIN.
WELCOME HOME.

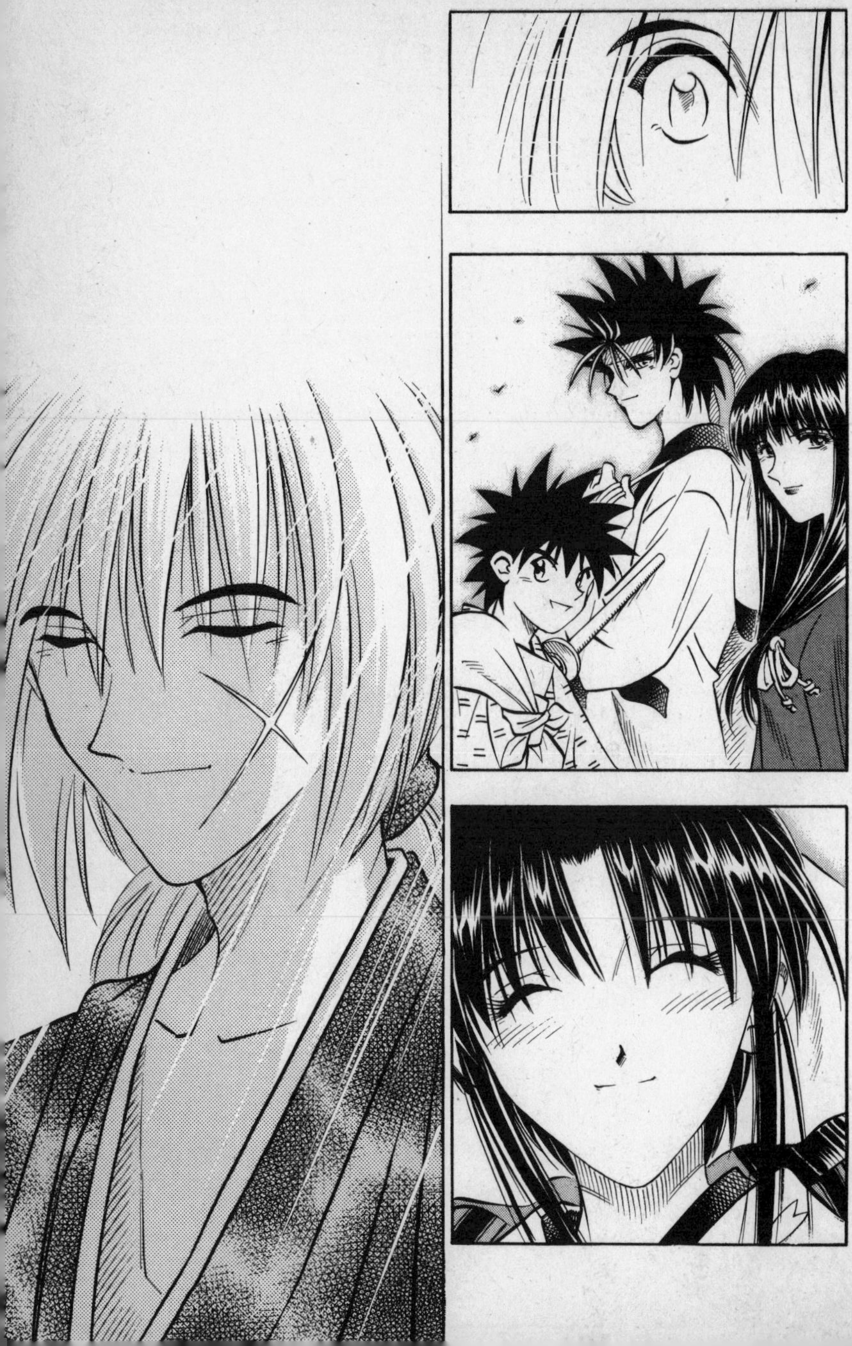

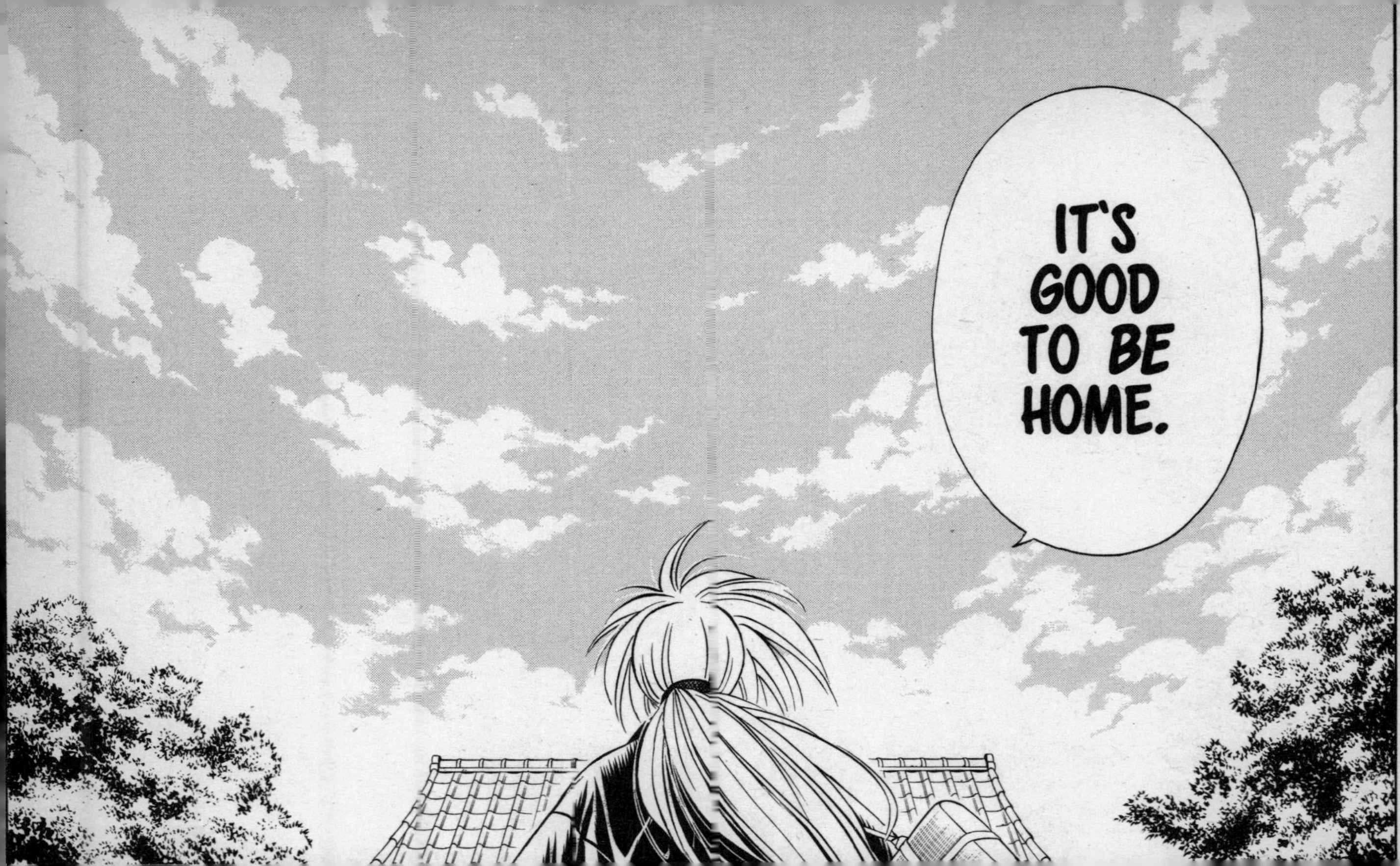
IT'S GOOD TO BE HOME.

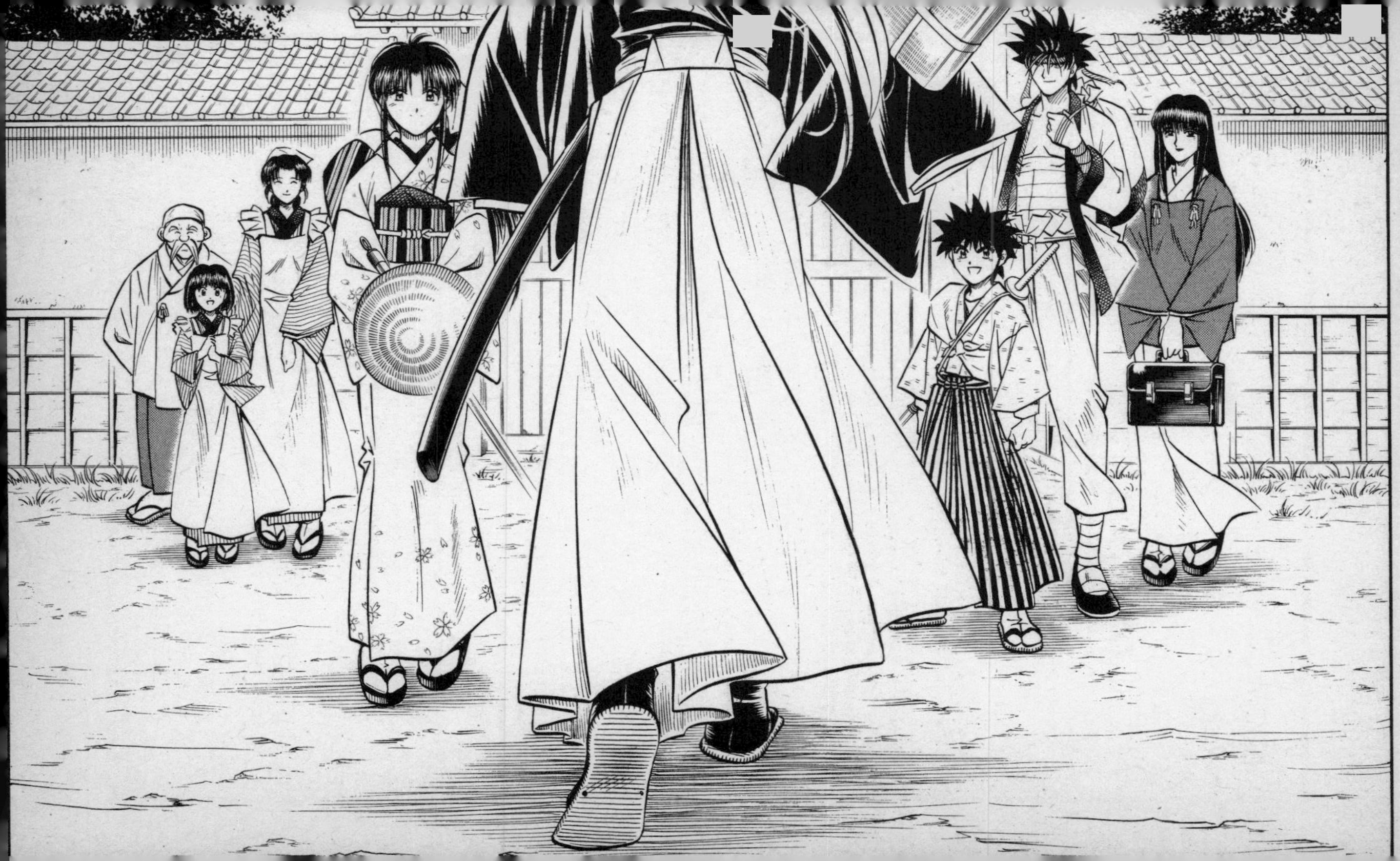

"FREE TALK"⟨PART I⟩

Long time no see. Watsuki here. It's been getting colder lately—and I *like* the cold—so I've started shifting into gear. Or...so I thought, but now here it is, the end of the year. My life's passing by at lightning speed.

"In the Blue Sky," the title of the final episode in the Kyoto Arc, was borrowed from the BGM of Temjin's stage in "Den'nō Senki Virtual On." I used it because of the blue sky in the last scene, but also because this BGM (or, I should say, the arranged version from the soundtrack) is a piece that perfectly fits my image of the *Kenshin* Kyoto episodes. In that Watsuki listened to it over and over while writing—especially during the "Kenshin vs. Shishio" scenes—it seemed the ideal closing title. Also, as many of you may have noticed, that last (manga) scene came from the final (anime) scene of the original TV series opening. I'd been planning to wrap up the Kyoto episodes with "It's good to *be* home," but there I was, struggling with the scene, and then I saw *that*, and thought, "This is it."

So, the Kyoto Arc is finally over. I'd planned to stretch it out over a year, but once the ideas started, it ended up going over two. It all paid off in the end, though, as it was a turning point, bringing my thinking processes and abilities as a manga artist up two or three levels. Those of you who supported me, thank you very much. Please continue to do so!

And now for the silliness, starting with games. "Polygon Samurai Spirits": At the time of this writing, the release date is still unknown. Waiting for it is hard, but for something this much fun, I guess I'll tough it out. "*Gekka no Kenshi* (The Last Blade)," on the other hand, has been coming into focus...no! Let's not *talk* about it, let's *play* it! Incidentally, Watsuki's favorite character—or so he anticipates—is Washizuka Kei'chirō (heh). As said in the previous volume, I hope they sharpen each other, both developing into great games.

To be honest, I've been so busy lately that I haven't played much of anything. I *did* play "TenSamu" on the NeoGeo CD so much that the stick broke, though. (Now I have to wait to buy a replacement.) I'm not really a gamer, so I can't say I'm experiencing withdrawal, but there are good days, and there are bad days....

Act 152
Cross-Shaped Scar

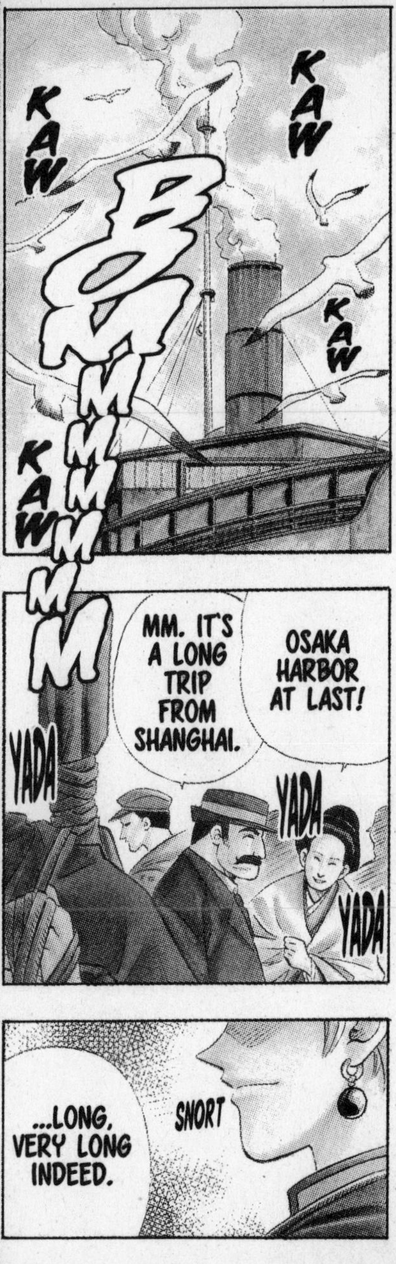
KAW
KAW
KAW
KAW
BOMMMMMMMM
OSAKA HARBOR AT LAST!
MM. IT'S A LONG TRIP FROM SHANGHAI.
YADA
YADA
YADA
SNORT
...LONG, VERY LONG INDEED.

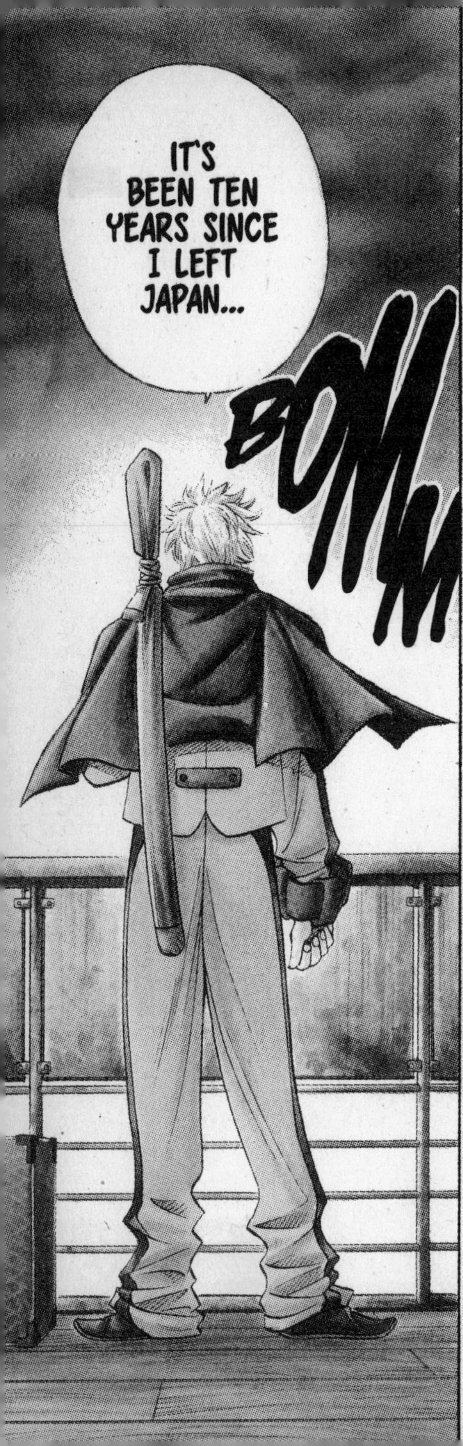
IT'S BEEN TEN YEARS SINCE I LEFT JAPAN...
BOMM

Act 152 Cross-Shaped Scar

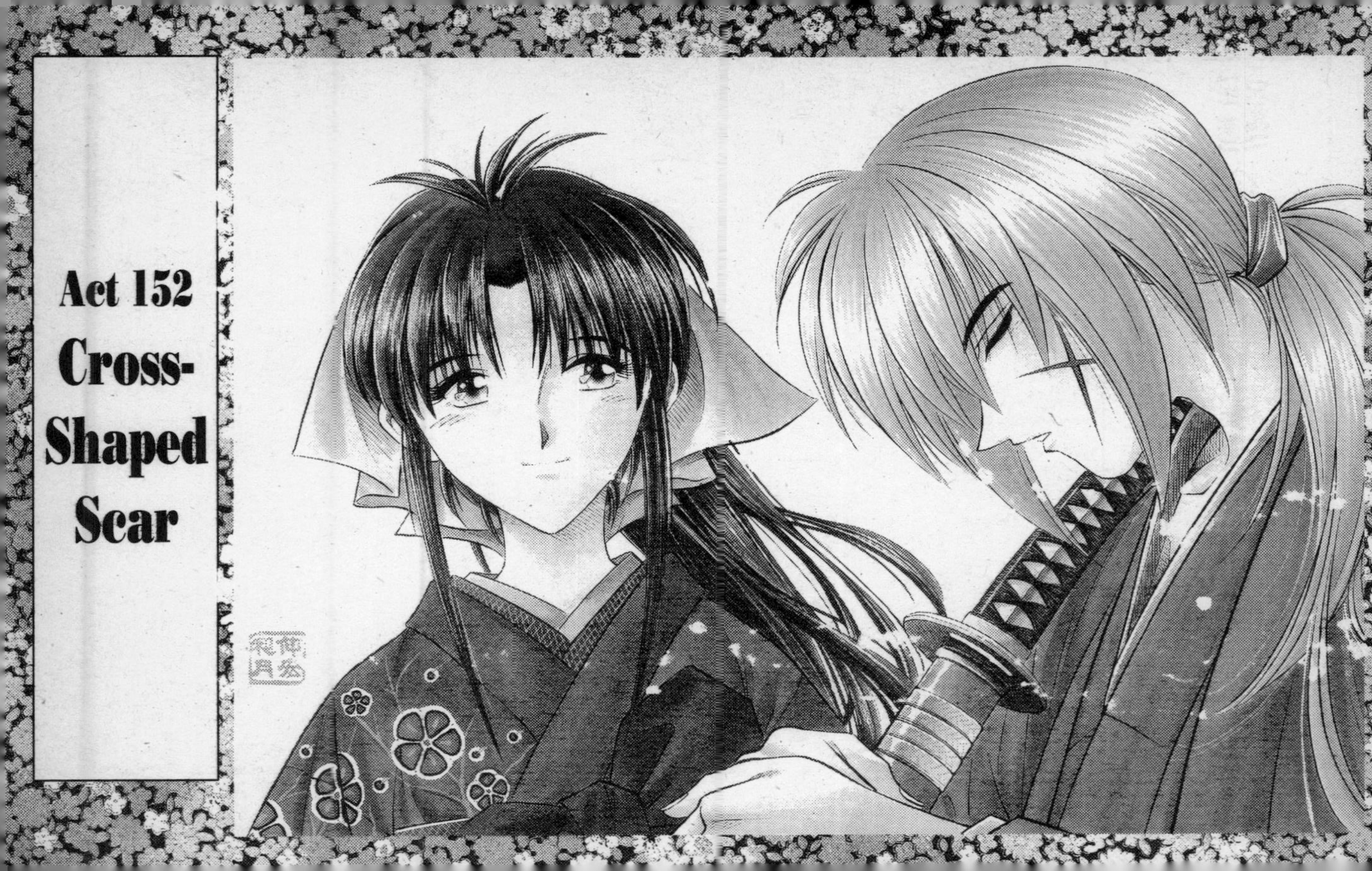

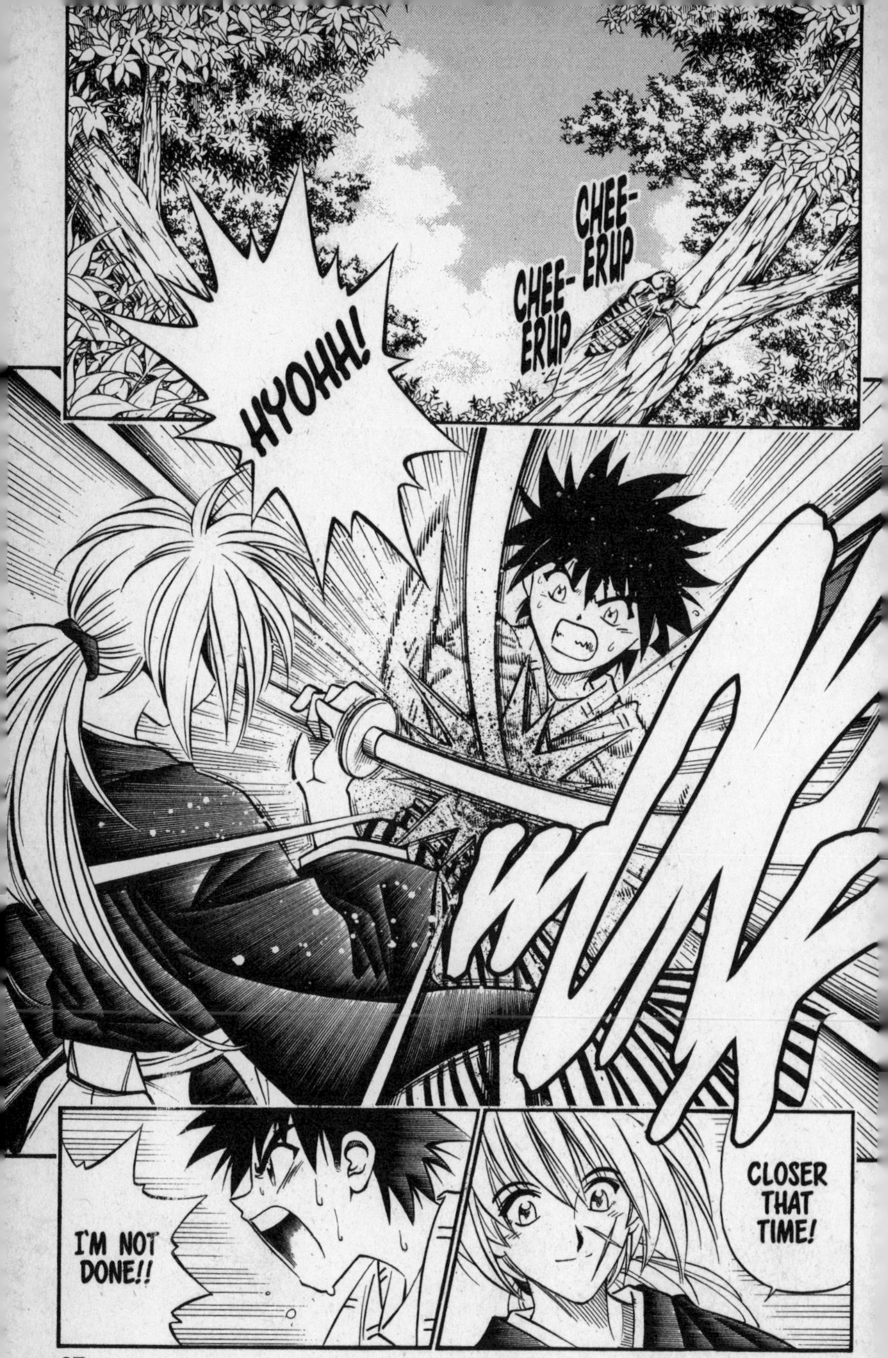
CHEE-ERUP
CHEE-ERUP
HYOHH!
CLOSER THAT TIME!
I'M NOT DONE!!

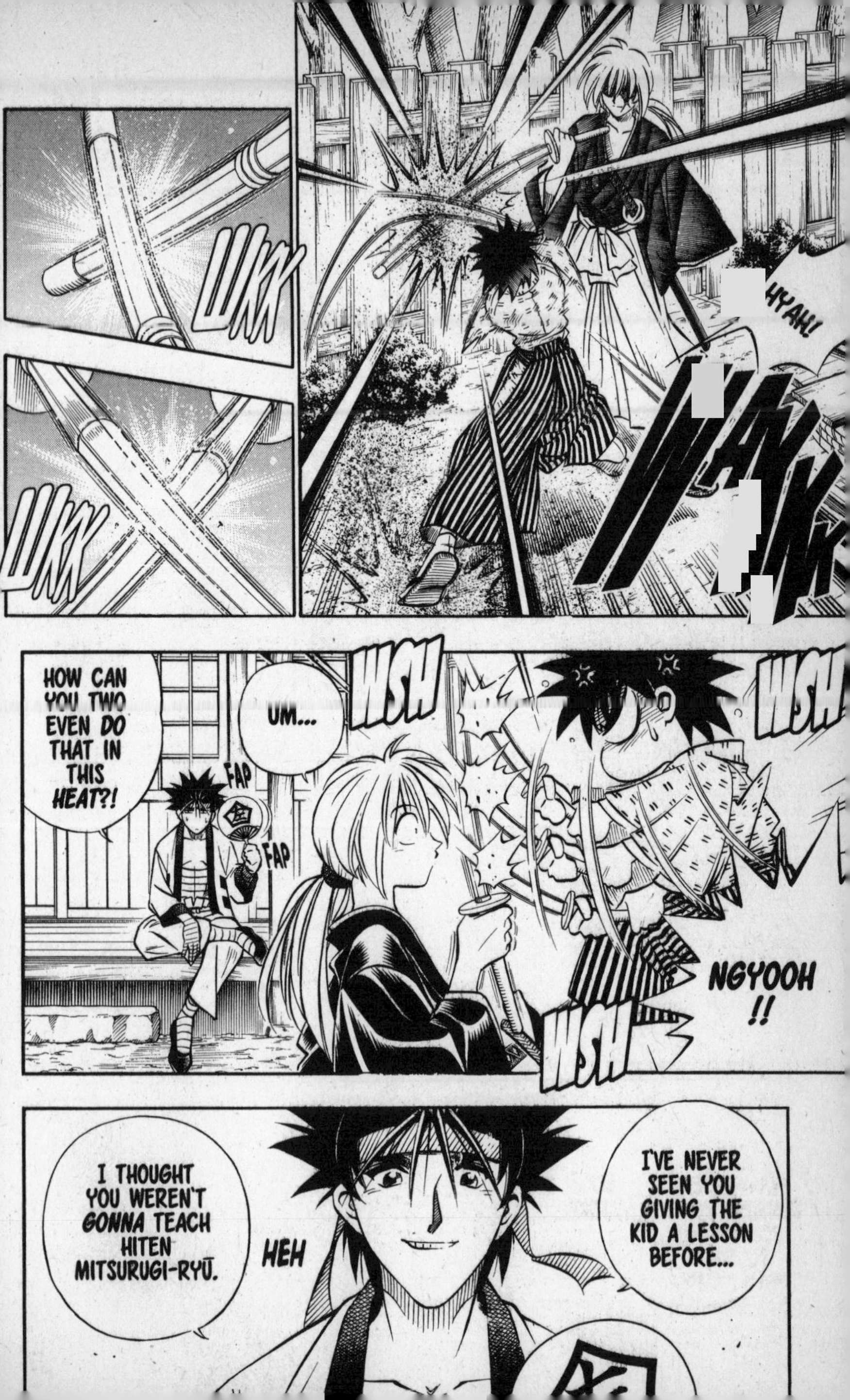
HYAH!
WSH
NGYOOH !!
WSH
UM...
WSH
HOW CAN YOU TWO EVEN DO THAT IN THIS HEAT?!
FAP
FAP
I'VE NEVER SEEN YOU GIVING THE KID A LESSON BEFORE...
HEH
I THOUGHT YOU WEREN'T GONNA TEACH HITEN MITSURUGI-RYŪ.

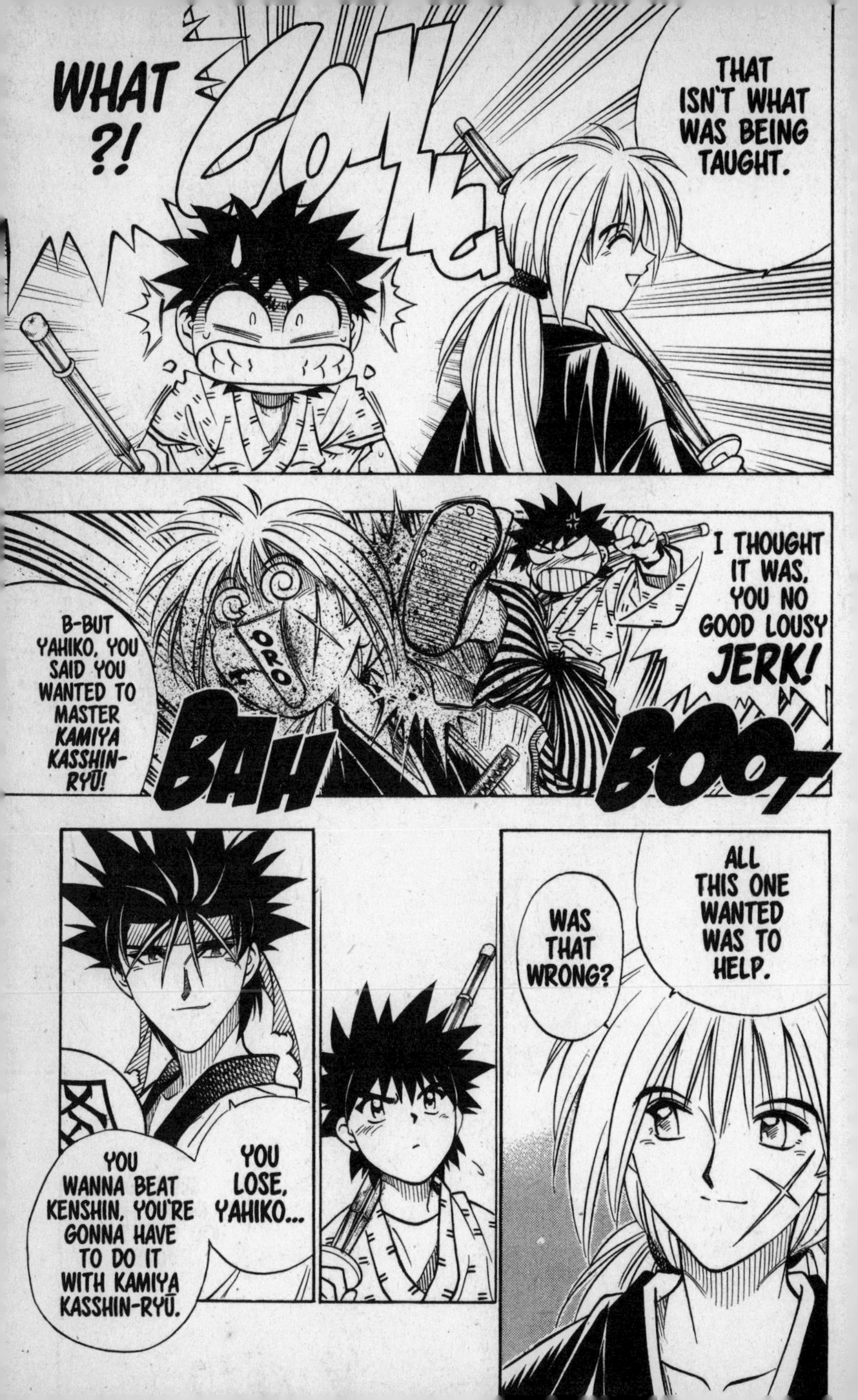
THAT ISN'T WHAT WAS BEING TAUGHT.
GON
WHAT ?!
I THOUGHT IT WAS, YOU NO GOOD LOUSY JERK!
BOOT
ORO
BAH
B-BUT YAHIKO, YOU SAID YOU WANTED TO MASTER KAMIYA KASSHIN-RYŪ!
ALL THIS ONE WANTED WAS TO HELP.
WAS THAT WRONG?
YOU LOSE, YAHIKO...
YOU WANNA BEAT KENSHIN, YOU'RE GONNA HAVE TO DO IT WITH KAMIYA KASSHIN-RYŪ.

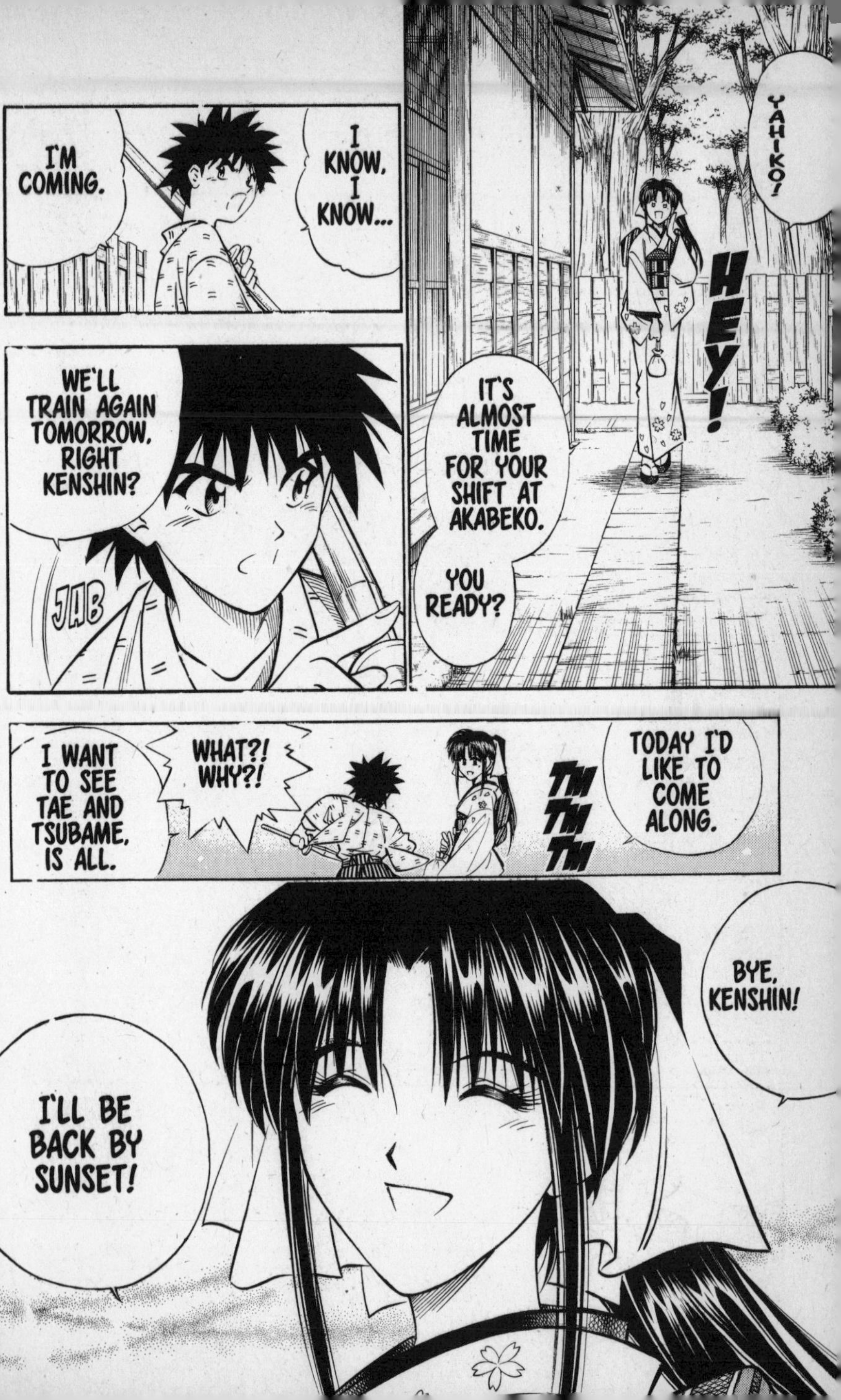
YAHIKO!
HEY!
IT'S ALMOST TIME FOR YOUR SHIFT AT AKABEKO.
YOU READY?
I KNOW, I KNOW...
I'M COMING.
WE'LL TRAIN AGAIN TOMORROW, RIGHT KENSHIN?
JAB
TODAY I'D LIKE TO COME ALONG.
TM TM TM
WHAT?! WHY?!
I WANT TO SEE TAE AND TSUBAME, IS ALL.
BYE, KENSHIN!
I'LL BE BACK BY SUNSET!

READ THIS WAY

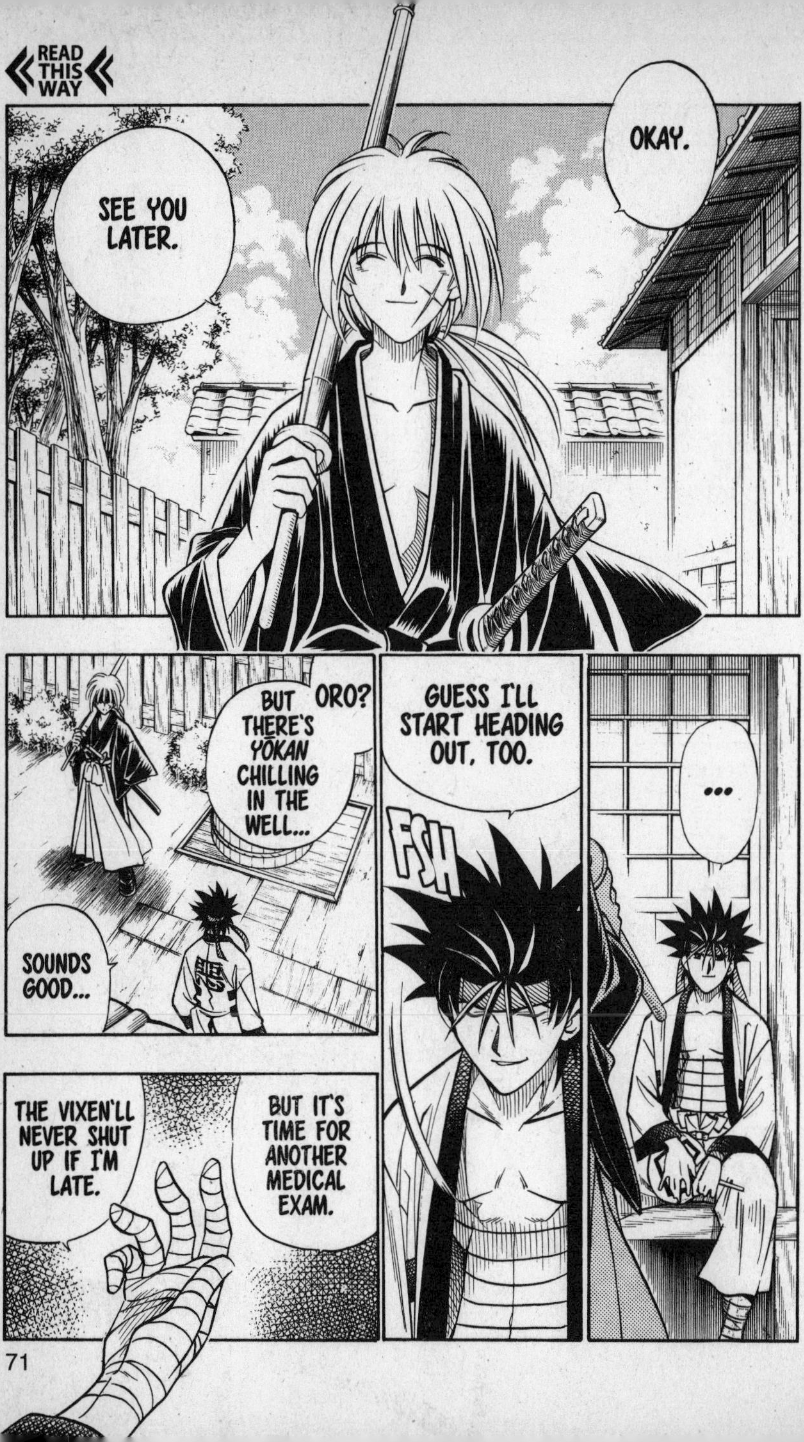
OKAY.
SEE YOU LATER.
...
GUESS I'LL START HEADING OUT, TOO.
FSH
ORO?
BUT THERE'S YŌKAN CHILLING IN THE WELL...
SOUNDS GOOD...
BUT IT'S TIME FOR ANOTHER MEDICAL EXAM.
THE VIXEN'LL NEVER SHUT UP IF I'M LATE.

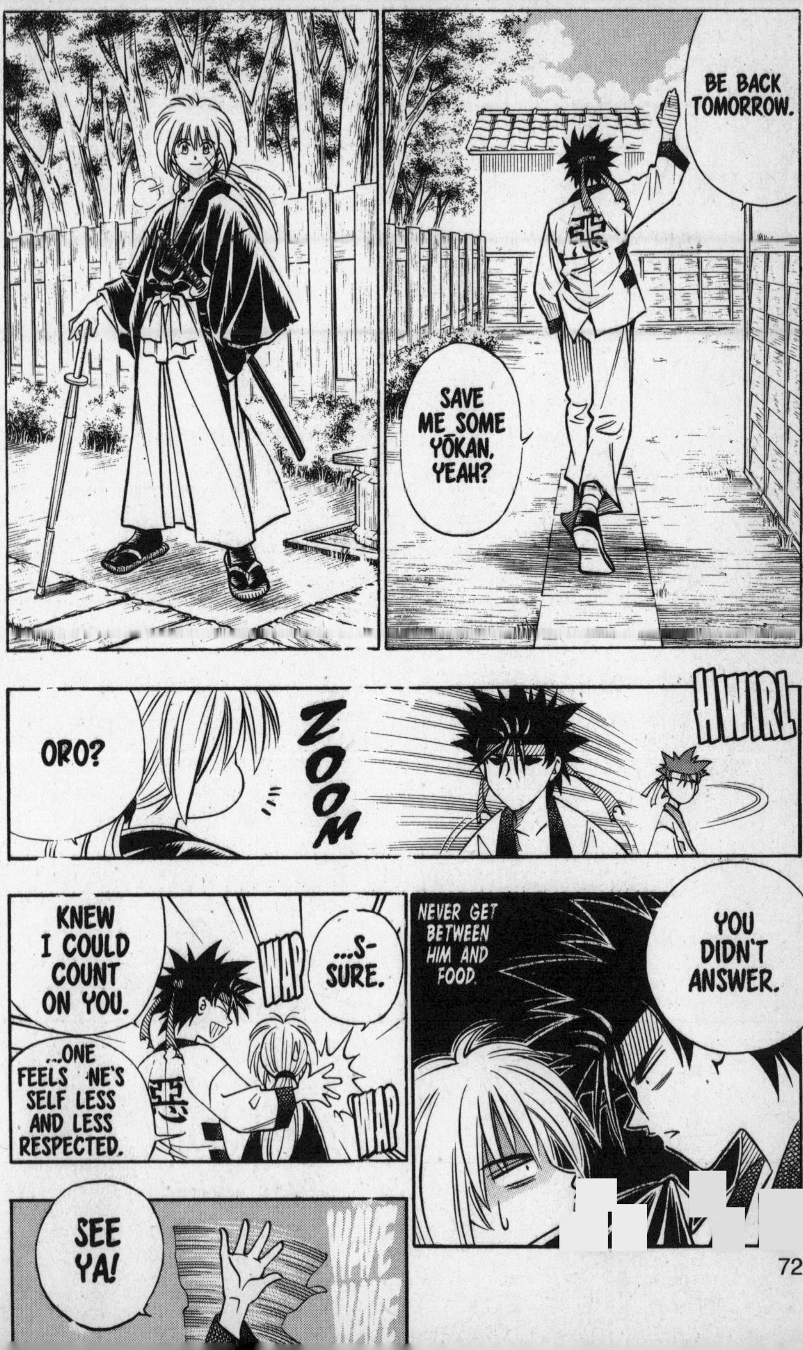
BE BACK TOMORROW.
SAVE ME SOME YŌKAN, YEAH?
HWIRL
ZOOM
ORO?
YOU DIDN'T ANSWER.
NEVER GET BETWEEN HIM AND FOOD.
...S-SURE.
WAP
KNEW I COULD COUNT ON YOU.
...ONE FEELS NE'S SELF LESS AND LESS RESPECTED.
WAP
WAVE
WAVE
SEE YA!

READ THIS WAY

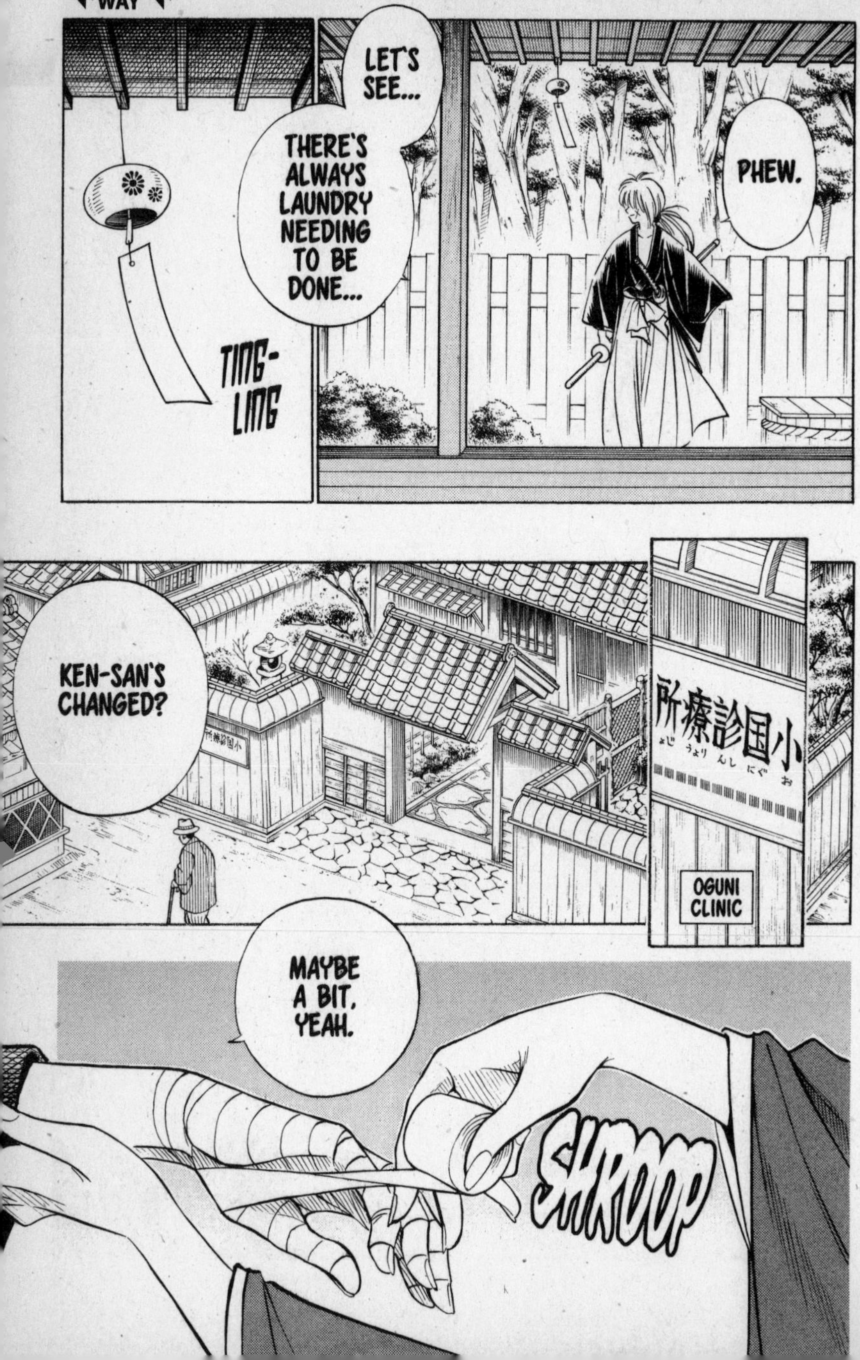

PHEW.
LET'S SEE...
THERE'S ALWAYS LAUNDRY NEEDING TO BE DONE...
TING-LING
小国診療所
おぐにしんりょうじょ
OGUNI CLINIC
KEN-SAN'S CHANGED?
MAYBE A BIT, YEAH.
SHROOP

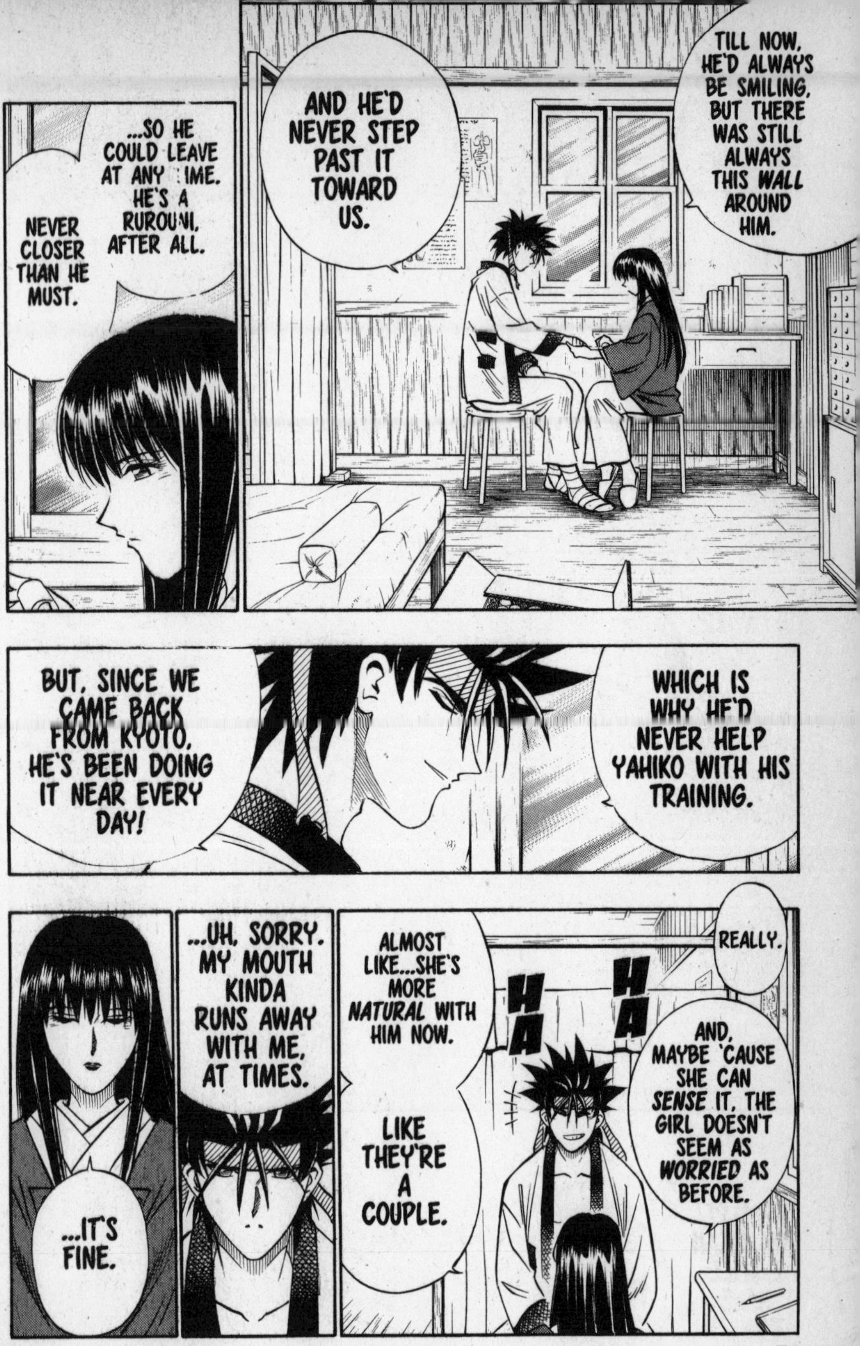
TILL NOW, HE'D ALWAYS BE SMILING, BUT THERE WAS STILL ALWAYS THIS *WALL* AROUND HIM.
AND HE'D NEVER STEP PAST IT TOWARD US.
...SO HE COULD LEAVE AT ANY TIME. HE'S A RUROUNI, AFTER ALL.
NEVER CLOSER THAN HE MUST.
WHICH IS WHY HE'D NEVER HELP YAHIKO WITH HIS TRAINING.
BUT, SINCE WE CAME BACK FROM KYOTO, HE'S BEEN DOING IT NEAR EVERY DAY!
REALLY.
HA
HA
AND, MAYBE 'CAUSE SHE CAN *SENSE* IT, THE GIRL DOESN'T SEEM AS *WORRIED* AS BEFORE.
ALMOST LIKE...SHE'S MORE *NATURAL* WITH HIM NOW.
LIKE THEY'RE A COUPLE.
...UH, SORRY. MY MOUTH KINDA RUNS AWAY WITH ME, AT TIMES.
...IT'S FINE.

READ THIS WAY

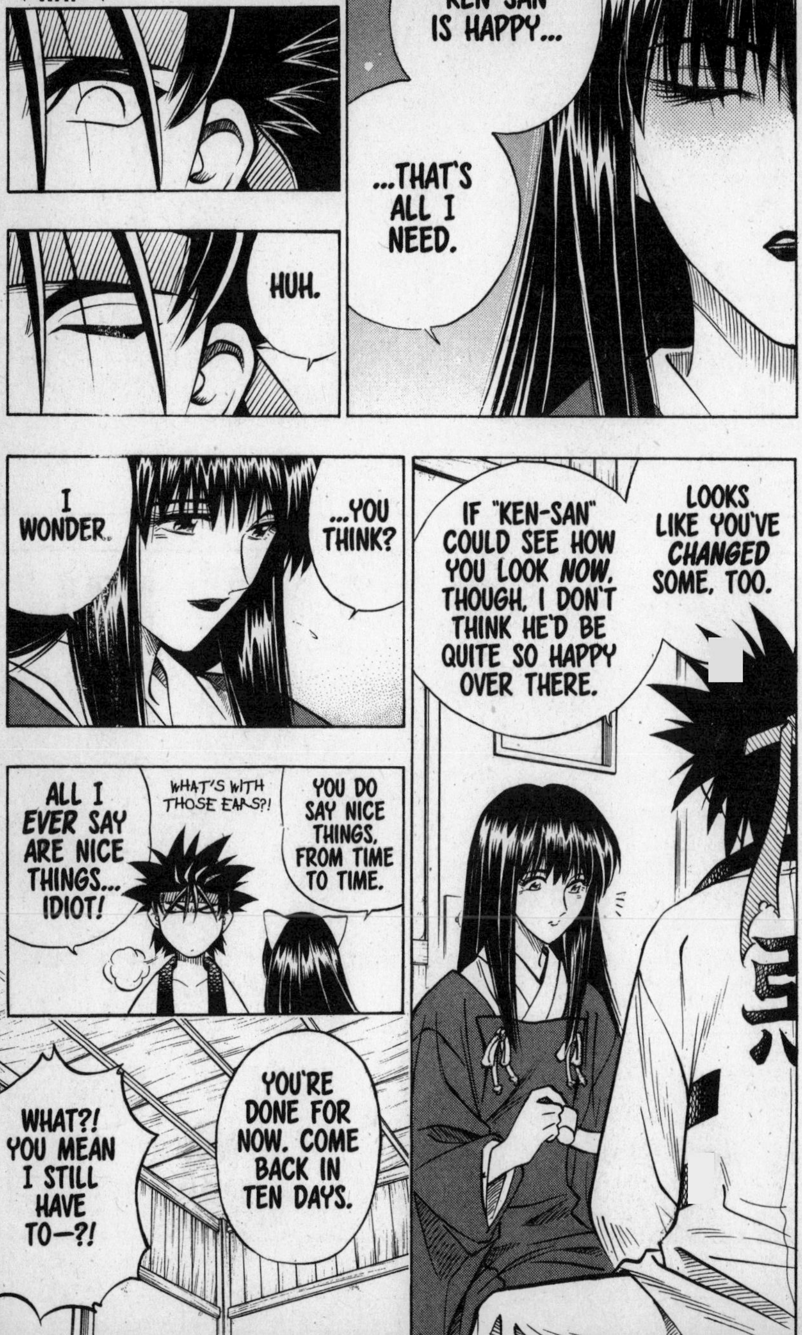
IF KEN-SAN IS HAPPY...
...THAT'S ALL I NEED.
HUH.
LOOKS LIKE YOU'VE *CHANGED* SOME, TOO.
IF "KEN-SAN" COULD SEE HOW YOU LOOK *NOW*, THOUGH, I DON'T THINK HE'D BE QUITE SO HAPPY OVER THERE.
...YOU THINK?
I WONDER.
YOU DO SAY NICE THINGS, FROM TIME TO TIME.
WHAT'S WITH THOSE EARS?!
ALL I EVER SAY ARE NICE THINGS... IDIOT!
YOU'RE DONE FOR NOW. COME BACK IN TEN DAYS.
WHAT?! YOU MEAN I STILL HAVE TO—?!

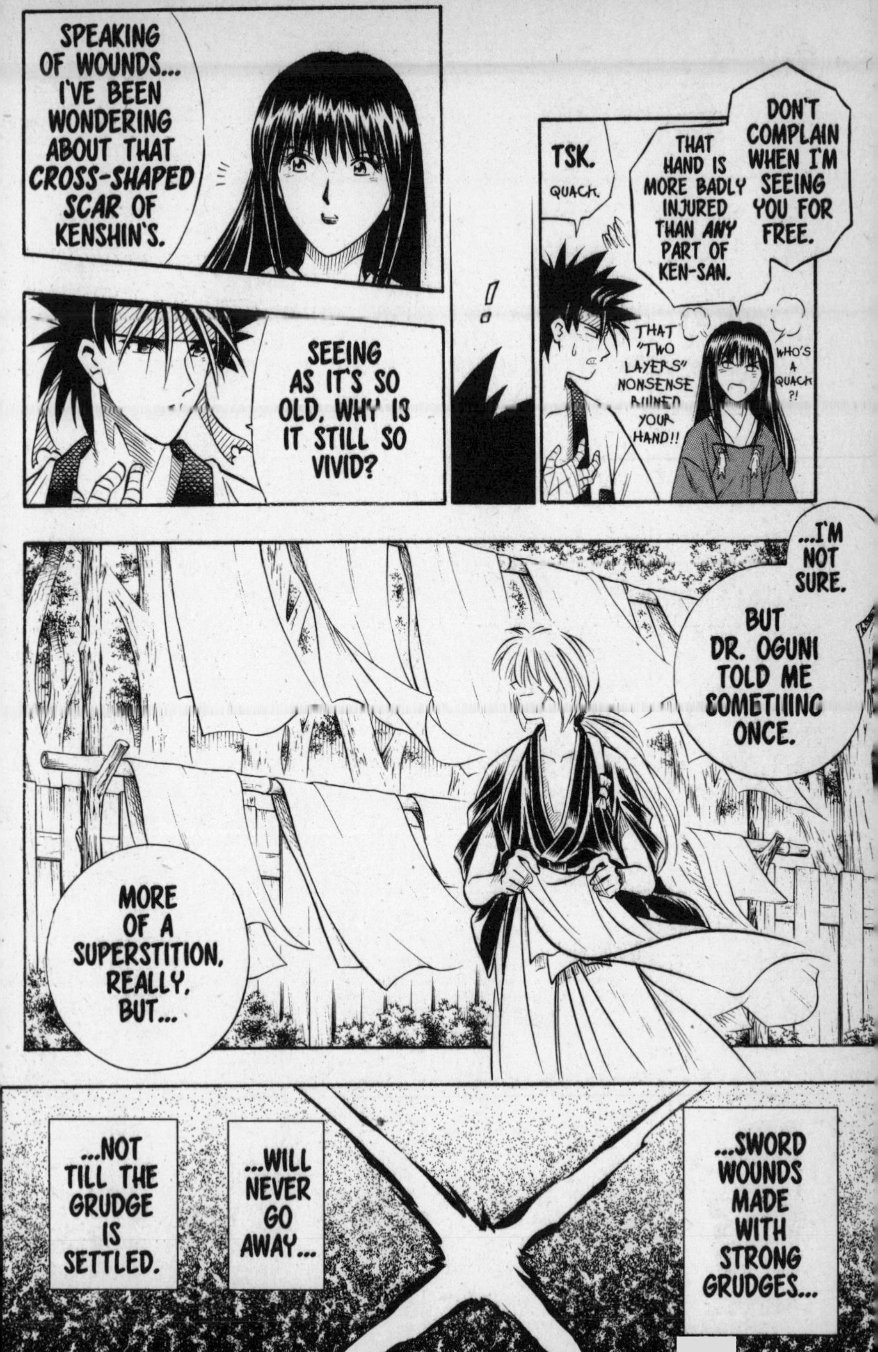
THAT HAND IS MORE BADLY INJURED THAN ANY PART OF KEN-SAN. DON'T COMPLAIN WHEN I'M SEEING YOU FOR FREE.
TSK.
QUACK.
WHO'S A QUACK?!
THAT "TWO LAYERS" NONSENSE RUINED YOUR HAND!!
SPEAKING OF WOUNDS... I'VE BEEN WONDERING ABOUT THAT CROSS-SHAPED SCAR OF KENSHIN'S.
SEEING AS IT'S SO OLD, WHY IS IT STILL SO VIVID?
...I'M NOT SURE.
BUT DR. OGUNI TOLD ME SOMETHING ONCE.
MORE OF A SUPERSTITION, REALLY, BUT...
...SWORD WOUNDS MADE WITH STRONG GRUDGES...
...WILL NEVER GO AWAY...
...NOT TILL THE GRUDGE IS SETTLED.

READ THIS WAY

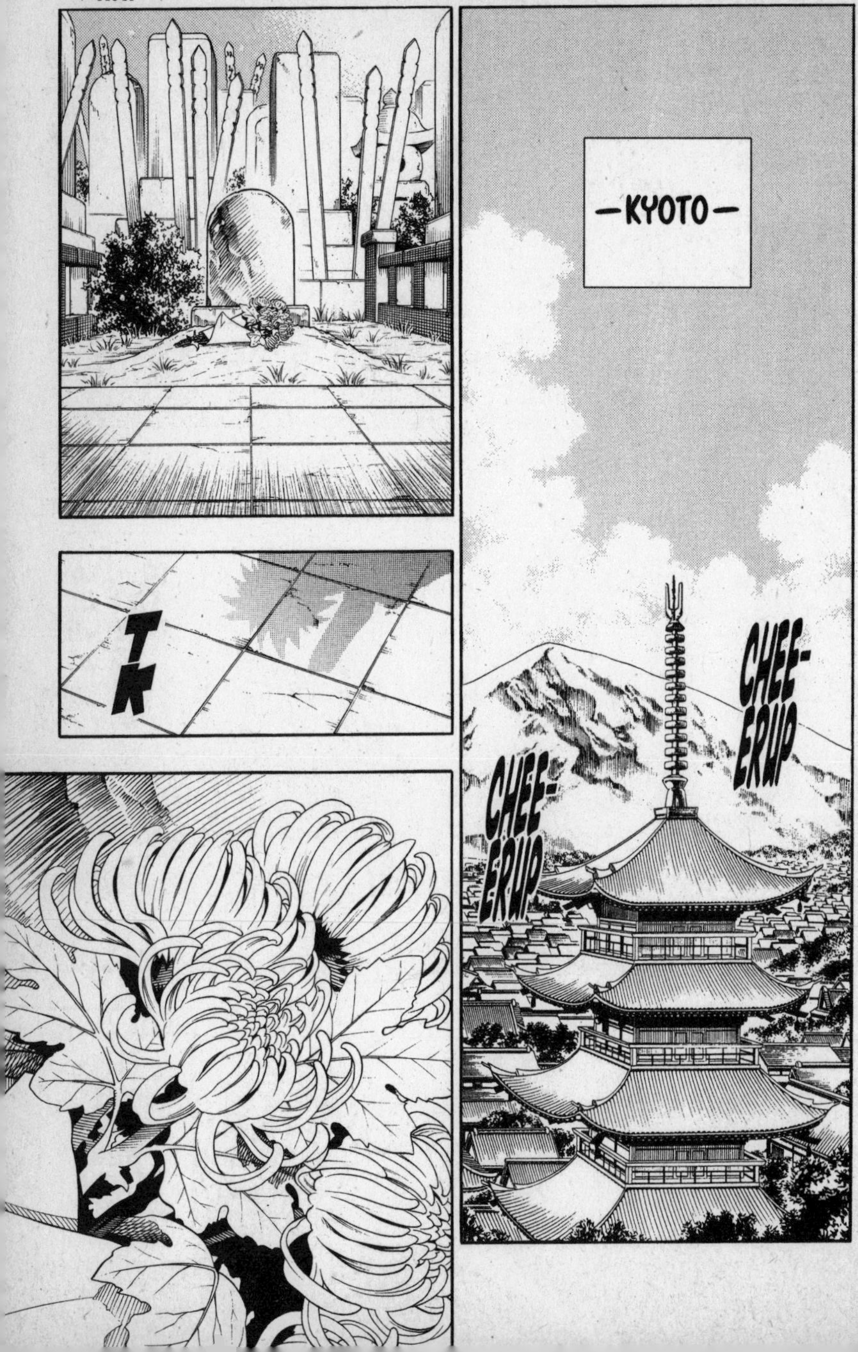

-KYOTO-
CHEE-ERUP
CHEE-ERUP
TK

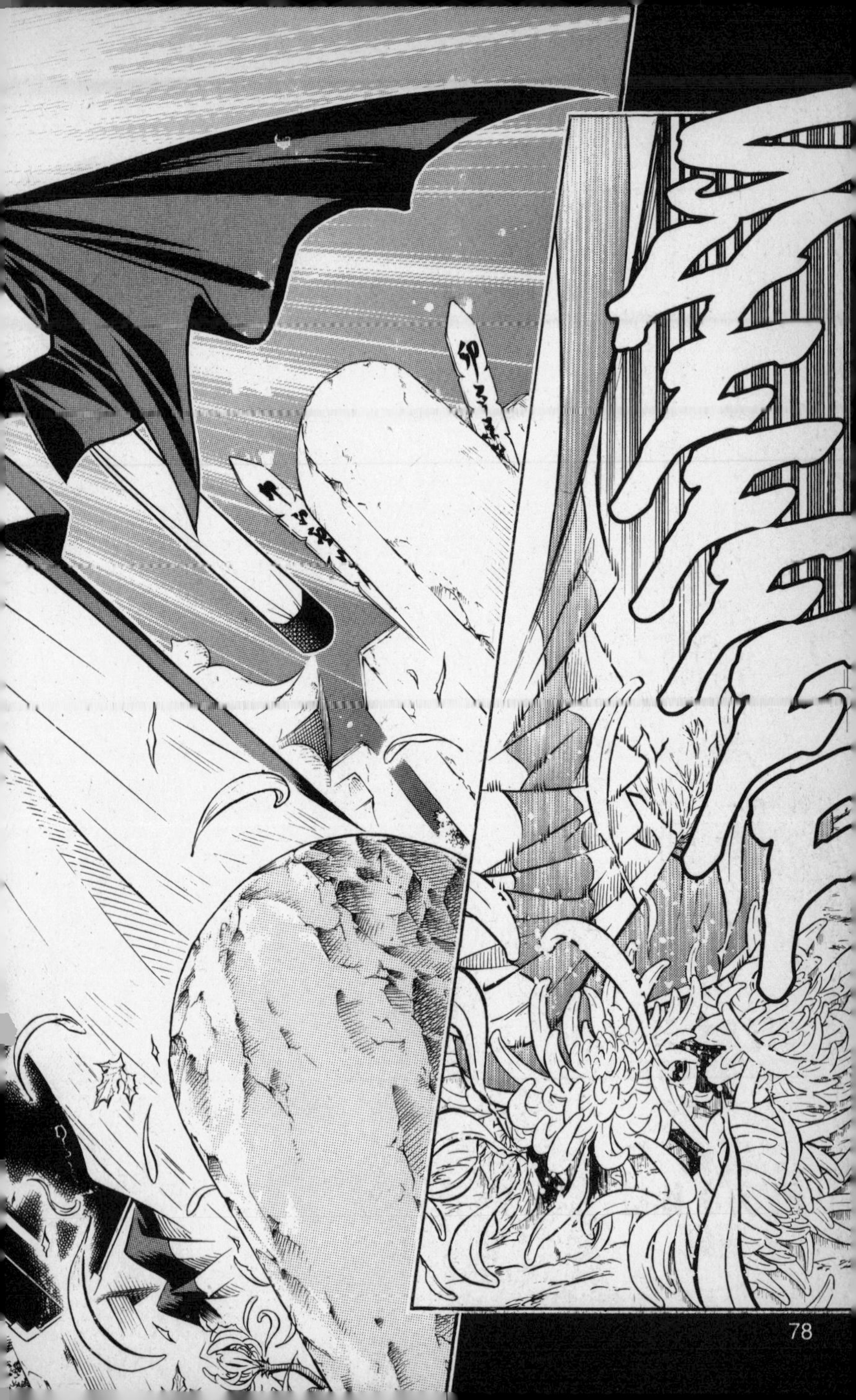

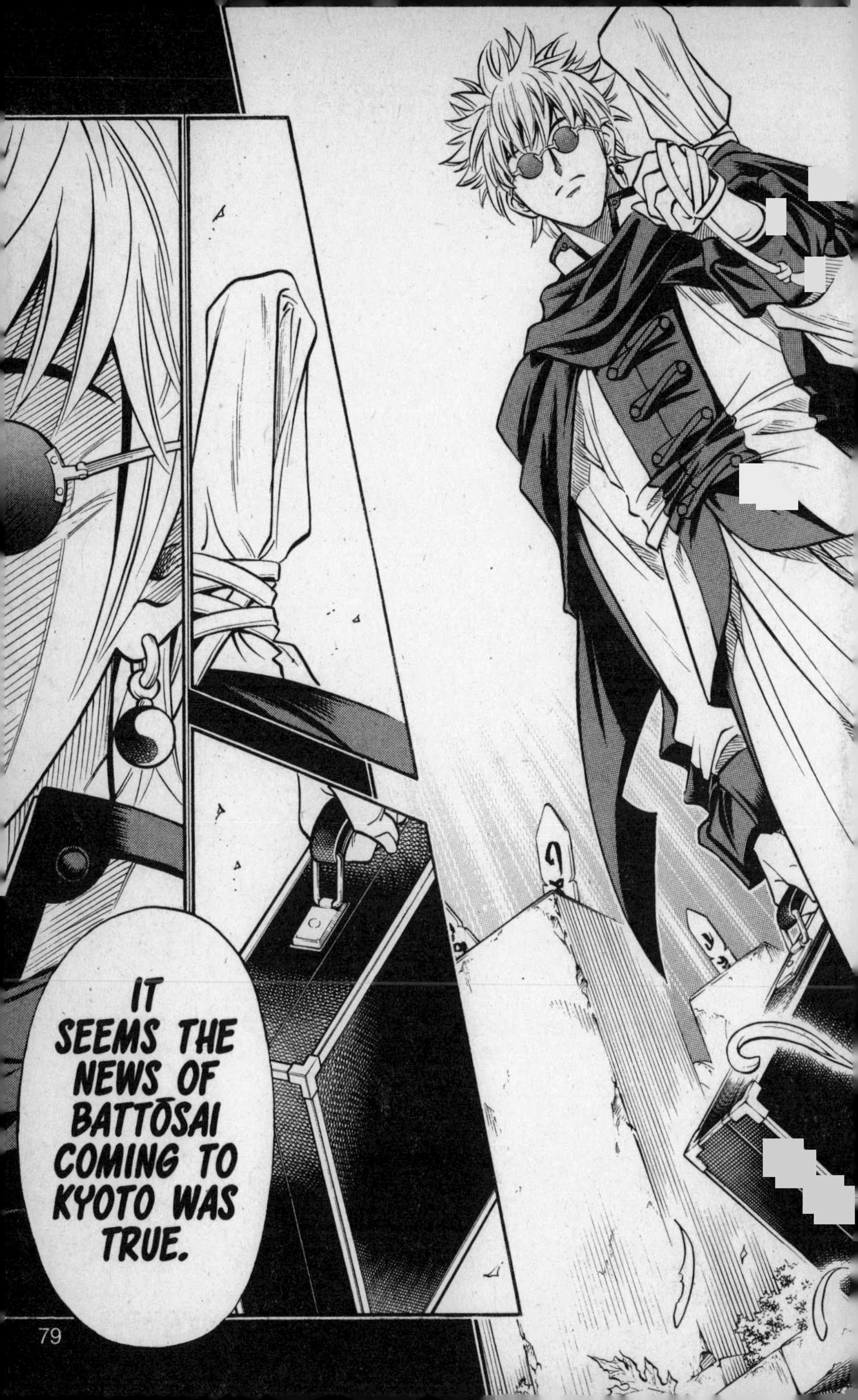
IT SEEMS THE NEWS OF BATTŌSAI COMING TO KYOTO WAS TRUE.

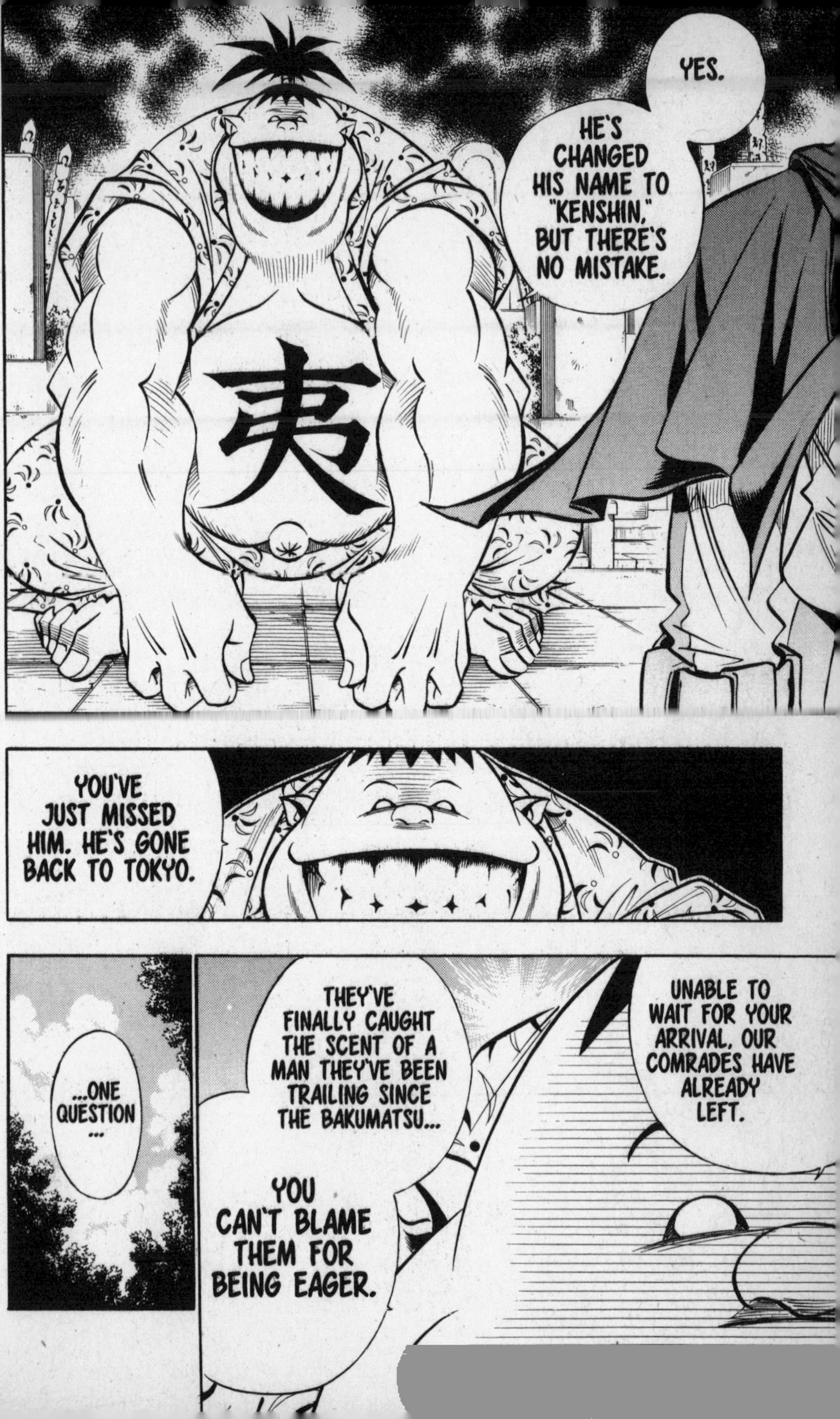
YES.
HE'S CHANGED HIS NAME TO "KENSHIN," BUT THERE'S NO MISTAKE.
YOU'VE JUST MISSED HIM. HE'S GONE BACK TO TOKYO.
UNABLE TO WAIT FOR YOUR ARRIVAL, OUR COMRADES HAVE ALREADY LEFT.
THEY'VE FINALLY CAUGHT THE SCENT OF A MAN THEY'VE BEEN TRAILING SINCE THE BAKUMATSU...
YOU CAN'T BLAME THEM FOR BEING EAGER.
...ONE QUESTION ...

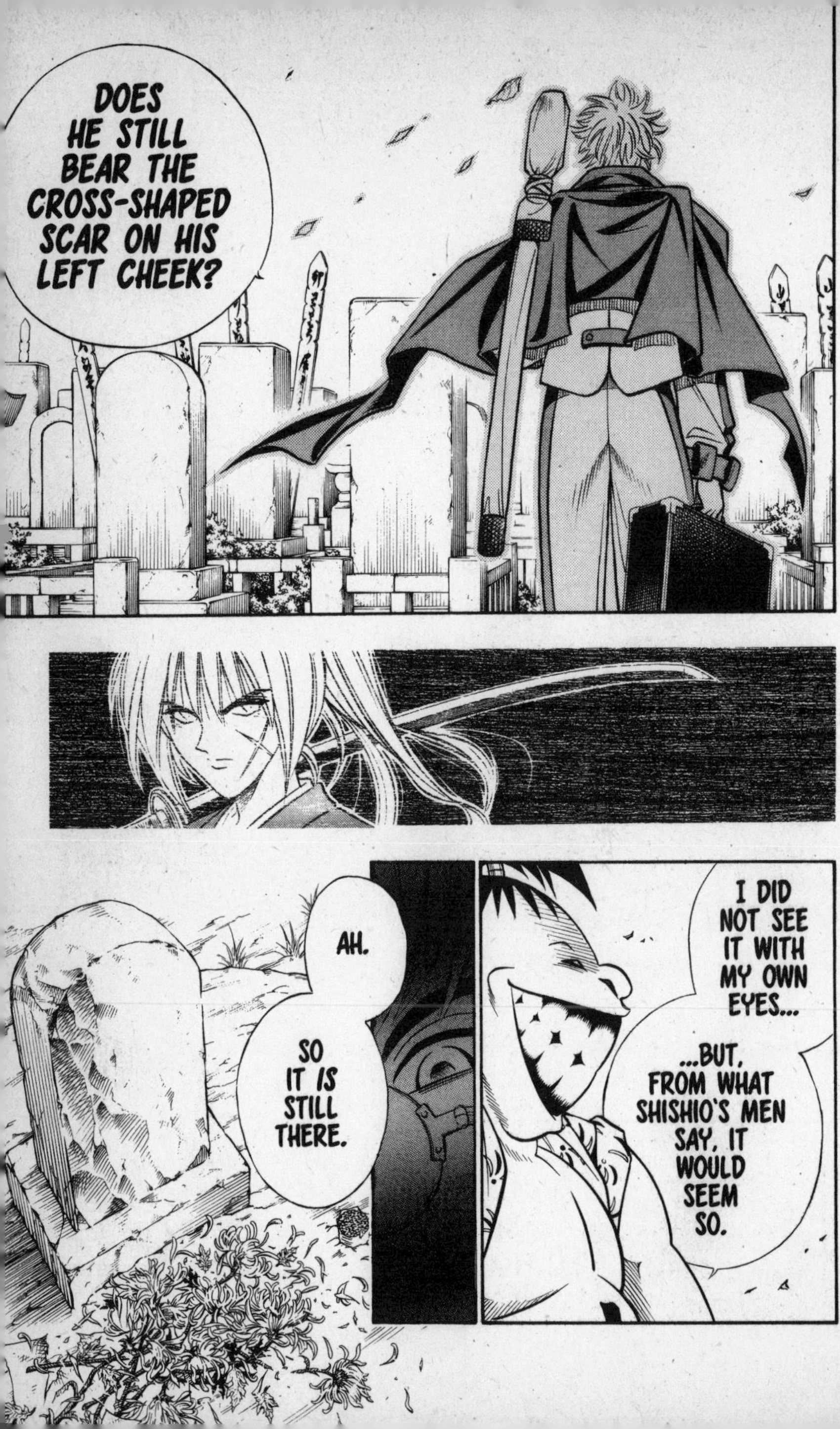
DOES HE STILL BEAR THE CROSS-SHAPED SCAR ON HIS LEFT CHEEK?
I DID NOT SEE IT WITH MY OWN EYES...
...BUT, FROM WHAT SHISHIO'S MEN SAY, IT WOULD SEEM SO.
AH.
SO IT IS STILL THERE.

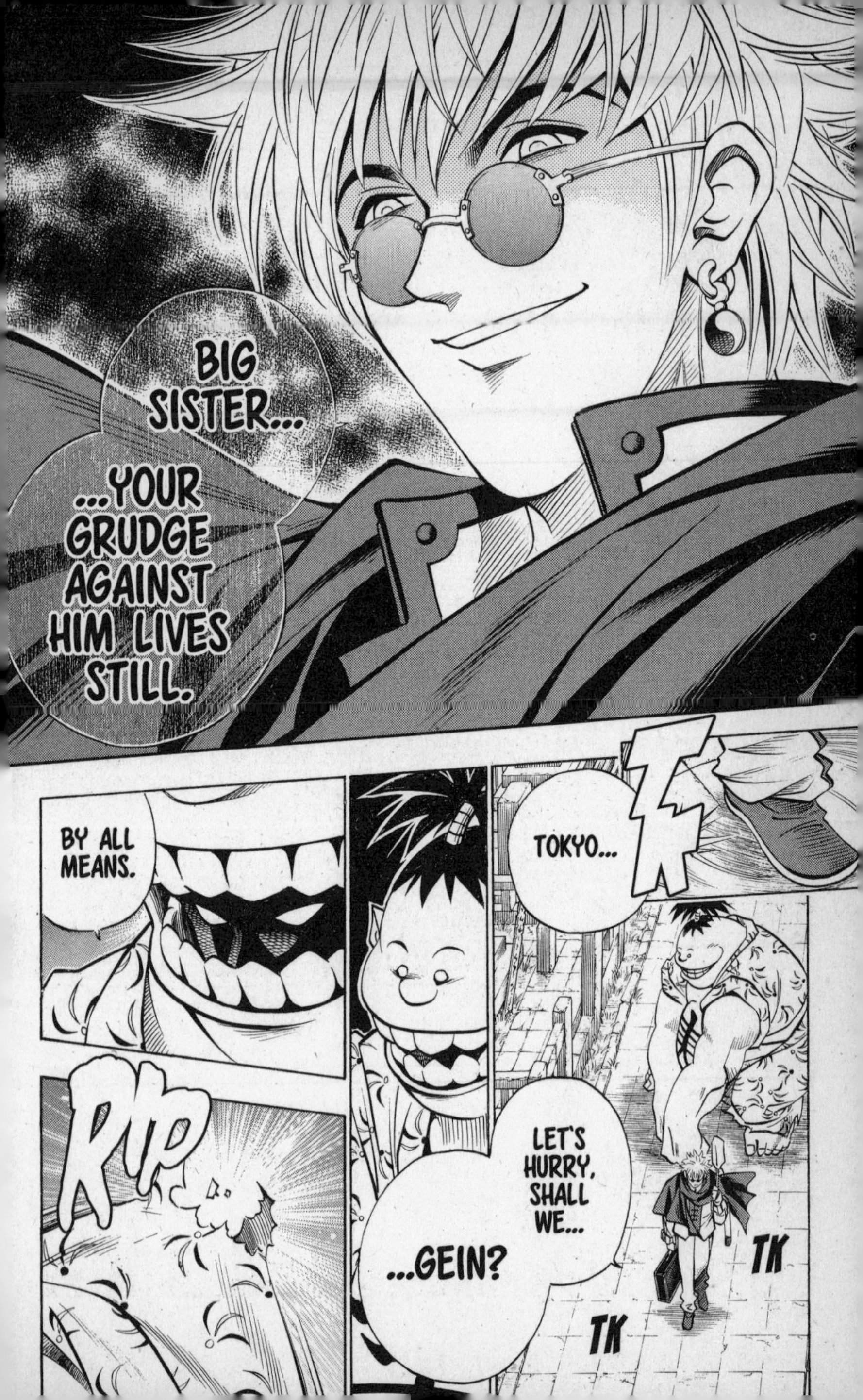
BIG SISTER...
...YOUR GRUDGE AGAINST HIM LIVES STILL.
TOKYO...
TK
TK
TK
LET'S HURRY, SHALL WE...
...GEIN?
BY ALL MEANS.
RIP

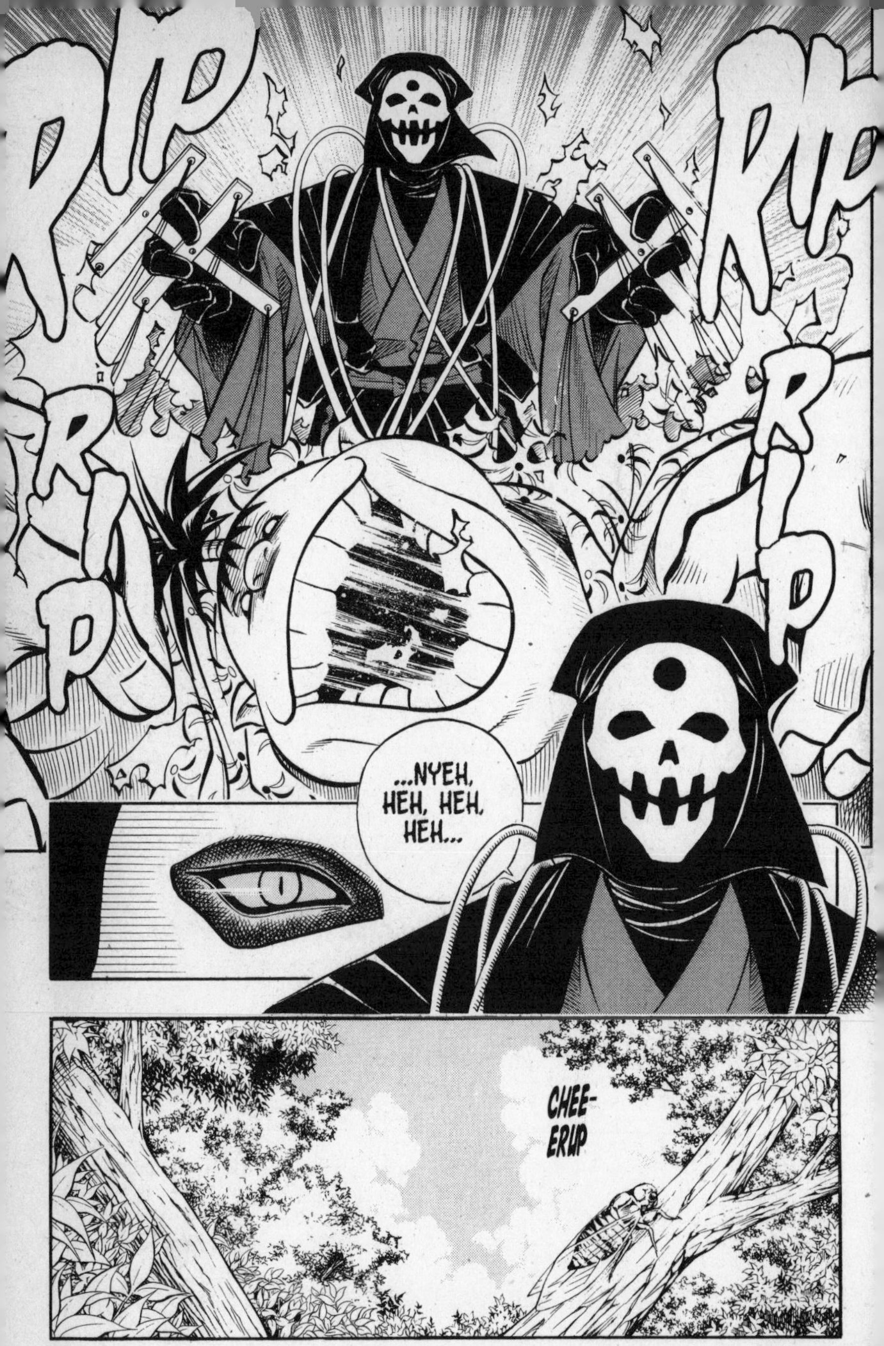
RIP
RIP
RIP
RIP
...NYEH, HEH, HEH, HEH...
CHEE-ERUP

Rurouni Kenshin

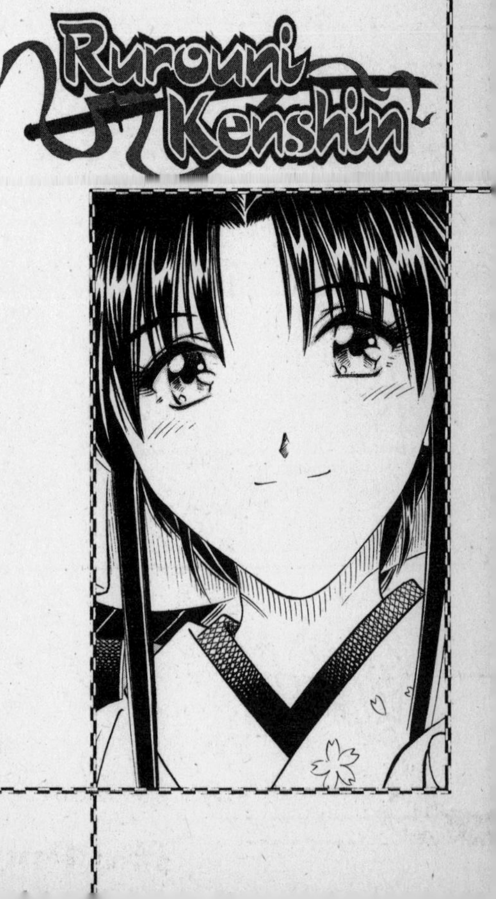

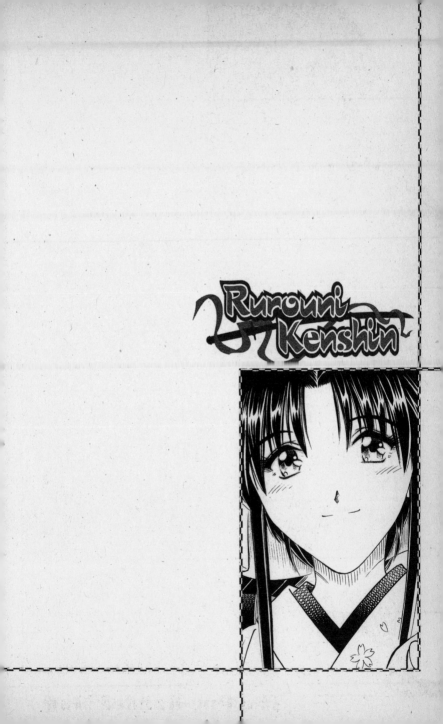

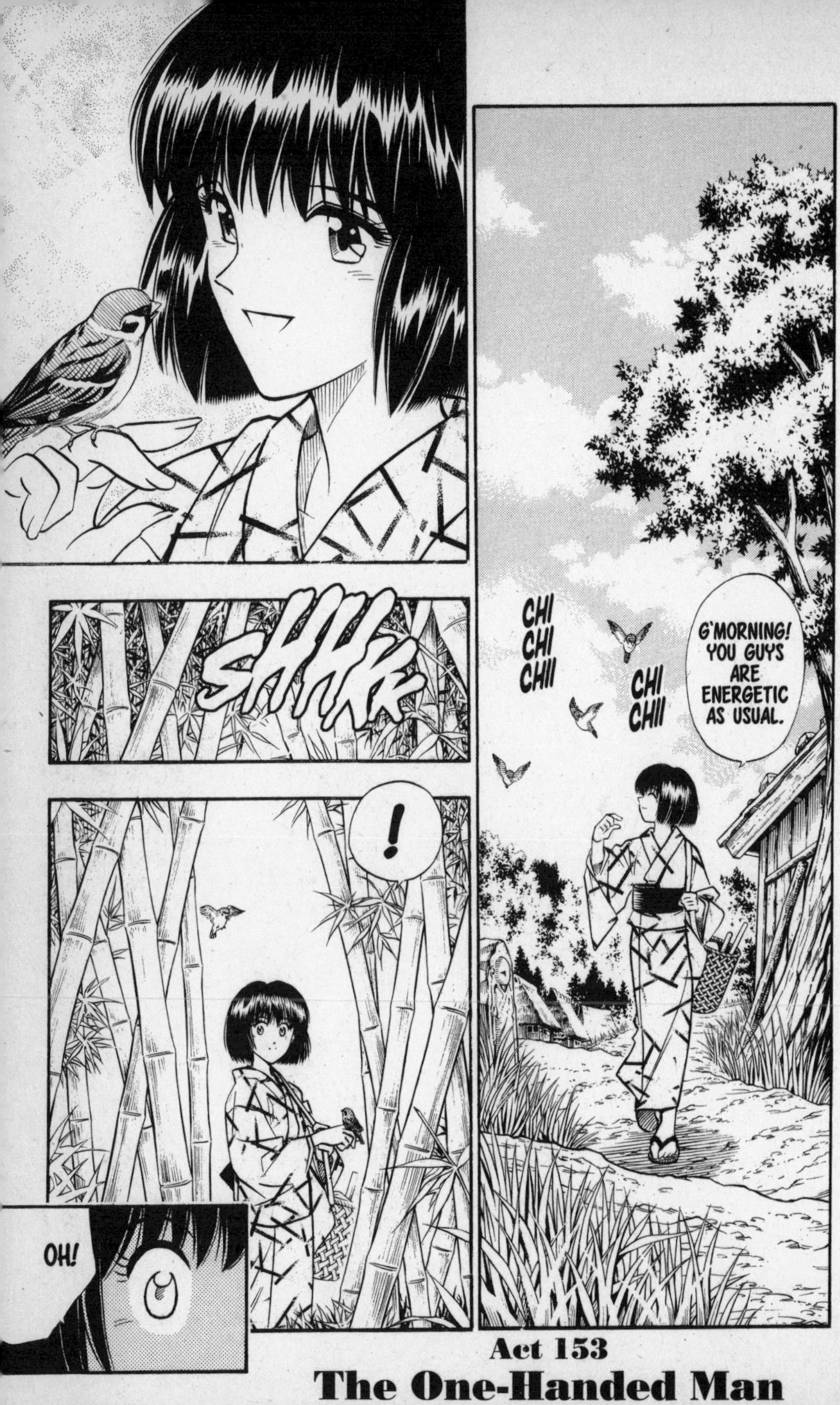
G'MORNING! YOU GUYS ARE ENERGETIC AS USUAL.
CHI CHII
CHI CHI CHII
SHHK
!
OH!

Act 153
The One-Handed Man

Act 153—The One-Handed Man

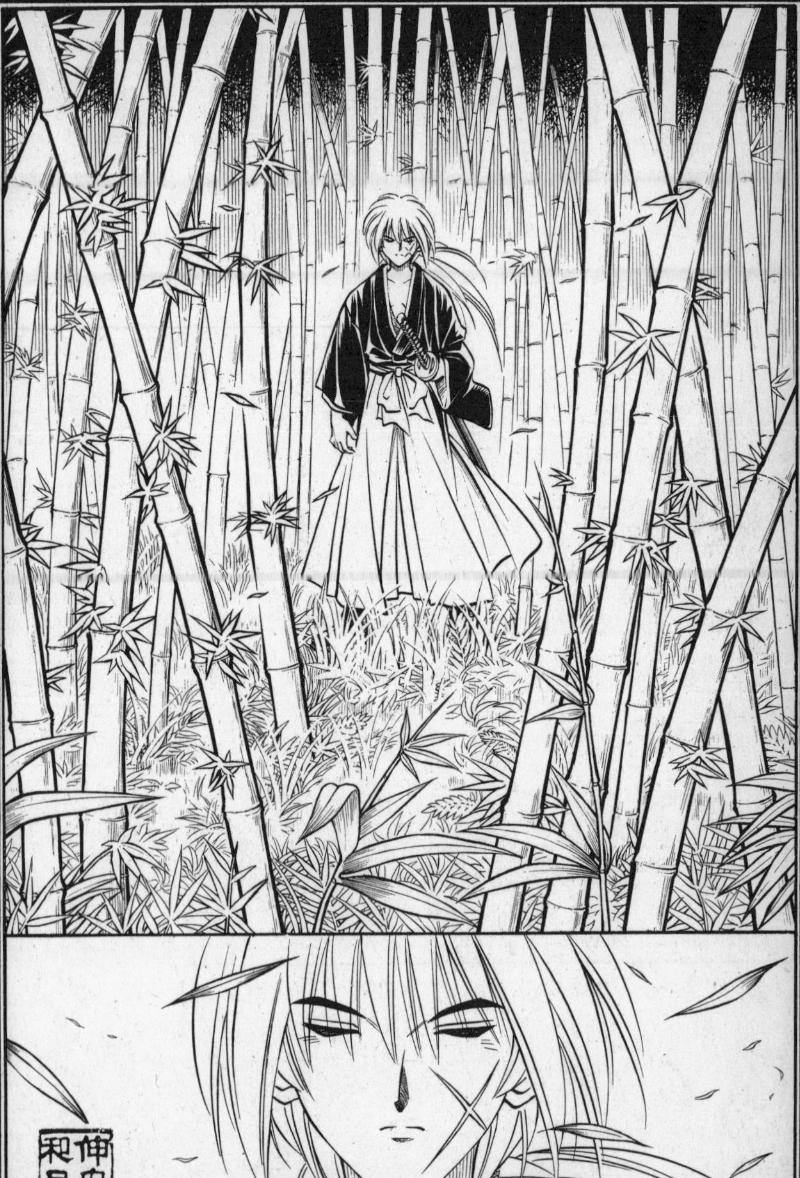
伸宏和月

READ THIS WAY

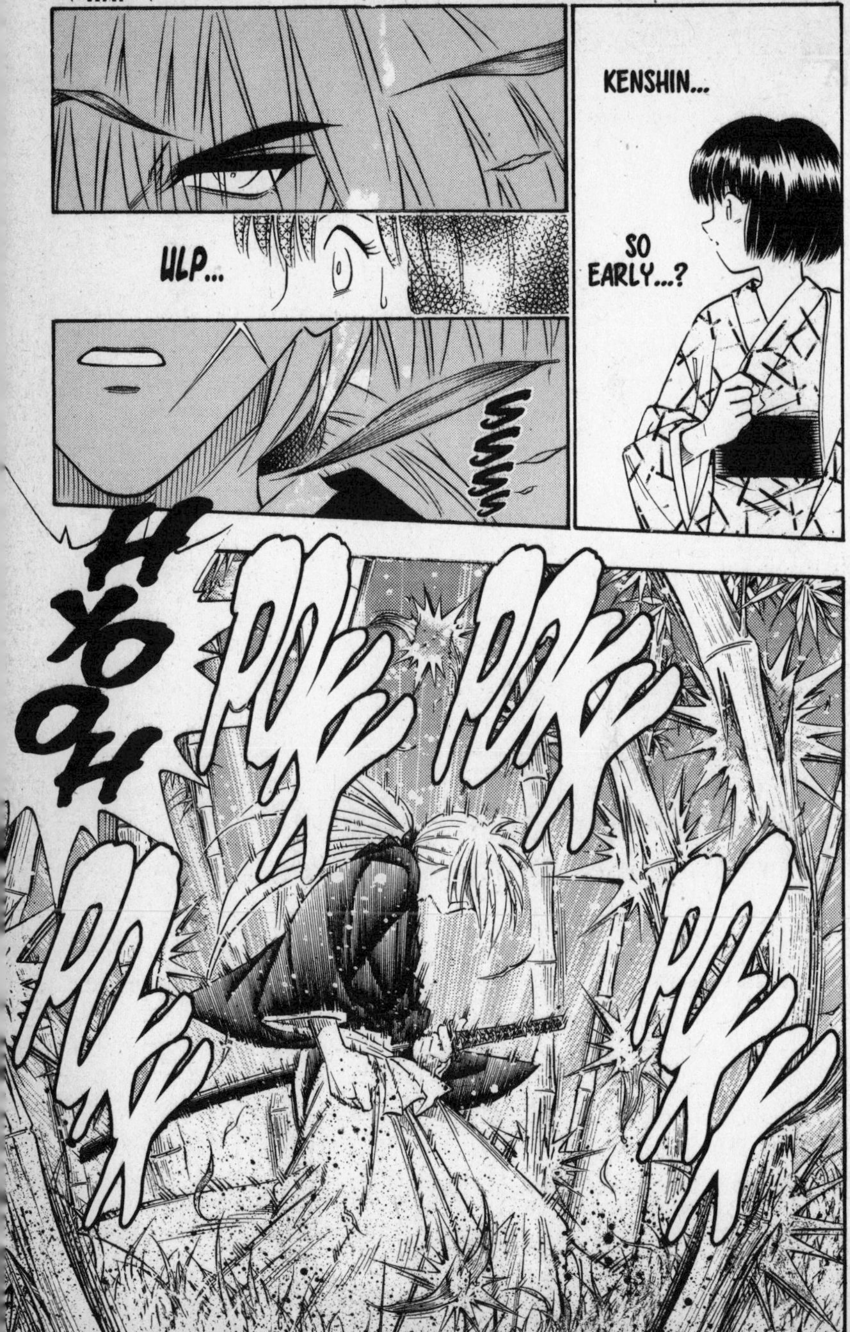
KENSHIN...
SO EARLY...?
ULP...
SSSSS

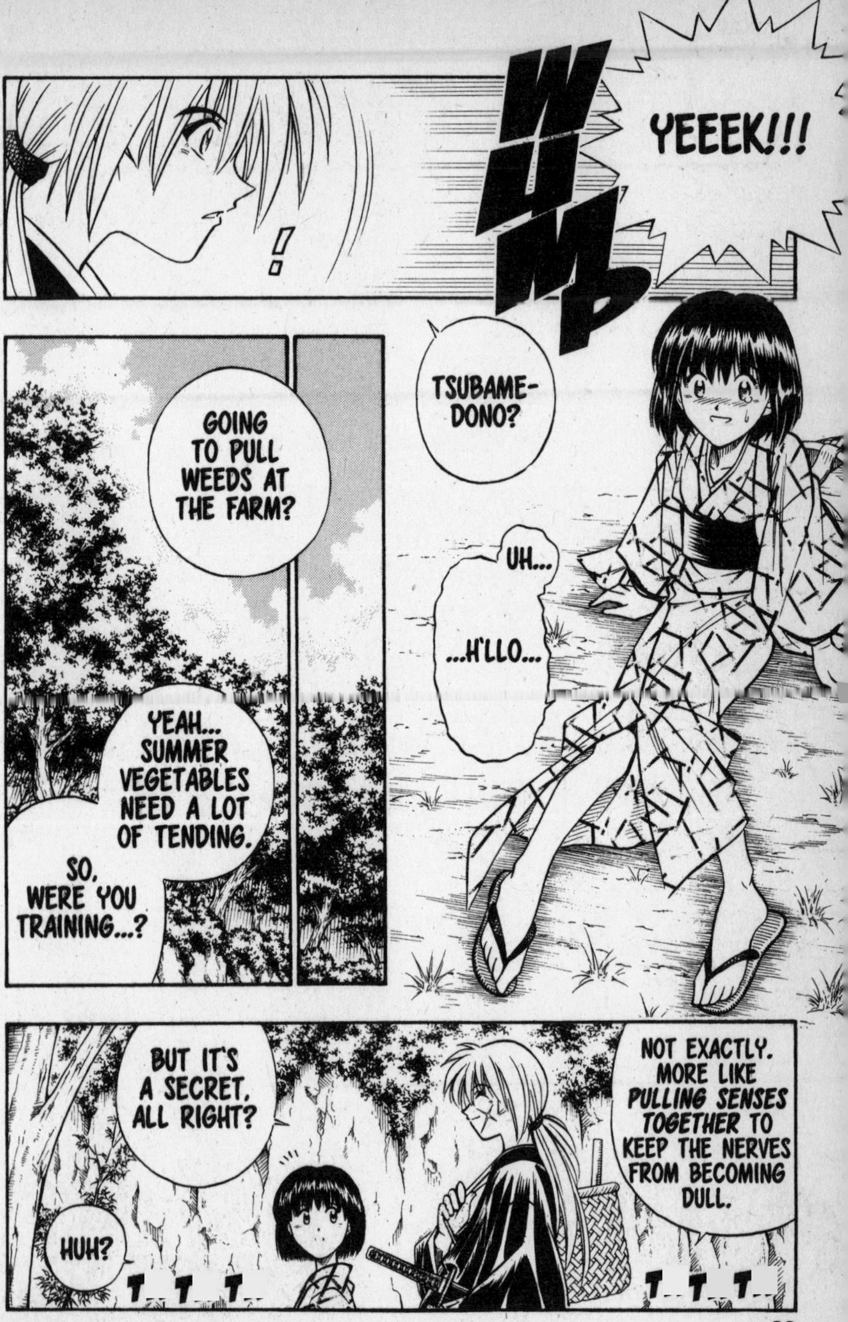
YEEEK!!!
WUMP
!
TSUBAME-DONO?
UH...
...H'LLO...
GOING TO PULL WEEDS AT THE FARM?
YEAH... SUMMER VEGETABLES NEED A LOT OF TENDING.
SO, WERE YOU TRAINING...?
NOT EXACTLY. MORE LIKE PULLING SENSES TOGETHER TO KEEP THE NERVES FROM BECOMING DULL.
T.. T.. T..
BUT IT'S A SECRET, ALL RIGHT?
HUH?
T.. T.. T..

READ THIS WAY

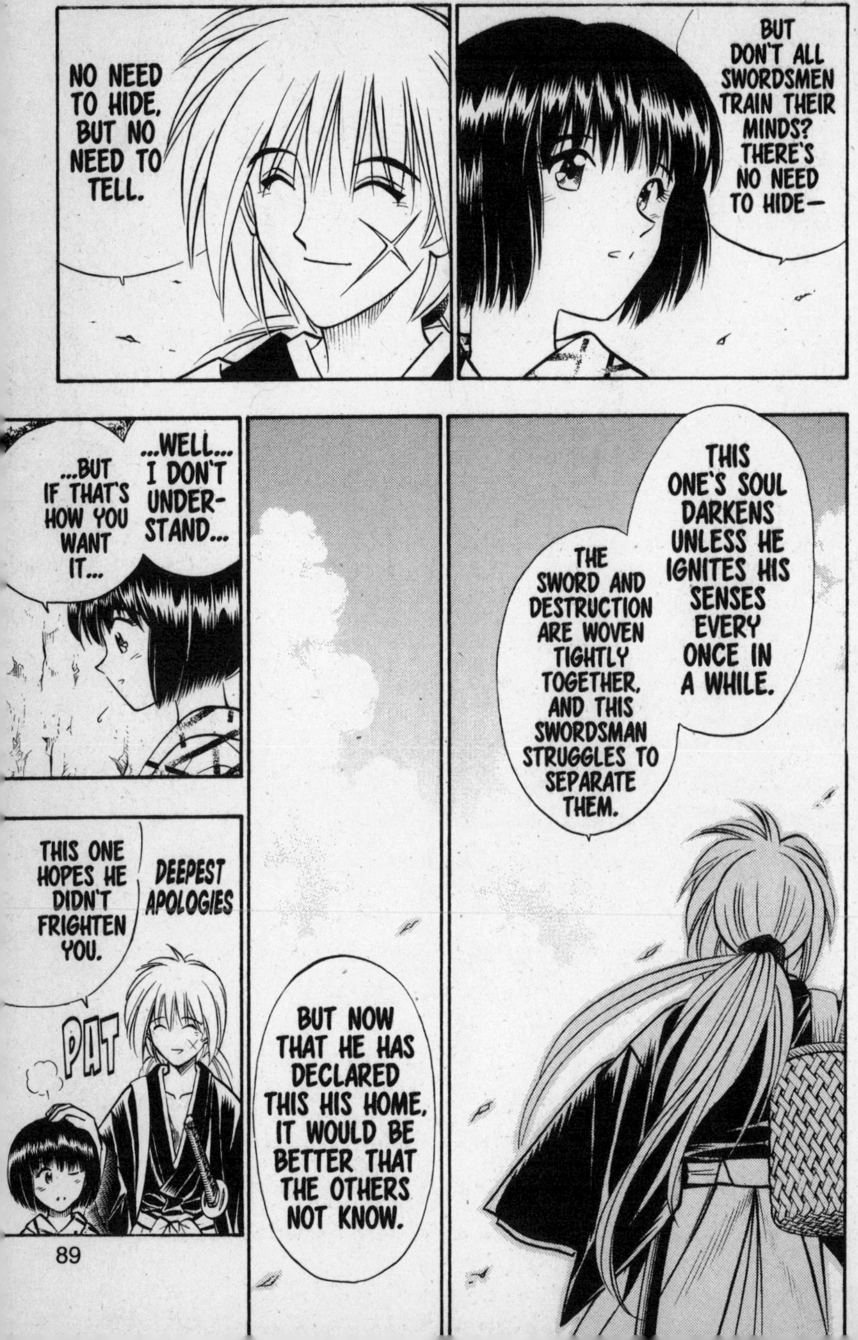
BUT DON'T ALL SWORDSMEN TRAIN THEIR MINDS? THERE'S NO NEED TO HIDE—
NO NEED TO HIDE, BUT NO NEED TO TELL.
THIS ONE'S SOUL DARKENS UNLESS HE IGNITES HIS SENSES EVERY ONCE IN A WHILE.
THE SWORD AND DESTRUCTION ARE WOVEN TIGHTLY TOGETHER, AND THIS SWORDSMAN STRUGGLES TO SEPARATE THEM.
BUT NOW THAT HE HAS DECLARED THIS HIS HOME, IT WOULD BE BETTER THAT THE OTHERS NOT KNOW.
...WELL... I DON'T UNDERSTAND...
...BUT IF THAT'S HOW YOU WANT IT...
DEEPEST APOLOGIES
THIS ONE HOPES HE DIDN'T FRIGHTEN YOU.
PAT

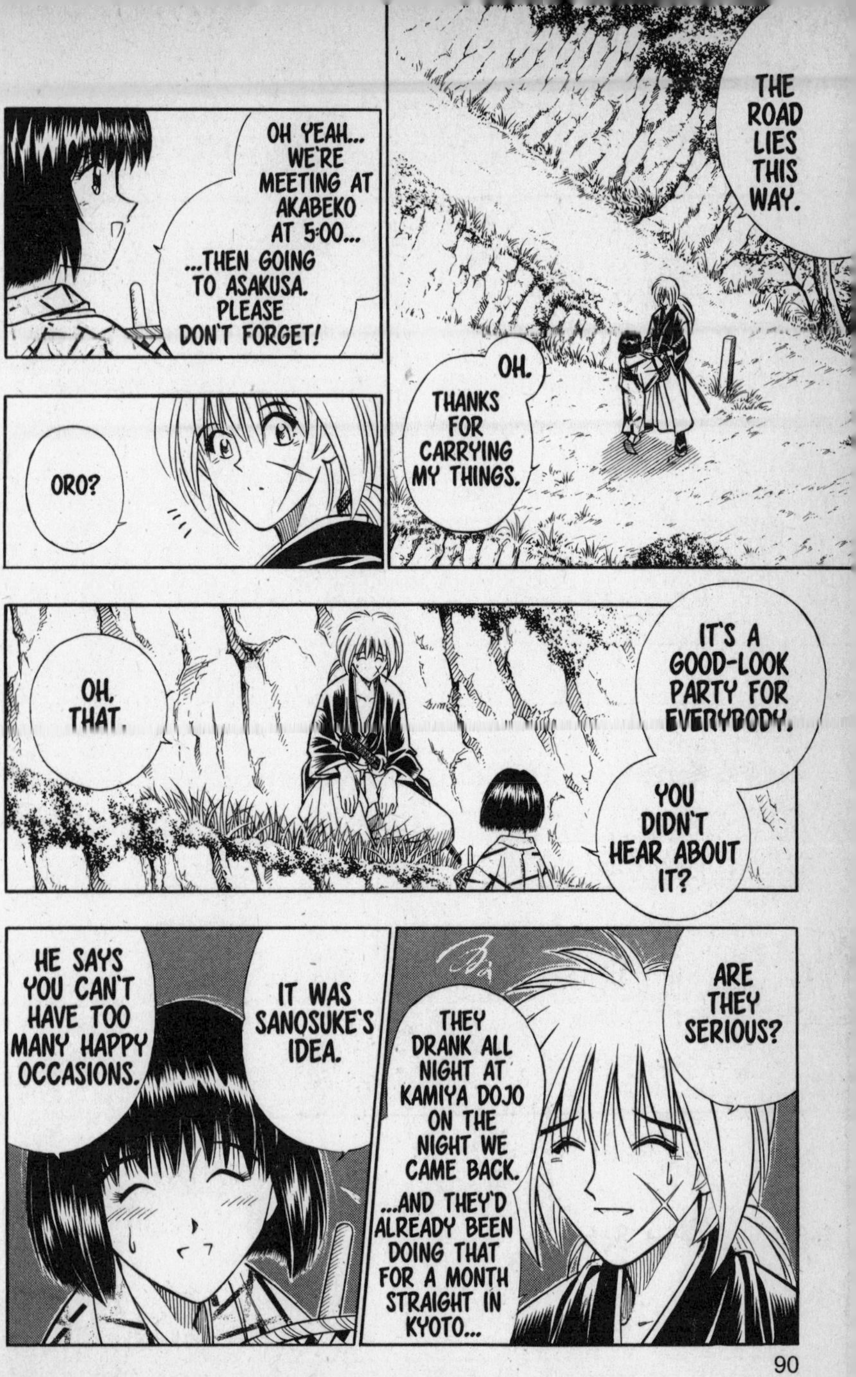
THE ROAD LIES THIS WAY.
OH. THANKS FOR CARRYING MY THINGS.
OH YEAH... WE'RE MEETING AT AKABEKO AT 5:00...
...THEN GOING TO ASAKUSA. PLEASE DON'T FORGET!
ORO?
IT'S A GOOD-LOOK PARTY FOR EVERYBODY.
YOU DIDN'T HEAR ABOUT IT?
OH, THAT.
ARE THEY SERIOUS?
THEY DRANK ALL NIGHT AT KAMIYA DOJO ON THE NIGHT WE CAME BACK.
...AND THEY'D ALREADY BEEN DOING THAT FOR A MONTH STRAIGHT IN KYOTO...
IT WAS SANOSUKE'S IDEA.
HE SAYS YOU CAN'T HAVE TOO MANY HAPPY OCCASIONS.

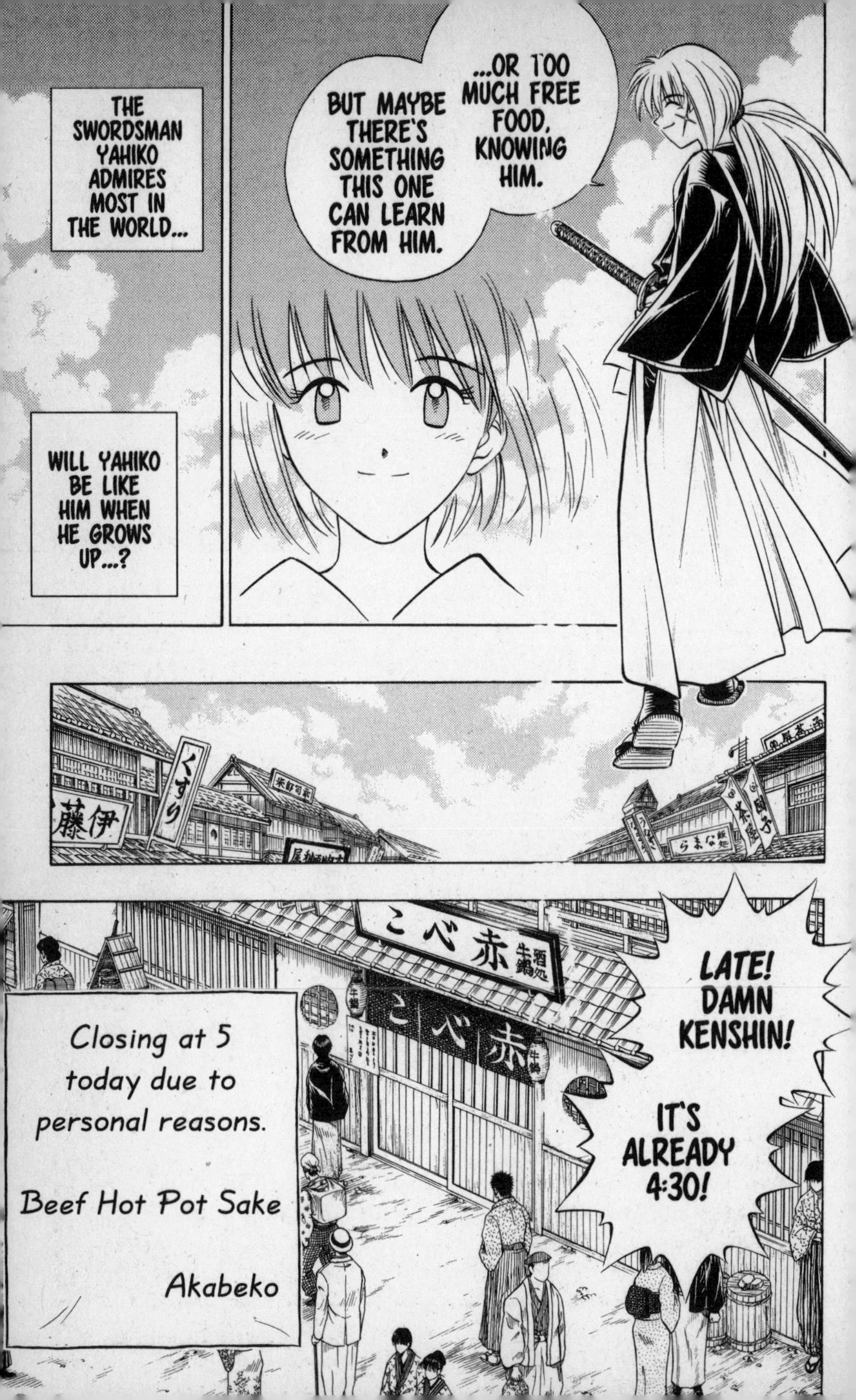
BUT MAYBE THERE'S SOMETHING THIS ONE CAN LEARN FROM HIM.
...OR TOO MUCH FREE FOOD, KNOWING HIM.
THE SWORDSMAN YAHIKO ADMIRES MOST IN THE WORLD...
WILL YAHIKO BE LIKE HIM WHEN HE GROWS UP...?
くすり
赤べこ
LATE! DAMN KENSHIN!
IT'S ALREADY 4:30!
Closing at 5 today due to personal reasons.
Beef Hot Pot Sake
Akabeko

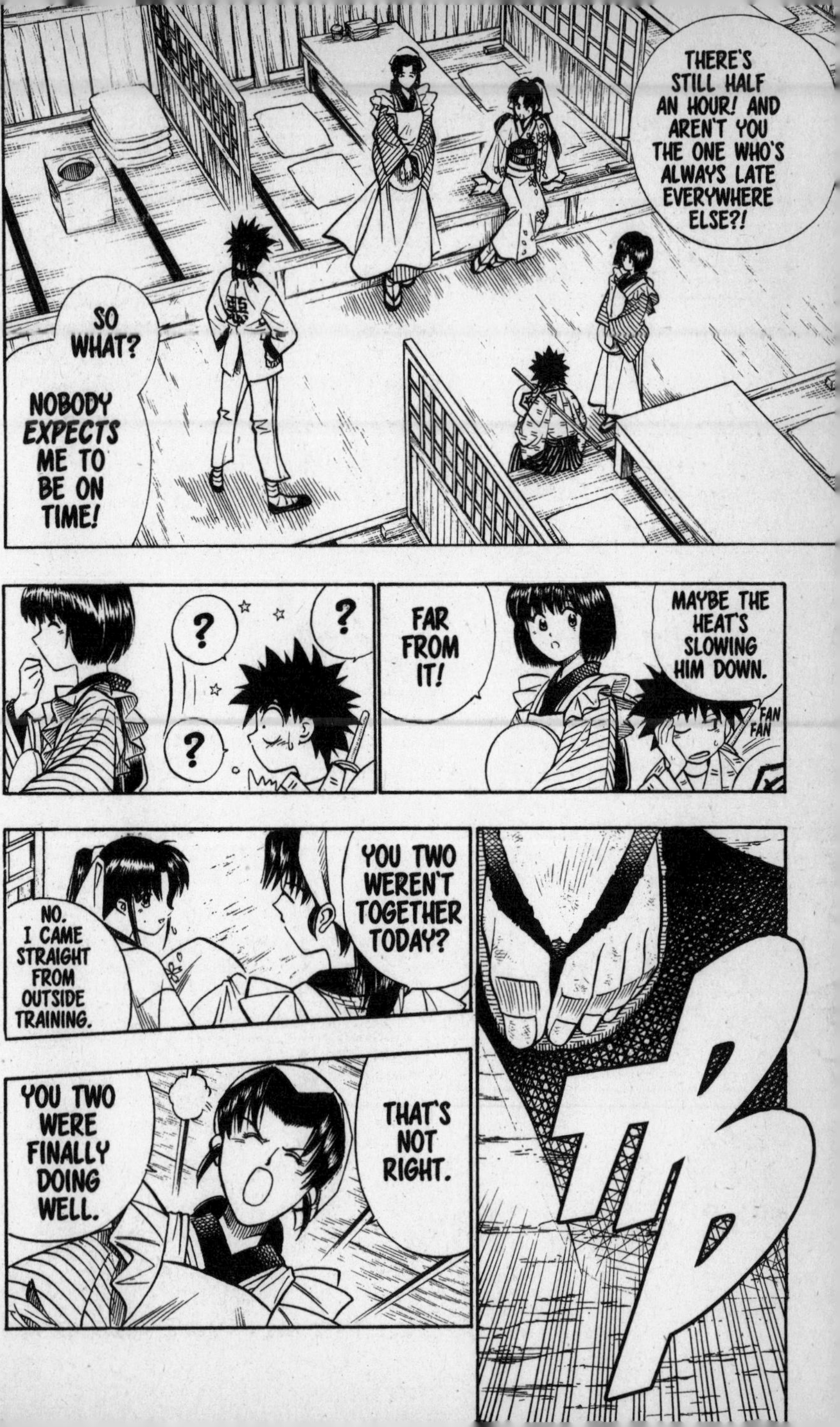
THERE'S STILL HALF AN HOUR! AND AREN'T YOU THE ONE WHO'S ALWAYS LATE EVERYWHERE ELSE?!
SO WHAT?
NOBODY EXPECTS ME TO BE ON TIME!
MAYBE THE HEAT'S SLOWING HIM DOWN.
FAN FAN
FAR FROM IT!
?
?
?
YOU TWO WEREN'T TOGETHER TODAY?
NO. I CAME STRAIGHT FROM OUTSIDE TRAINING.
THAT'S NOT RIGHT.
YOU TWO WERE FINALLY DOING WELL.

READ THIS WAY

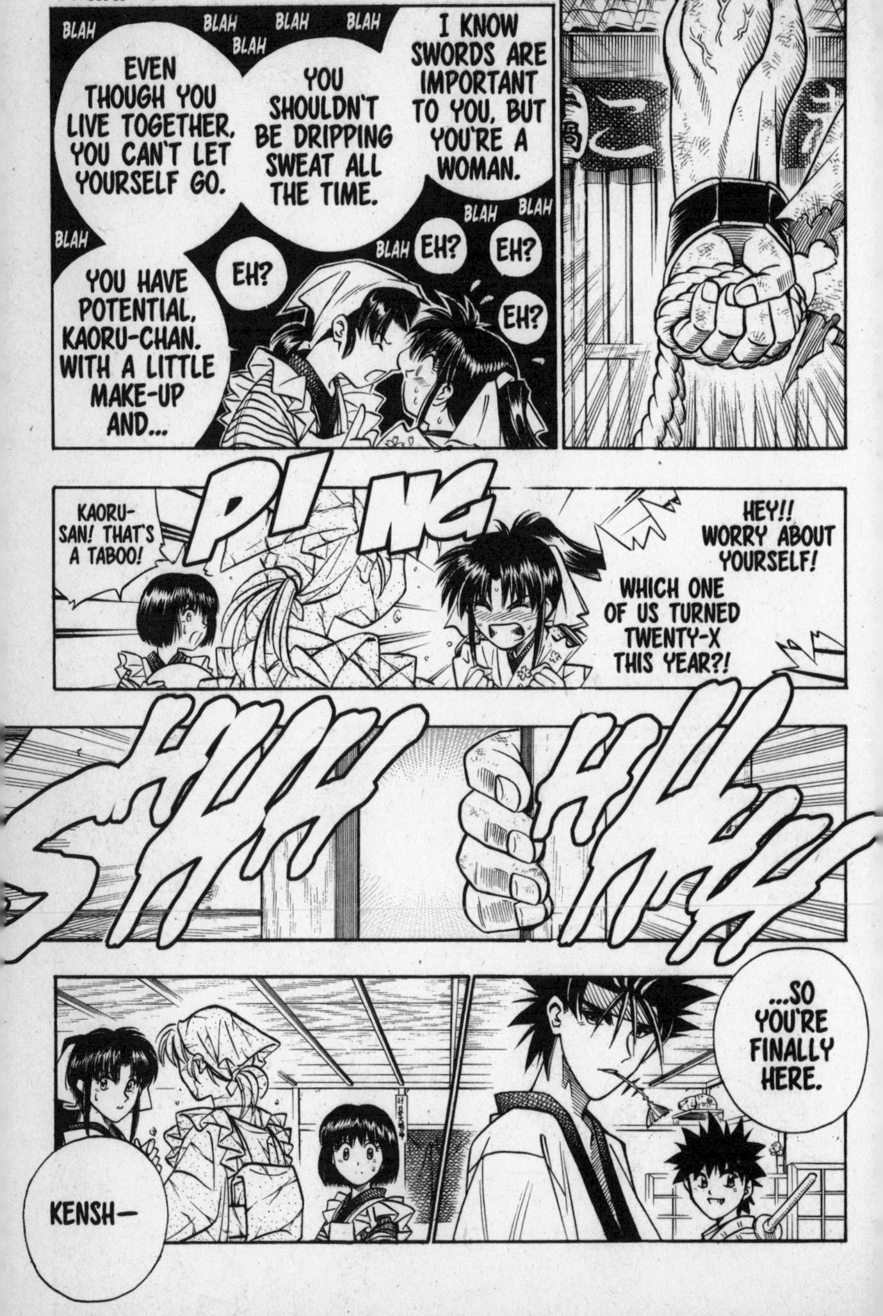
BLAH BLAH BLAH BLAH BLAH
I KNOW SWORDS ARE IMPORTANT TO YOU, BUT YOU'RE A WOMAN.
YOU SHOULDN'T BE DRIPPING SWEAT ALL THE TIME.
EVEN THOUGH YOU LIVE TOGETHER, YOU CAN'T LET YOURSELF GO.
BLAH BLAH BLAH BLAH
EH?
EH?
EH?
EH?
YOU HAVE POTENTIAL, KAORU-CHAN. WITH A LITTLE MAKE-UP AND...
HEY!! WORRY ABOUT YOURSELF!
WHICH ONE OF US TURNED TWENTY-X THIS YEAR?!
PING
KAORU-SAN! THAT'S A TABOO!
...SO YOU'RE FINALLY HERE.
KENSH—

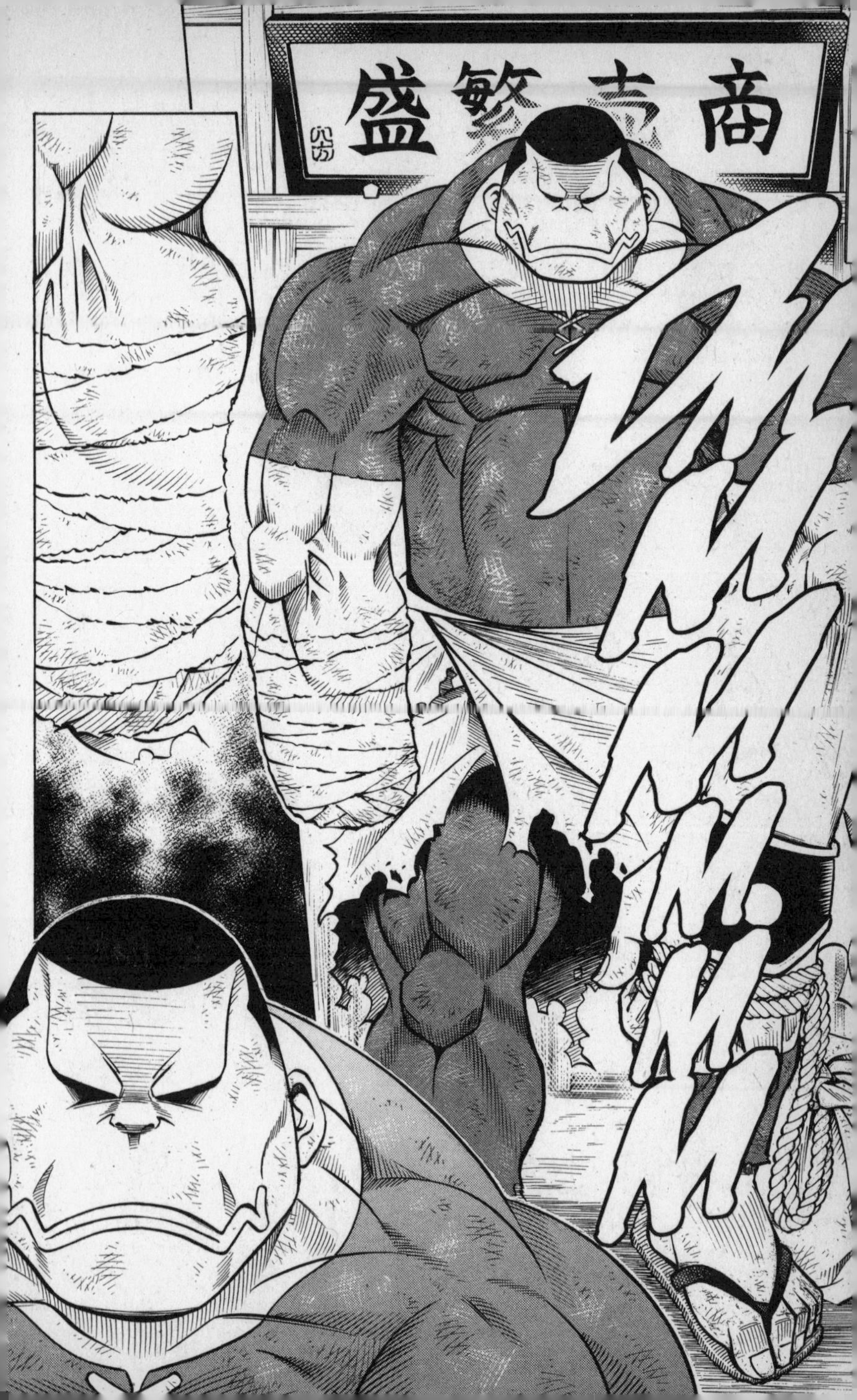

READ THIS WAY

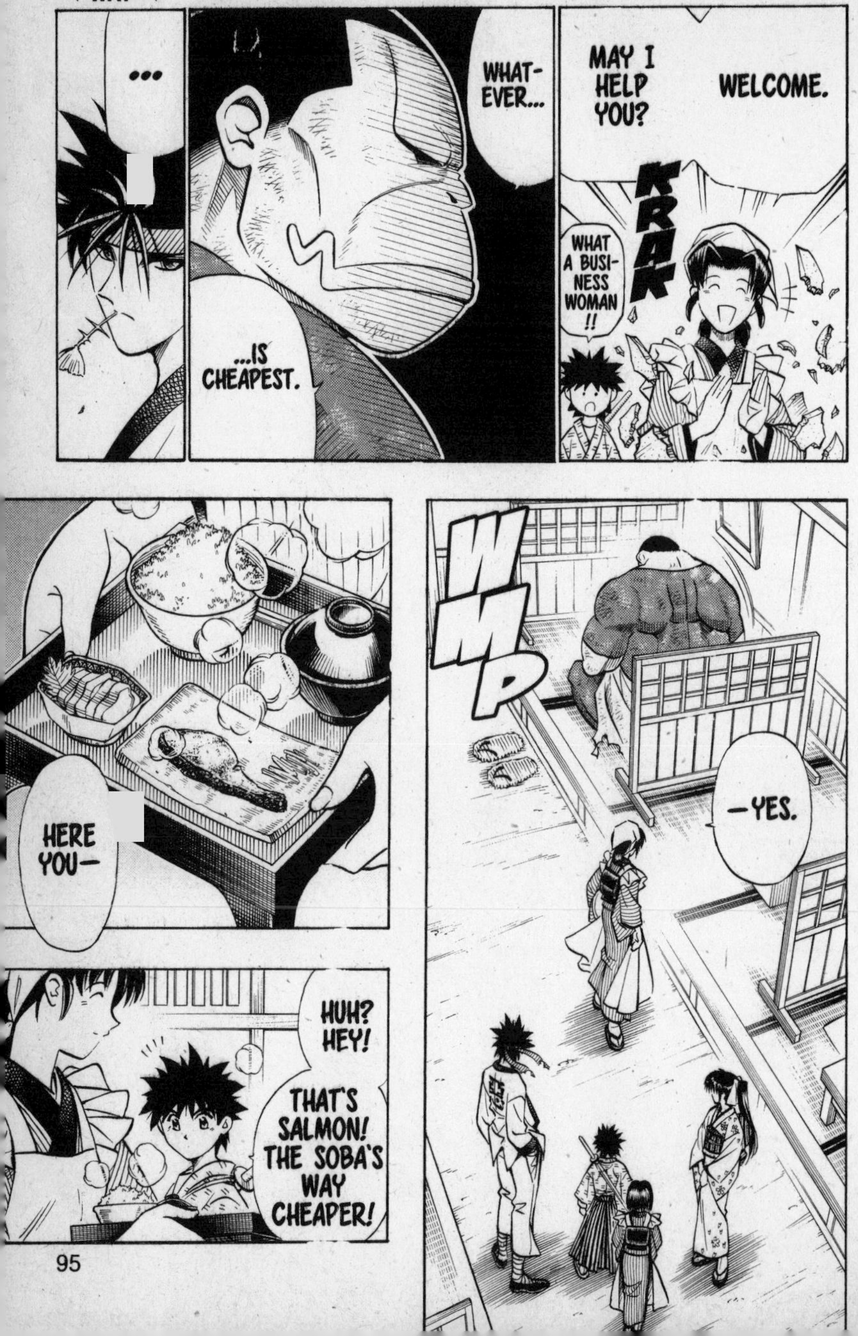

WELCOME.
MAY I HELP YOU?
KRAK
WHAT A BUSINESS WOMAN !!
WHAT-EVER...
...IS CHEAPEST.
...
WMP
—YES.
HERE YOU—
HUH? HEY!
THAT'S SALMON! THE SOBA'S WAY CHEAPER!

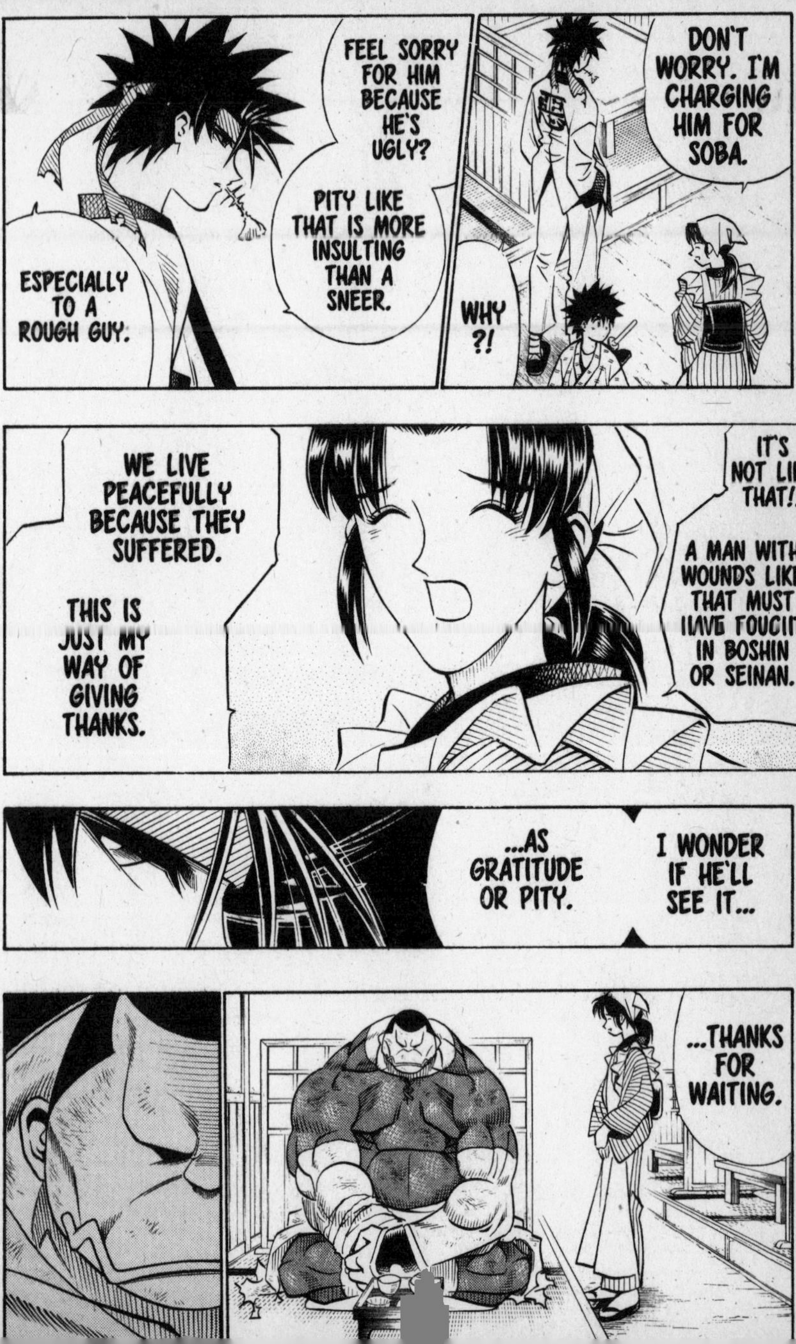
DON'T WORRY. I'M CHARGING HIM FOR SOBA.
WHY?!
FEEL SORRY FOR HIM BECAUSE HE'S UGLY?
PITY LIKE THAT IS MORE INSULTING THAN A SNEER.
ESPECIALLY TO A ROUGH GUY.
IT'S NOT LIKE THAT!!
A MAN WITH WOUNDS LIKE THAT MUST HAVE FOUGHT IN BOSHIN OR SEINAN.
WE LIVE PEACEFULLY BECAUSE THEY SUFFERED.
THIS IS JUST MY WAY OF GIVING THANKS.
I WONDER IF HE'LL SEE IT...
...AS GRATITUDE OR PITY.
...THANKS FOR WAITING.

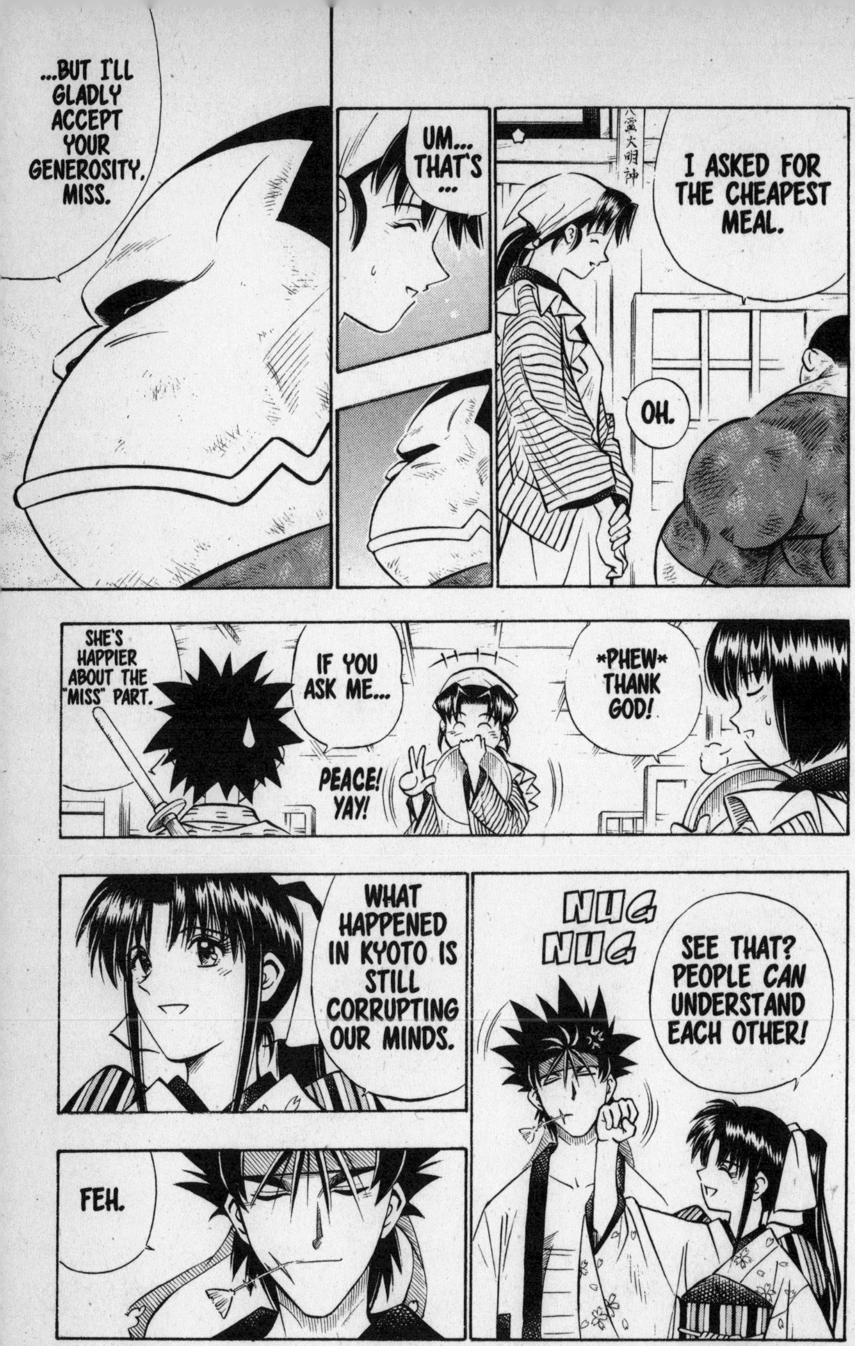
I ASKED FOR THE CHEAPEST MEAL.
OH.
UM... THAT'S ...
...BUT I'LL GLADLY ACCEPT YOUR GENEROSITY, MISS.
PHEW THANK GOD!
IF YOU ASK ME...
PEACE! YAY!
SHE'S HAPPIER ABOUT THE "MISS" PART.
NUG NUG
SEE THAT? PEOPLE CAN UNDERSTAND EACH OTHER!
WHAT HAPPENED IN KYOTO IS STILL CORRUPTING OUR MINDS.
FEH.

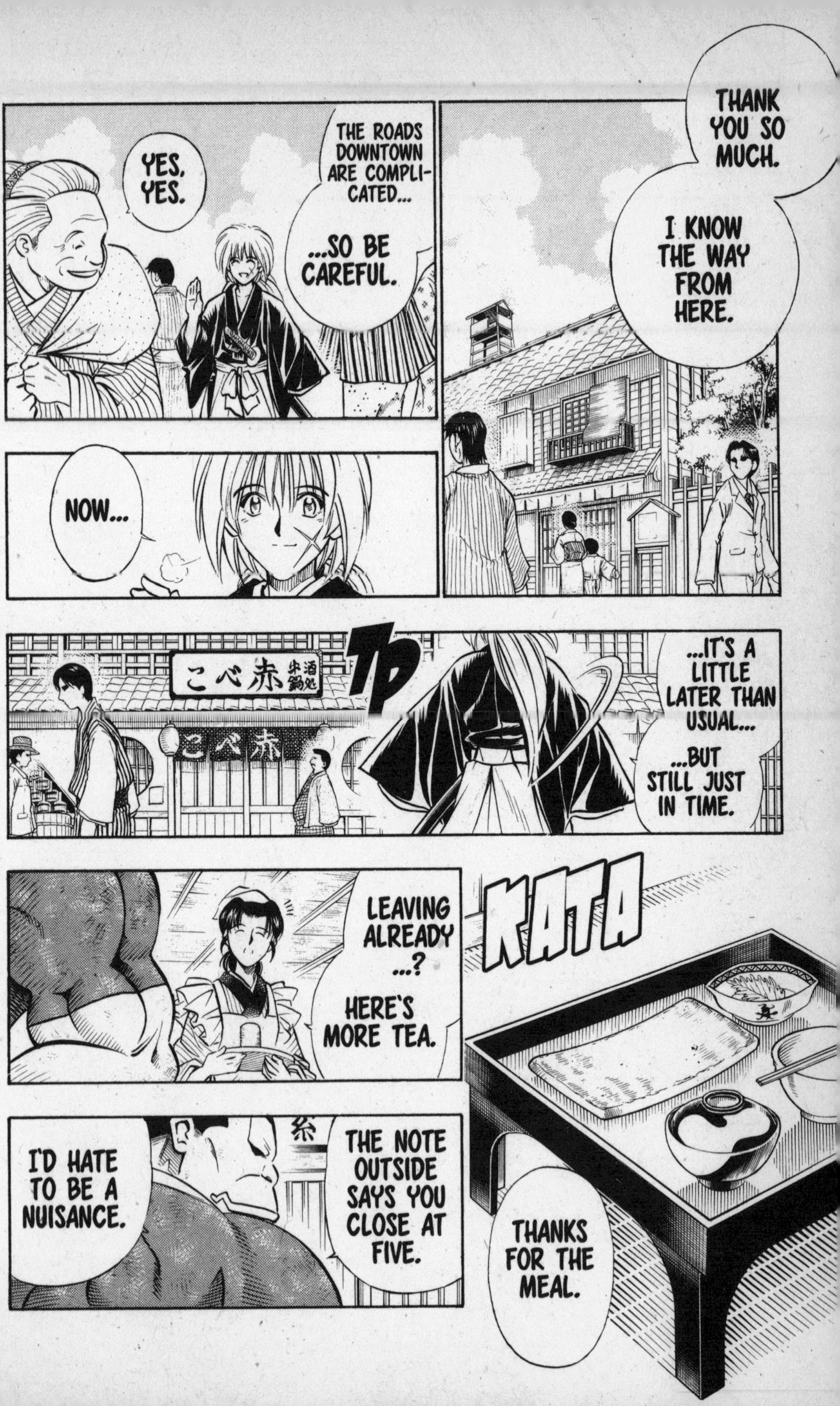
THANK YOU SO MUCH.
I KNOW THE WAY FROM HERE.
THE ROADS DOWNTOWN ARE COMPLICATED...
...SO BE CAREFUL.
YES, YES.
NOW...
...IT'S A LITTLE LATER THAN USUAL...
...BUT STILL JUST IN TIME.
TP
赤べこ
赤べこ
KATA
THANKS FOR THE MEAL.
LEAVING ALREADY ...?
HERE'S MORE TEA.
THE NOTE OUTSIDE SAYS YOU CLOSE AT FIVE.
I'D HATE TO BE A NUISANCE.

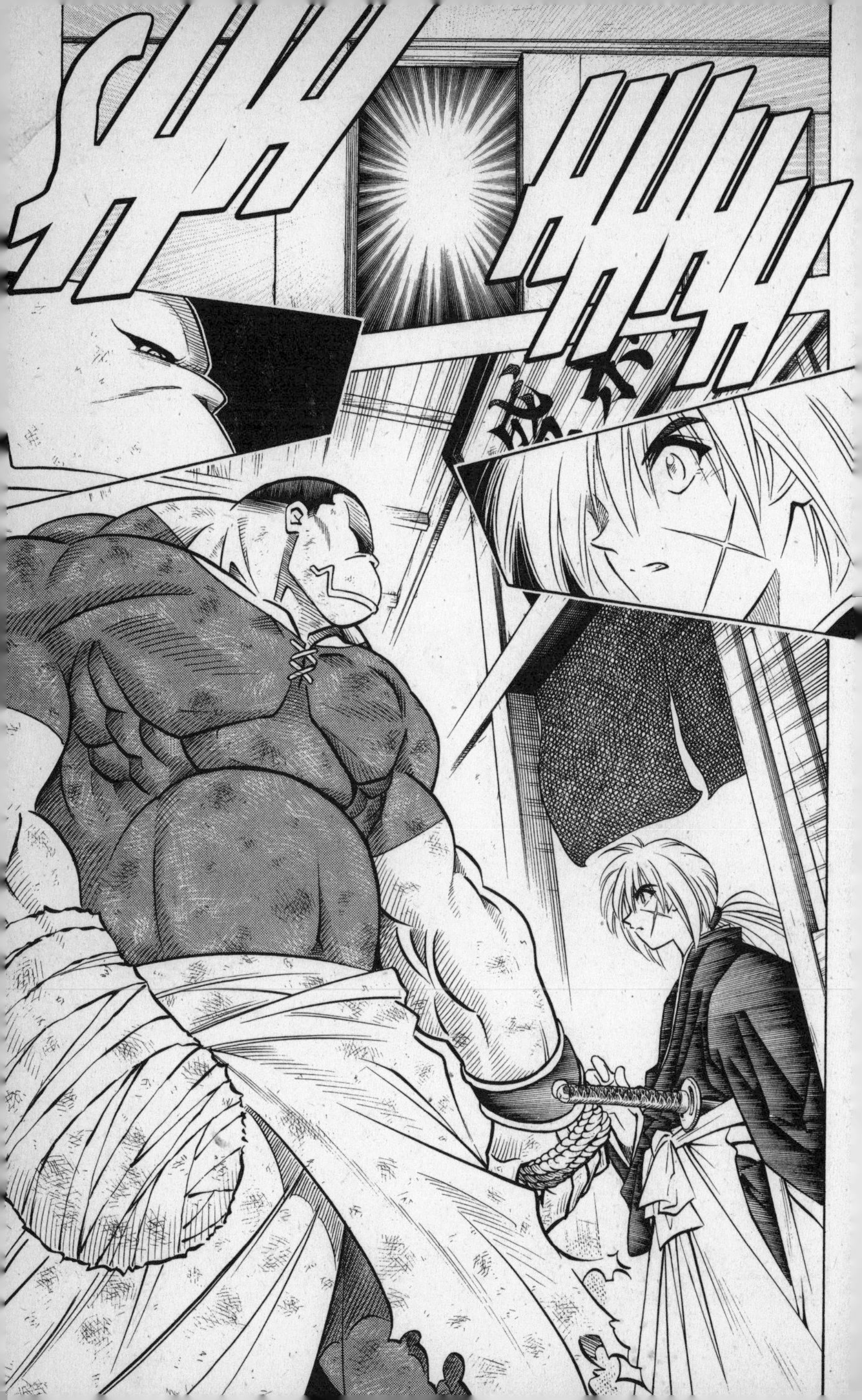
SHH
HHHHHH

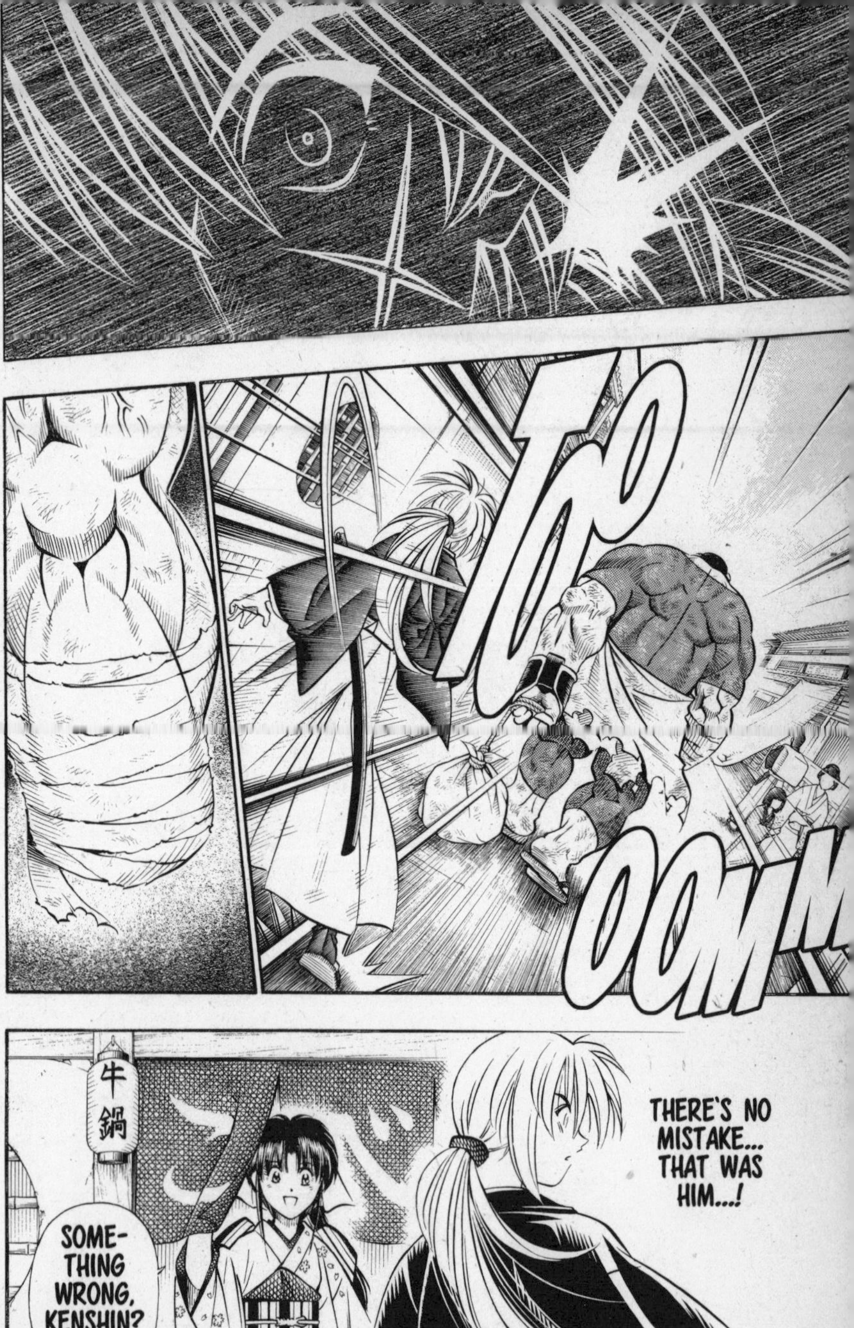
TOOOM...
THERE'S NO MISTAKE... THAT WAS HIM...!
牛鍋
SOME-THING WRONG, KENSHIN?

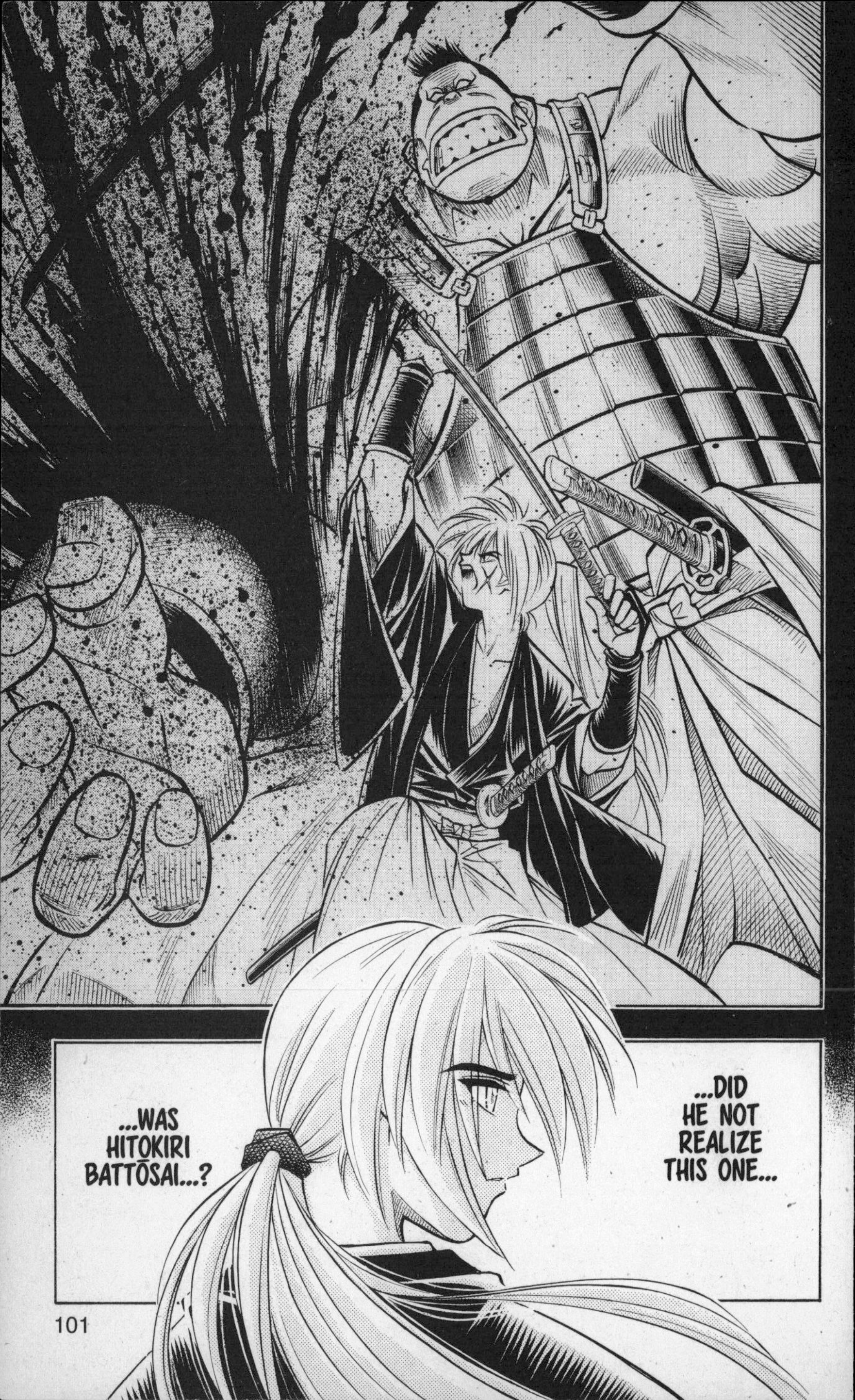
...DID HE NOT REALIZE THIS ONE...
...WAS HITOKIRI BATTŌSAI...?

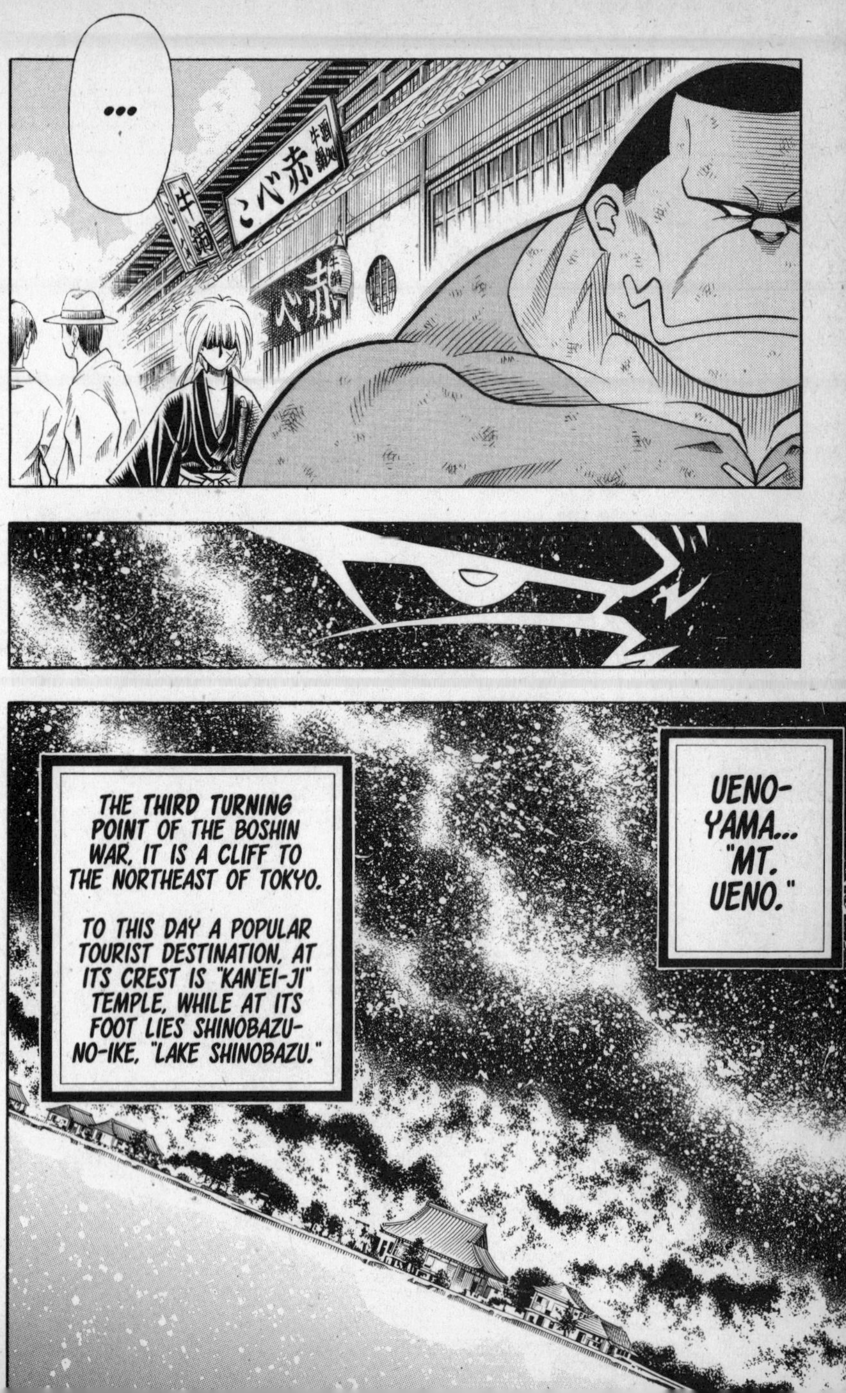
...
UENO-YAMA... "MT. UENO."
THE THIRD TURNING POINT OF THE BOSHIN WAR, IT IS A CLIFF TO THE NORTHEAST OF TOKYO.
TO THIS DAY A POPULAR TOURIST DESTINATION, AT ITS CREST IS "KAN'EI-JI" TEMPLE, WHILE AT ITS FOOT LIES SHINOBAZU-NO-IKE, "LAKE SHINOBAZU."

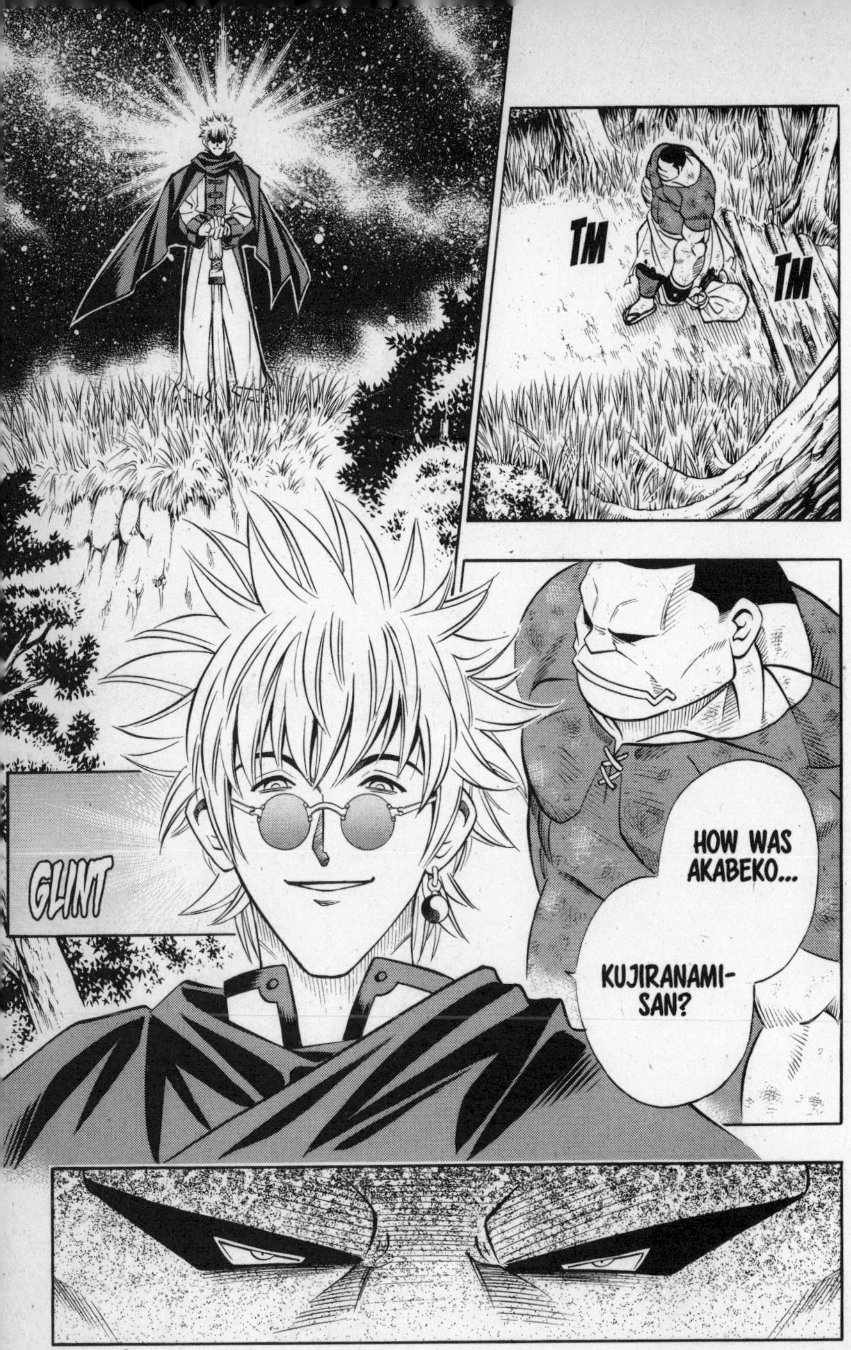
TM
TM
HOW WAS AKABEKO...
KUJIRANAMI-SAN?
GLINT

Rurouni Kenshin

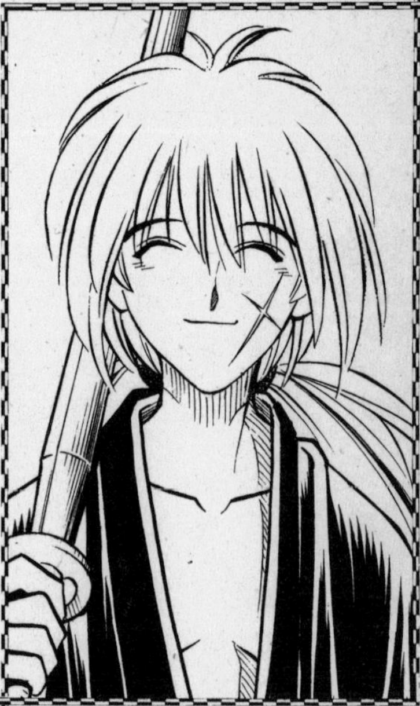

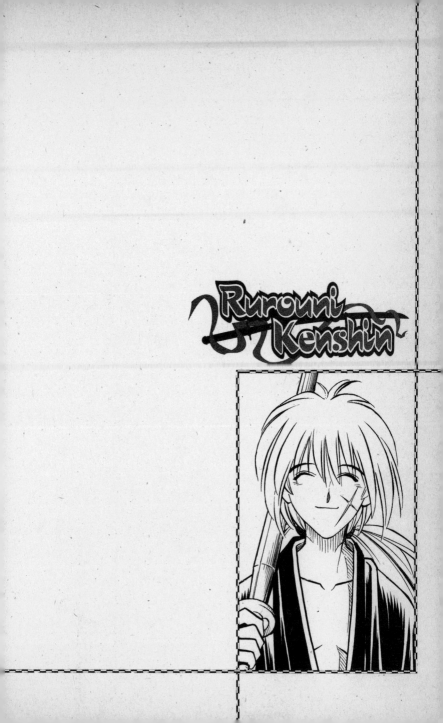

Act 154
The Signal Fire of Revenge

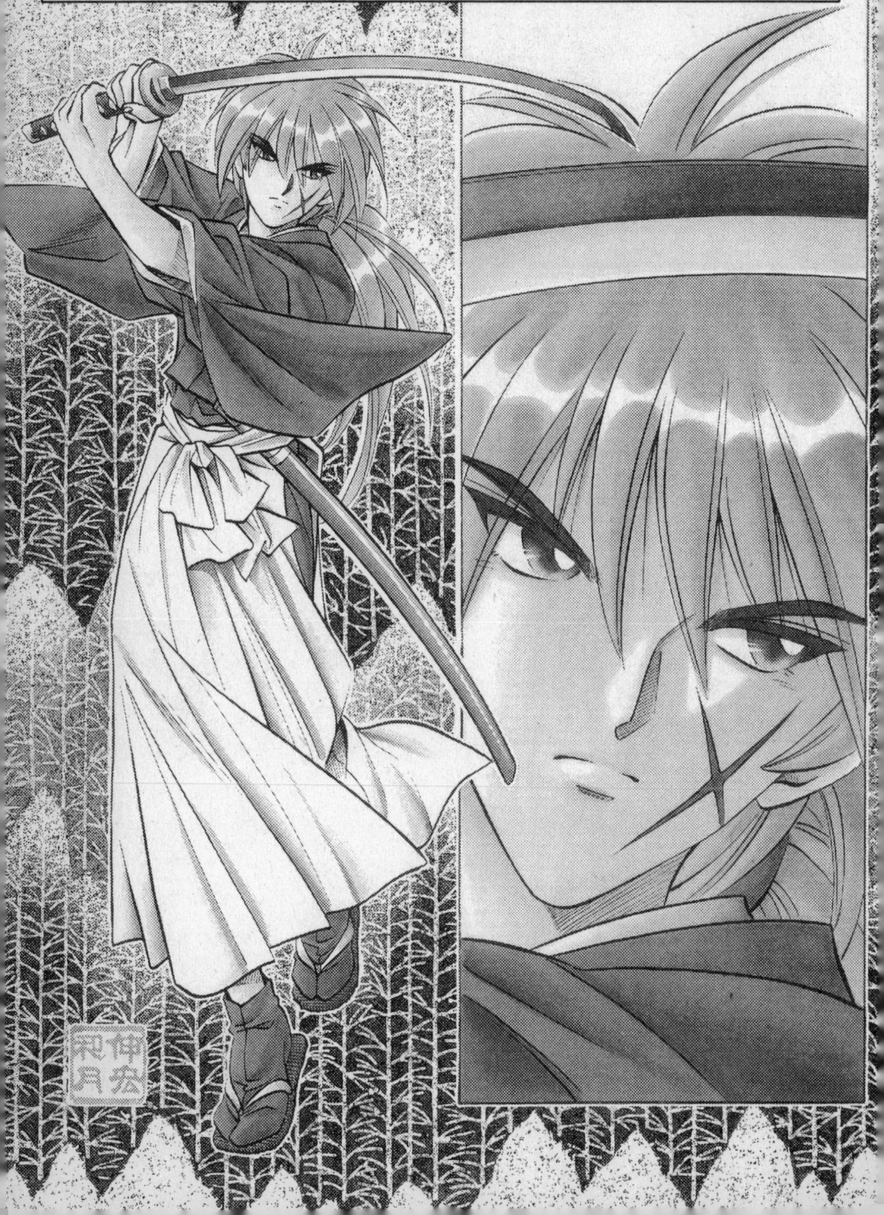

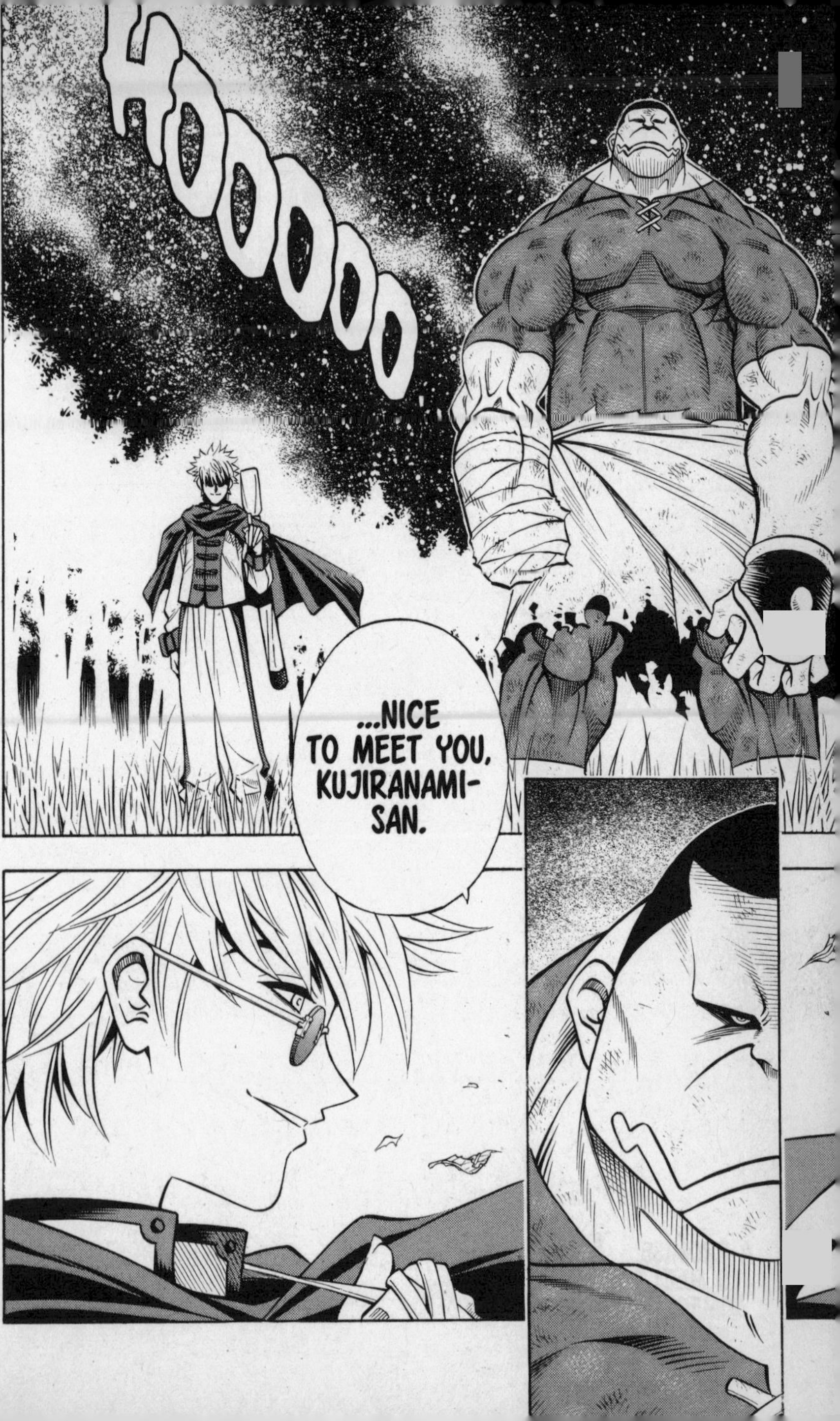
HOOOOOO
...NICE TO MEET YOU, KUJIRANAMI-SAN.

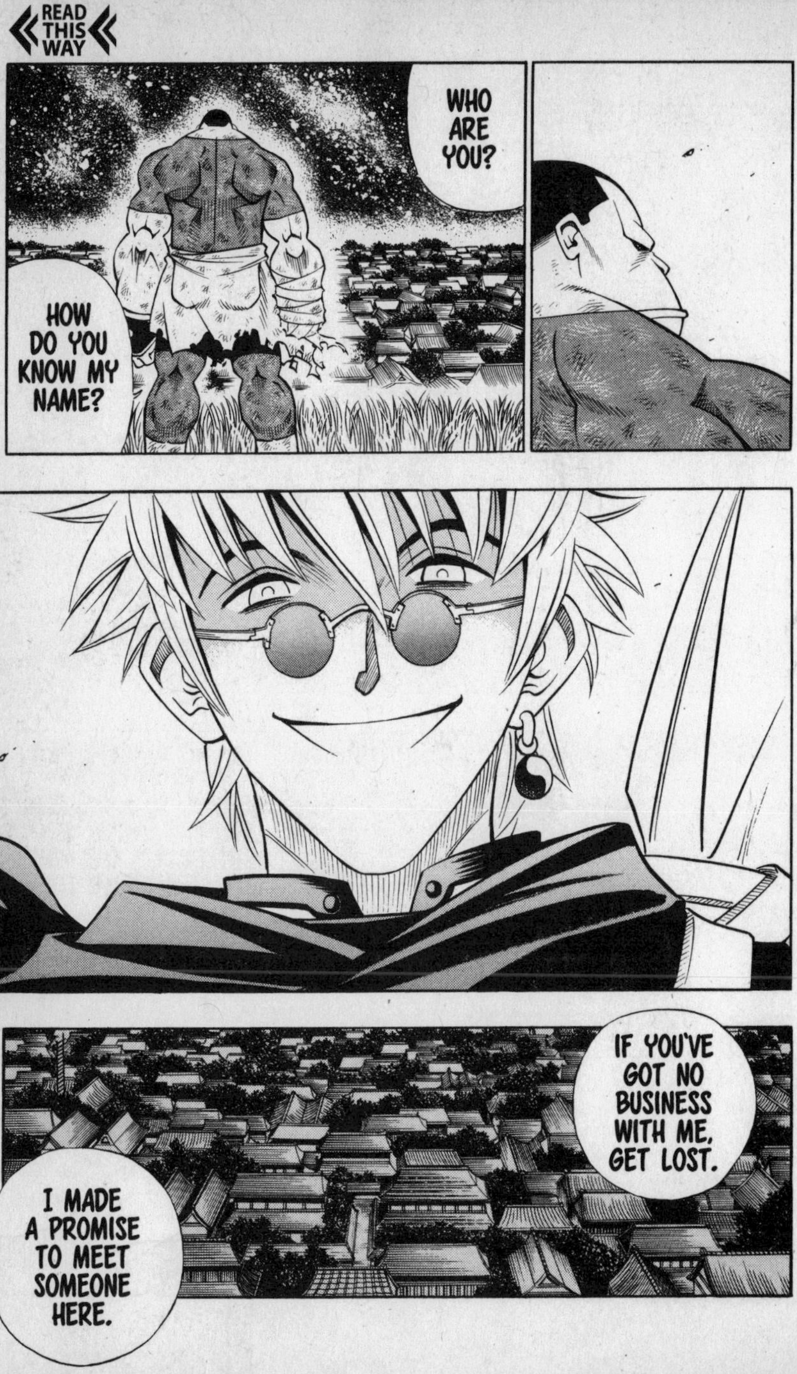
READ THIS WAY
WHO ARE YOU?
HOW DO YOU KNOW MY NAME?
IF YOU'VE GOT NO BUSINESS WITH ME, GET LOST.
I MADE A PROMISE TO MEET SOMEONE HERE.

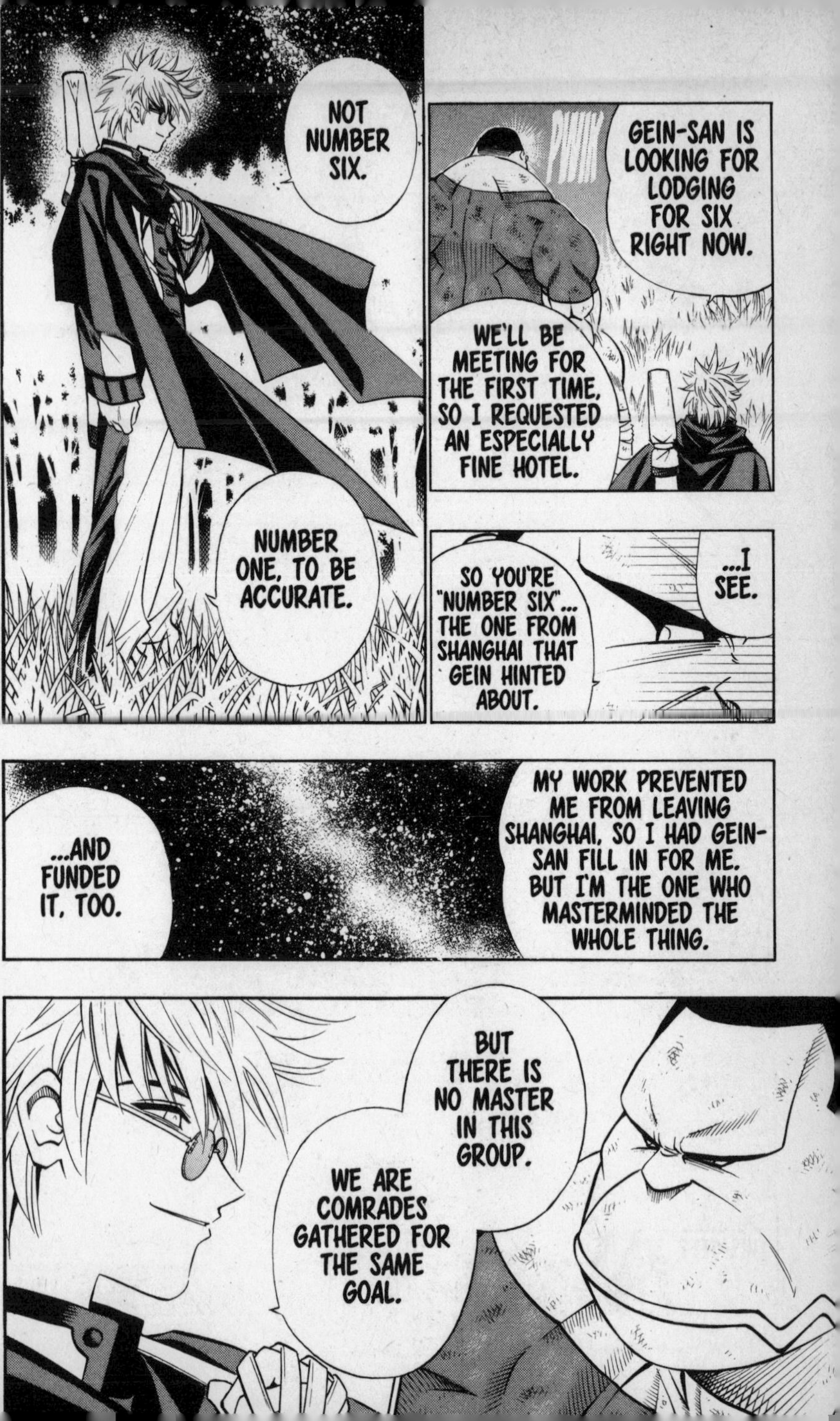
GEIN-SAN IS LOOKING FOR LODGING FOR SIX RIGHT NOW.
WE'LL BE MEETING FOR THE FIRST TIME, SO I REQUESTED AN ESPECIALLY FINE HOTEL.
...I SEE.
SO YOU'RE "NUMBER SIX"... THE ONE FROM SHANGHAI THAT GEIN HINTED ABOUT.
NOT NUMBER SIX.
NUMBER ONE, TO BE ACCURATE.
MY WORK PREVENTED ME FROM LEAVING SHANGHAI, SO I HAD GEIN-SAN FILL IN FOR ME. BUT I'M THE ONE WHO MASTERMINDED THE WHOLE THING.
...AND FUNDED IT, TOO.
BUT THERE IS NO MASTER IN THIS GROUP.
WE ARE COMRADES GATHERED FOR THE SAME GOAL.

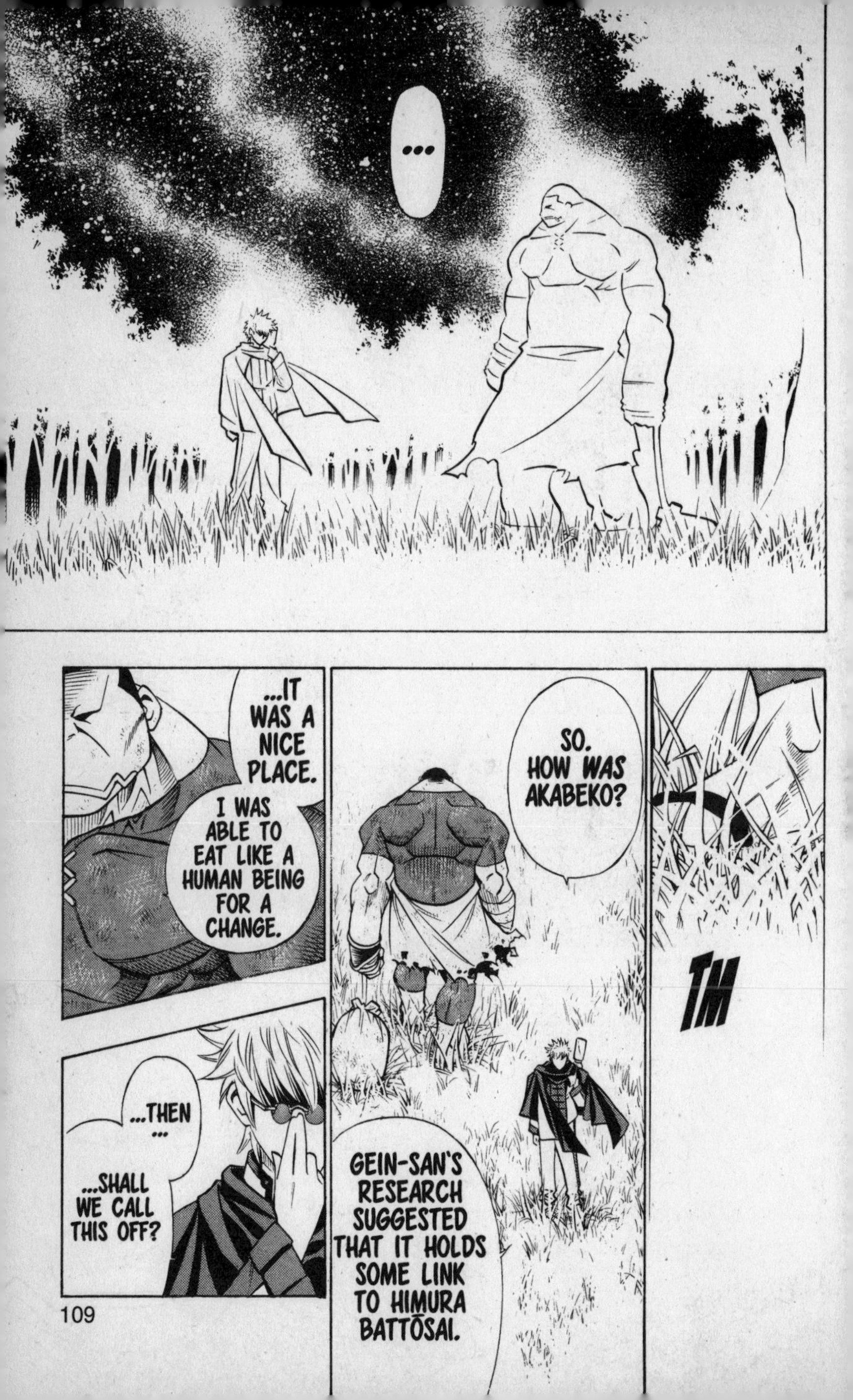
...
TM
SO. HOW WAS AKABEKO?
...IT WAS A NICE PLACE.
I WAS ABLE TO EAT LIKE A HUMAN BEING FOR A CHANGE.
GEIN-SAN'S RESEARCH SUGGESTED THAT IT HOLDS SOME LINK TO HIMURA BATTŌSAI.
...THEN ...
...SHALL WE CALL THIS OFF?

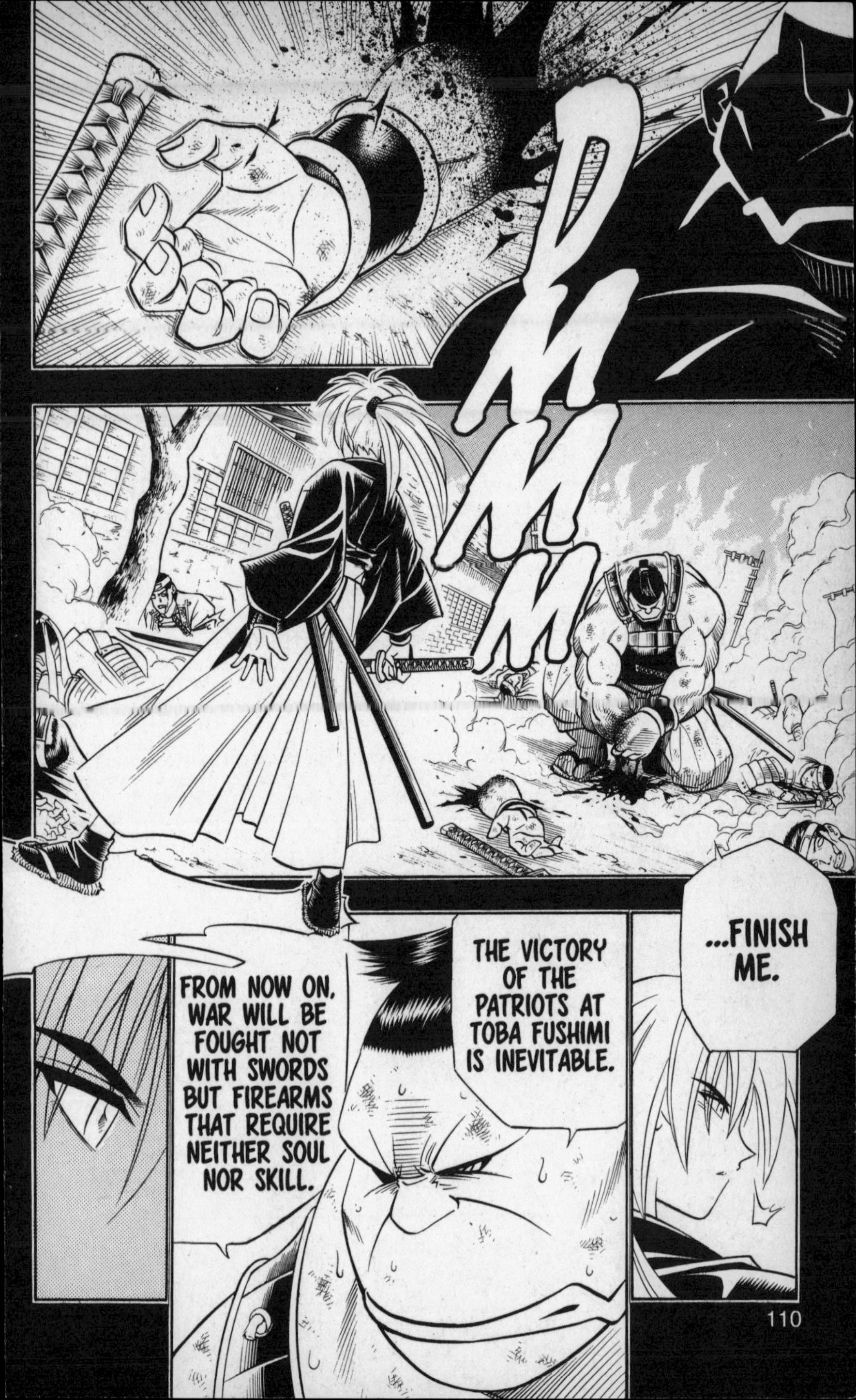
DMMM
...FINISH ME.
THE VICTORY OF THE PATRIOTS AT TOBA FUSHIMI IS INEVITABLE.
FROM NOW ON, WAR WILL BE FOUGHT NOT WITH SWORDS BUT FIREARMS THAT REQUIRE NEITHER SOUL NOR SKILL.

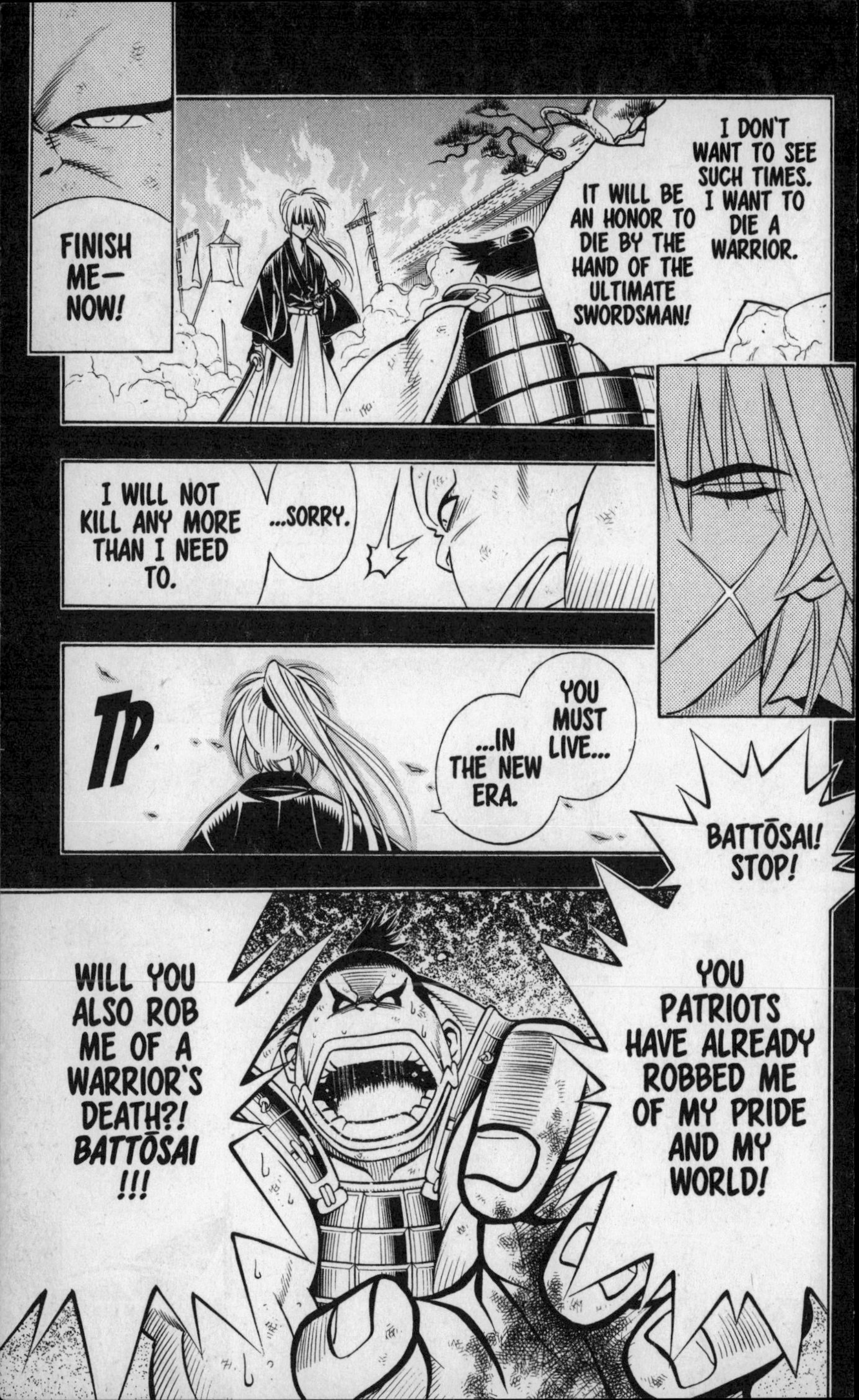
I DON'T WANT TO SEE SUCH TIMES. I WANT TO DIE A WARRIOR.
IT WILL BE AN HONOR TO DIE BY THE HAND OF THE ULTIMATE SWORDSMAN!
FINISH ME—NOW!
...SORRY.
I WILL NOT KILL ANY MORE THAN I NEED TO.
YOU MUST LIVE...
...IN THE NEW ERA.
TP
BATTŌSAI! STOP!
YOU PATRIOTS HAVE ALREADY ROBBED ME OF MY PRIDE AND MY WORLD!
WILL YOU ALSO ROB ME OF A WARRIOR'S DEATH?! BATTŌSAI !!!

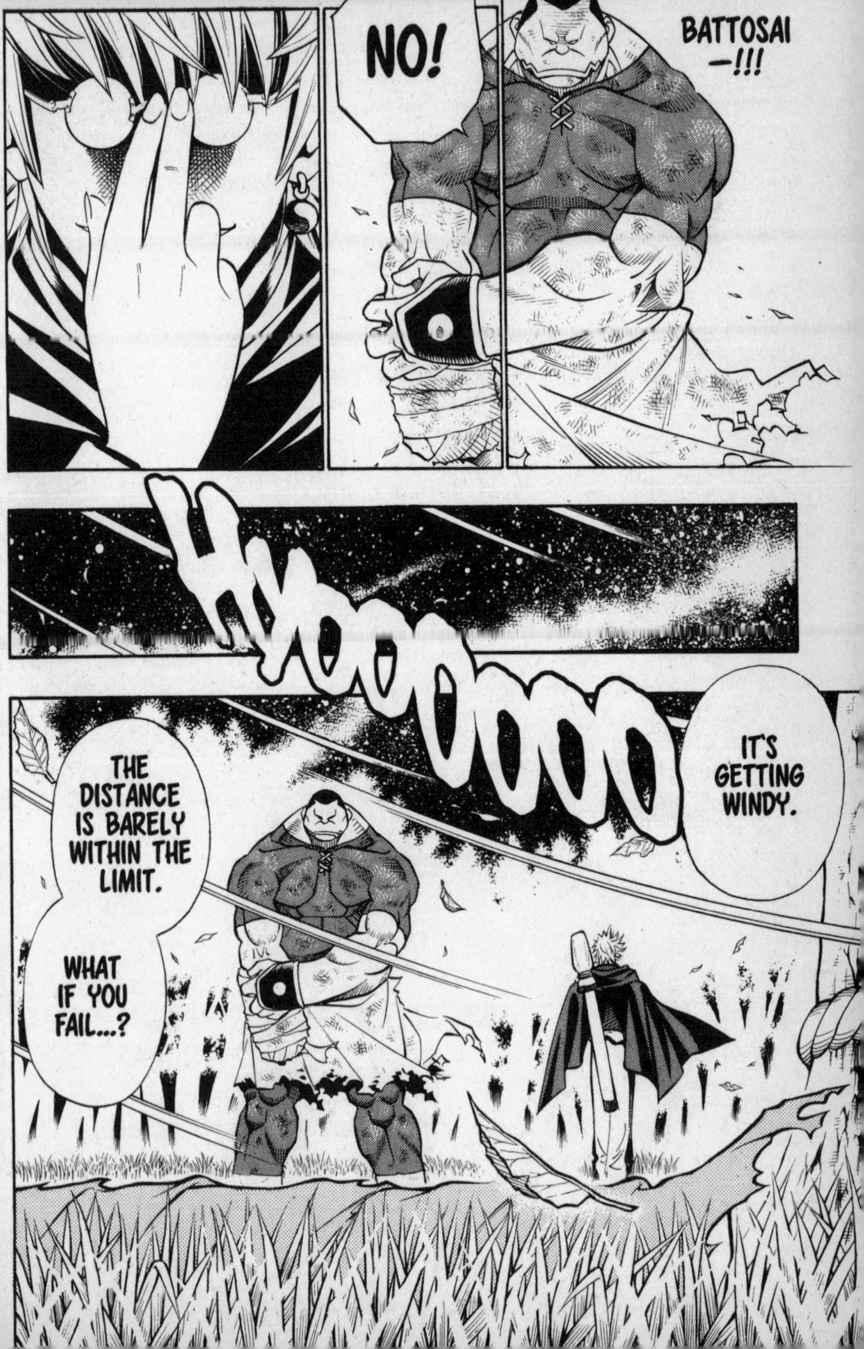
BATTOSAI—!!!
NO!
HYOOOOOO
IT'S GETTING WINDY.
THE DISTANCE IS BARELY WITHIN THE LIMIT.
WHAT IF YOU FAIL...?

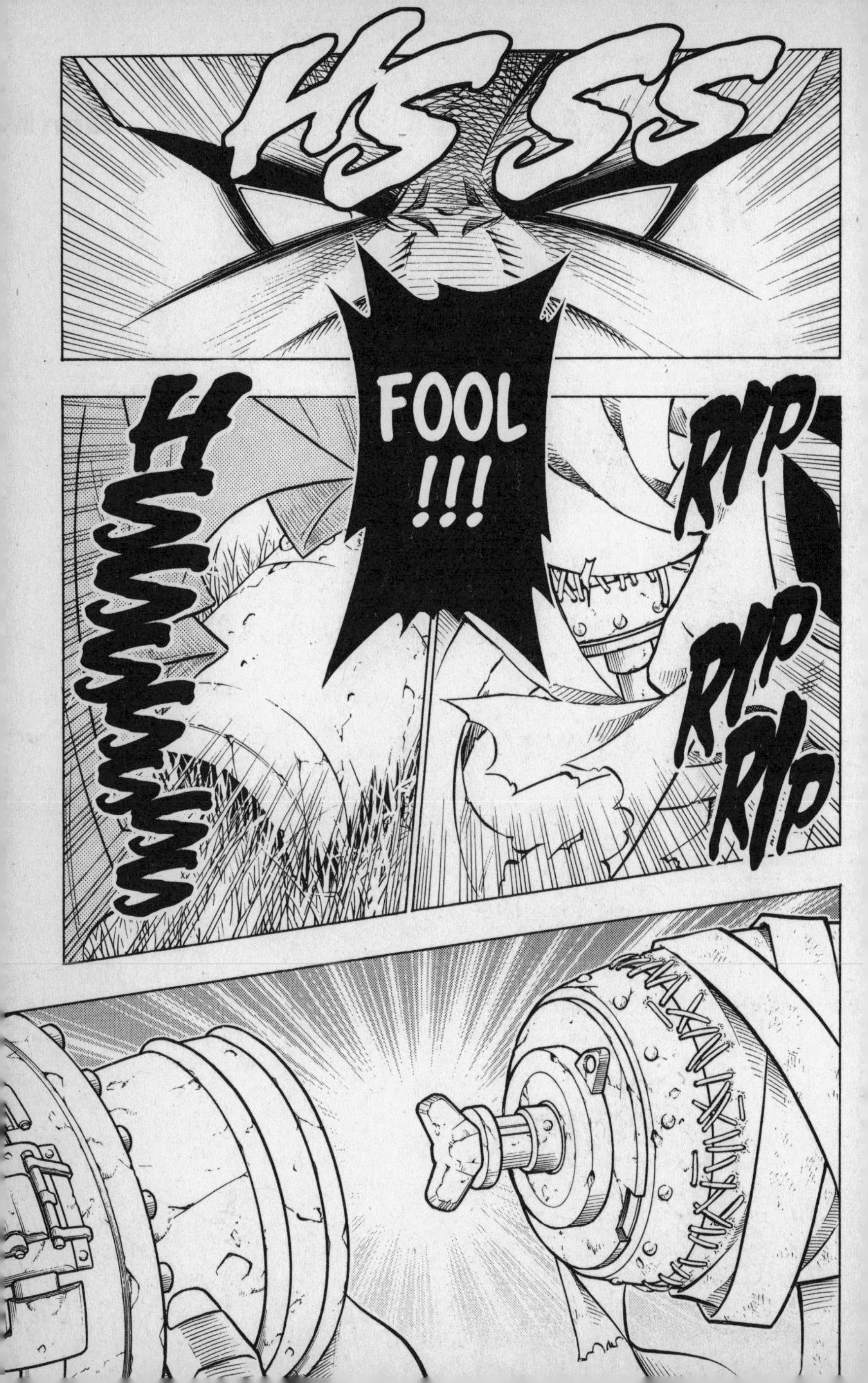
HSSS
FOOL !!!
RIP
RIP RIP RIP
HSWSWSWSWS

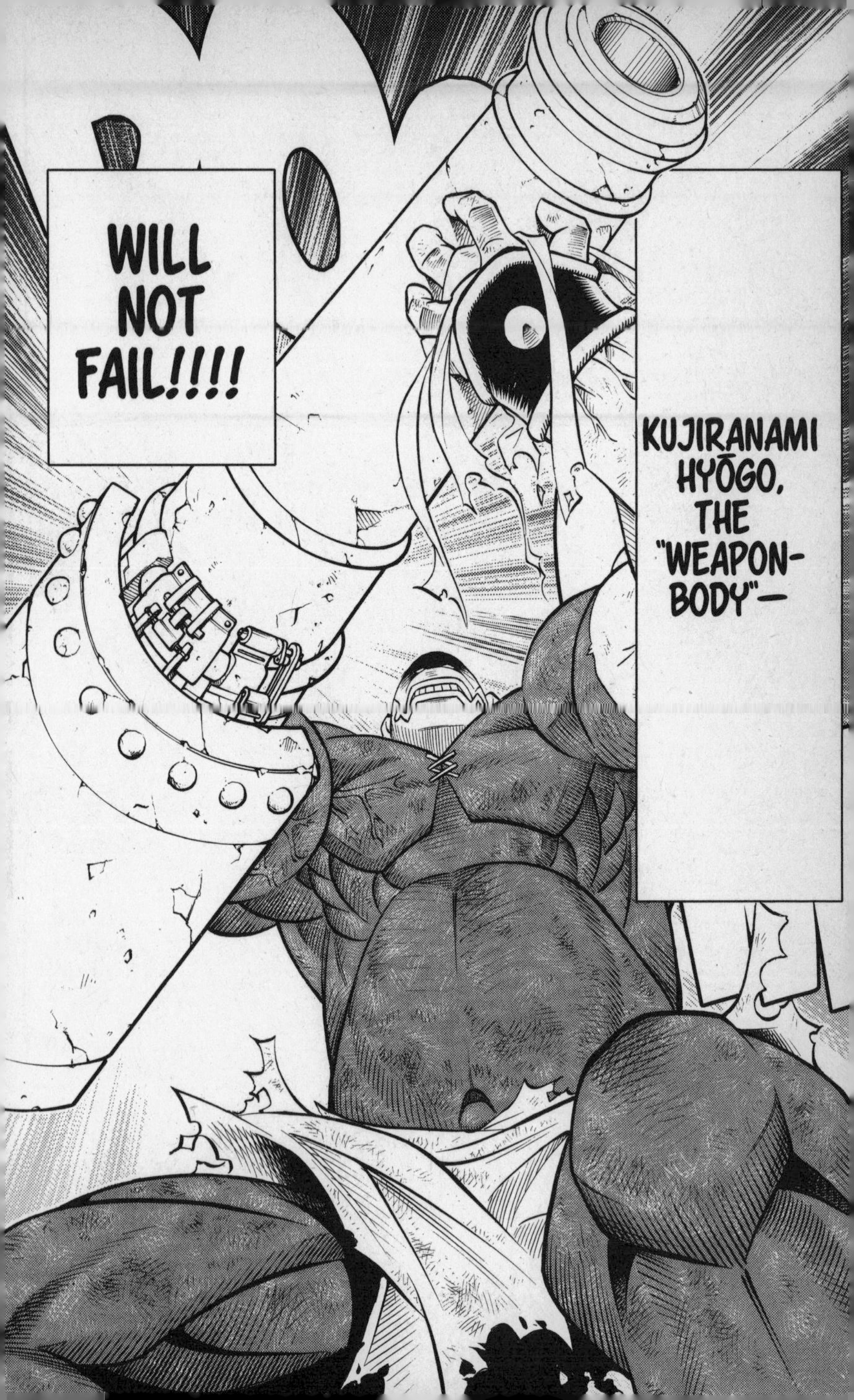
KUJIRANAMI HYŌGO, THE "WEAPON-BODY"—
WILL NOT FAIL!!!!

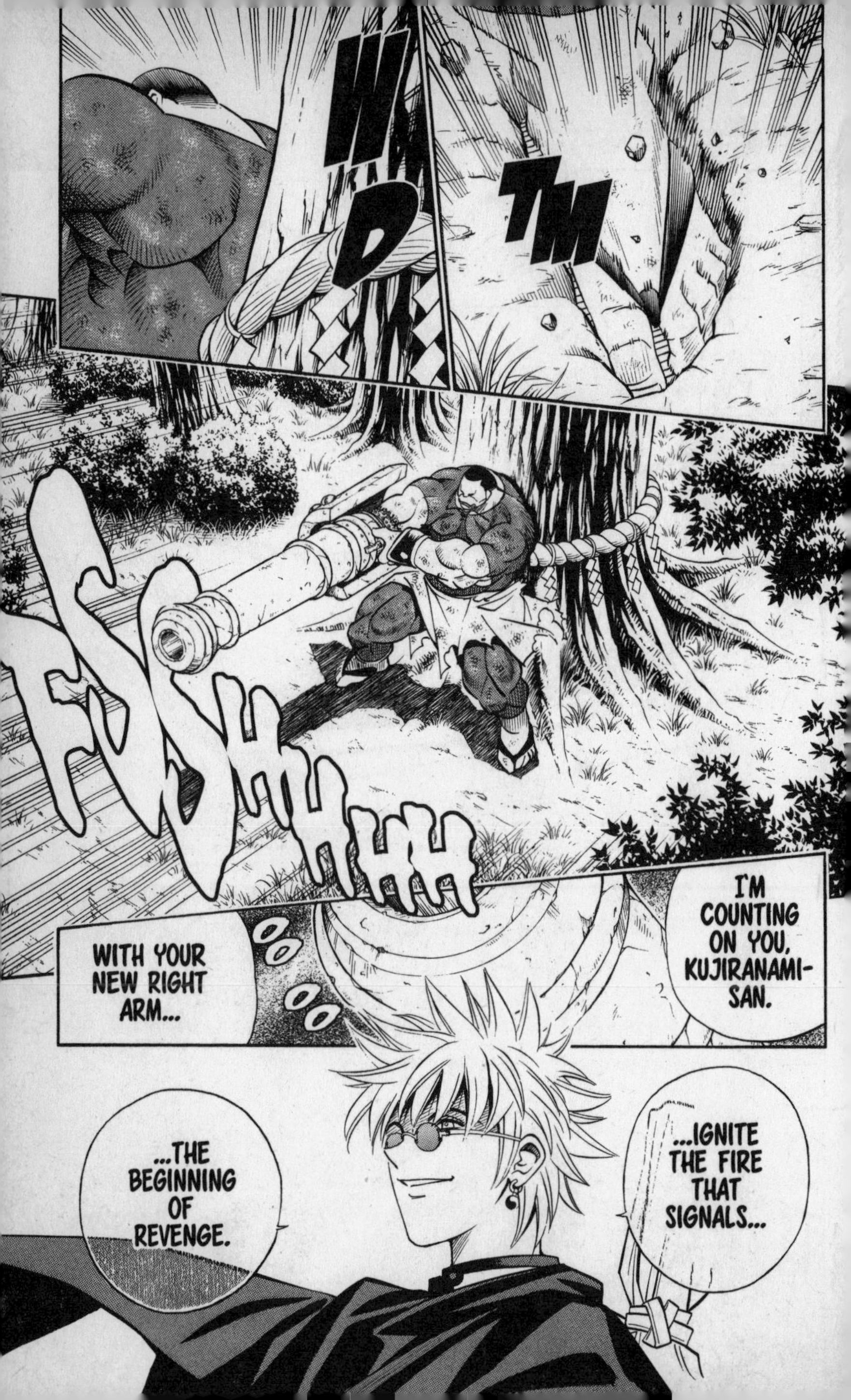
I'M COUNTING ON YOU, KUJIRANAMI-SAN.
WITH YOUR NEW RIGHT ARM...
...IGNITE THE FIRE THAT SIGNALS...
...THE BEGINNING OF REVENGE.

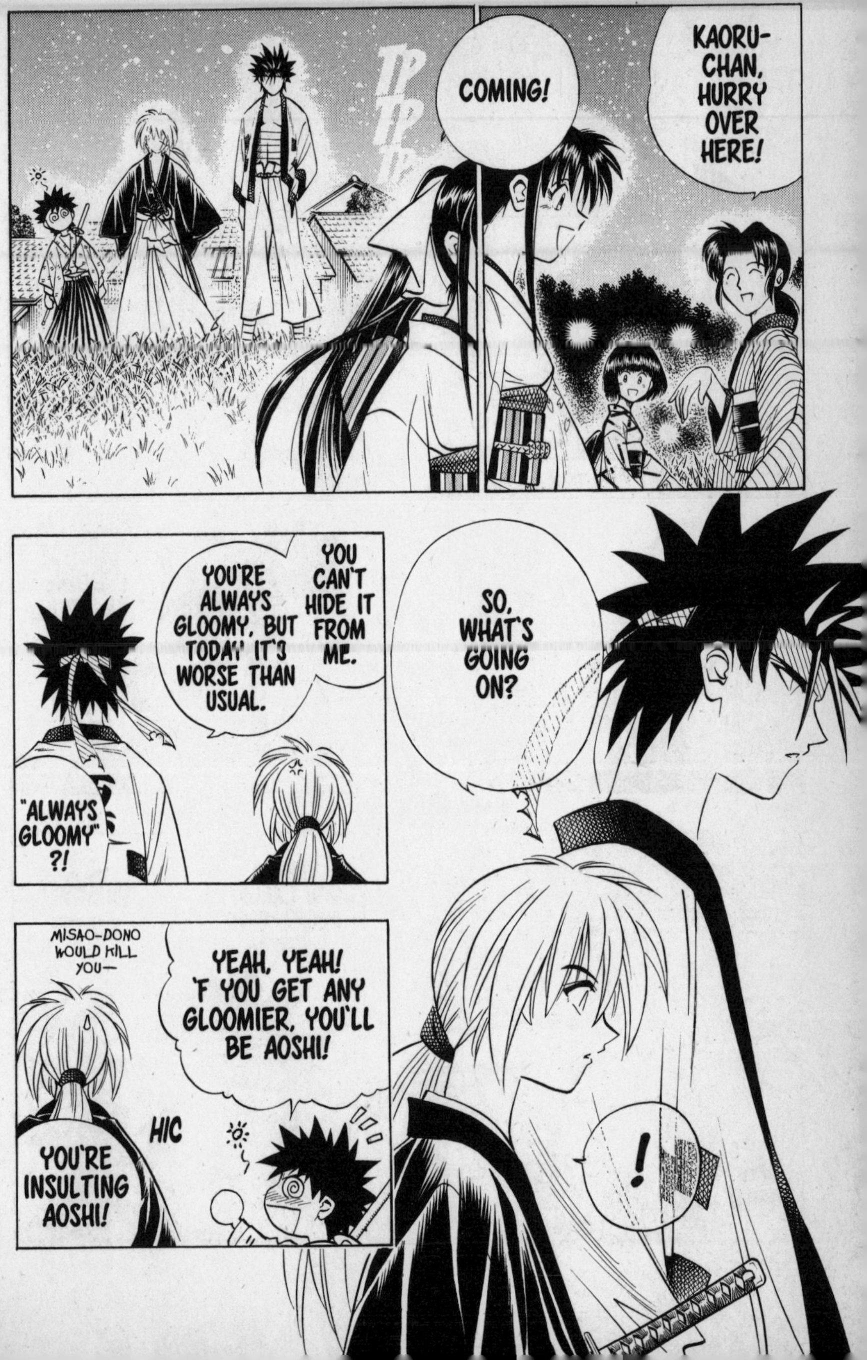
KAORU-CHAN, HURRY OVER HERE!
COMING!
TP TP TP
SO, WHAT'S GOING ON?
!
YOU CAN'T HIDE IT FROM ME.
YOU'RE ALWAYS GLOOMY, BUT TODAY IT'S WORSE THAN USUAL.
"ALWAYS GLOOMY" ?!
YEAH, YEAH! 'F YOU GET ANY GLOOMIER, YOU'LL BE AOSHI!
MISAO-DONO WOULD KILL YOU—
HIC
YOU'RE INSULTING AOSHI!

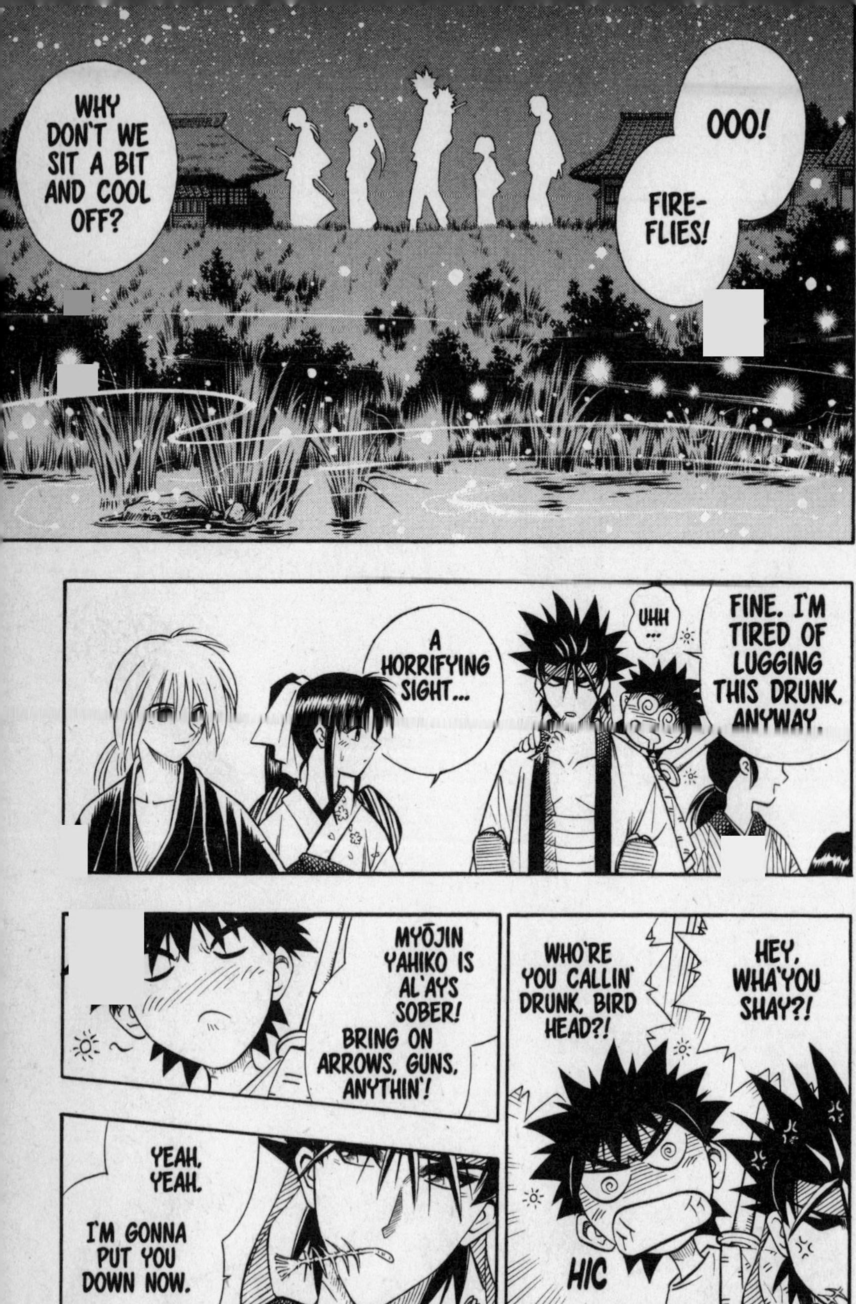
OOO!
FIRE-FLIES!
WHY DON'T WE SIT A BIT AND COOL OFF?
FINE. I'M TIRED OF LUGGING THIS DRUNK, ANYWAY.
UHH ...
A HORRIFYING SIGHT...
HEY, WHA'YOU SHAY?!
WHO'RE YOU CALLIN' DRUNK, BIRD HEAD?!
HIC
MYŌJIN YAHIKO IS AL'AYS SOBER! BRING ON ARROWS, GUNS, ANYTHIN'!
YEAH, YEAH.
I'M GONNA PUT YOU DOWN NOW.

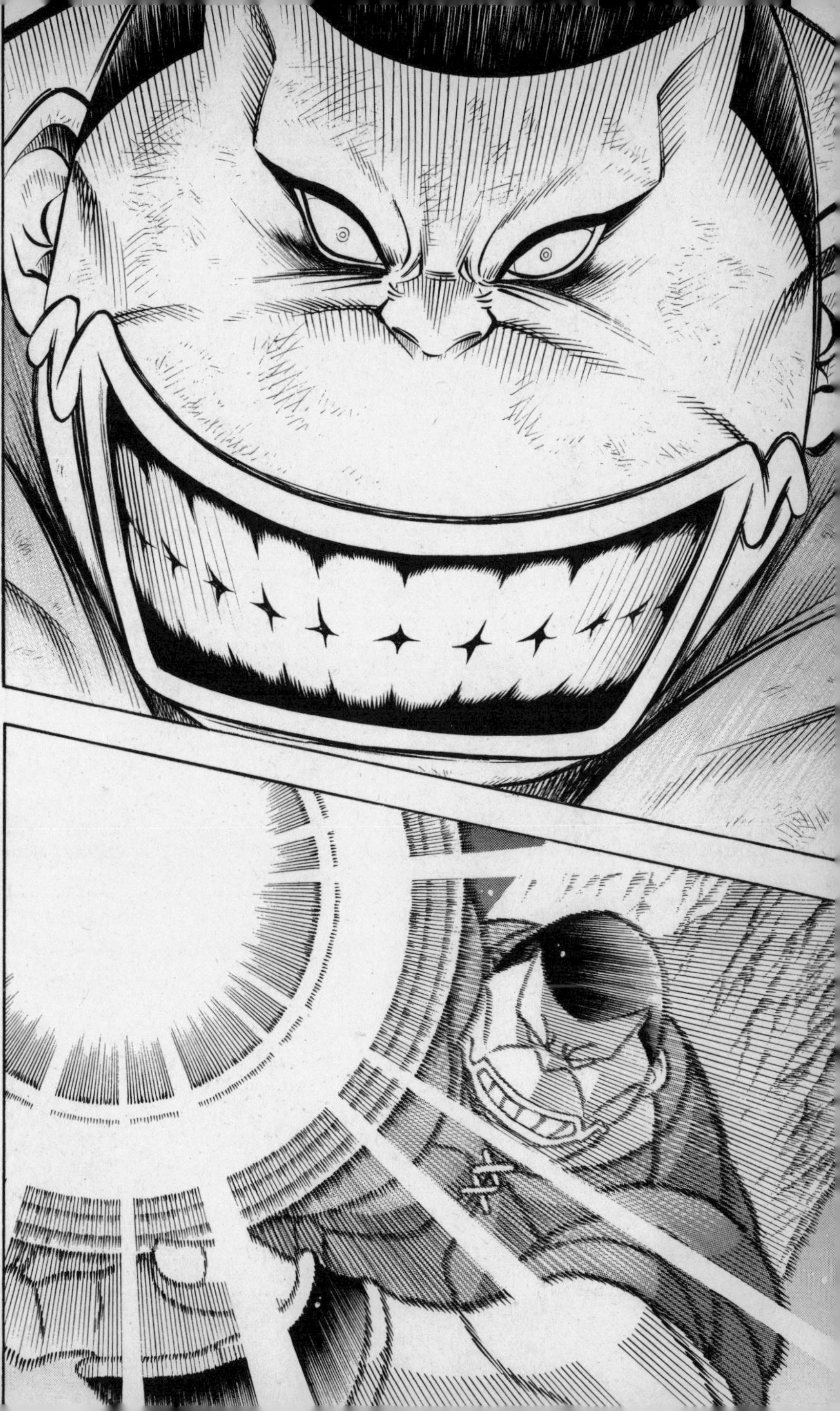

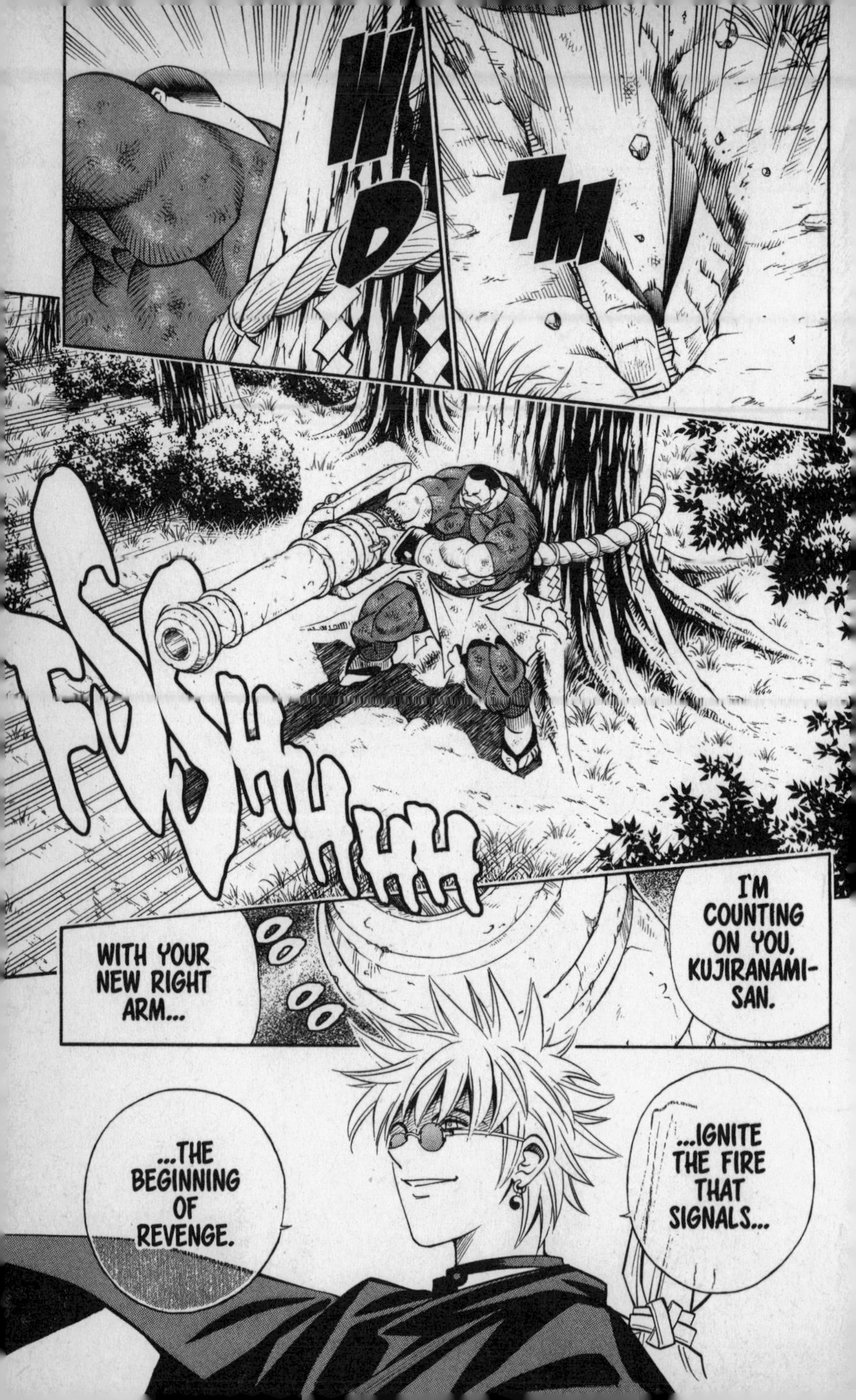

TM
WHD
FSHHHH
I'M COUNTING ON YOU, KUJIRANAMI-SAN.
WITH YOUR NEW RIGHT ARM...
...IGNITE THE FIRE THAT SIGNALS...
...THE BEGINNING OF REVENGE.

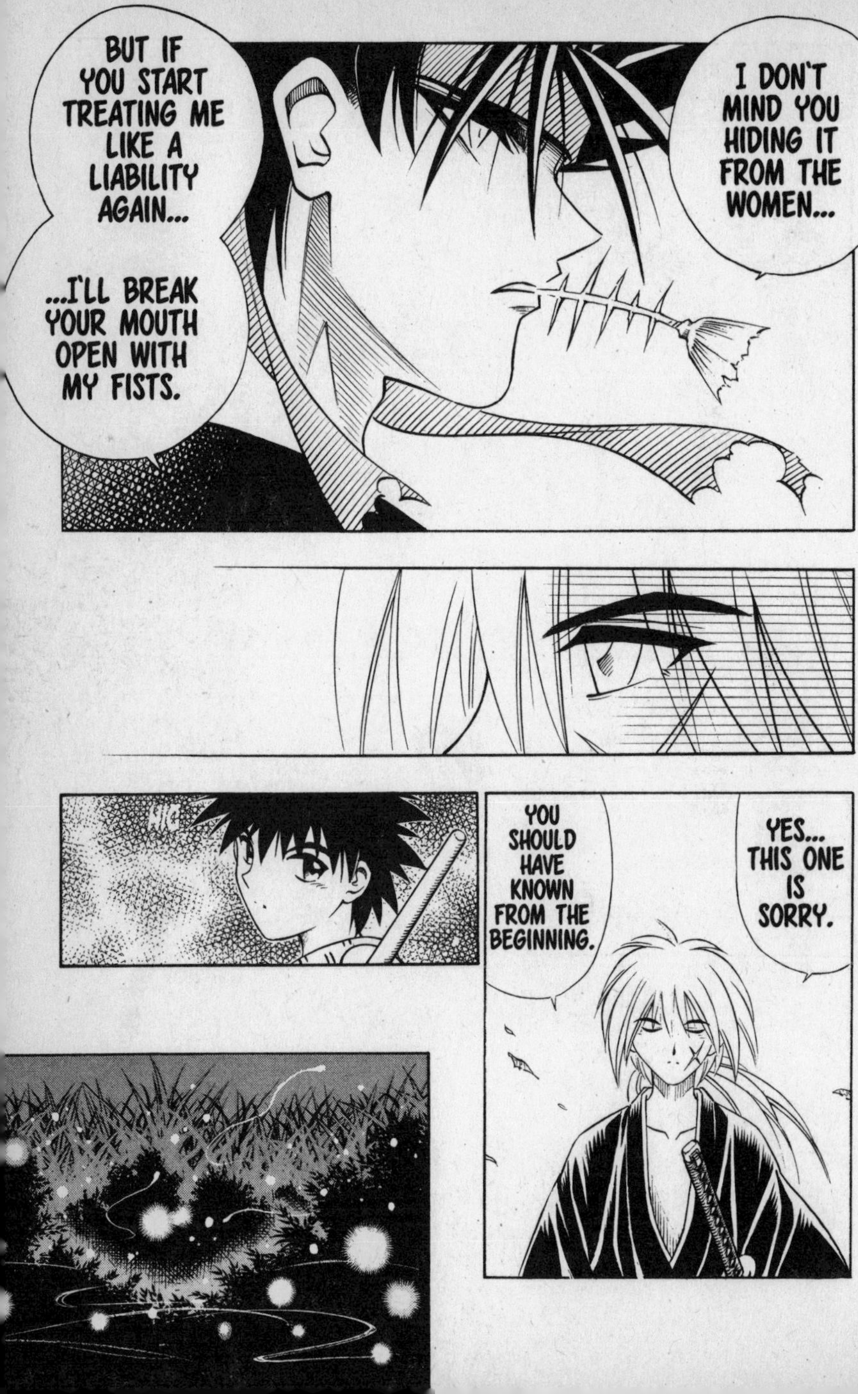
I DON'T MIND YOU HIDING IT FROM THE WOMEN...
BUT IF YOU START TREATING ME LIKE A LIABILITY AGAIN...
...I'LL BREAK YOUR MOUTH OPEN WITH MY FISTS.
YES... THIS ONE IS SORRY.
YOU SHOULD HAVE KNOWN FROM THE BEGINNING.

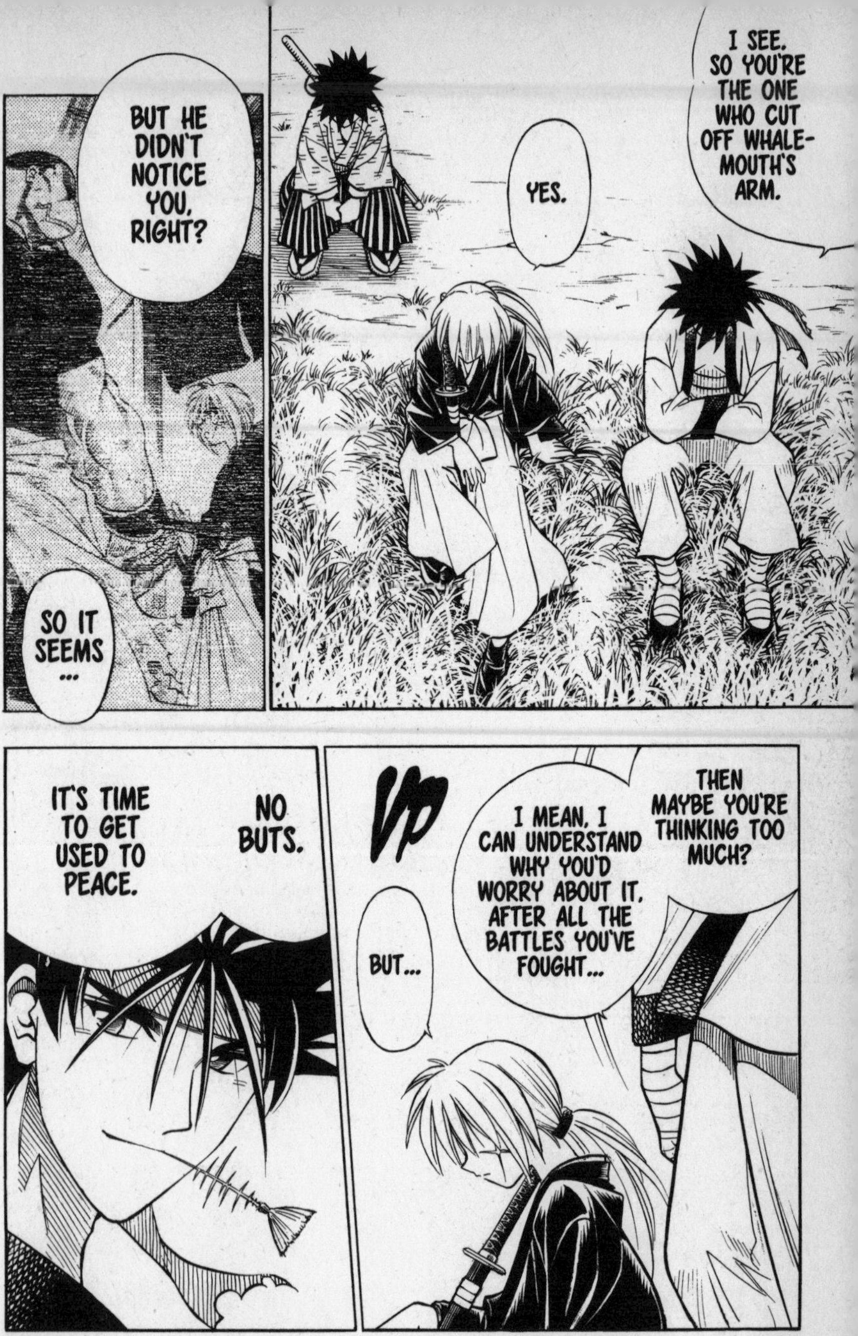
I SEE. SO YOU'RE THE ONE WHO CUT OFF WHALE-MOUTH'S ARM.
YES.
BUT HE DIDN'T NOTICE YOU, RIGHT?
SO IT SEEMS...
THEN MAYBE YOU'RE THINKING TOO MUCH?
I MEAN, I CAN UNDERSTAND WHY YOU'D WORRY ABOUT IT, AFTER ALL THE BATTLES YOU'VE FOUGHT...
BUT...
NO BUTS.
IT'S TIME TO GET USED TO PEACE.

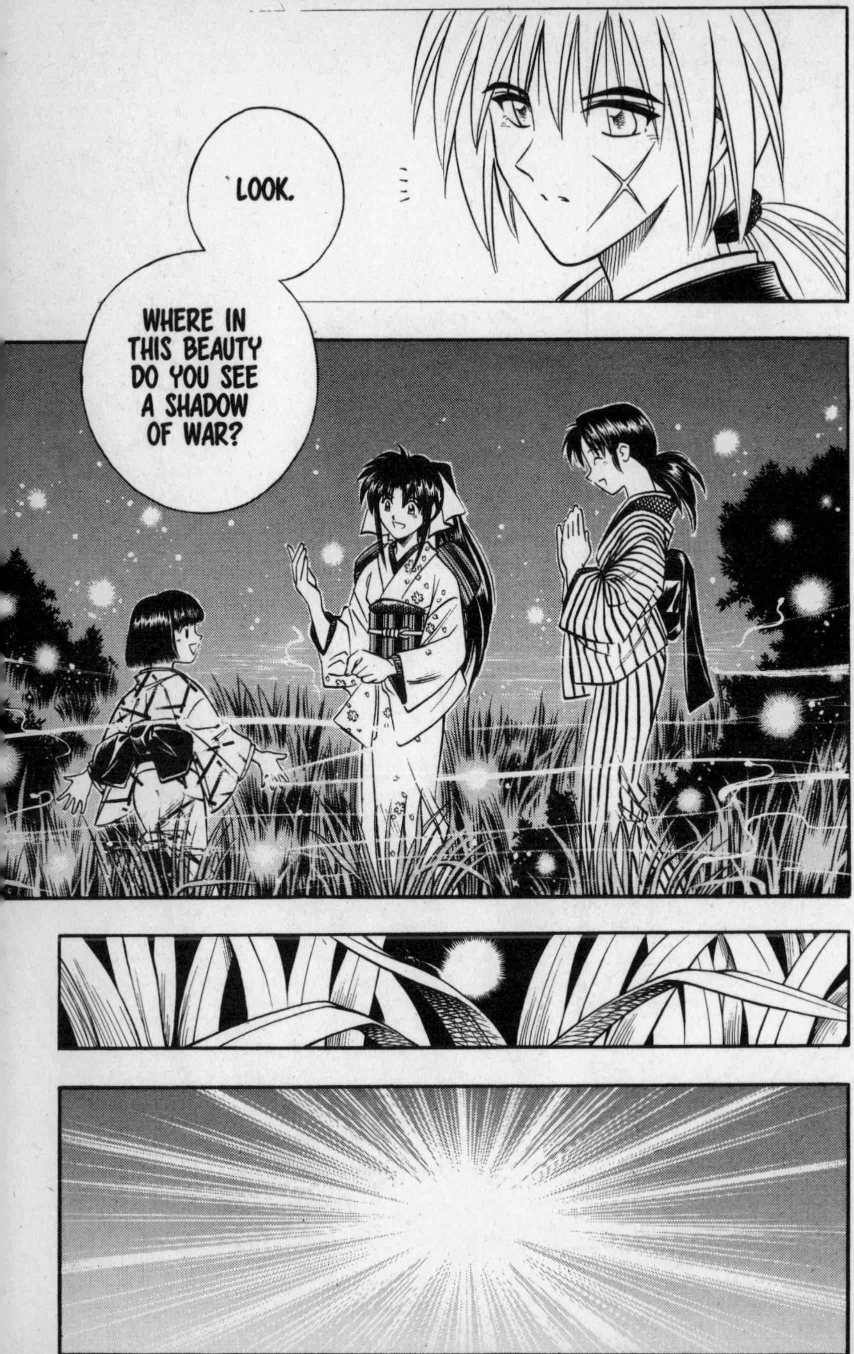

LOOK.
WHERE IN THIS BEAUTY DO YOU SEE A SHADOW OF WAR?

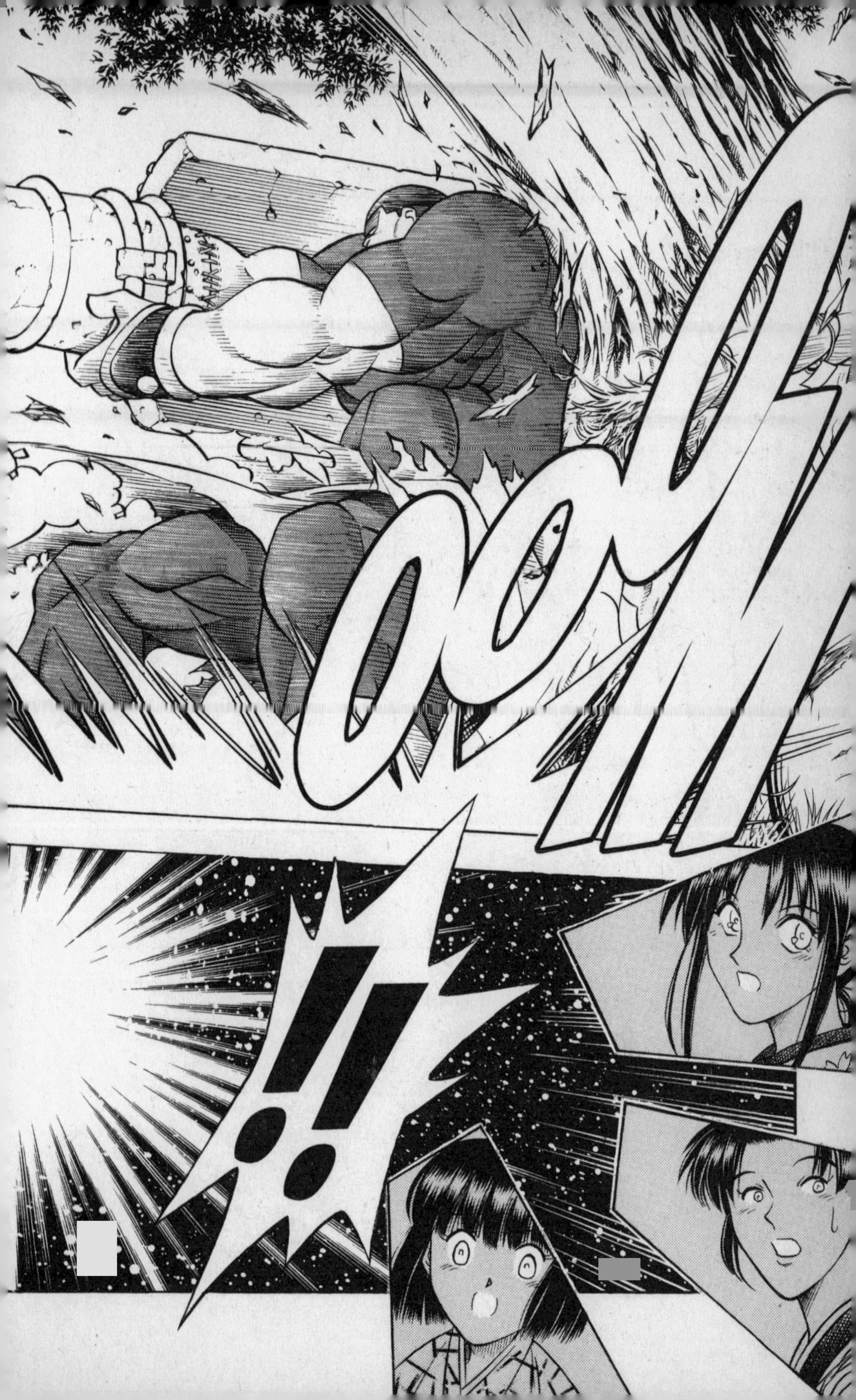
!!

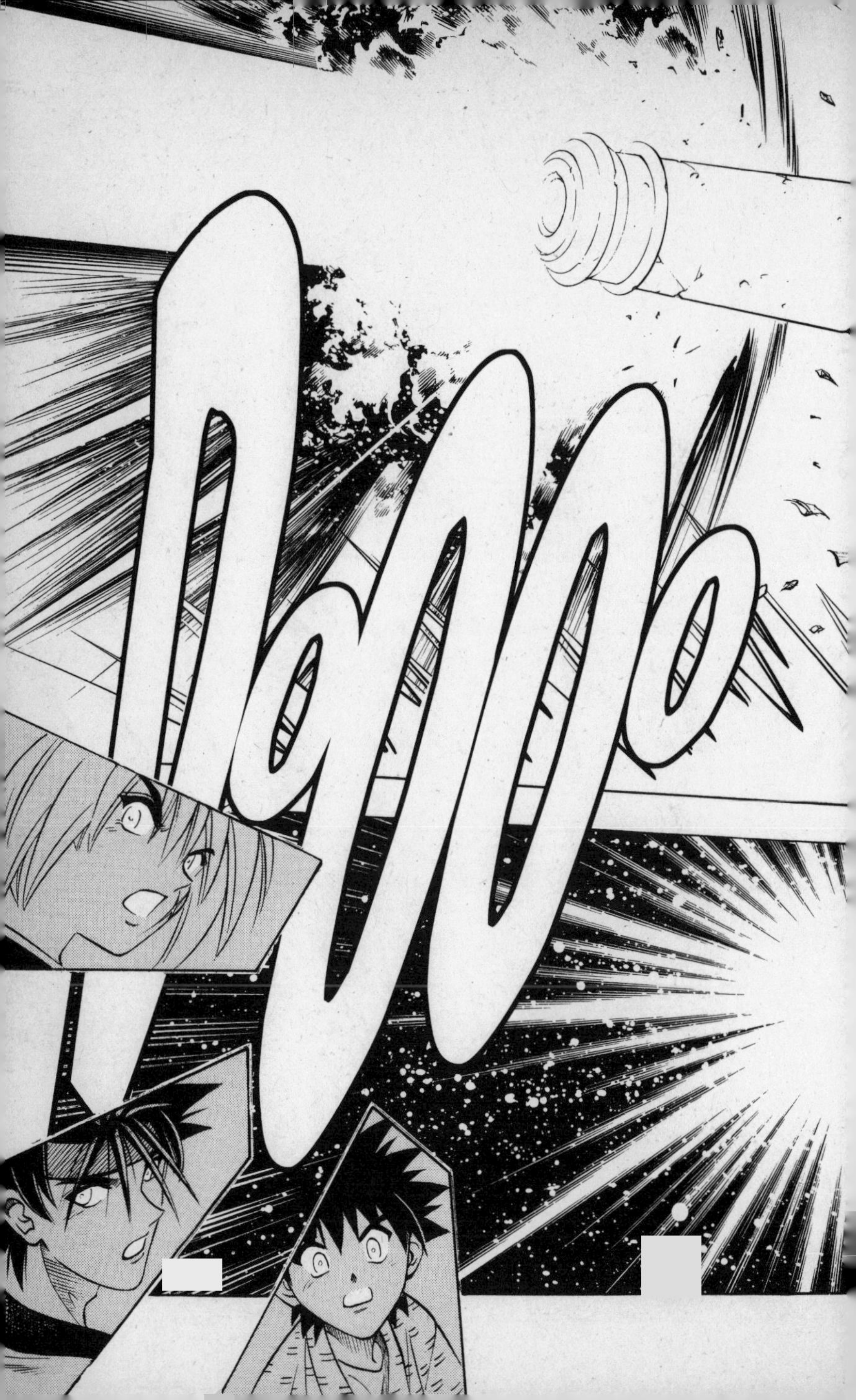

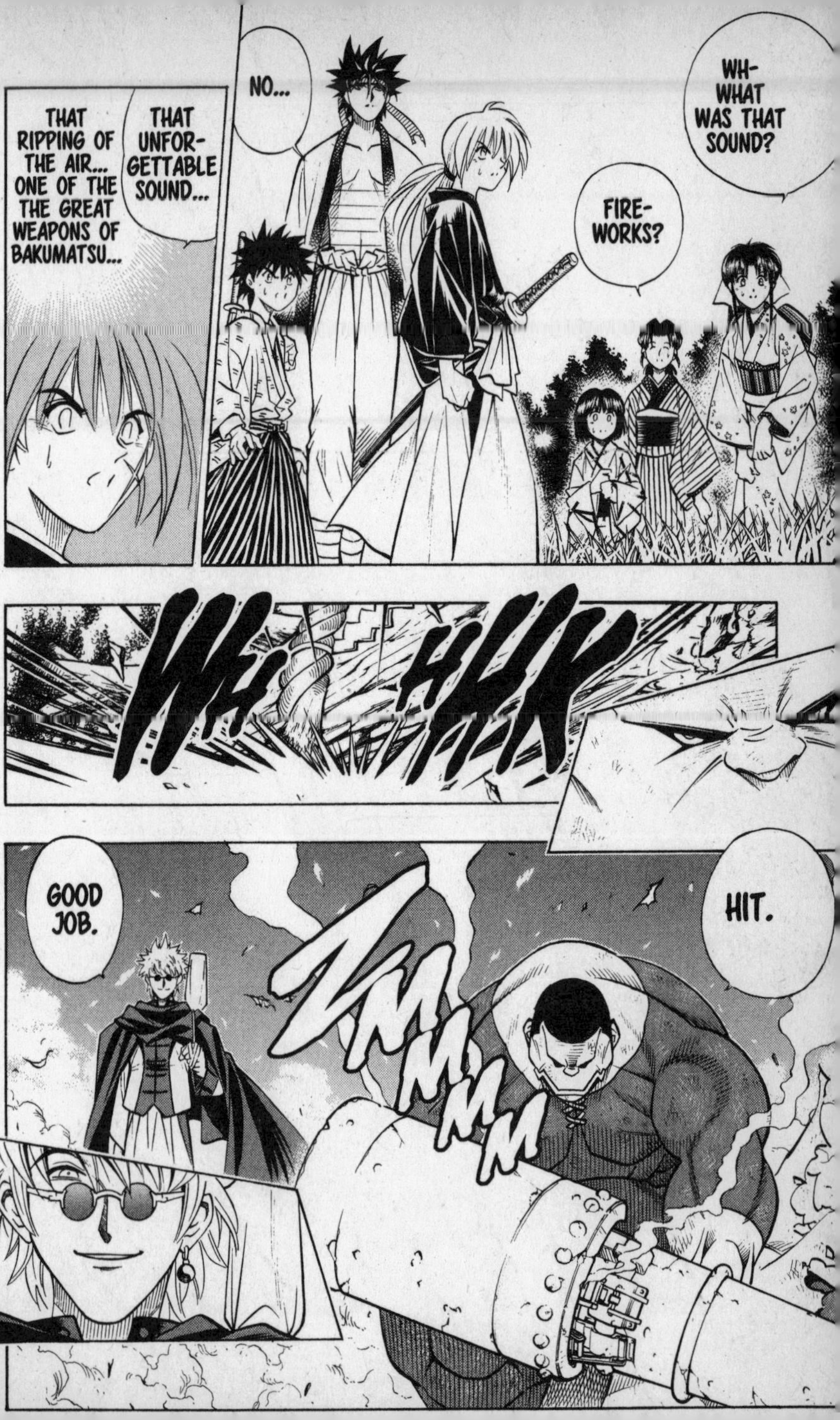
WH- WHAT WAS THAT SOUND?
FIRE-WORKS?
NO...
THAT UNFOR-GETTABLE SOUND...
THAT RIPPING OF THE AIR... ONE OF THE THE GREAT WEAPONS OF BAKUMATSU...
WHHHK
HIT.
ZMMMMM
GOOD JOB.

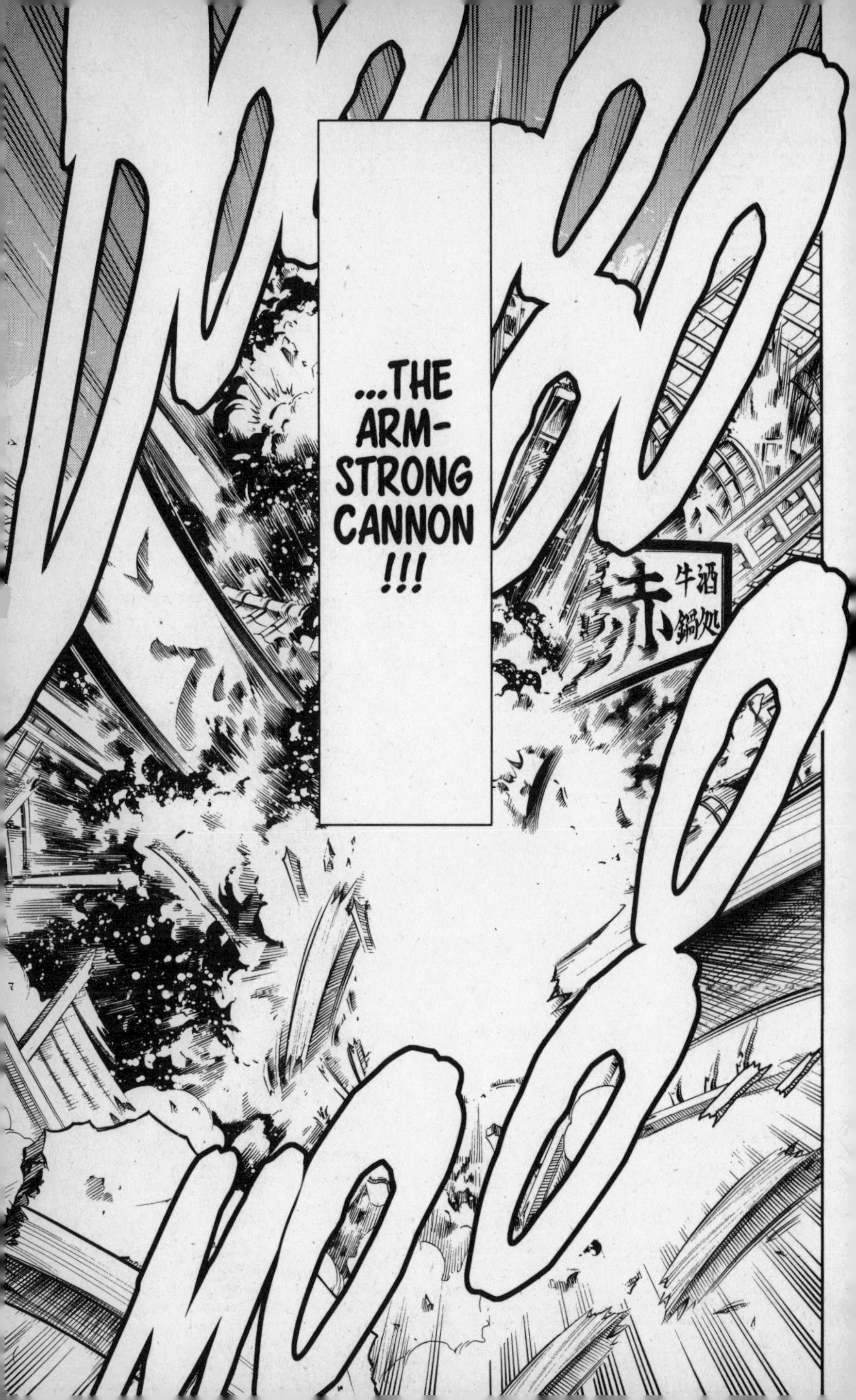
...THE ARM-STRONG CANNON !!!
酒処
牛鍋
赤

Rurouni Kenshin

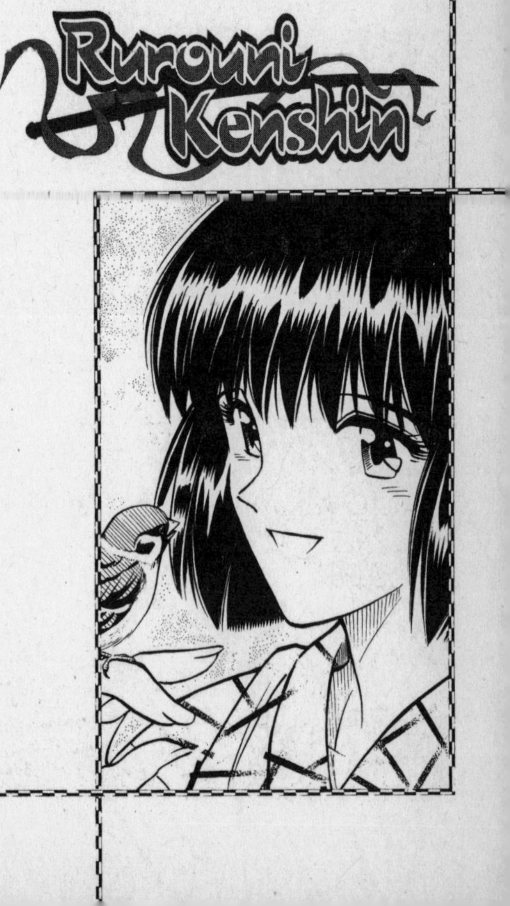

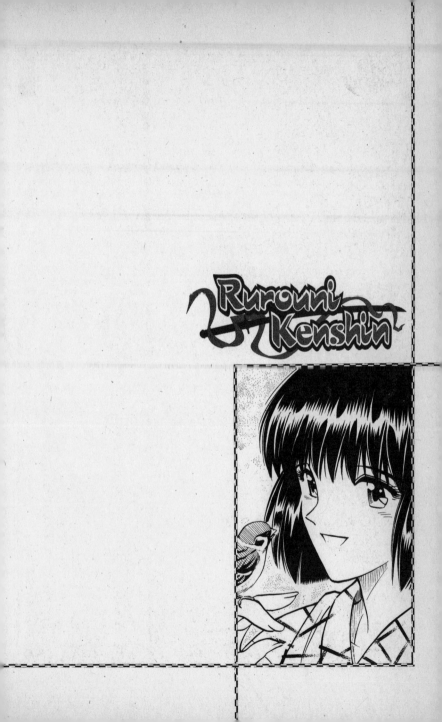

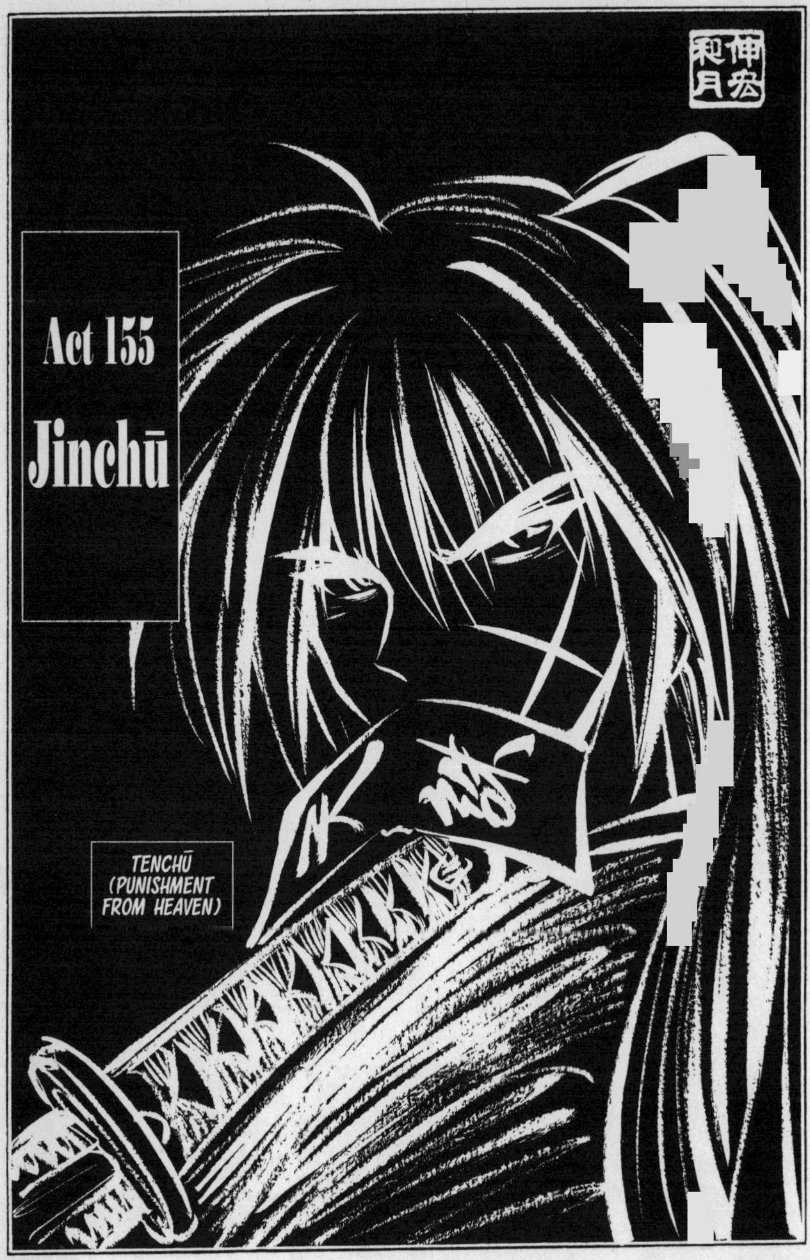
Act 155
Jinchū
TENCHŪ (PUNISHMENT FROM HEAVEN)

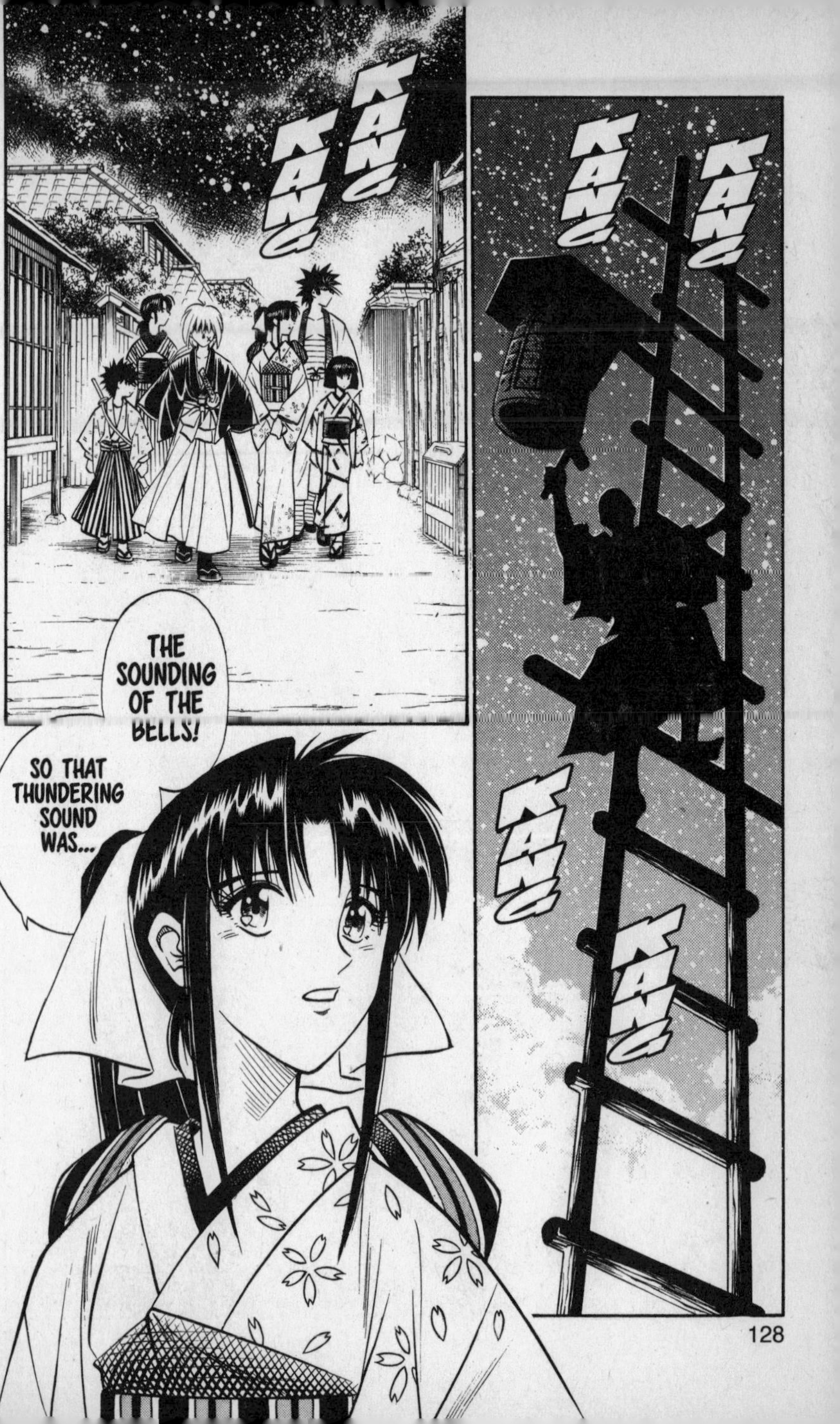
KANG
KANG
KANG
KANG
KANG
KANG
THE SOUNDING OF THE BELLS!
SO THAT THUNDERING SOUND WAS...

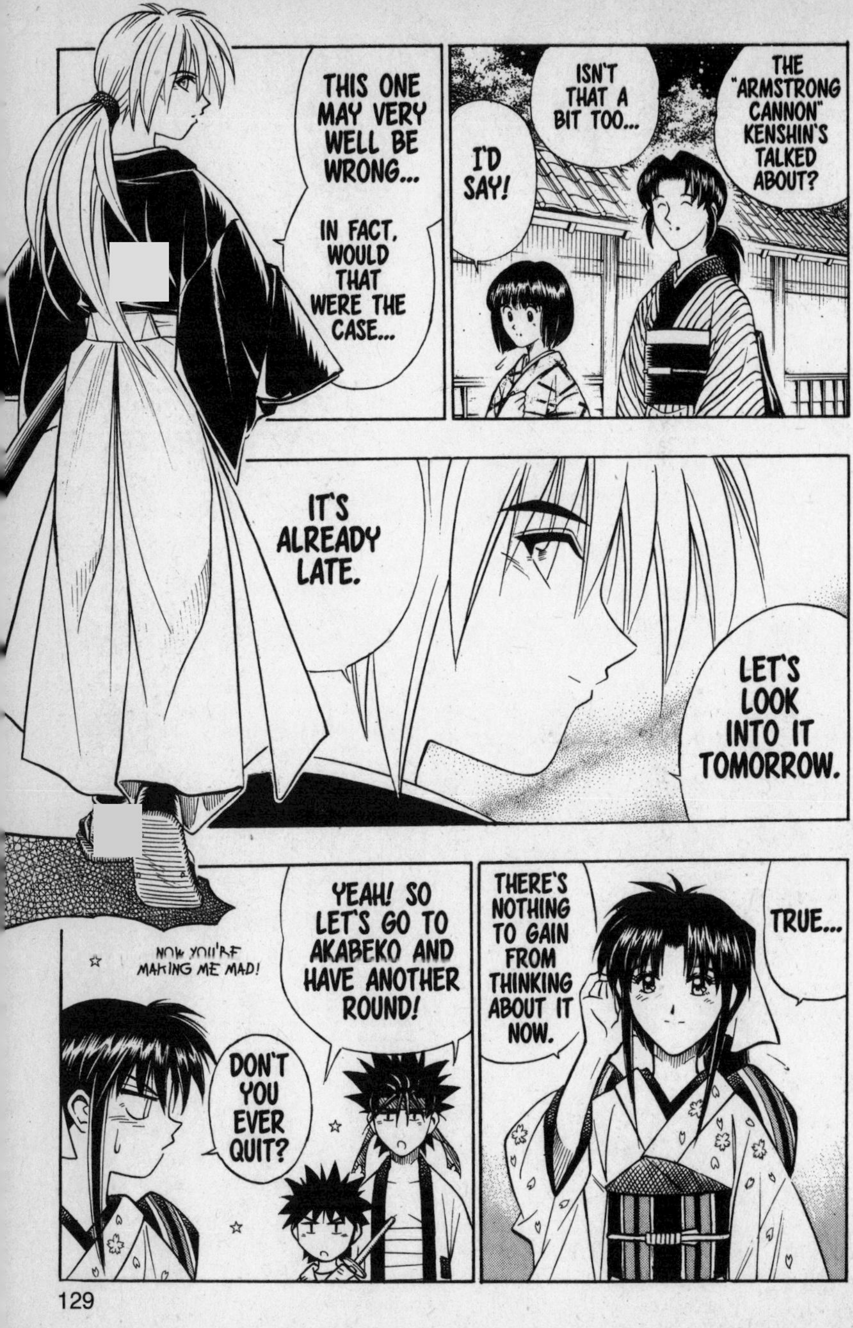
THE "ARMSTRONG CANNON" KENSHIN'S TALKED ABOUT?
ISN'T THAT A BIT TOO...
I'D SAY!
THIS ONE MAY VERY WELL BE WRONG...
IN FACT, WOULD THAT WERE THE CASE...
IT'S ALREADY LATE.
LET'S LOOK INTO IT TOMORROW.
TRUE...
THERE'S NOTHING TO GAIN FROM THINKING ABOUT IT NOW.
YEAH! SO LET'S GO TO AKABEKO AND HAVE ANOTHER ROUND!
NOW YOU'RE MAKING ME MAD!
DON'T YOU EVER QUIT?

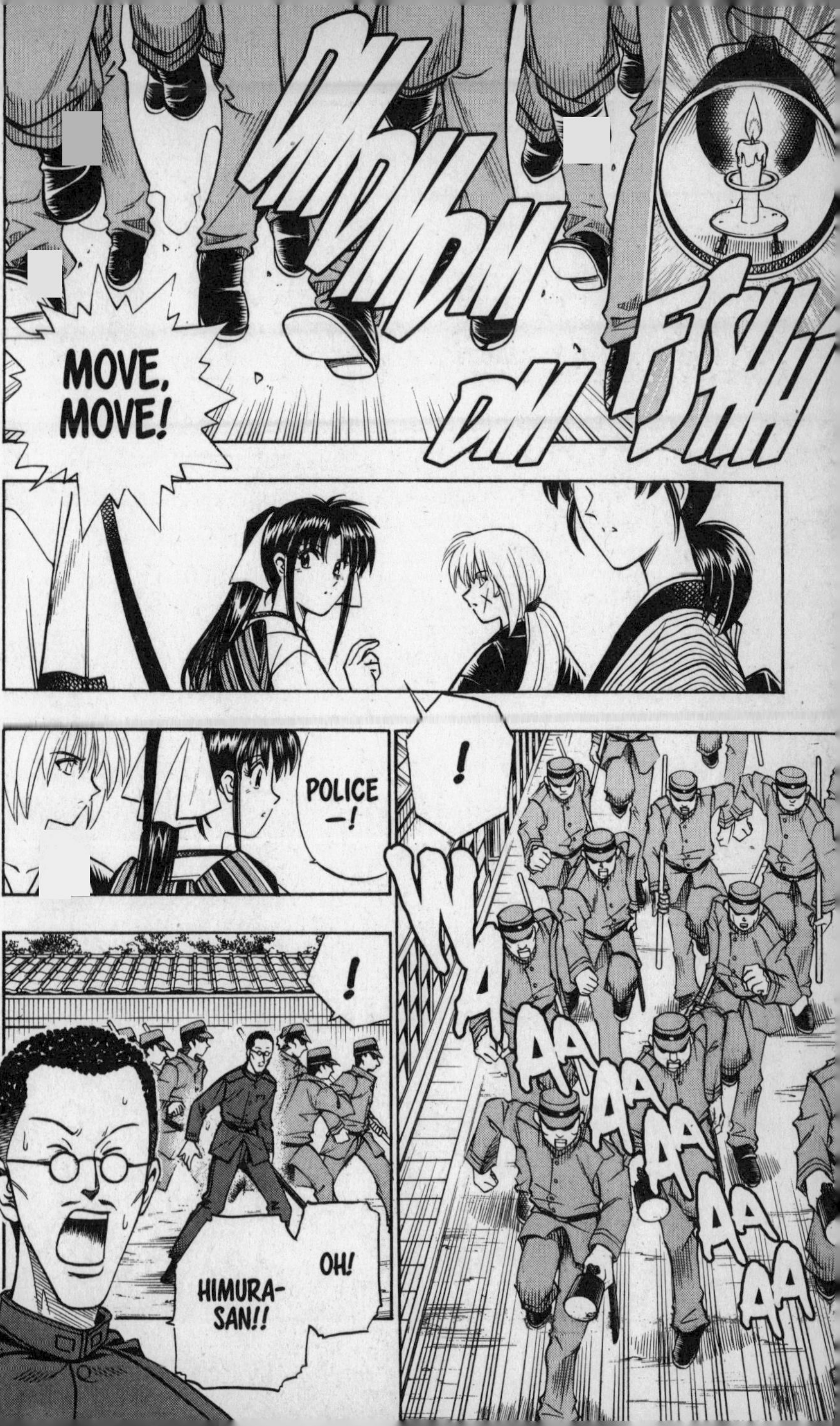
MOVE, MOVE!
!
POLICE —!
!
OH!
HIMURA-SAN!!

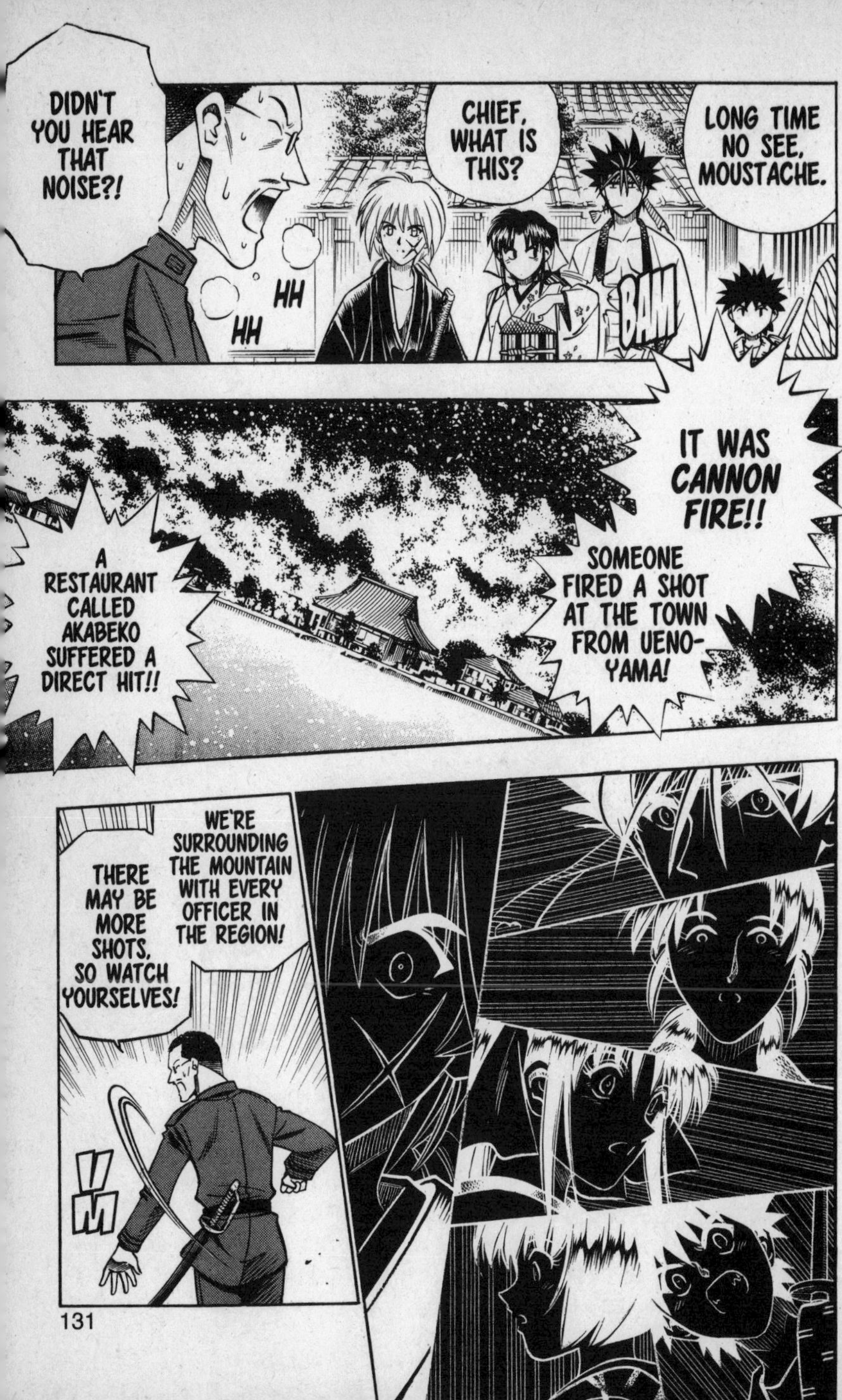
LONG TIME NO SEE, MOUSTACHE.
CHIEF, WHAT IS THIS?
DIDN'T YOU HEAR THAT NOISE?!
BAM
HH
HH
IT WAS CANNON FIRE!!
SOMEONE FIRED A SHOT AT THE TOWN FROM UENO-YAMA!
A RESTAURANT CALLED AKABEKO SUFFERED A DIRECT HIT!!
WE'RE SURROUNDING THE MOUNTAIN WITH EVERY OFFICER IN THE REGION!
THERE MAY BE MORE SHOTS, SO WATCH YOURSELVES!

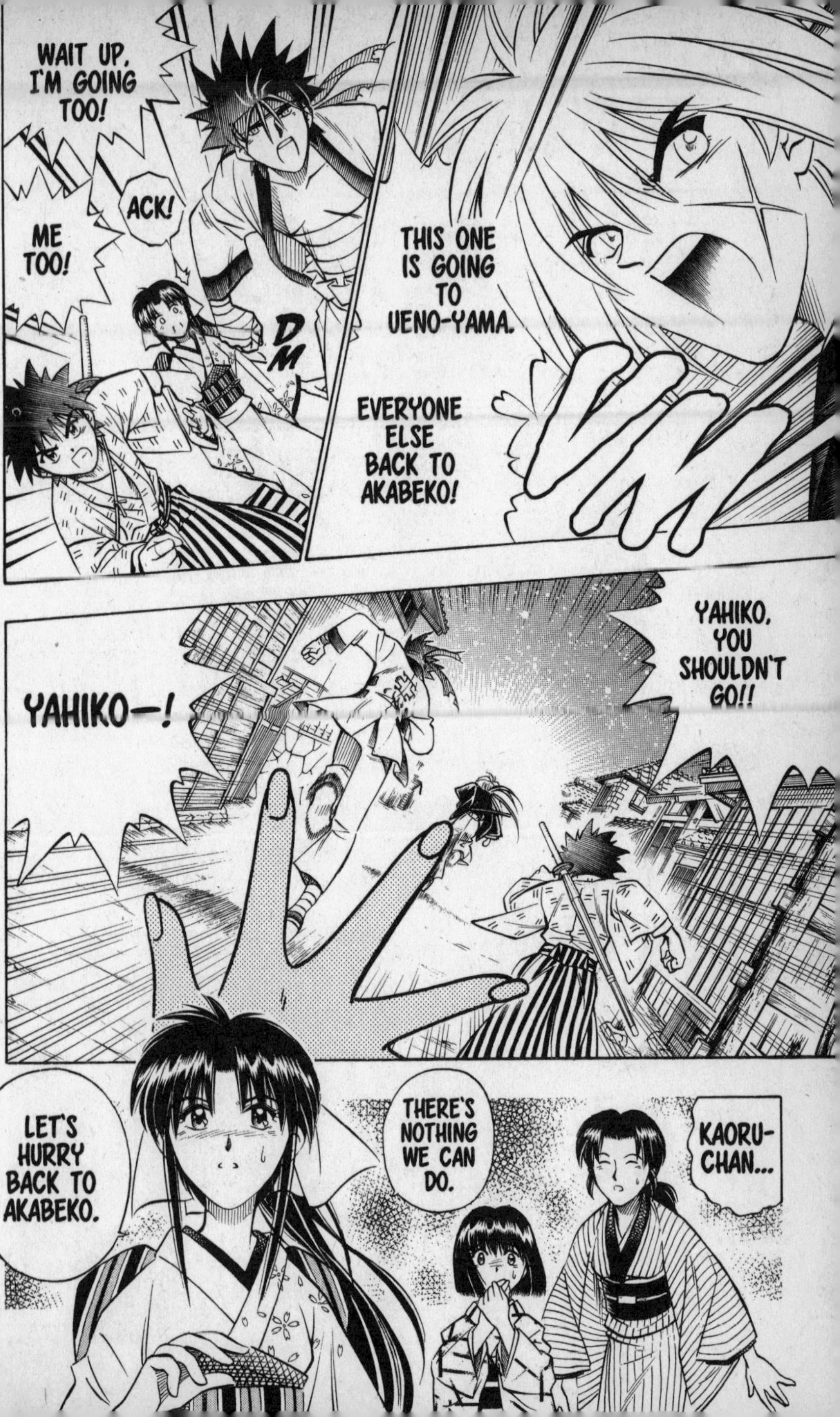
THIS ONE IS GOING TO UENO-YAMA.
EVERYONE ELSE BACK TO AKABEKO!
WAIT UP, I'M GOING TOO!
ACK!
ME TOO!
DM
YAHIKO, YOU SHOULDN'T GO!!
YAHIKO—!
KAORU-CHAN...
THERE'S NOTHING WE CAN DO.
LET'S HURRY BACK TO AKABEKO.

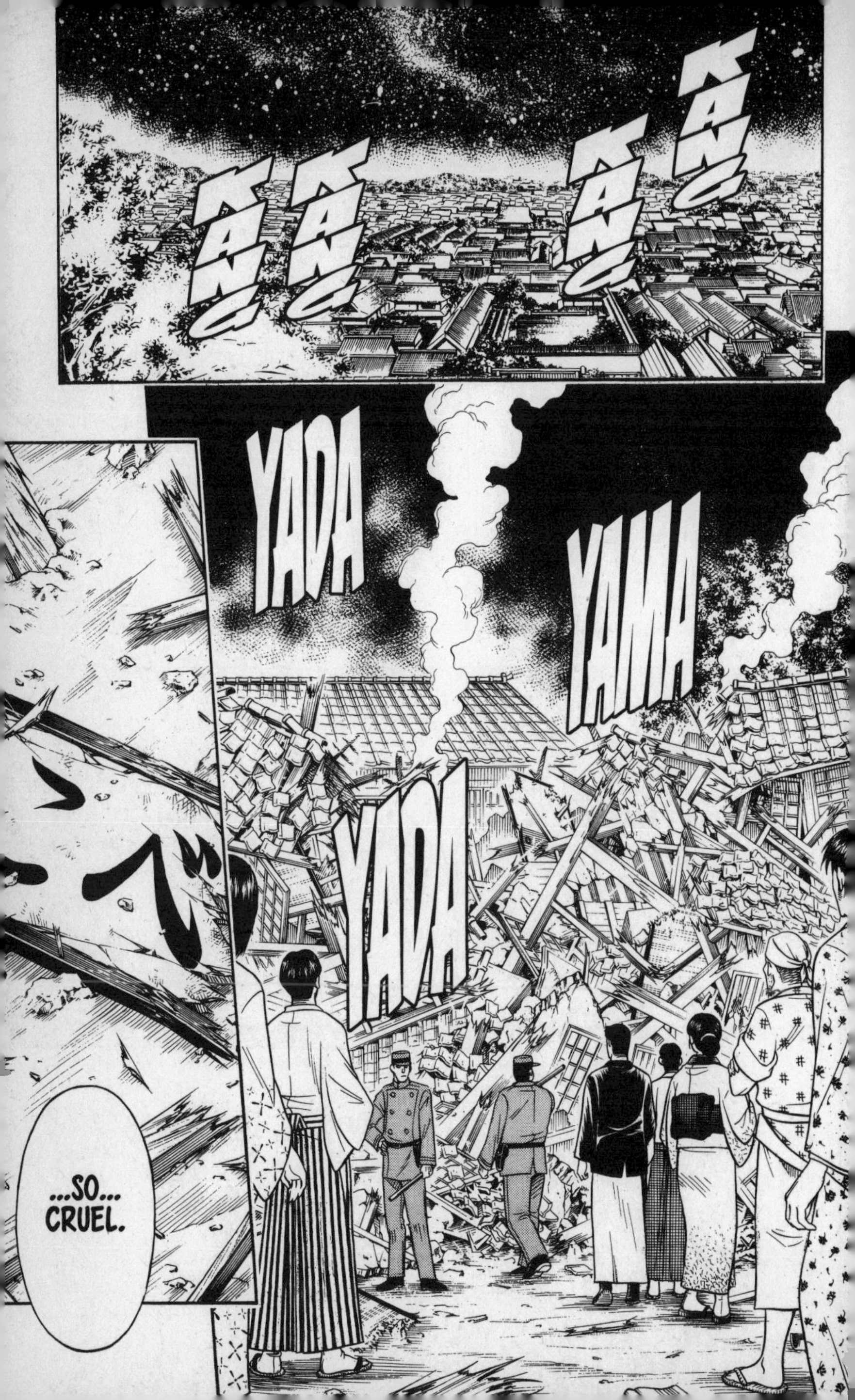
KANG
KANG
KANG
KANG
YADA
YAMA
YADA
...SO... CRUEL.

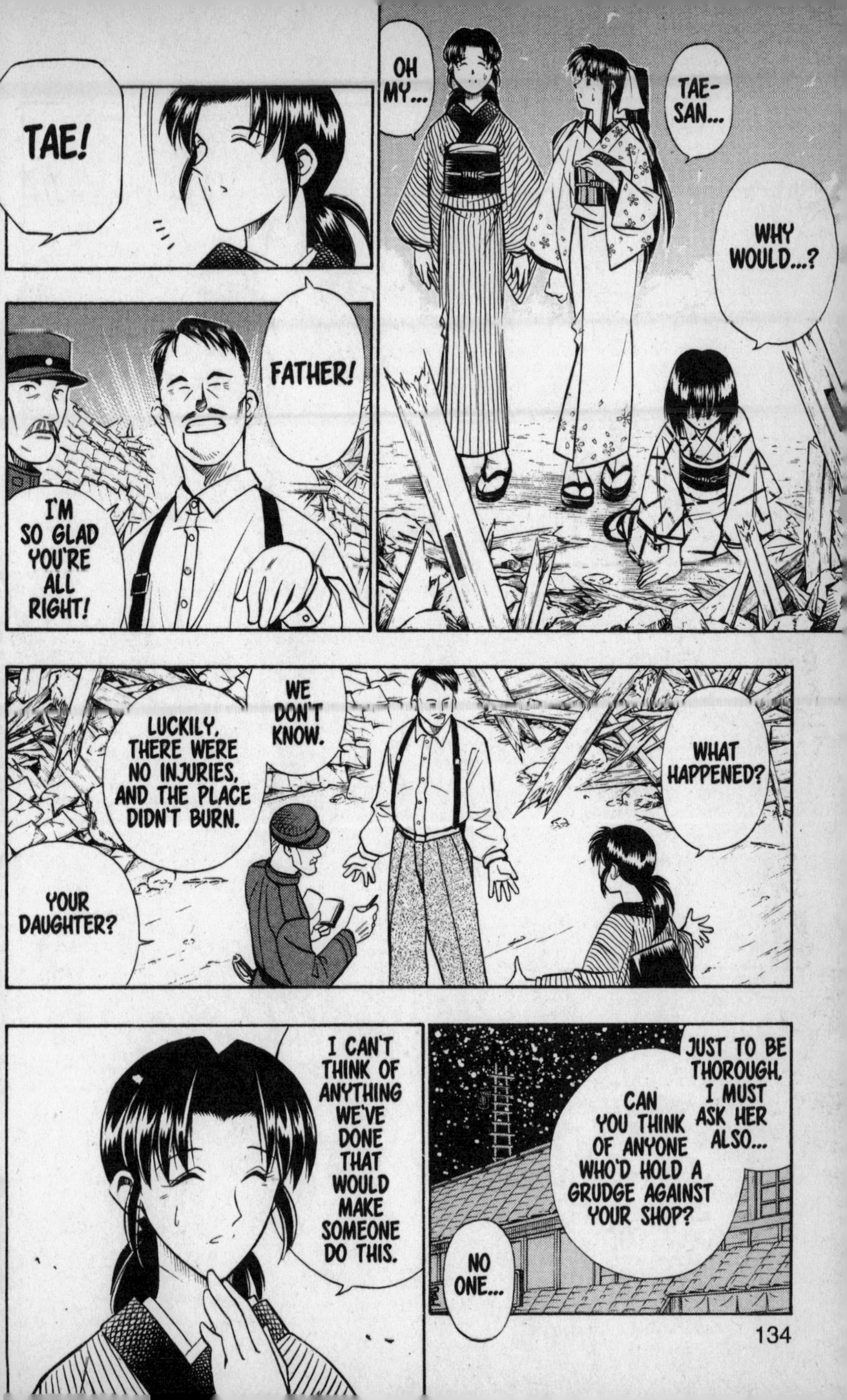
TAE-SAN...
OH MY...
WHY WOULD...?
TAE!
FATHER!
I'M SO GLAD YOU'RE ALL RIGHT!
WHAT HAPPENED?
WE DON'T KNOW.
LUCKILY, THERE WERE NO INJURIES, AND THE PLACE DIDN'T BURN.
YOUR DAUGHTER?
JUST TO BE THOROUGH, I MUST ASK HER ALSO...
CAN YOU THINK OF ANYONE WHO'D HOLD A GRUDGE AGAINST YOUR SHOP?
NO ONE...
I CAN'T THINK OF ANYTHING WE'VE DONE THAT WOULD MAKE SOMEONE DO THIS.

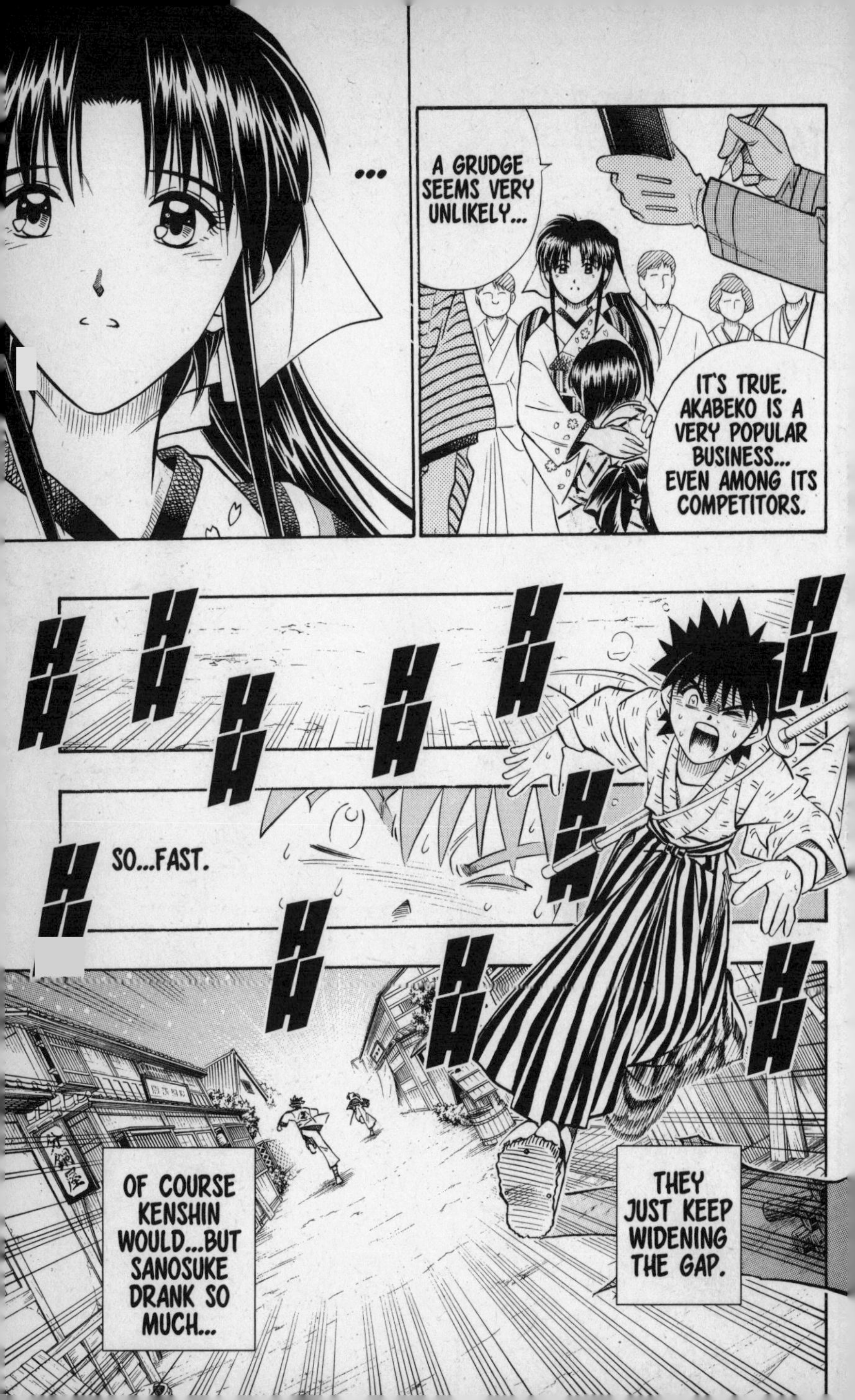
A GRUDGE SEEMS VERY UNLIKELY...
IT'S TRUE. AKABEKO IS A VERY POPULAR BUSINESS... EVEN AMONG ITS COMPETITORS.
...
SO...FAST.
THEY JUST KEEP WIDENING THE GAP.
OF COURSE KENSHIN WOULD...BUT SANOSUKE DRANK SO MUCH...

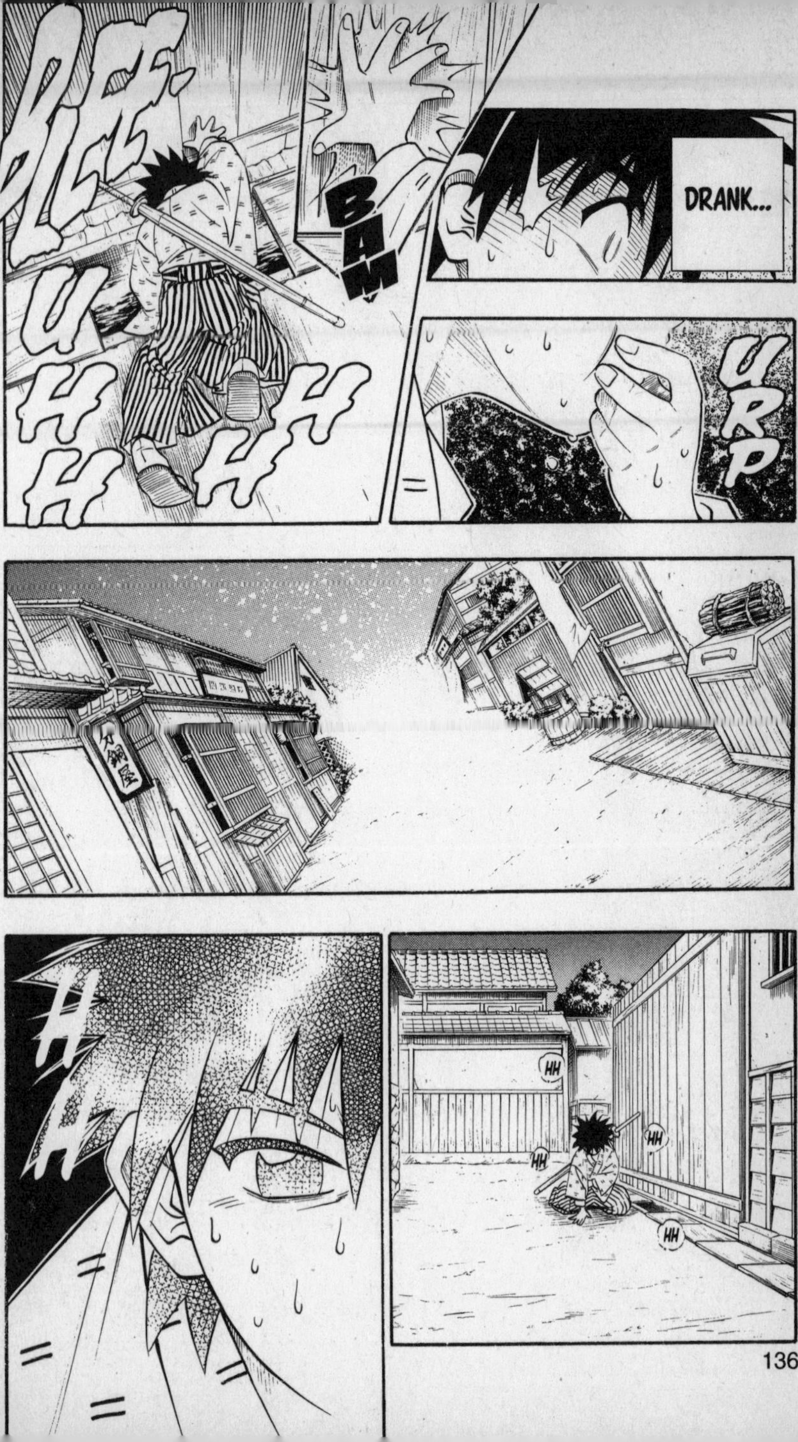
DRANK...
URP
BAM
UHHHH
HH
HH
HH
HH

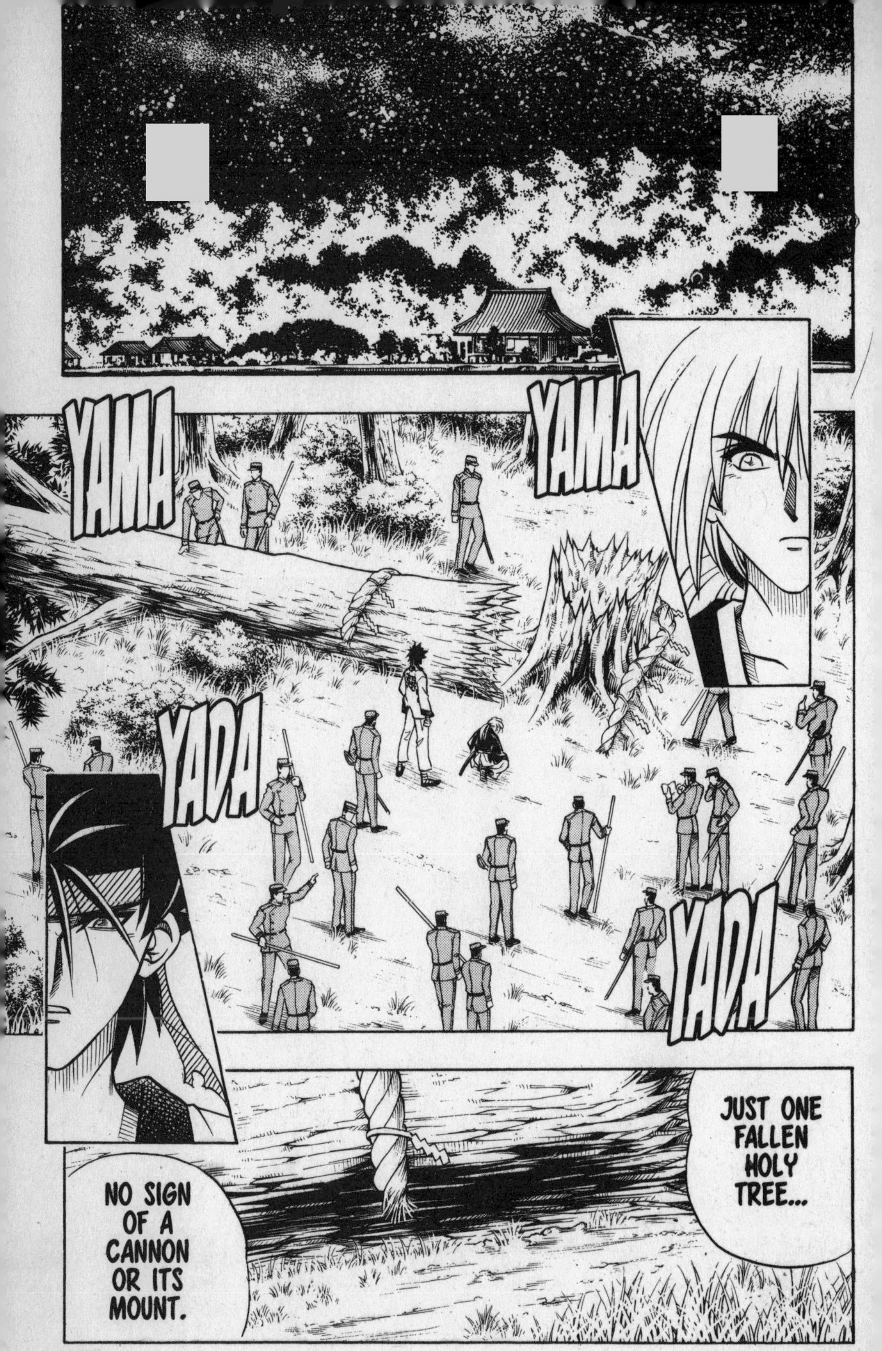
YAMA
YAMA
YADA
YADA
JUST ONE FALLEN HOLY TREE...
NO SIGN OF A CANNON OR ITS MOUNT.

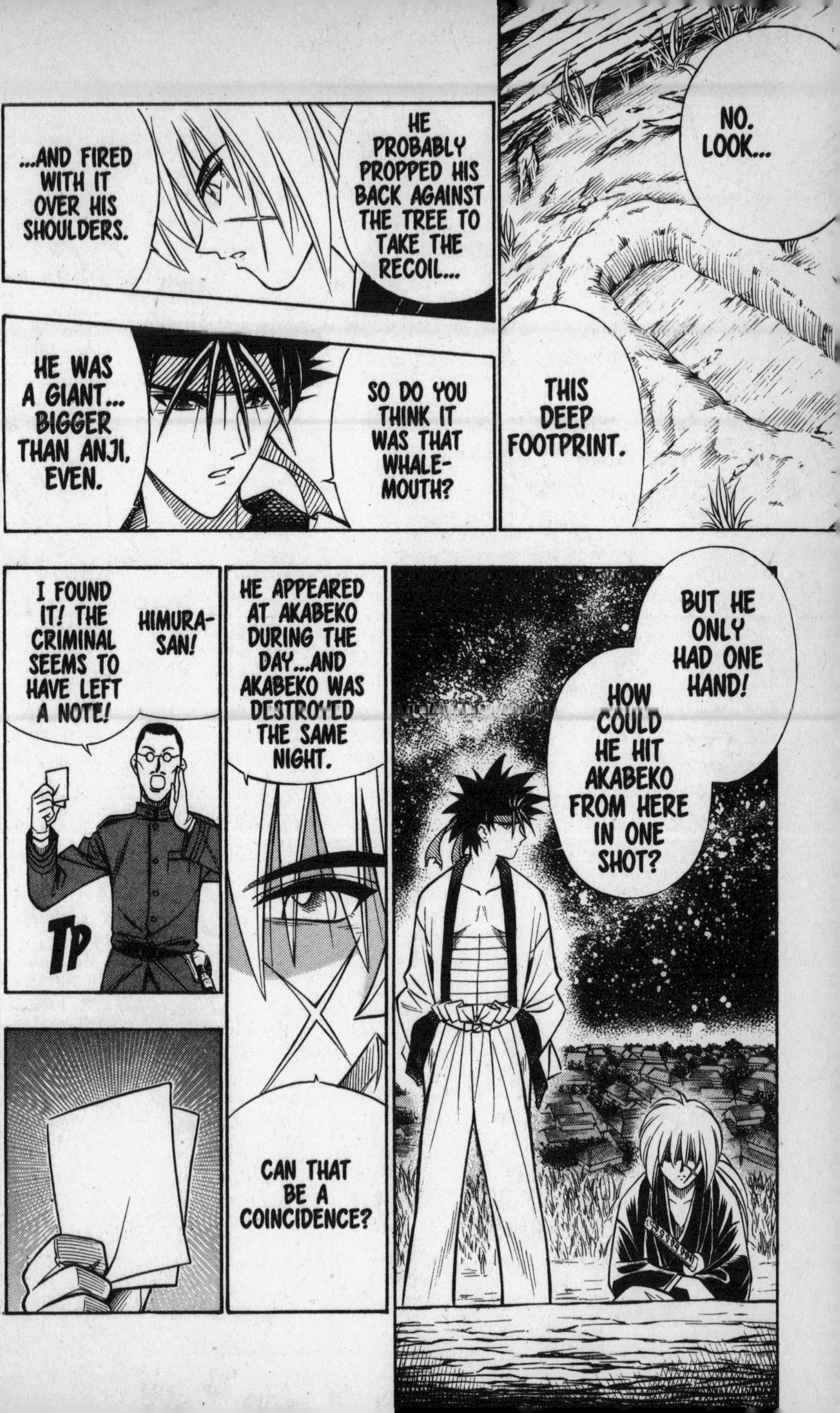
NO. LOOK...
THIS DEEP FOOTPRINT.
HE PROBABLY PROPPED HIS BACK AGAINST THE TREE TO TAKE THE RECOIL...
...AND FIRED WITH IT OVER HIS SHOULDERS.
SO DO YOU THINK IT WAS THAT WHALE-MOUTH?
HE WAS A GIANT... BIGGER THAN ANJI, EVEN.
BUT HE ONLY HAD ONE HAND!
HOW COULD HE HIT AKABEKO FROM HERE IN ONE SHOT?
HE APPEARED AT AKABEKO DURING THE DAY...AND AKABEKO WAS DESTROYED THE SAME NIGHT.
CAN THAT BE A COINCIDENCE?
HIMURA-SAN!
I FOUND IT! THE CRIMINAL SEEMS TO HAVE LEFT A NOTE!
TP

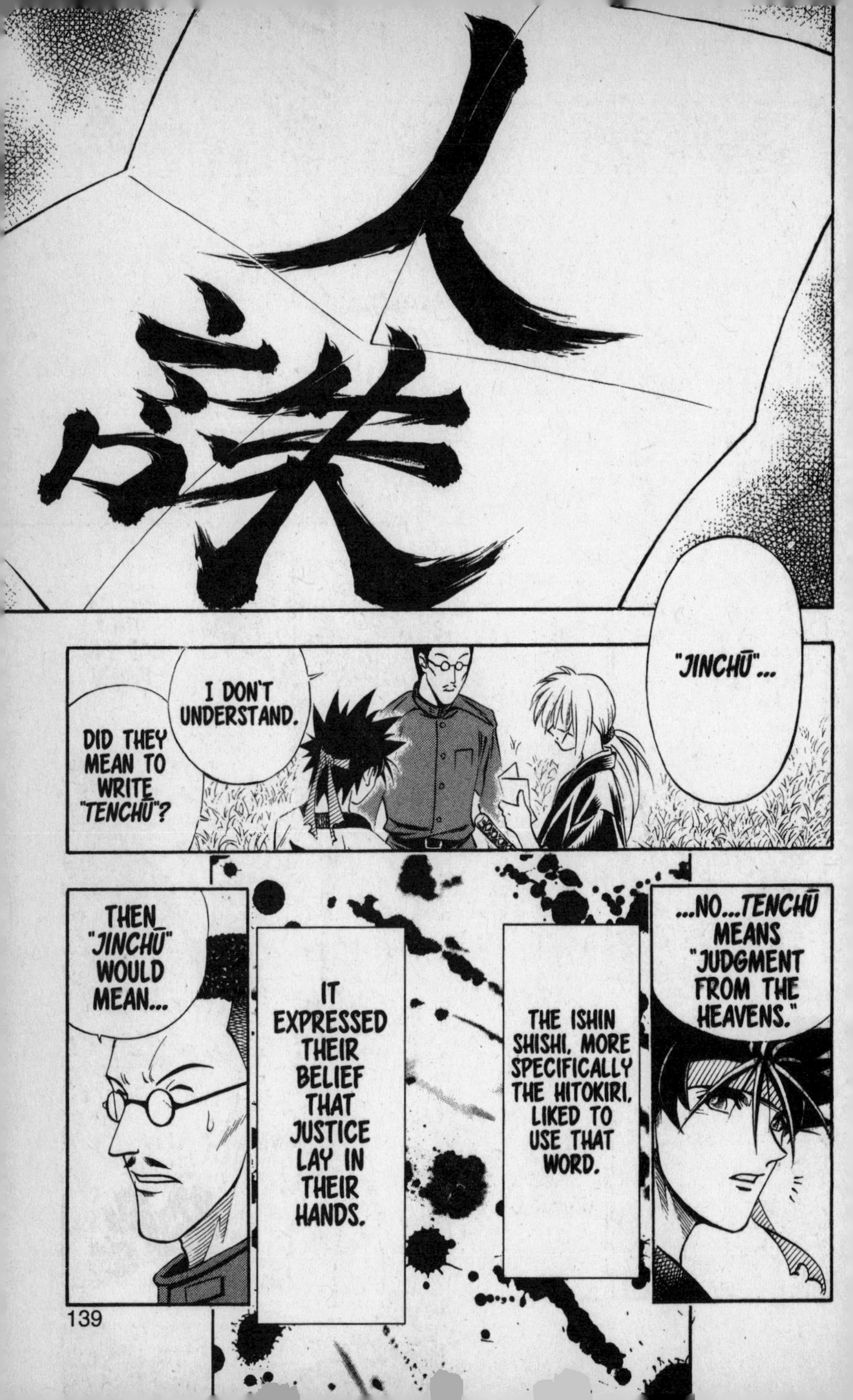
人誅
"JINCHŪ"...
I DON'T UNDERSTAND.
DID THEY MEAN TO WRITE "TENCHŪ"?
...NO...TENCHŪ MEANS "JUDGMENT FROM THE HEAVENS."
THE ISHIN SHISHI, MORE SPECIFICALLY THE HITOKIRI, LIKED TO USE THAT WORD.
IT EXPRESSED THEIR BELIEF THAT JUSTICE LAY IN THEIR HANDS.
THEN "JINCHŪ" WOULD MEAN...

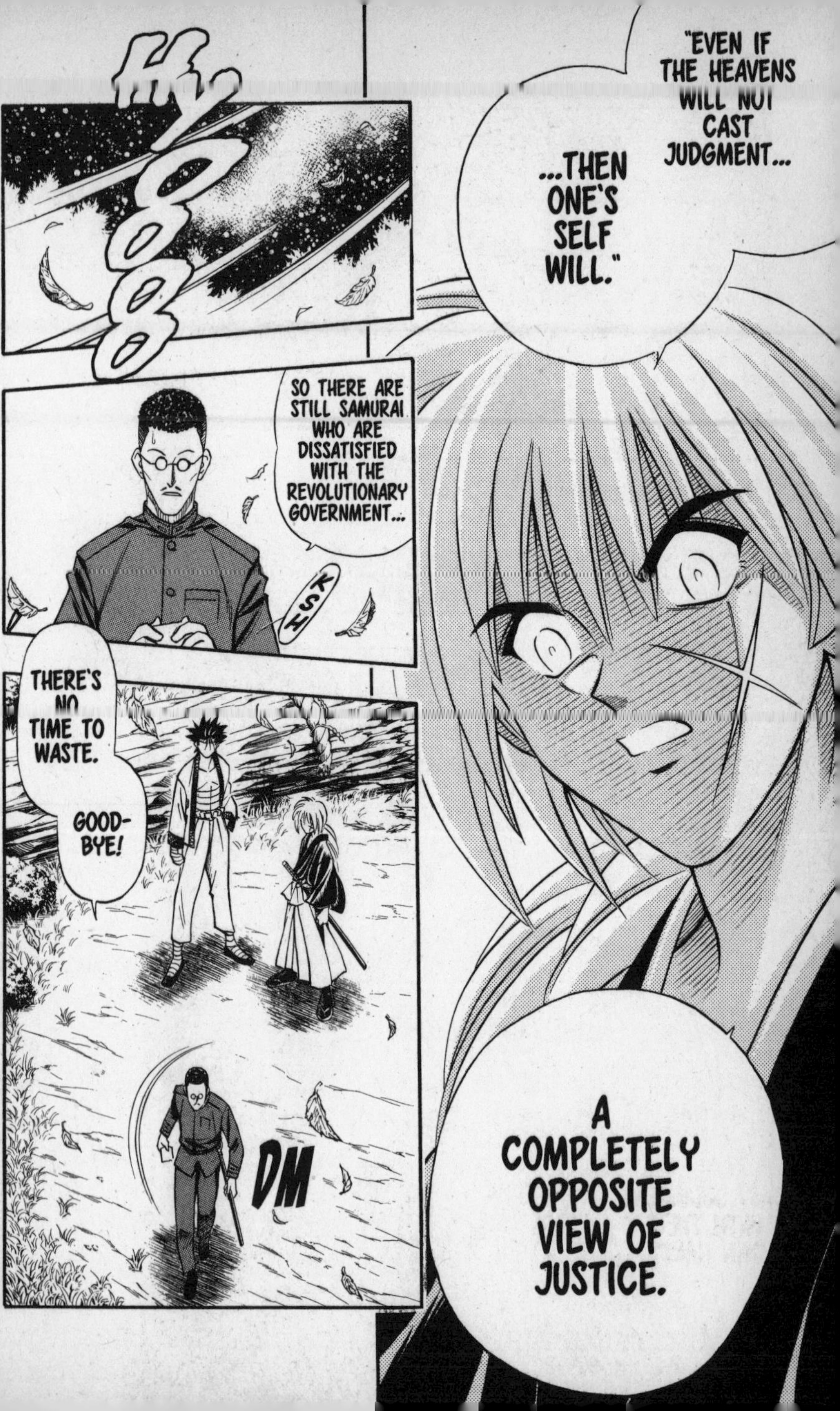
"EVEN IF THE HEAVENS WILL NOT CAST JUDGMENT...
...THEN ONE'S SELF WILL."
A COMPLETELY OPPOSITE VIEW OF JUSTICE.
HYOOOOO
SO THERE ARE STILL SAMURAI WHO ARE DISSATISFIED WITH THE REVOLUTIONARY GOVERNMENT...
KSH
THERE'S NO TIME TO WASTE.
GOOD-BYE!
DM

READ THIS WAY

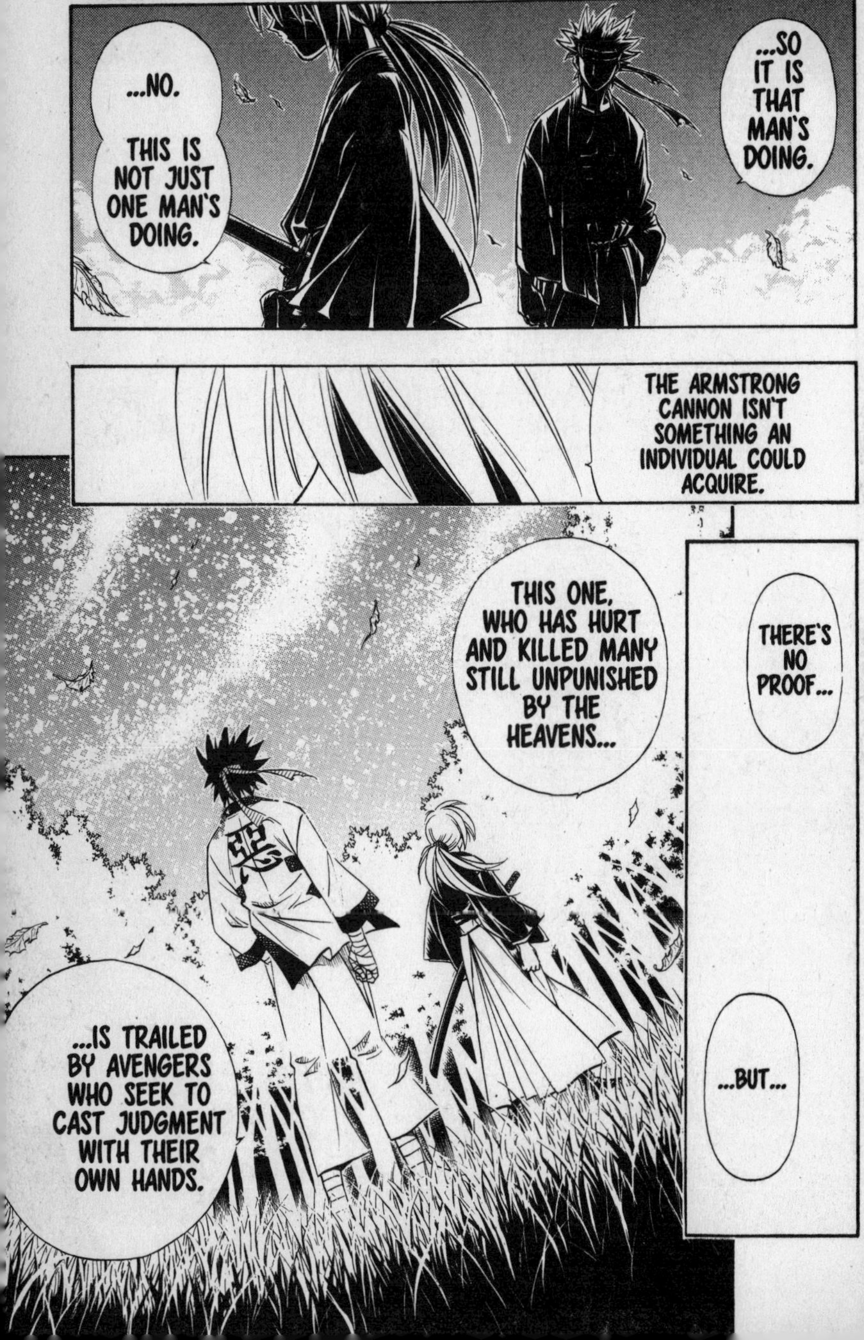
...SO IT IS THAT MAN'S DOING.
...NO.
THIS IS NOT JUST ONE MAN'S DOING.
THE ARMSTRONG CANNON ISN'T SOMETHING AN INDIVIDUAL COULD ACQUIRE.
THERE'S NO PROOF...
...BUT...
THIS ONE, WHO HAS HURT AND KILLED MANY STILL UNPUNISHED BY THE HEAVENS...
...IS TRAILED BY AVENGERS WHO SEEK TO CAST JUDGMENT WITH THEIR OWN HANDS.

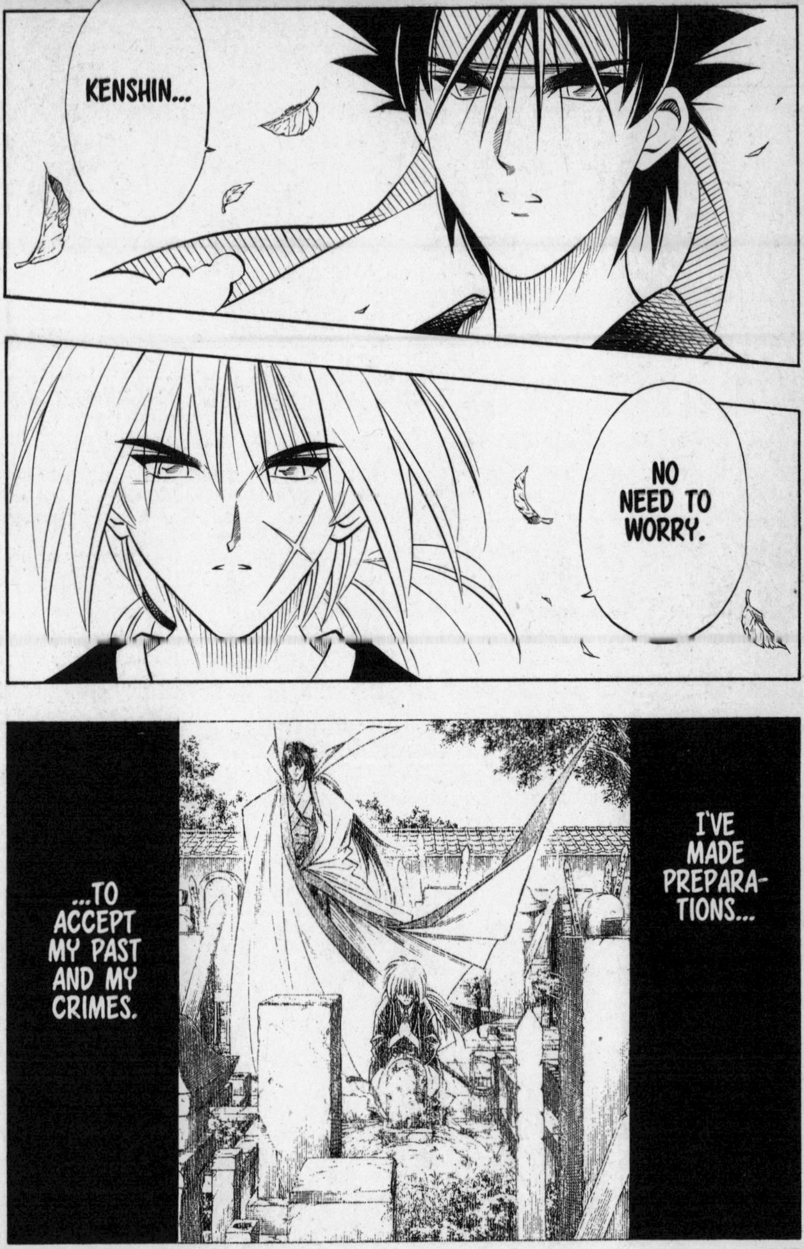
KENSHIN...
NO NEED TO WORRY.
I'VE MADE PREPARATIONS...
...TO ACCEPT MY PAST AND MY CRIMES.

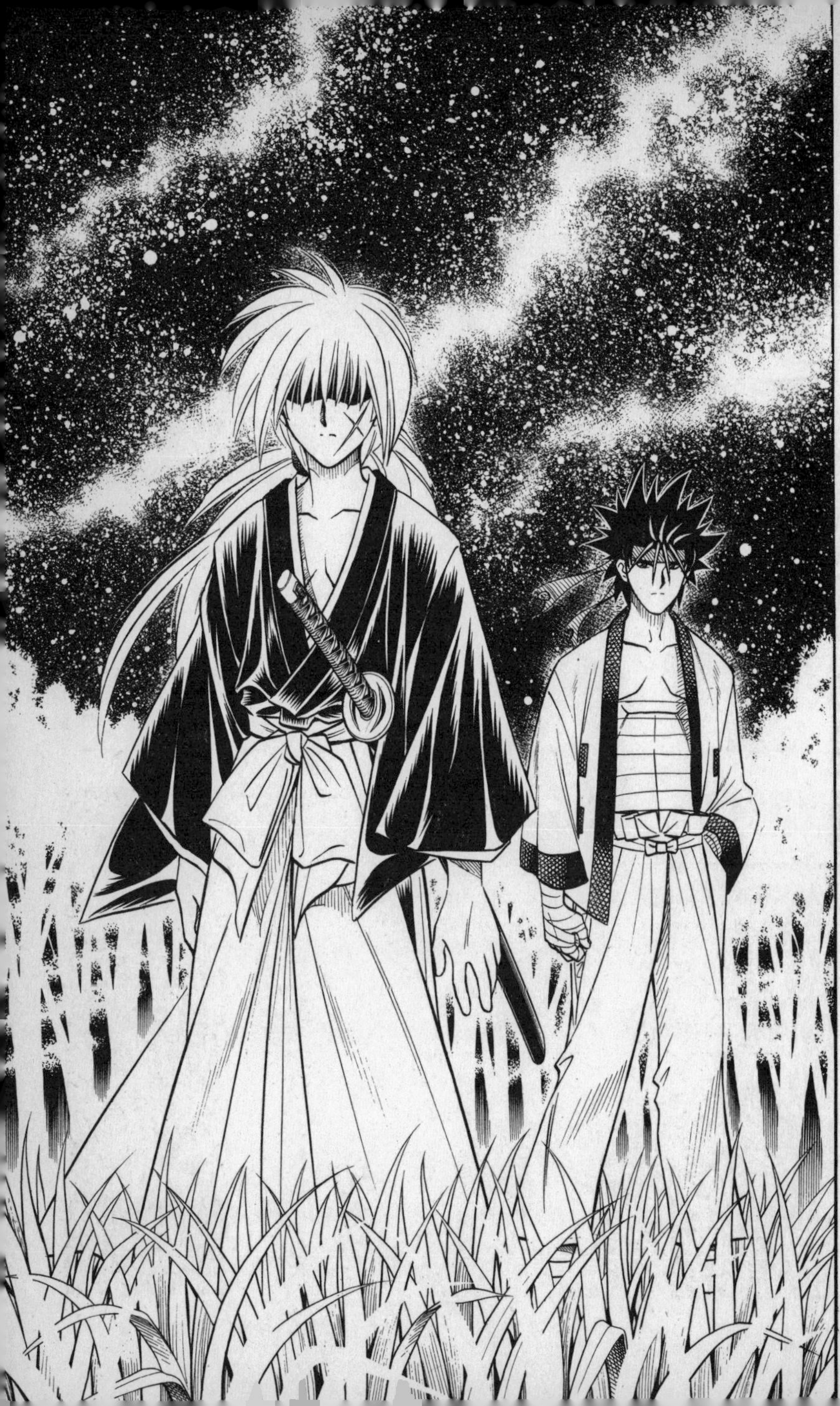

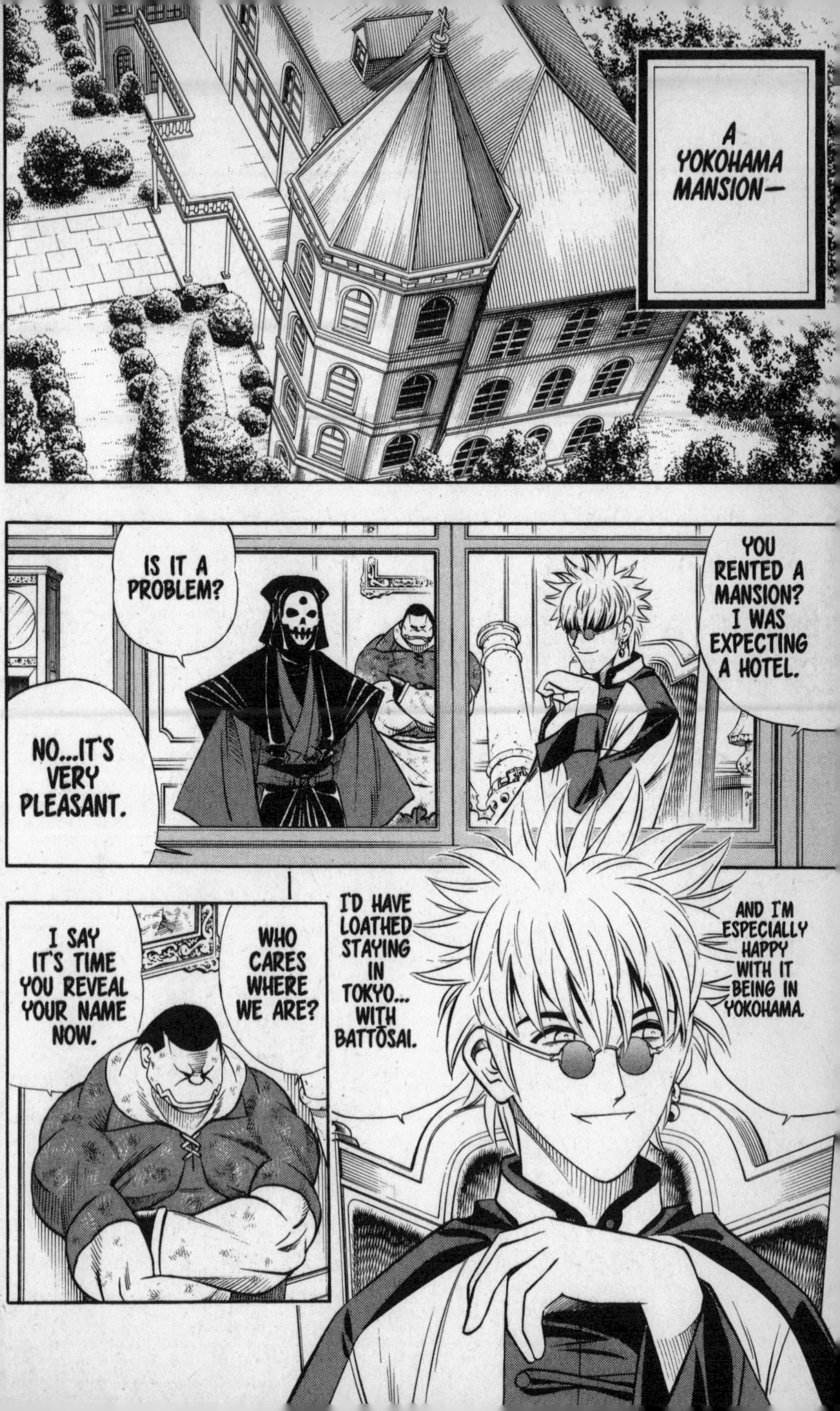
A YOKOHAMA MANSION—
YOU RENTED A MANSION? I WAS EXPECTING A HOTEL.
IS IT A PROBLEM?
NO...IT'S VERY PLEASANT.
AND I'M ESPECIALLY HAPPY WITH IT BEING IN YOKOHAMA.
I'D HAVE LOATHED STAYING IN TOKYO... WITH BATTŌSAI.
WHO CARES WHERE WE ARE?
I SAY IT'S TIME YOU REVEAL YOUR NAME NOW.

READ THIS WAY

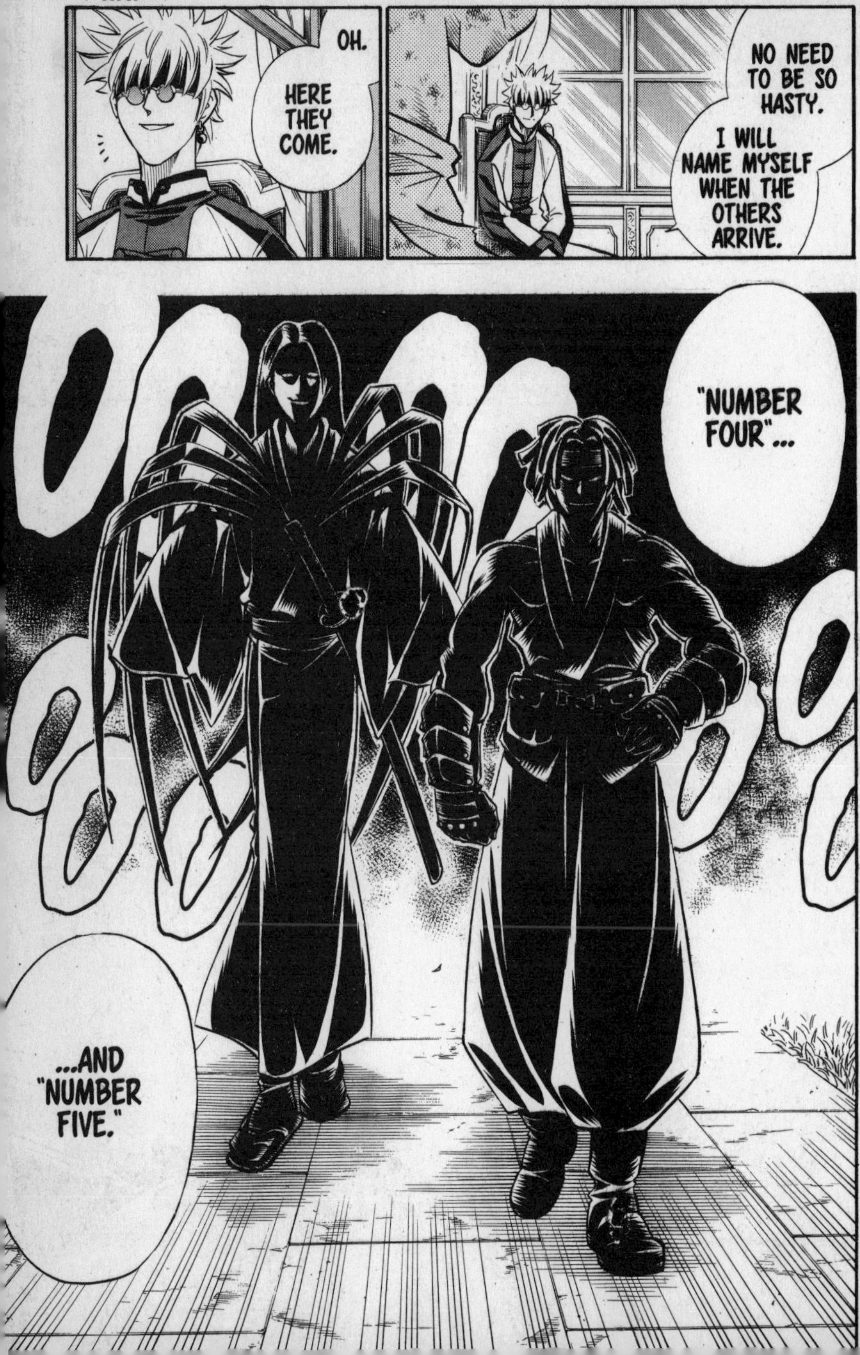
NO NEED TO BE SO HASTY.
I WILL NAME MYSELF WHEN THE OTHERS ARRIVE.
OH.
HERE THEY COME.
"NUMBER FOUR"...
...AND "NUMBER FIVE."

Rurouni Kenshin

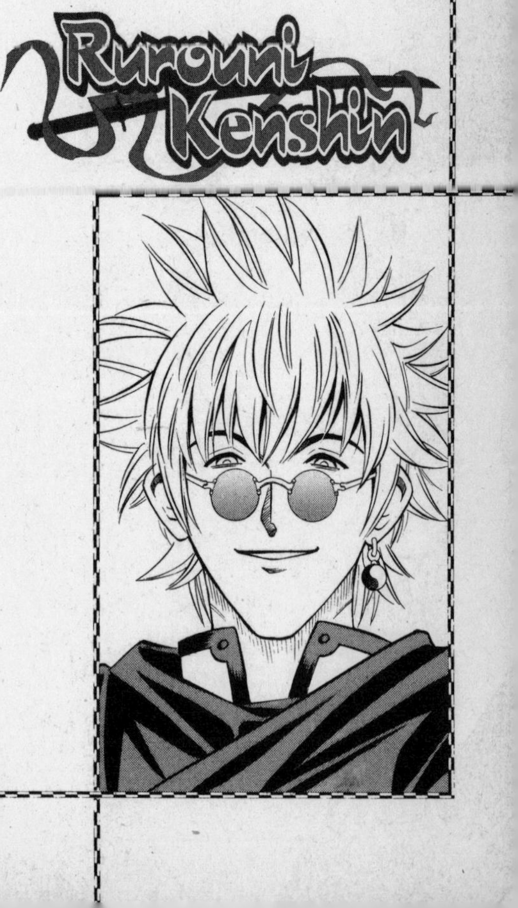

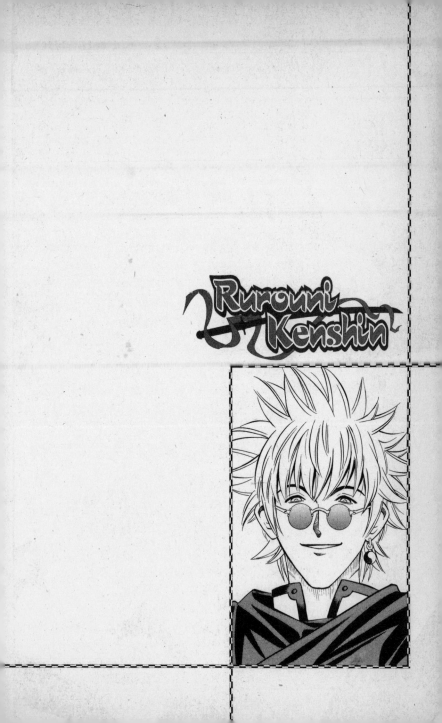

Act 156—Comrades

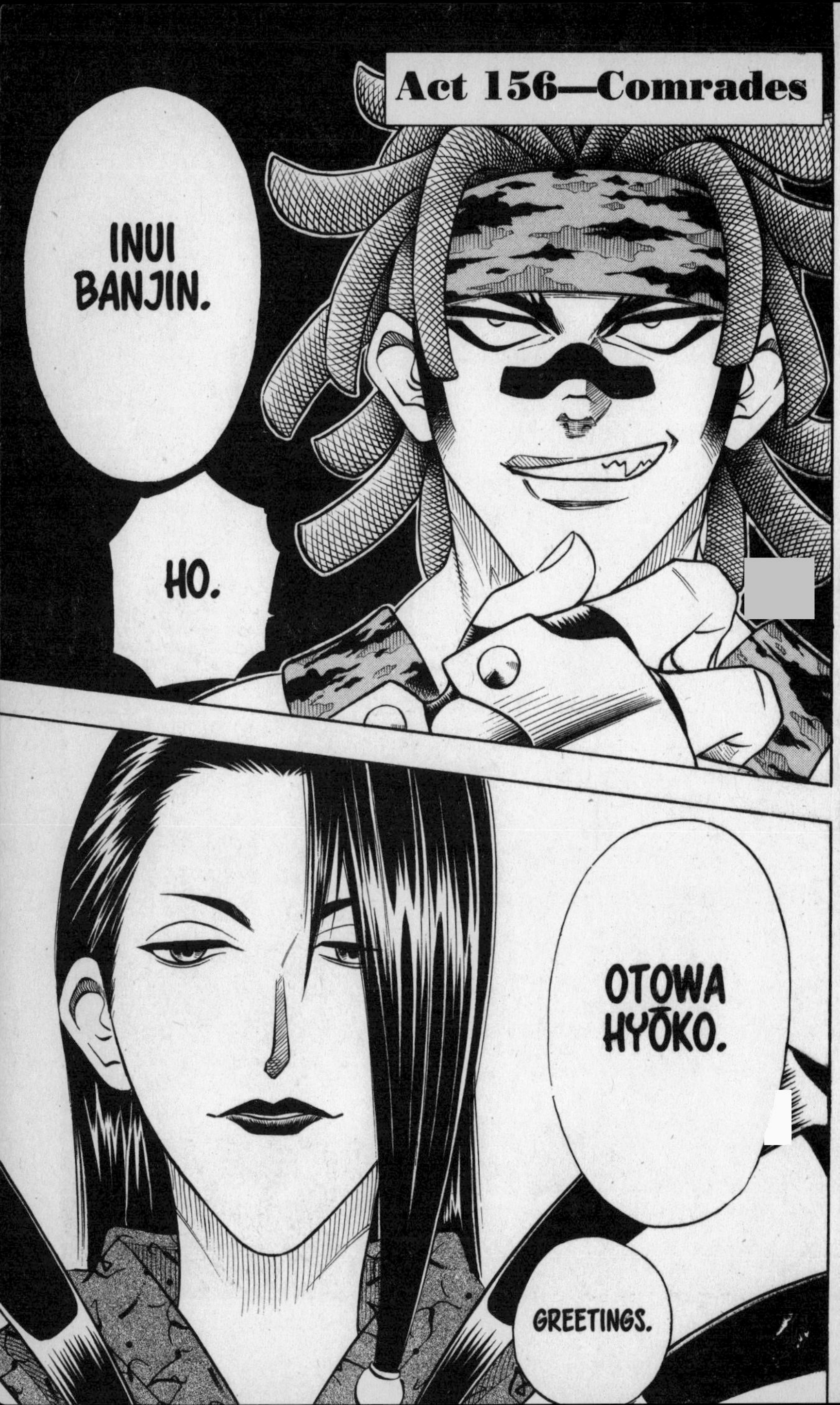
INUI BANJIN.
HO.
OTOWA HYŌKO.
GREETINGS.

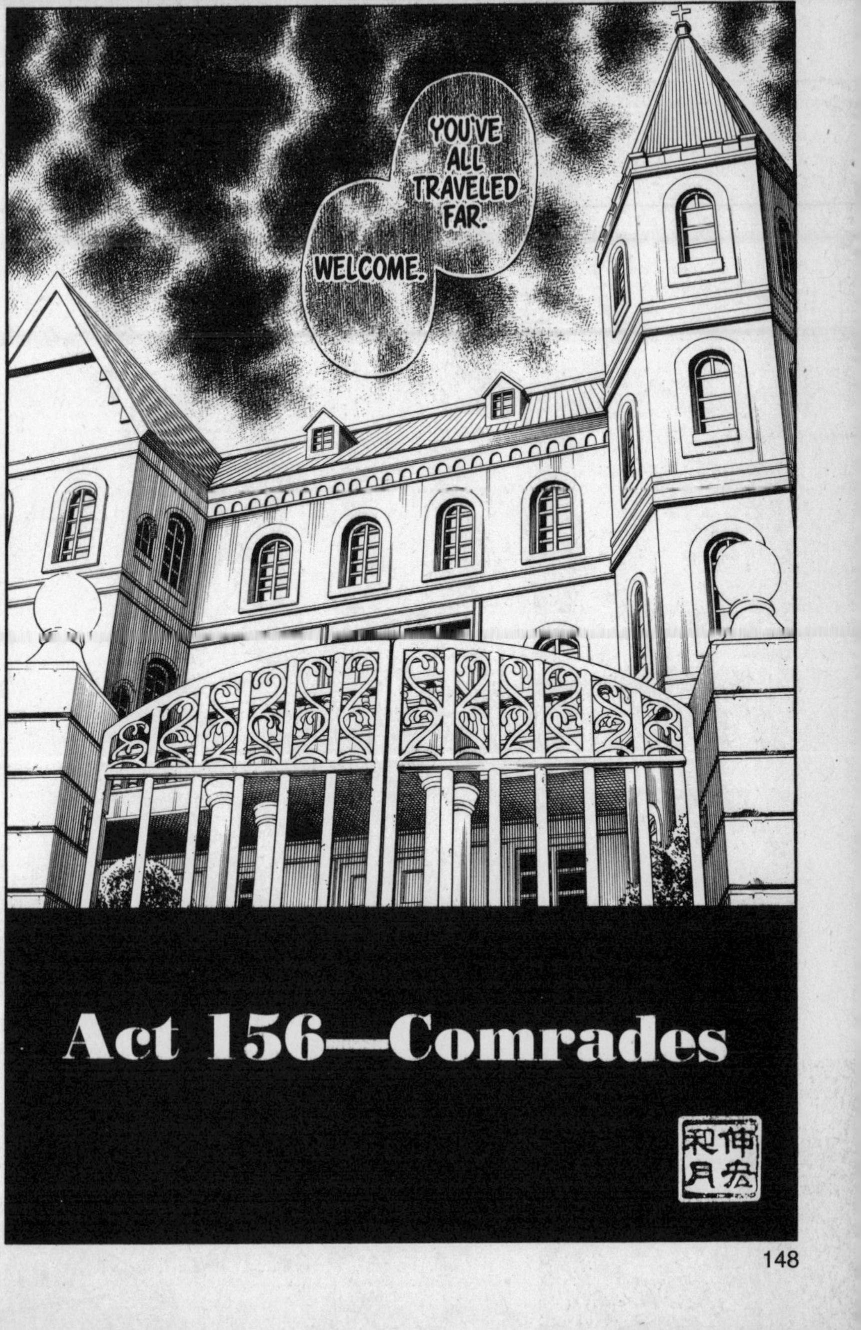
YOU'VE ALL TRAVELED FAR.
WELCOME.

Act 156—Comrades

伸宏和月

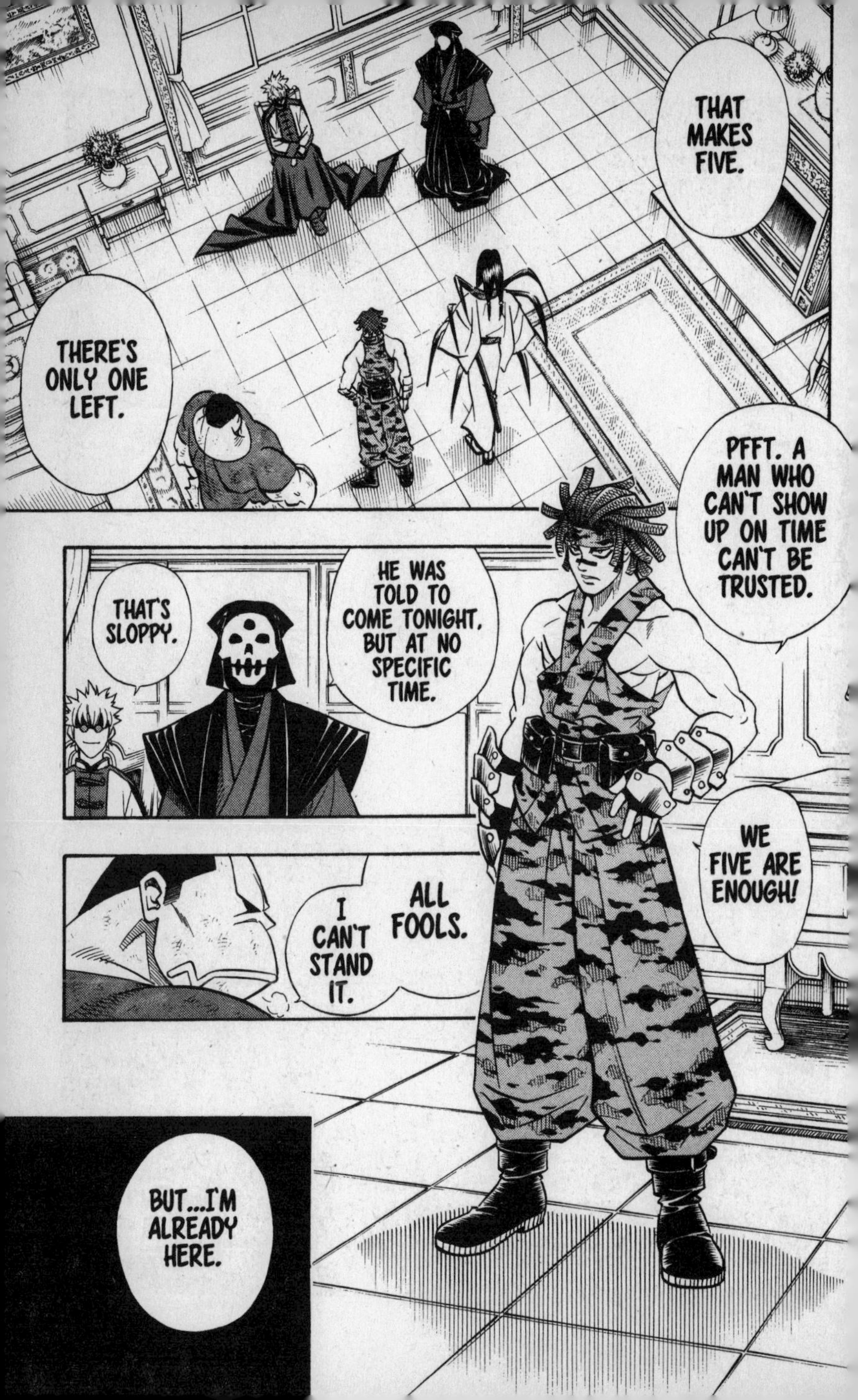
THAT MAKES FIVE.
THERE'S ONLY ONE LEFT.
PFFT. A MAN WHO CAN'T SHOW UP ON TIME CAN'T BE TRUSTED.
WE FIVE ARE ENOUGH!
HE WAS TOLD TO COME TONIGHT, BUT AT NO SPECIFIC TIME.
THAT'S SLOPPY.
ALL FOOLS.
I CAN'T STAND IT.
BUT...I'M ALREADY HERE.

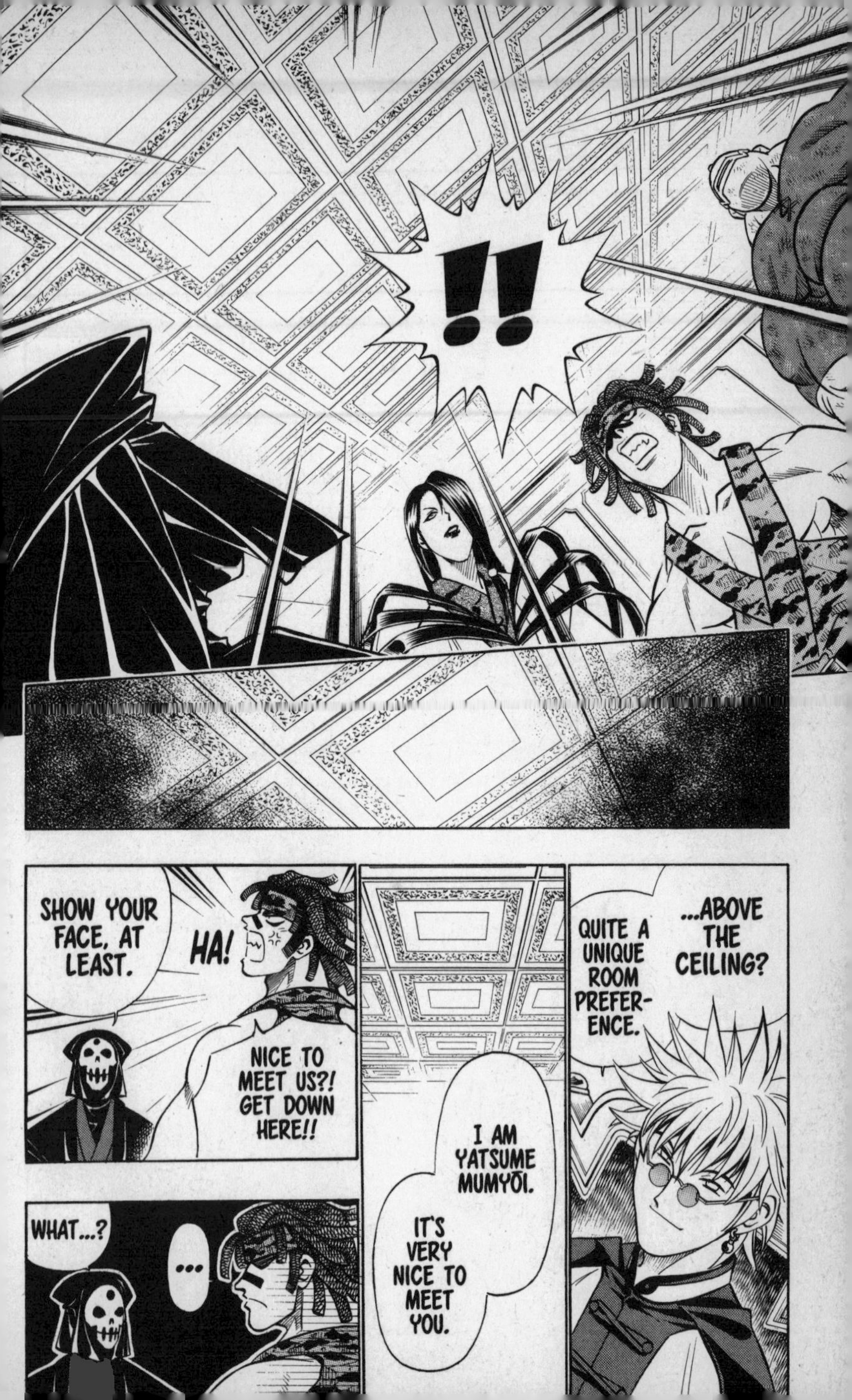
!!
...ABOVE THE CEILING?
QUITE A UNIQUE ROOM PREFERENCE.
I AM YATSUME MUMYŌI.
IT'S VERY NICE TO MEET YOU.
HA!
NICE TO MEET US?! GET DOWN HERE!!
SHOW YOUR FACE, AT LEAST.
...
WHAT...?

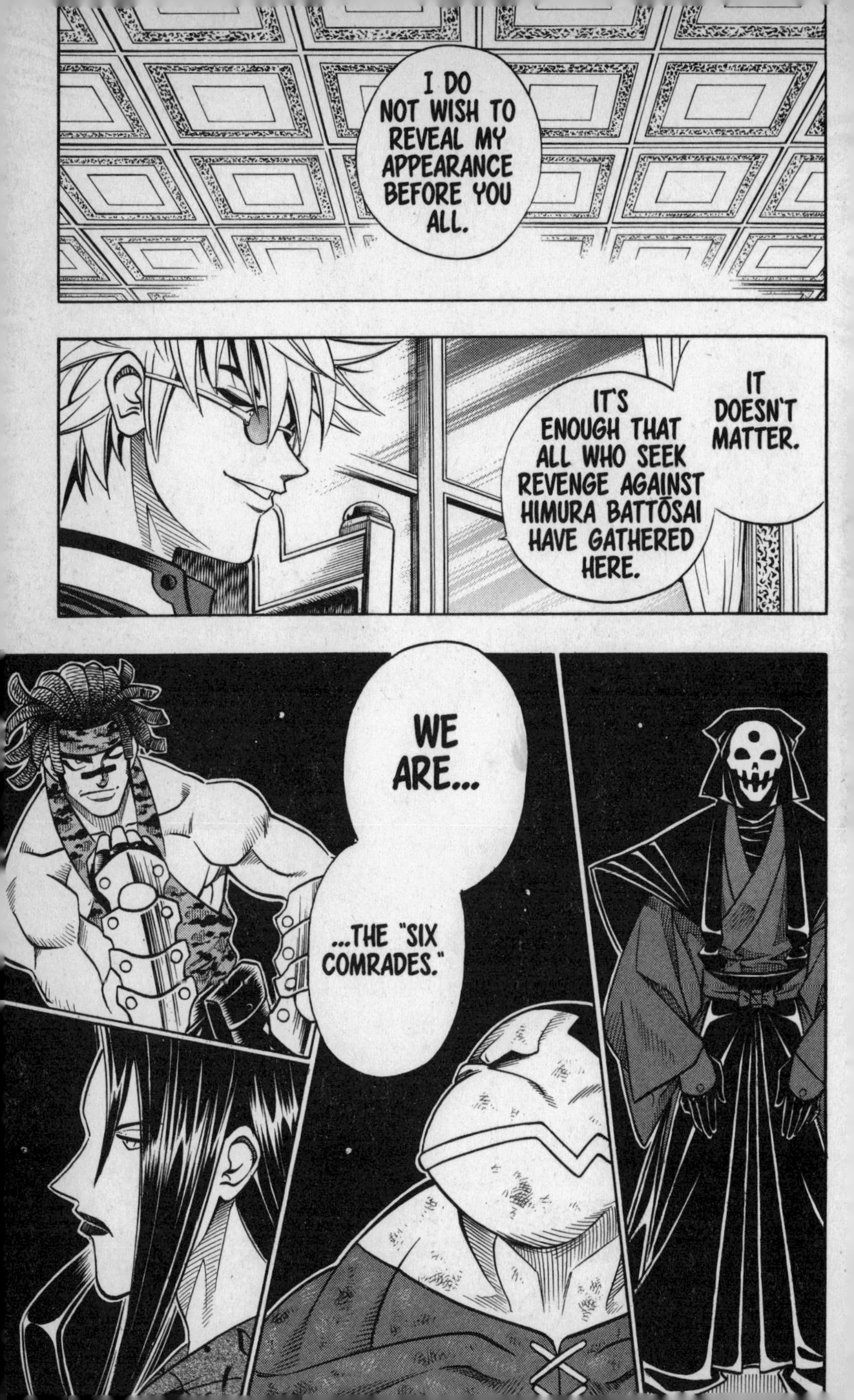
I DO NOT WISH TO REVEAL MY APPEARANCE BEFORE YOU ALL.
IT DOESN'T MATTER.
IT'S ENOUGH THAT ALL WHO SEEK REVENGE AGAINST HIMURA BATTŌSAI HAVE GATHERED HERE.
WE ARE...
...THE "SIX COMRADES."

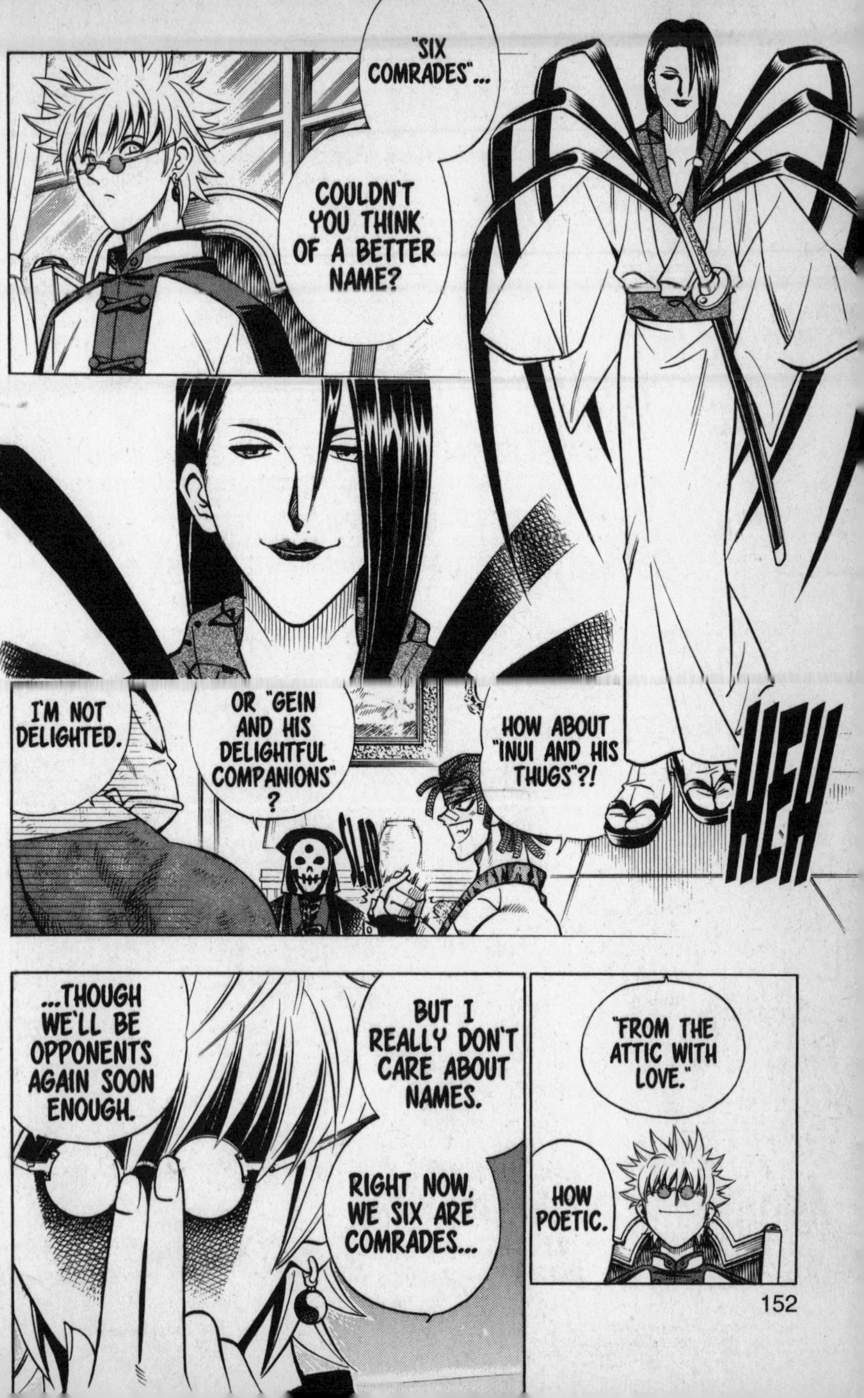
HEH
"SIX COMRADES"...
COULDN'T YOU THINK OF A BETTER NAME?
HOW ABOUT "INUI AND HIS THUGS"?!
SLAP
OR "GEIN AND HIS DELIGHTFUL COMPANIONS"?
I'M NOT DELIGHTED.
"FROM THE ATTIC WITH LOVE."
HOW POETIC.
BUT I REALLY DON'T CARE ABOUT NAMES.
RIGHT NOW, WE SIX ARE COMRADES...
...THOUGH WE'LL BE OPPONENTS AGAIN SOON ENOUGH.

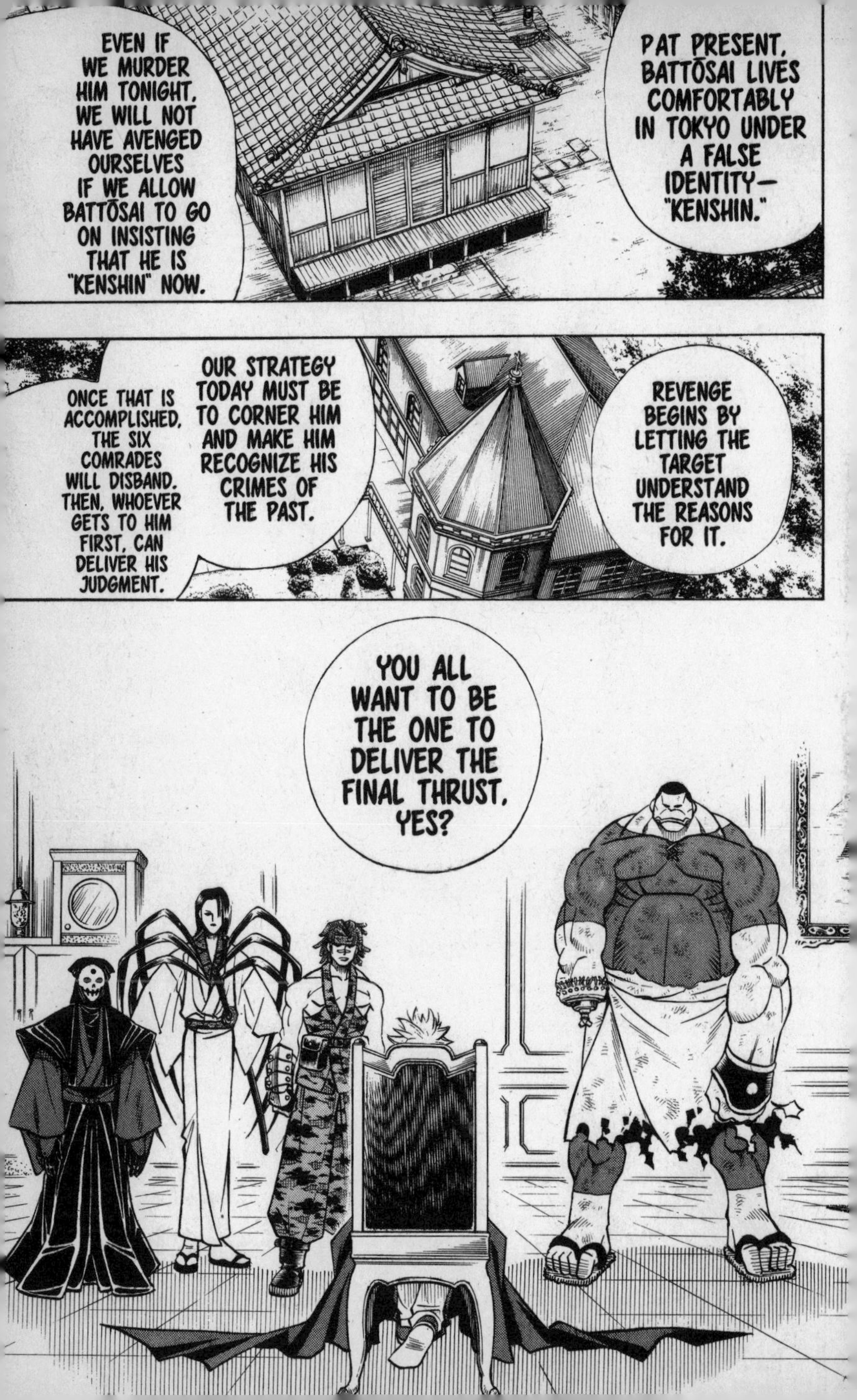
PAT PRESENT, BATTŌSAI LIVES COMFORTABLY IN TOKYO UNDER A FALSE IDENTITY— "KENSHIN."
EVEN IF WE MURDER HIM TONIGHT, WE WILL NOT HAVE AVENGED OURSELVES IF WE ALLOW BATTŌSAI TO GO ON INSISTING THAT HE IS "KENSHIN" NOW.
REVENGE BEGINS BY LETTING THE TARGET UNDERSTAND THE REASONS FOR IT.
OUR STRATEGY TODAY MUST BE TO CORNER HIM AND MAKE HIM RECOGNIZE HIS CRIMES OF THE PAST.
ONCE THAT IS ACCOMPLISHED, THE SIX COMRADES WILL DISBAND. THEN, WHOEVER GETS TO HIM FIRST, CAN DELIVER HIS JUDGMENT.
YOU ALL WANT TO BE THE ONE TO DELIVER THE FINAL THRUST, YES?

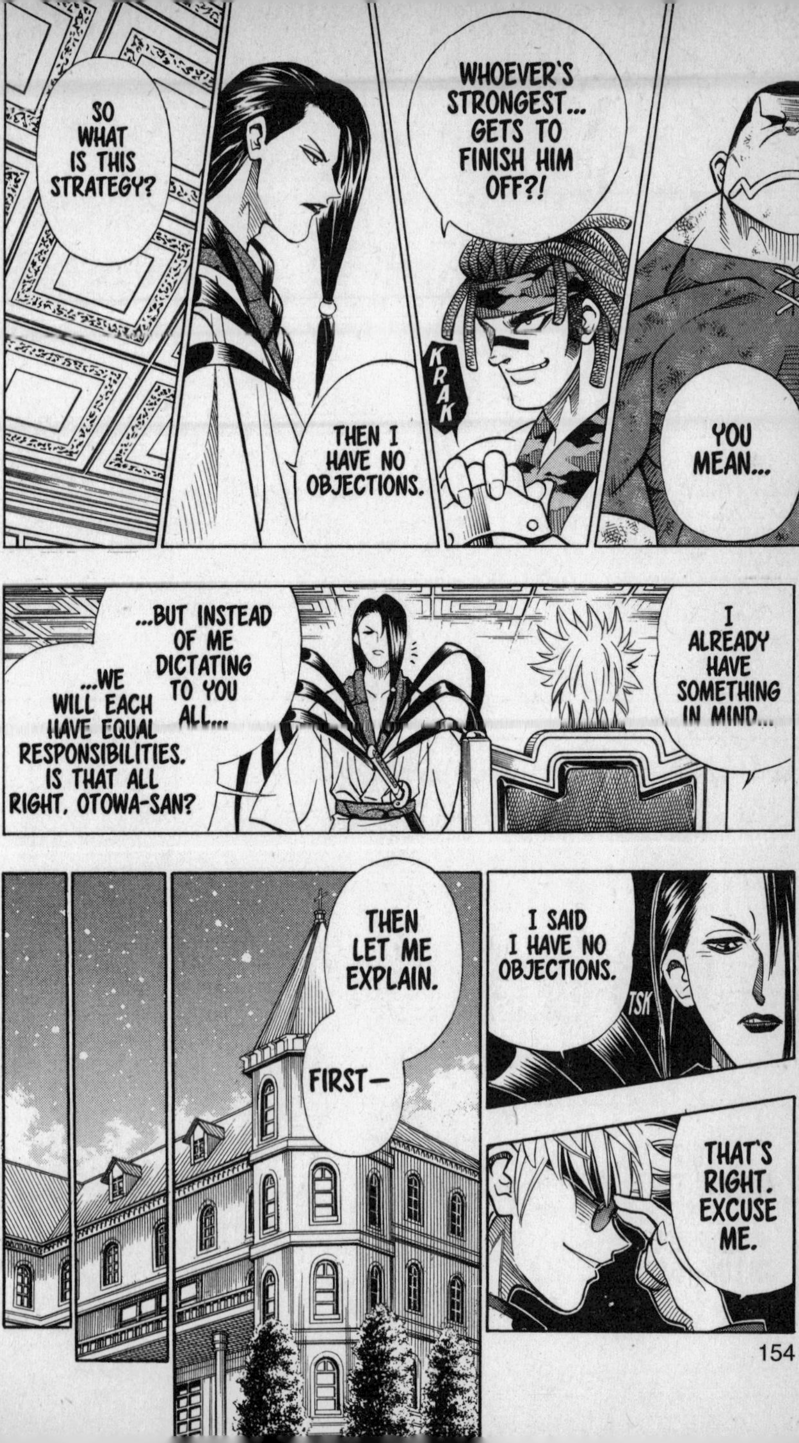
YOU MEAN...
WHOEVER'S STRONGEST... GETS TO FINISH HIM OFF?!
KRAK
THEN I HAVE NO OBJECTIONS.
SO WHAT IS THIS STRATEGY?
I ALREADY HAVE SOMETHING IN MIND...
...BUT INSTEAD OF ME DICTATING TO YOU ALL...
...WE WILL EACH HAVE EQUAL RESPONSIBILITIES. IS THAT ALL RIGHT, OTOWA-SAN?
I SAID I HAVE NO OBJECTIONS.
TSK
THAT'S RIGHT. EXCUSE ME.
THEN LET ME EXPLAIN.
FIRST—

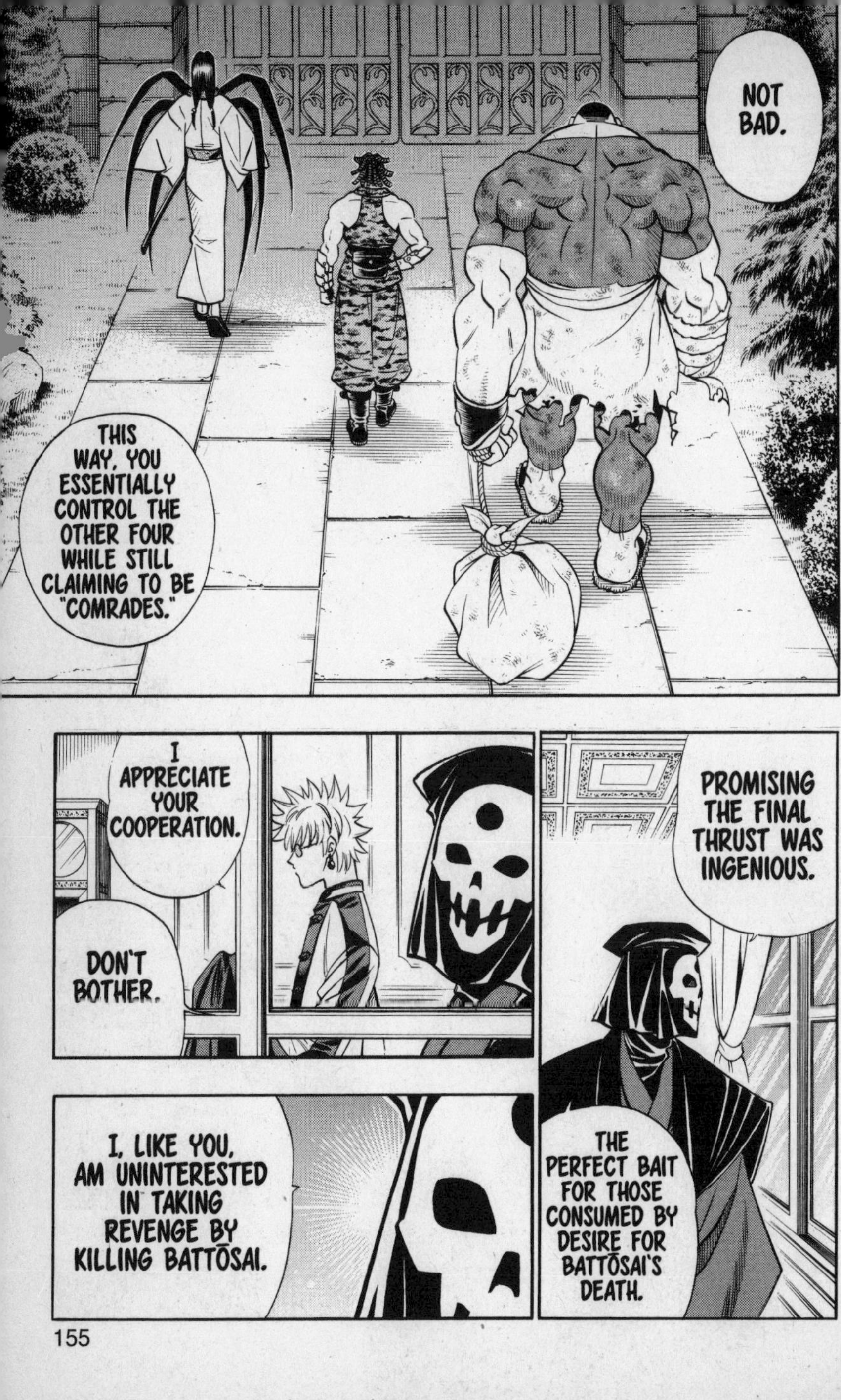
NOT BAD.
THIS WAY, YOU ESSENTIALLY CONTROL THE OTHER FOUR WHILE STILL CLAIMING TO BE "COMRADES."
PROMISING THE FINAL THRUST WAS INGENIOUS.
THE PERFECT BAIT FOR THOSE CONSUMED BY DESIRE FOR BATTŌSAI'S DEATH.
I APPRECIATE YOUR COOPERATION.
DON'T BOTHER.
I, LIKE YOU, AM UNINTERESTED IN TAKING REVENGE BY KILLING BATTŌSAI.

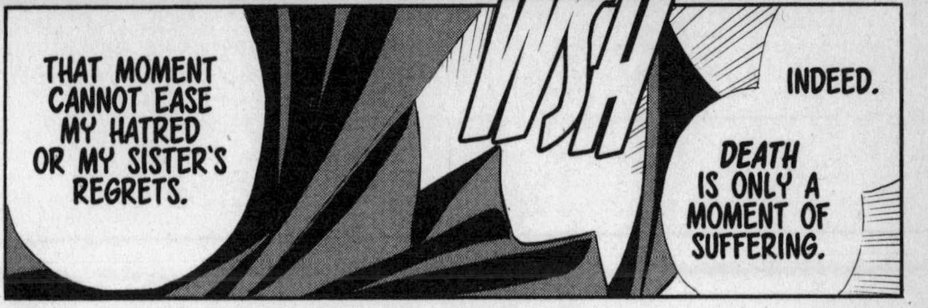
INDEED.
DEATH IS ONLY A MOMENT OF SUFFERING.
WSH
THAT MOMENT CANNOT EASE MY HATRED OR MY SISTER'S REGRETS.
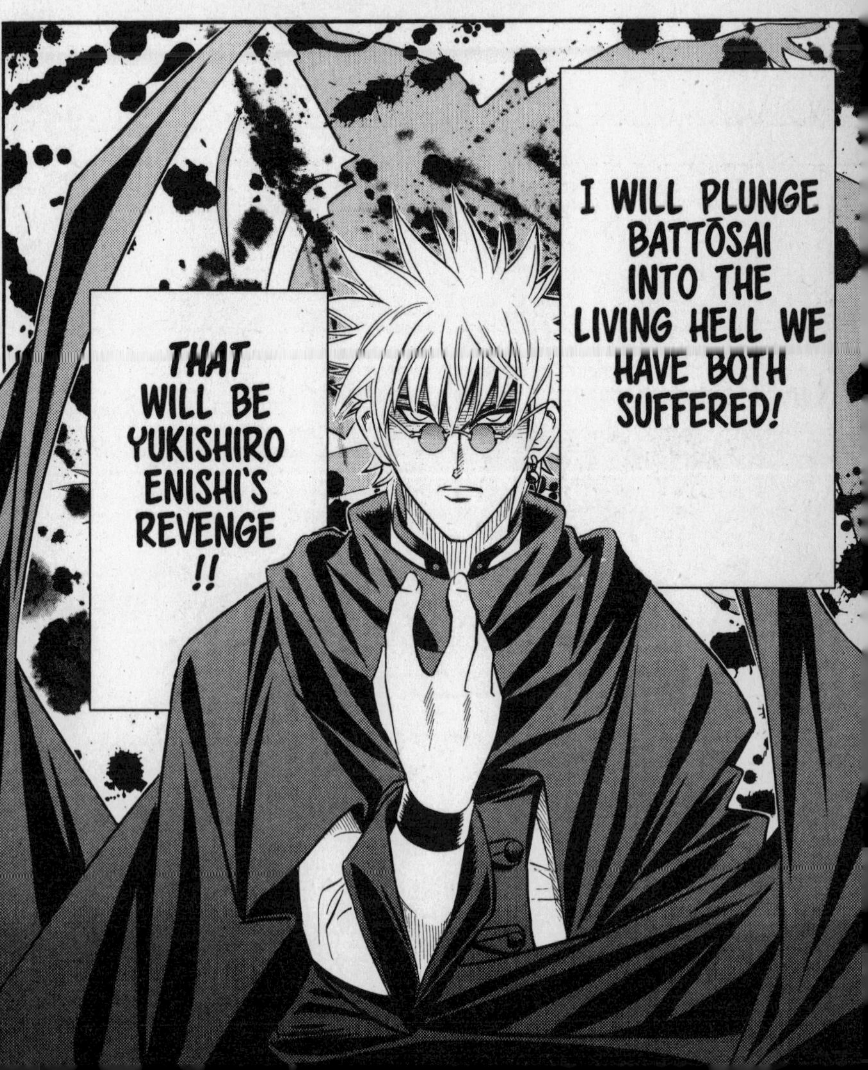
I WILL PLUNGE BATTŌSAI INTO THE LIVING HELL WE HAVE BOTH SUFFERED!
THAT WILL BE YUKISHIRO ENISHI'S REVENGE !!

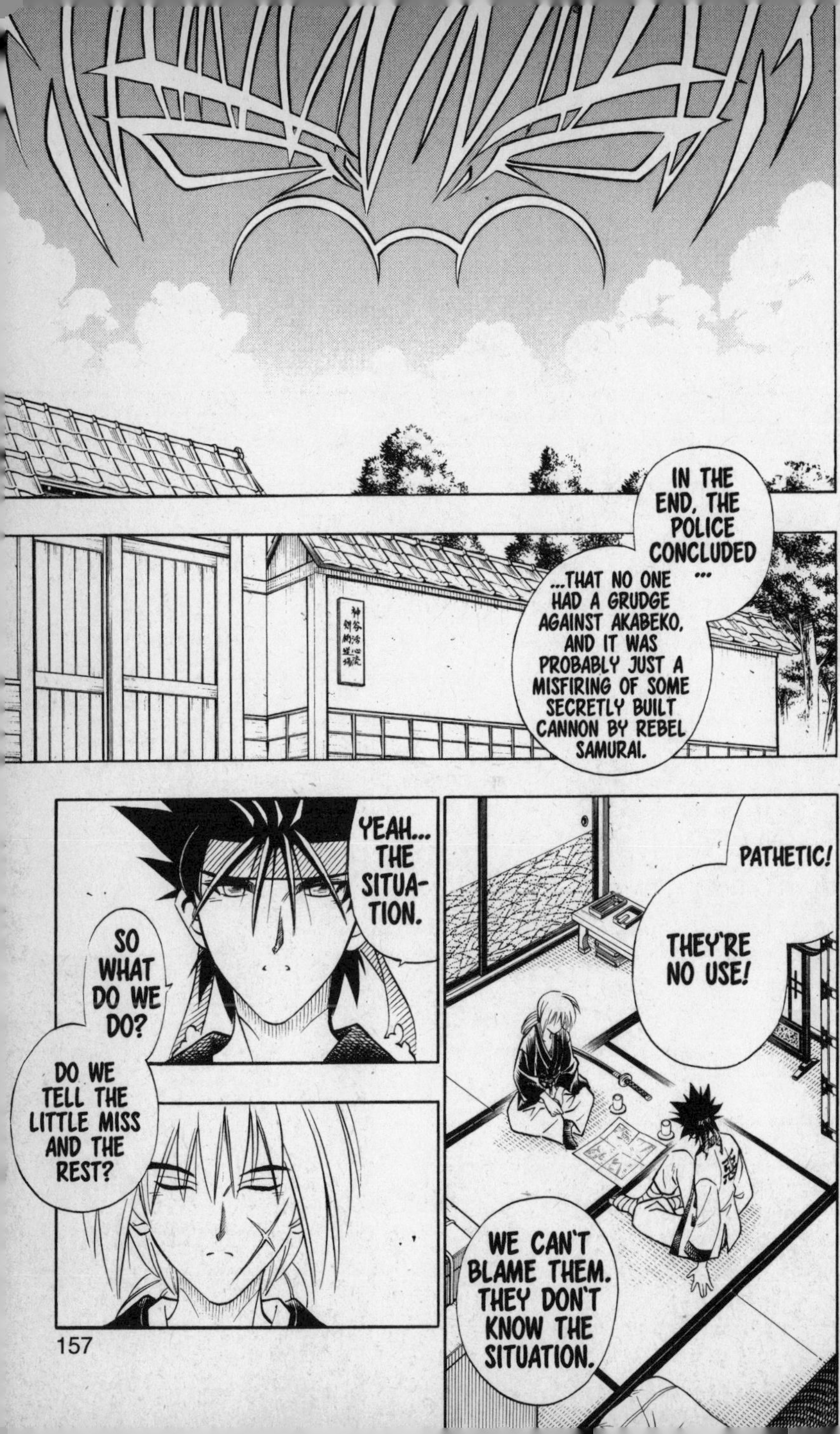
IN THE END, THE POLICE CONCLUDED...
...THAT NO ONE HAD A GRUDGE AGAINST AKABEKO, AND IT WAS PROBABLY JUST A MISFIRING OF SOME SECRETLY BUILT CANNON BY REBEL SAMURAI.
PATHETIC!
THEY'RE NO USE!
WE CAN'T BLAME THEM. THEY DON'T KNOW THE SITUATION.
YEAH... THE SITUATION.
SO WHAT DO WE DO?
DO WE TELL THE LITTLE MISS AND THE REST?

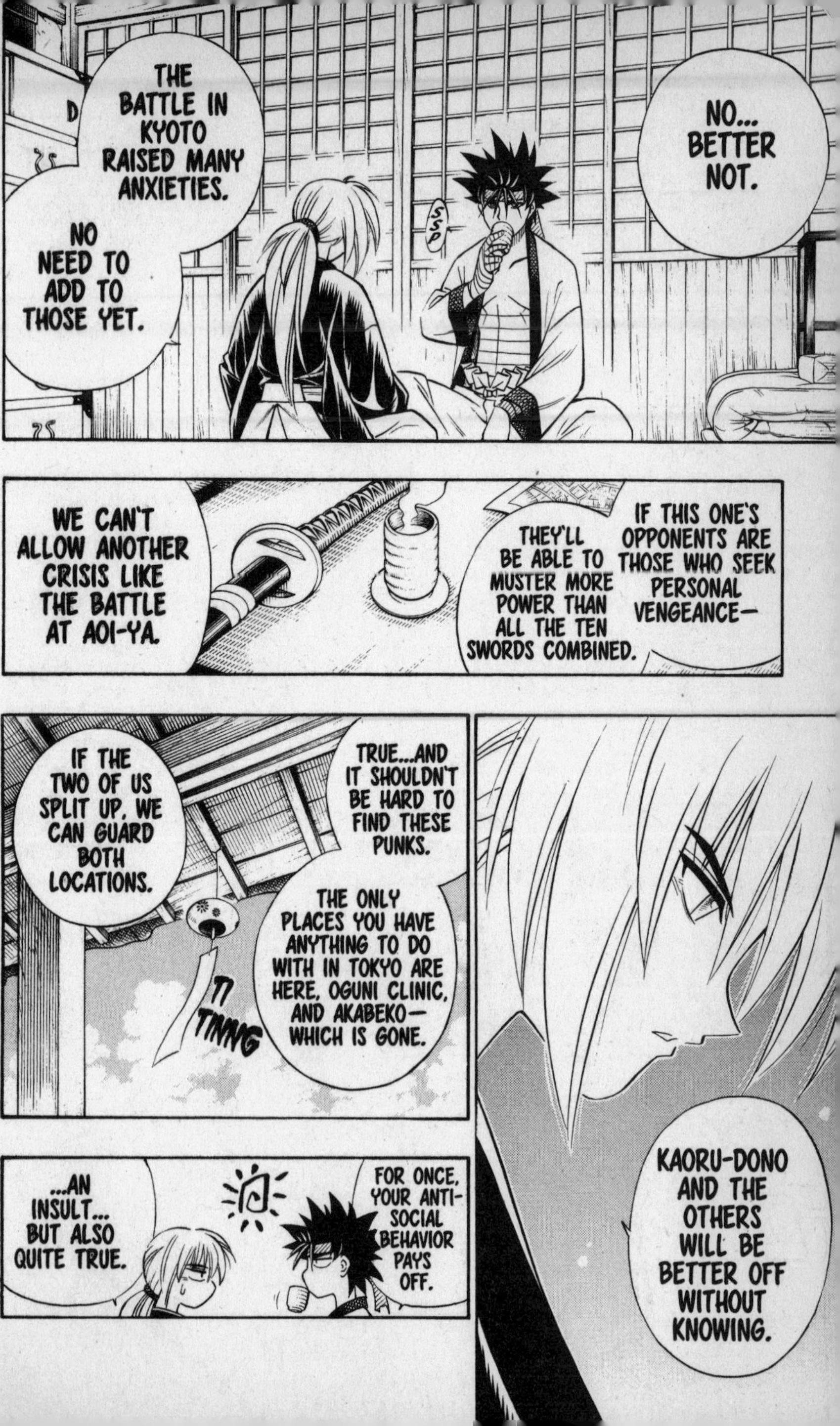
NO... BETTER NOT.
SSP
THE BATTLE IN KYOTO RAISED MANY ANXIETIES.
NO NEED TO ADD TO THOSE YET.
IF THIS ONE'S OPPONENTS ARE THOSE WHO SEEK PERSONAL VENGEANCE—
THEY'LL BE ABLE TO MUSTER MORE POWER THAN ALL THE TEN SWORDS COMBINED.
WE CAN'T ALLOW ANOTHER CRISIS LIKE THE BATTLE AT AOI-YA.
KAORU-DONO AND THE OTHERS WILL BE BETTER OFF WITHOUT KNOWING.
TRUE...AND IT SHOULDN'T BE HARD TO FIND THESE PUNKS.
THE ONLY PLACES YOU HAVE ANYTHING TO DO WITH IN TOKYO ARE HERE, OGUNI CLINIC, AND AKABEKO—WHICH IS GONE.
IF THE TWO OF US SPLIT UP, WE CAN GUARD BOTH LOCATIONS.
TI TINNG
FOR ONCE, YOUR ANTI-SOCIAL BEHAVIOR PAYS OFF.
...AN INSULT... BUT ALSO QUITE TRUE.

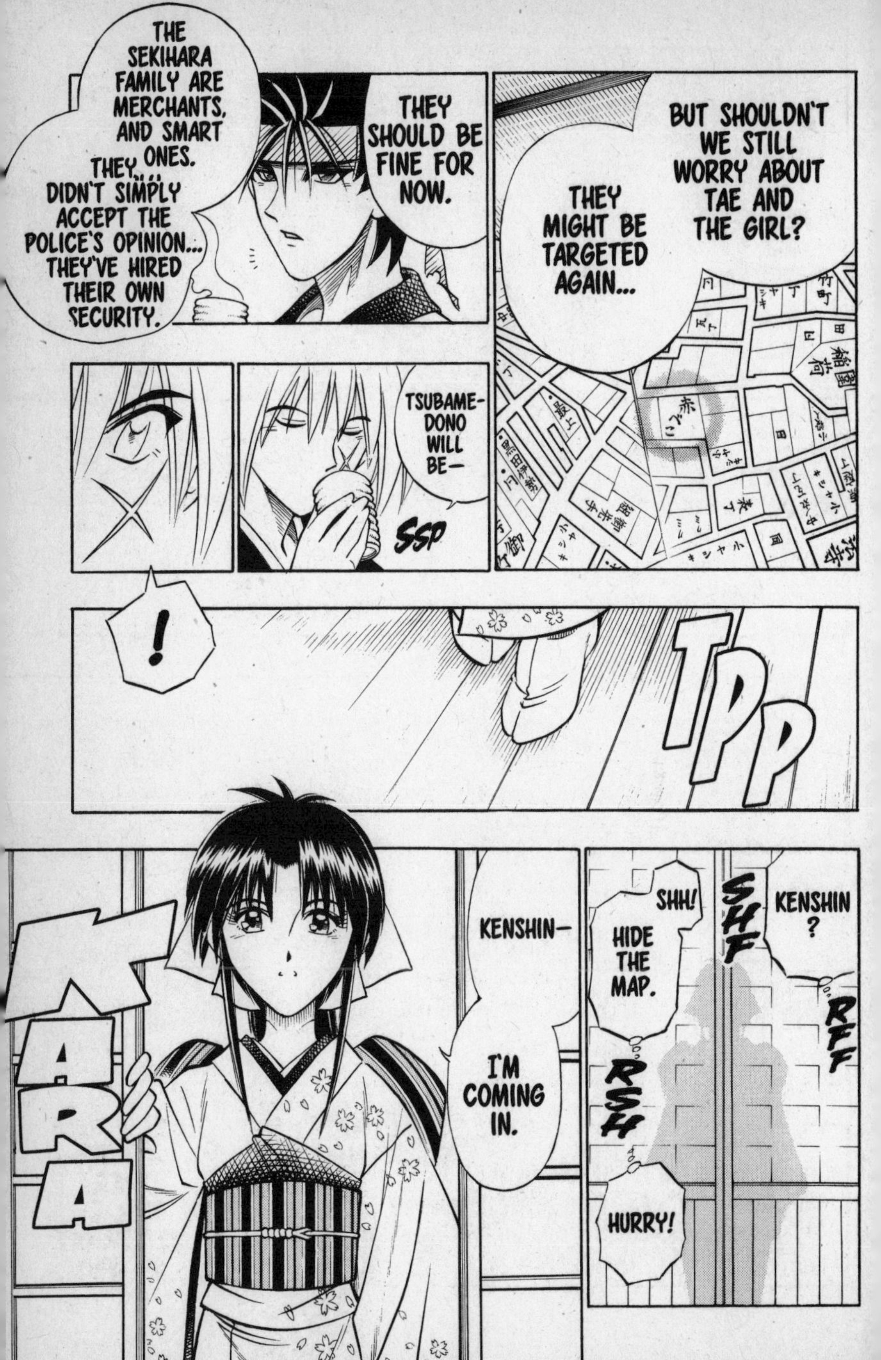
BUT SHOULDN'T WE STILL WORRY ABOUT TAE AND THE GIRL?
THEY MIGHT BE TARGETED AGAIN...
赤べこ
THEY SHOULD BE FINE FOR NOW.
THE SEKIHARA FAMILY ARE MERCHANTS, AND SMART ONES.
THEY... DIDN'T SIMPLY ACCEPT THE POLICE'S OPINION... THEY'VE HIRED THEIR OWN SECURITY.
TSUBAME-DONO WILL BE—
SSP
!
TPP
KENSHIN?
SHF
SHH!
HIDE THE MAP.
RFF
RSH
HURRY!
KENSHIN—
I'M COMING IN.
KARA

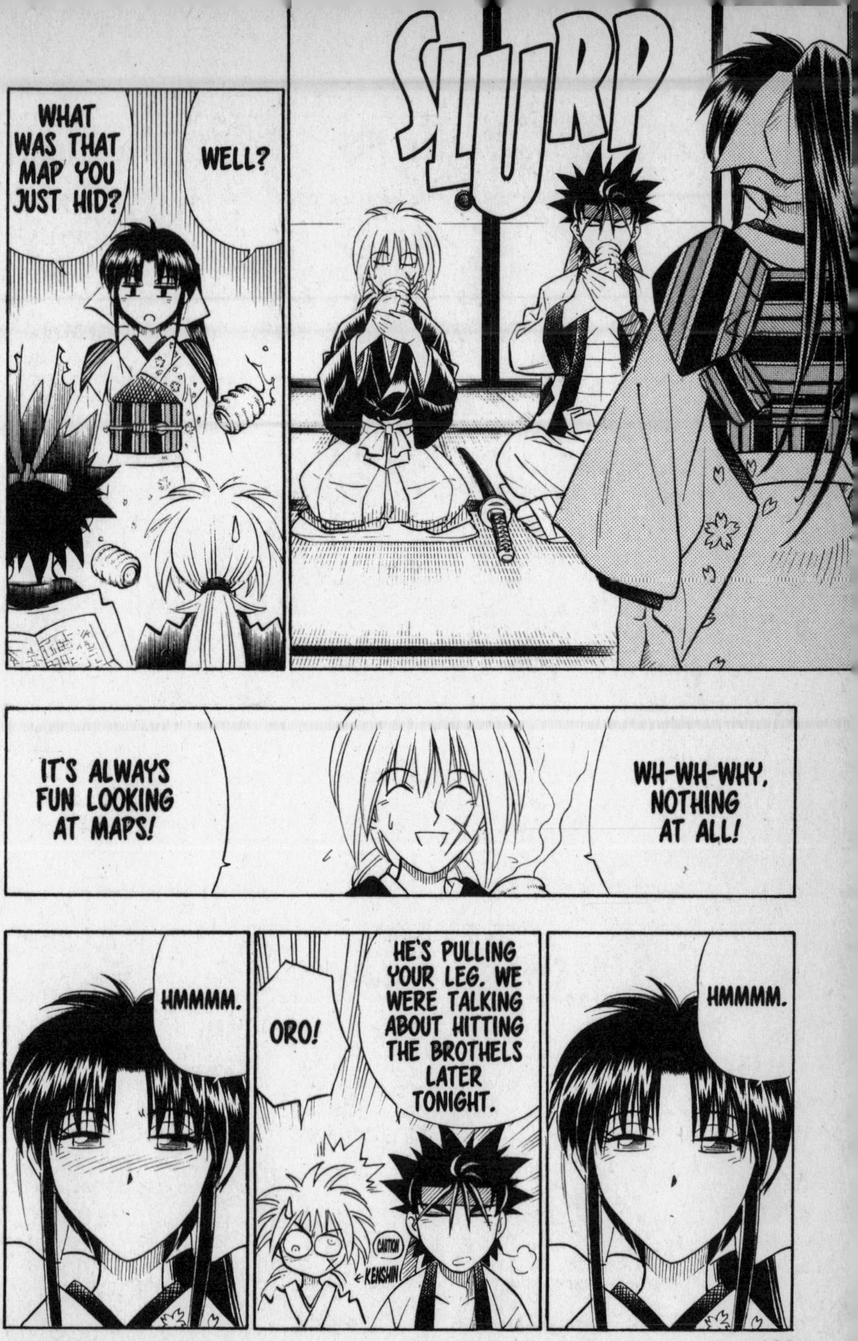
SLURP
WELL?
WHAT WAS THAT MAP YOU JUST HID?
WH-WH-WHY, NOTHING AT ALL!
IT'S ALWAYS FUN LOOKING AT MAPS!
HMMMM.
HE'S PULLING YOUR LEG. WE WERE TALKING ABOUT HITTING THE BROTHELS LATER TONIGHT.
ORO!
CAUTION
←KENSHIN
HMMMM.

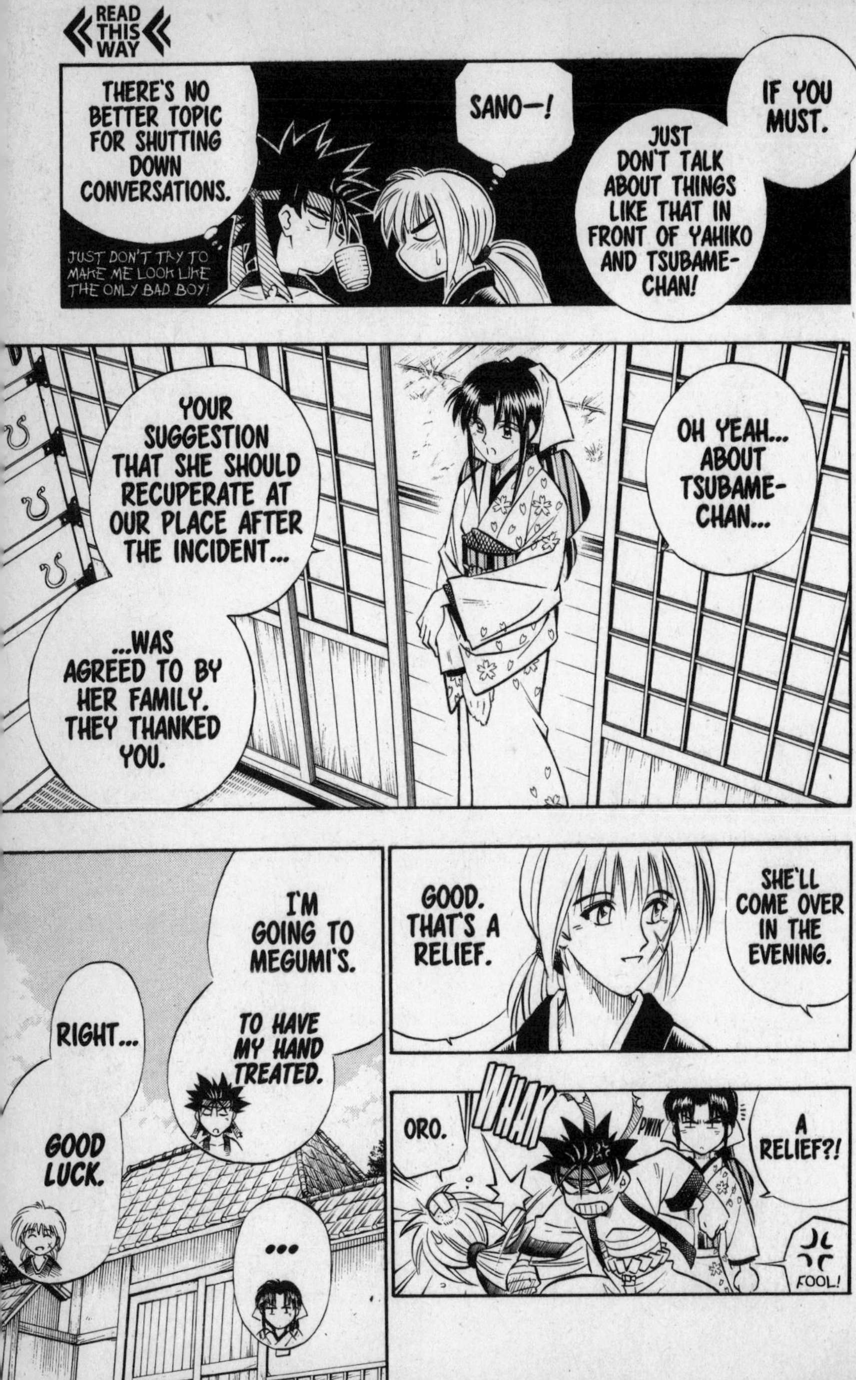
READ THIS WAY
IF YOU MUST.
JUST DON'T TALK ABOUT THINGS LIKE THAT IN FRONT OF YAHIKO AND TSUBAME-CHAN!
SANO—!
THERE'S NO BETTER TOPIC FOR SHUTTING DOWN CONVERSATIONS.
JUST DON'T TRY TO MAKE ME LOOK LIKE THE ONLY BAD BOY!
OH YEAH... ABOUT TSUBAME-CHAN...
YOUR SUGGESTION THAT SHE SHOULD RECUPERATE AT OUR PLACE AFTER THE INCIDENT...
...WAS AGREED TO BY HER FAMILY. THEY THANKED YOU.
SHE'LL COME OVER IN THE EVENING.
GOOD. THAT'S A RELIEF.
A RELIEF?!
FOOL!
PWIK
WHAK
ORO.
I'M GOING TO MEGUMI'S.
TO HAVE MY HAND TREATED.
RIGHT...
GOOD LUCK.
...

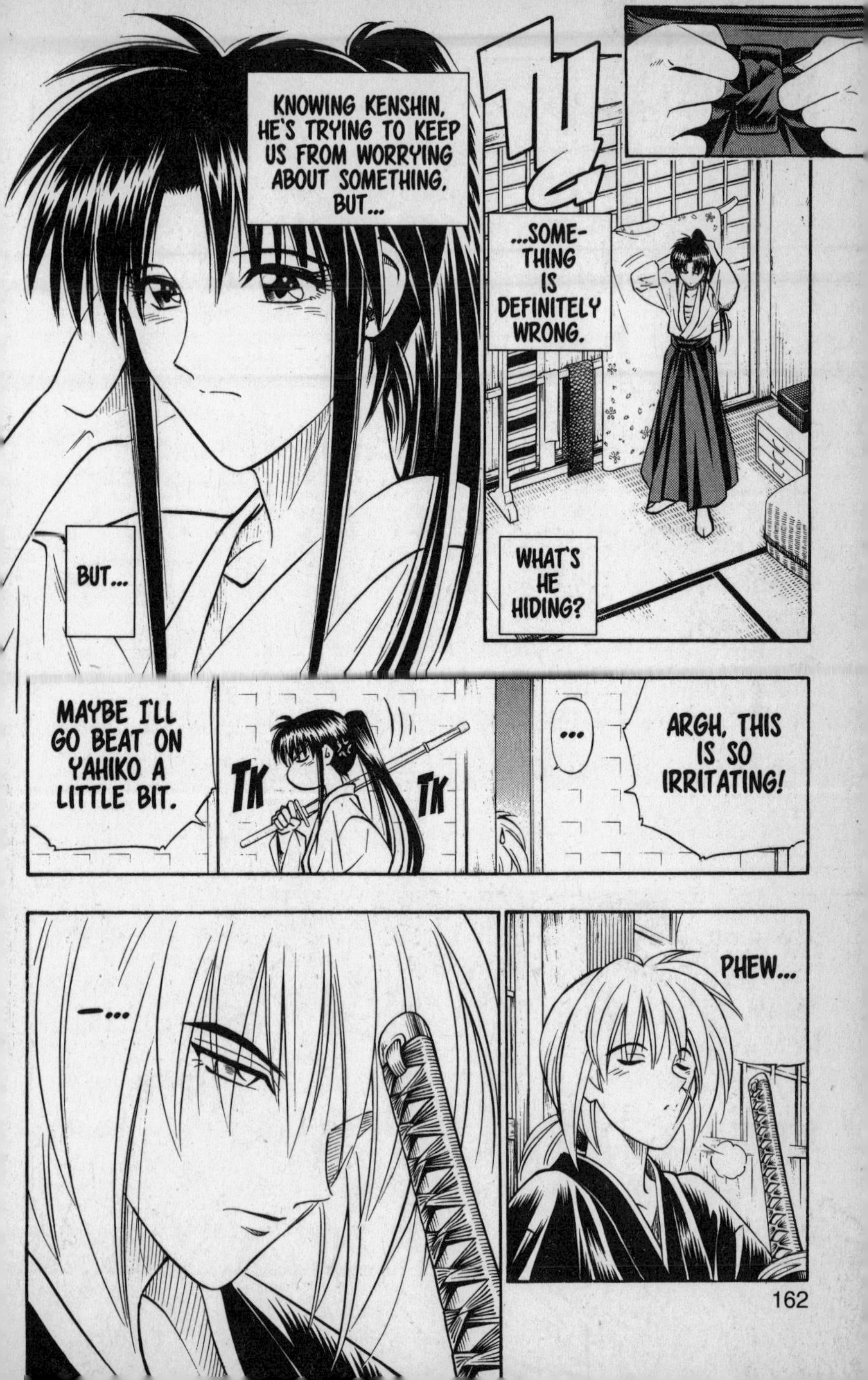
TUG
KNOWING KENSHIN, HE'S TRYING TO KEEP US FROM WORRYING ABOUT SOMETHING, BUT...
...SOMETHING IS DEFINITELY WRONG.
WHAT'S HE HIDING?
BUT...
ARGH, THIS IS SO IRRITATING!
...
TK
TK
MAYBE I'LL GO BEAT ON YAHIKO A LITTLE BIT.
PHEW...
—...

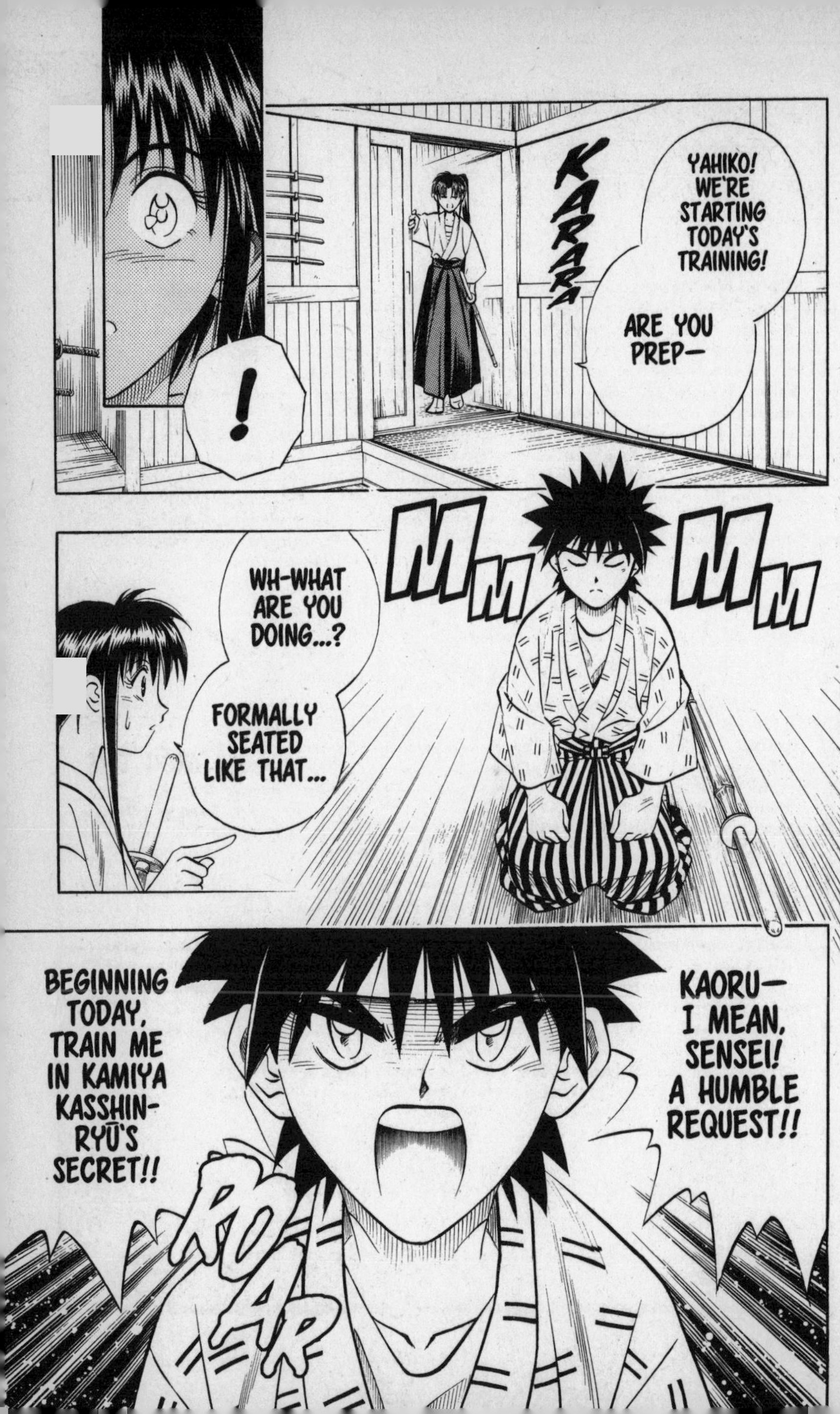
KARARA
YAHIKO! WE'RE STARTING TODAY'S TRAINING!
ARE YOU PREP—
!
MM
MM
WH-WHAT ARE YOU DOING...?
FORMALLY SEATED LIKE THAT...
KAORU— I MEAN, SENSEI! A HUMBLE REQUEST!!
BEGINNING TODAY, TRAIN ME IN KAMIYA KASSHIN-RYŪ'S SECRET!!
ROAR

"FREE TALK" ‹PART II›

Since I can't play many games, another outlet for my stress is collecting figures. The end of this year saw a flood of them, sending me shrieking in joy! The craftsmanship of McFarlane Toys knows no bounds, and the rest of the toy business is catching up, using its technology too...These aren't figures, but as someone who grew up during the *Gundam* boom, I have to mention Bandai's *Gundam* MG series and the *Eva* LM-HG series plastic models. And then there are the action dolls. No matter how impressive the product is, I have no interest in non-mobile dolls, but the ones that are mobile are a different story. I was really surprised by Takara's *Nako-Rimu* dolls when I bought them. (This is off topic, but my friend, Michimoto Munenori, was surprised too, especially by the quality of the hair.) The garage kit makers are also putting out action dolls, so even though I don't plan to start collecting them (collecting Yo-toys is already too much...) I'm anticipating a revolution in model technology in the future. If this keeps up, the birth of the "action doll with seamless joints" (with a mobile skeleton hidden under a layer of skin) may not be a dream!

Another stress reliever for me is the sunset. The air is clearer in the winter, making it very nice. But I can't get out to watch the sunset with my current schedule, so I'm enjoying the recorded version shown early in the morning. And now they're broadcasting scenery from the train. "Train windows of the world" is nice too, but Watsuki likes more close-to-home scenes like the Yamanote line, or the roads seen from cars driving in the city. I guess I like a "lightly taken night trip." I'm thinking I'll put that into action at the end of the year.

Finally, something serious. "Rurouni Kenshin" becomes more of a struggle with every new episode. There is an overall storyline all the way to the end, but I seem to keep getting dragged into the deepness of the story, and I'm not able to control it as much as I wish I could. However, the winter is lightening my spirits and allowing me to recover some. I plan to make a full sprint next year to make up for the shortfall this year. Please support me through next year, toward that happy ending I still promise. (Again, off topic. Michimoto and I share the motto, "Manga artists are DEAD or ALIVE, ALL or NOTHING"...) See you in the next volume!

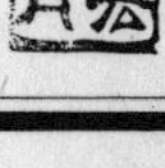

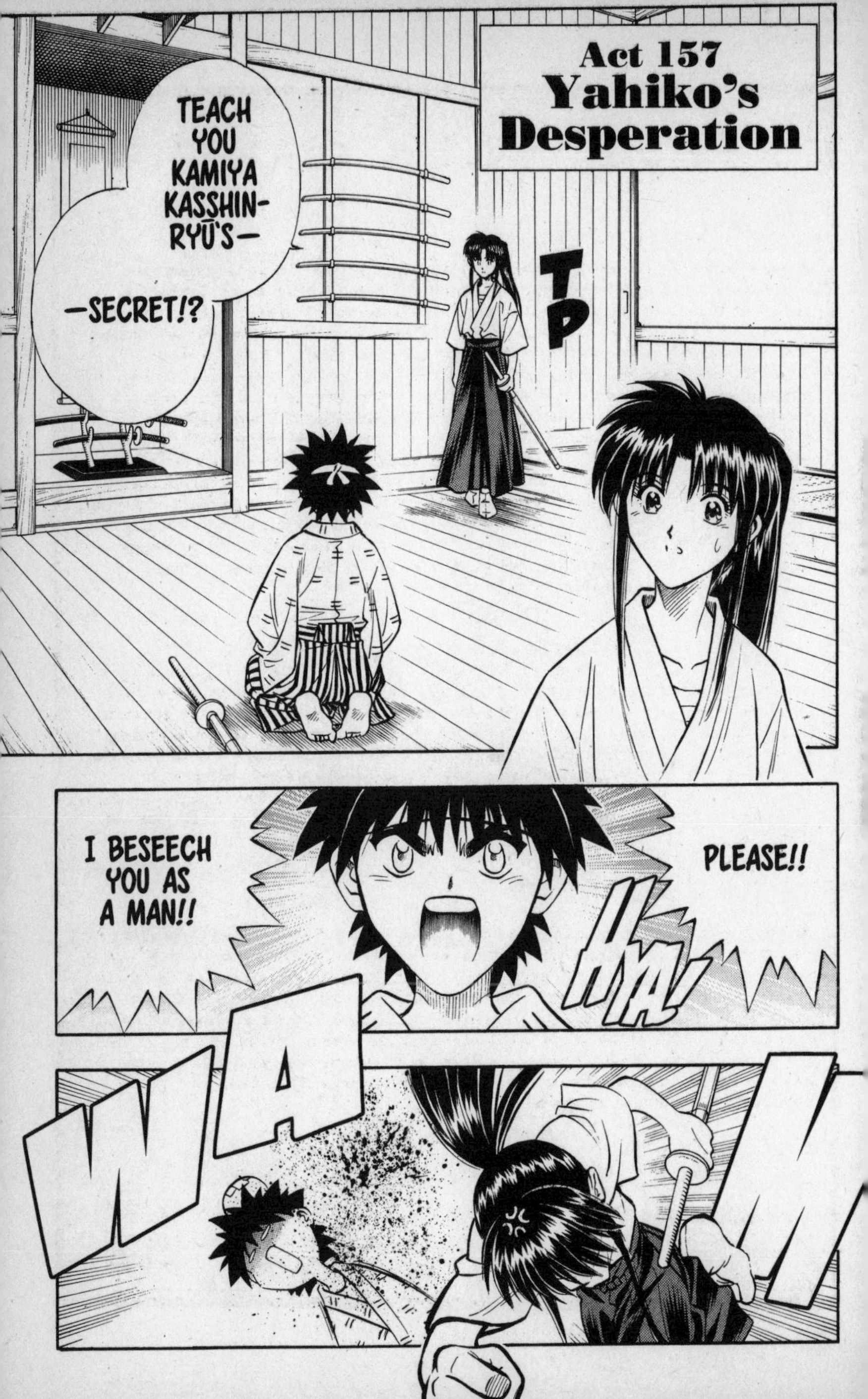
Act 157 Yahiko's Desperation
TP
TEACH YOU KAMIYA KASSHIN-RYŪ'S—
—SECRET!?
PLEASE!!
HYA
I BESEECH YOU AS A MAN!!
WHAM

Act 157
Yahiko's
Desperation

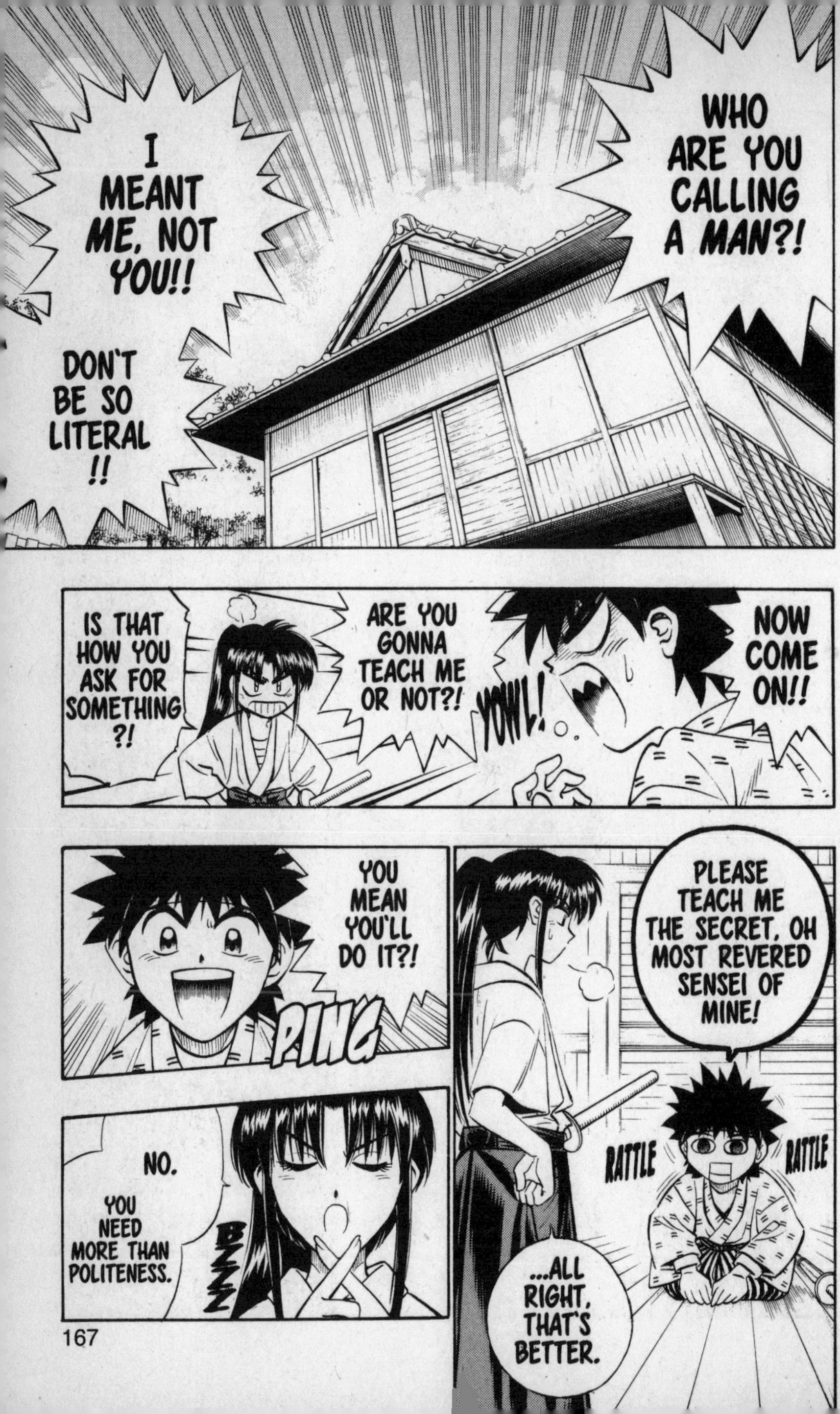
WHO ARE YOU CALLING A MAN?!
I MEANT ME, NOT YOU!!
DON'T BE SO LITERAL!!
NOW COME ON!!
YOWL!
ARE YOU GONNA TEACH ME OR NOT?!
IS THAT HOW YOU ASK FOR SOMETHING?!
PLEASE TEACH ME THE SECRET, OH MOST REVERED SENSEI OF MINE!
RATTLE
RATTLE
...ALL RIGHT, THAT'S BETTER.
YOU MEAN YOU'LL DO IT?!
PING
NO.
YOU NEED MORE THAN POLITENESS.
BZZZ

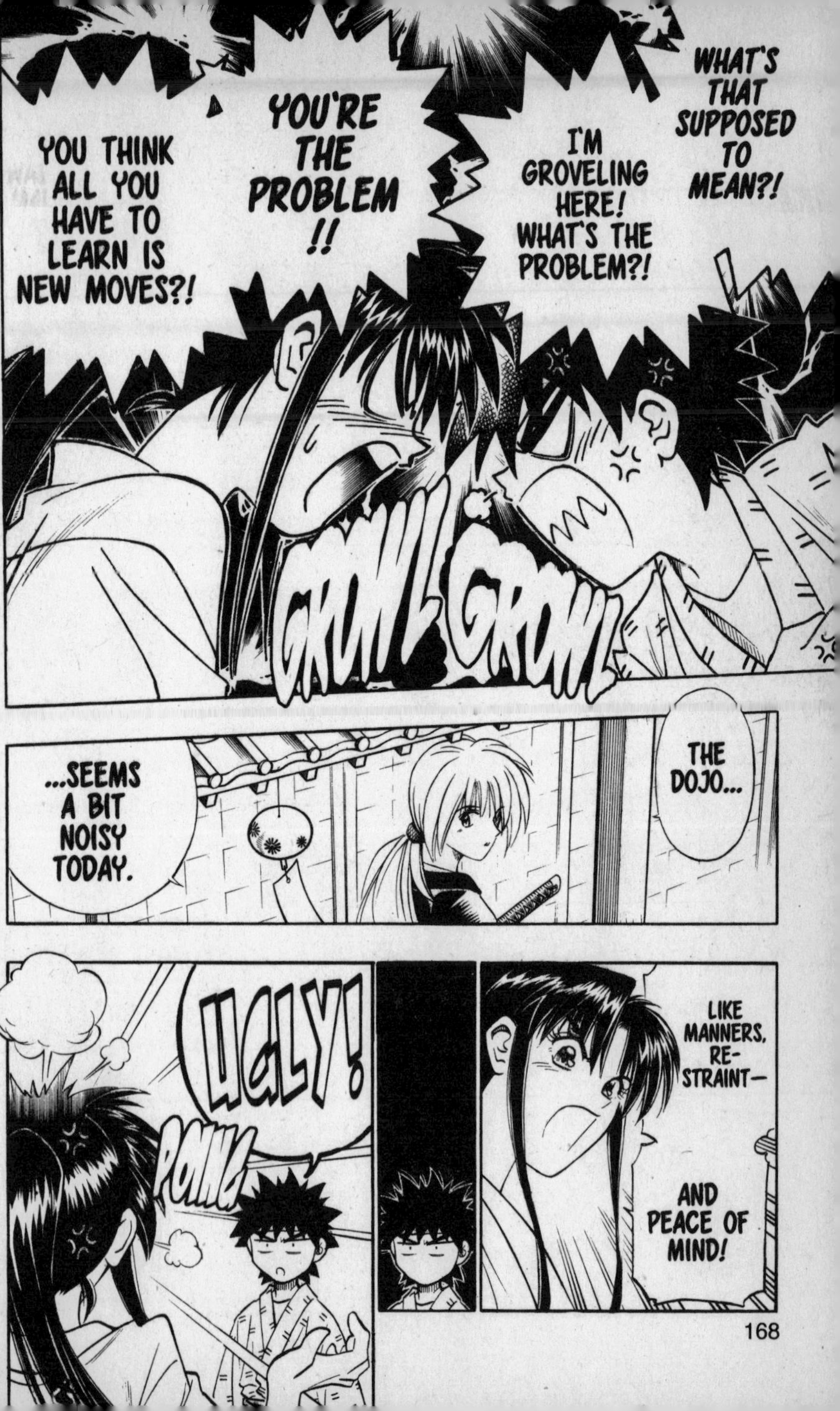
WHAT'S THAT SUPPOSED TO MEAN?!
I'M GROVELING HERE! WHAT'S THE PROBLEM?!
YOU'RE THE PROBLEM !!
YOU THINK ALL YOU HAVE TO LEARN IS NEW MOVES?!
GROWL GROWL
THE DOJO...
...SEEMS A BIT NOISY TODAY.
LIKE MANNERS, RE-STRAINT—
AND PEACE OF MIND!
UGLY!

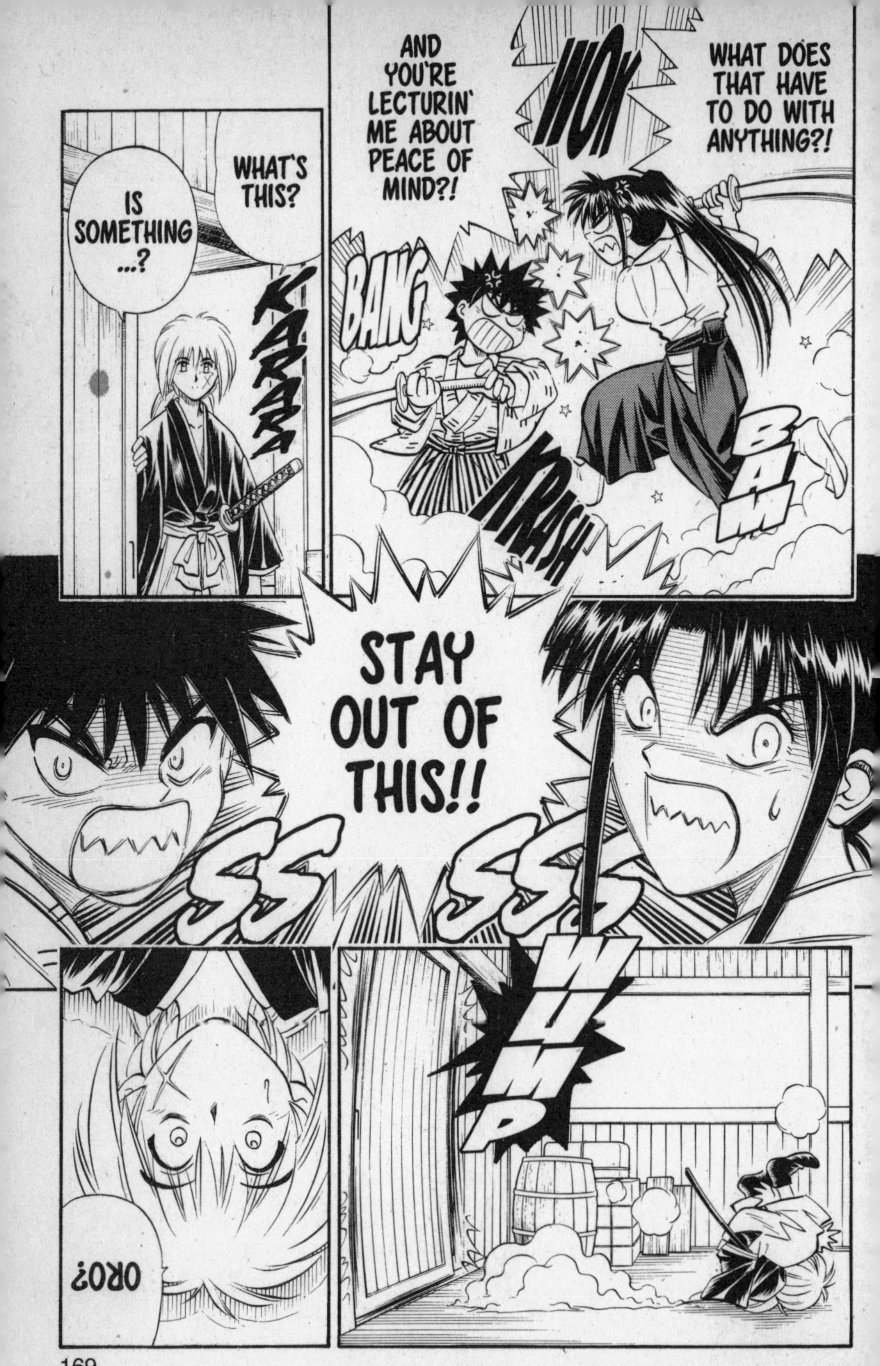

WHAT DOES THAT HAVE TO DO WITH ANYTHING?!
WOCK
AND YOU'RE LECTURIN' ME ABOUT PEACE OF MIND?!
BANG
KRASH
BAM
WHAT'S THIS?
KARARA
IS SOMETHING ...?
STAY OUT OF THIS!!
WHUMP
ORO?

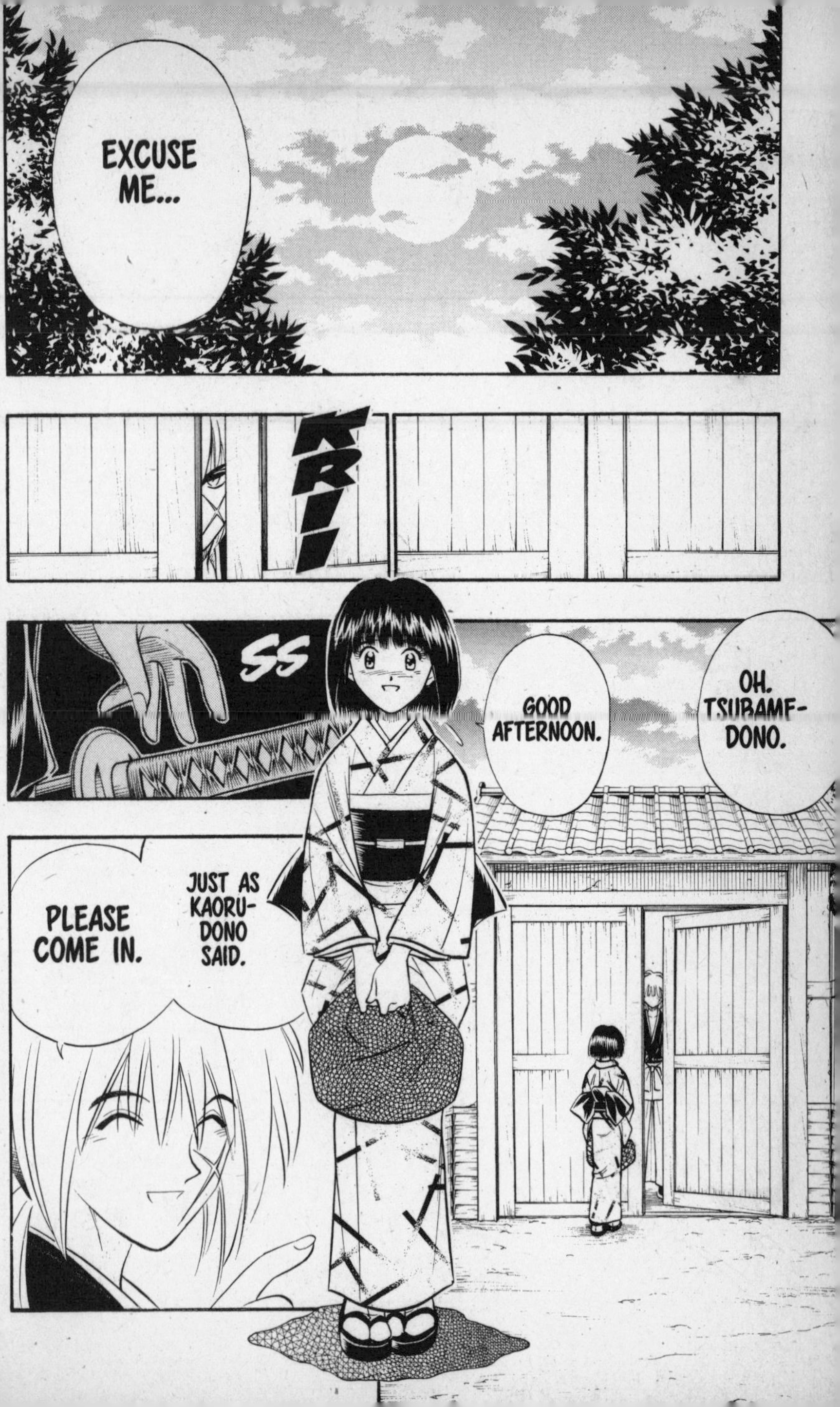
EXCUSE ME...
KRI
OH. TSUBAME-DONO.
GOOD AFTERNOON.
SS
JUST AS KAORU-DONO SAID.
PLEASE COME IN.

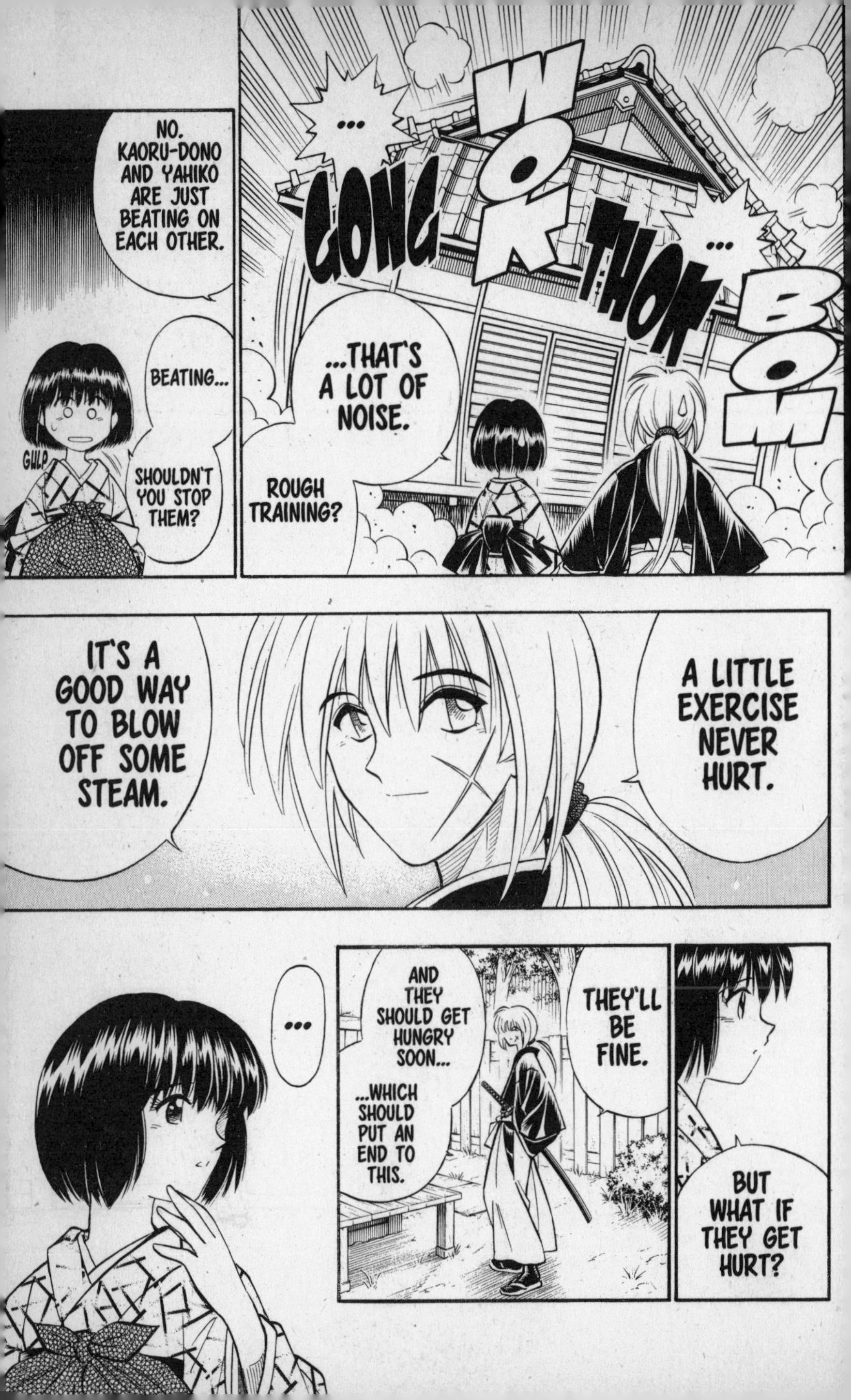
BOOM
THOM
...
WOK
GONG
...
...THAT'S A LOT OF NOISE.
ROUGH TRAINING?
NO. KAORU-DONO AND YAHIKO ARE JUST BEATING ON EACH OTHER.
BEATING...
SHOULDN'T YOU STOP THEM?
GULP
A LITTLE EXERCISE NEVER HURT.
IT'S A GOOD WAY TO BLOW OFF SOME STEAM.
BUT WHAT IF THEY GET HURT?
THEY'LL BE FINE.
AND THEY SHOULD GET HUNGRY SOON...
...WHICH SHOULD PUT AN END TO THIS.
...

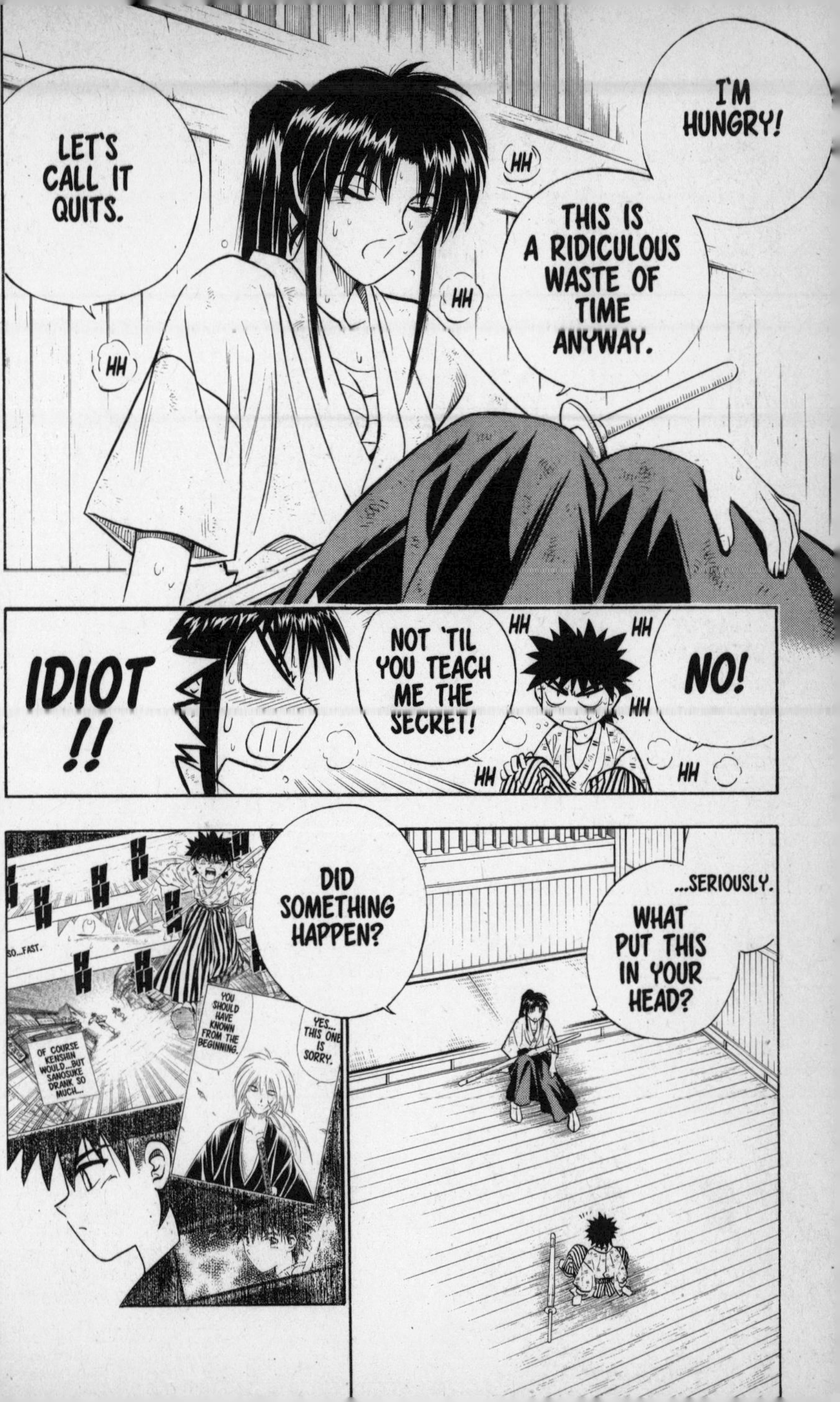
I'M HUNGRY!
HH
THIS IS A RIDICULOUS WASTE OF TIME ANYWAY.
HH
HH
LET'S CALL IT QUITS.
HH
NO!
HH
HH
HH
NOT 'TIL YOU TEACH ME THE SECRET!
HH
IDIOT !!
...SERIOUSLY.
WHAT PUT THIS IN YOUR HEAD?
DID SOMETHING HAPPEN?
SO...FAST.
YES... THIS ONE IS SORRY.
YOU SHOULD HAVE KNOWN FROM THE BEGINNING.
OF COURSE KENSHIN WOULD...BUT SANOSUKE DRANK SO MUCH...

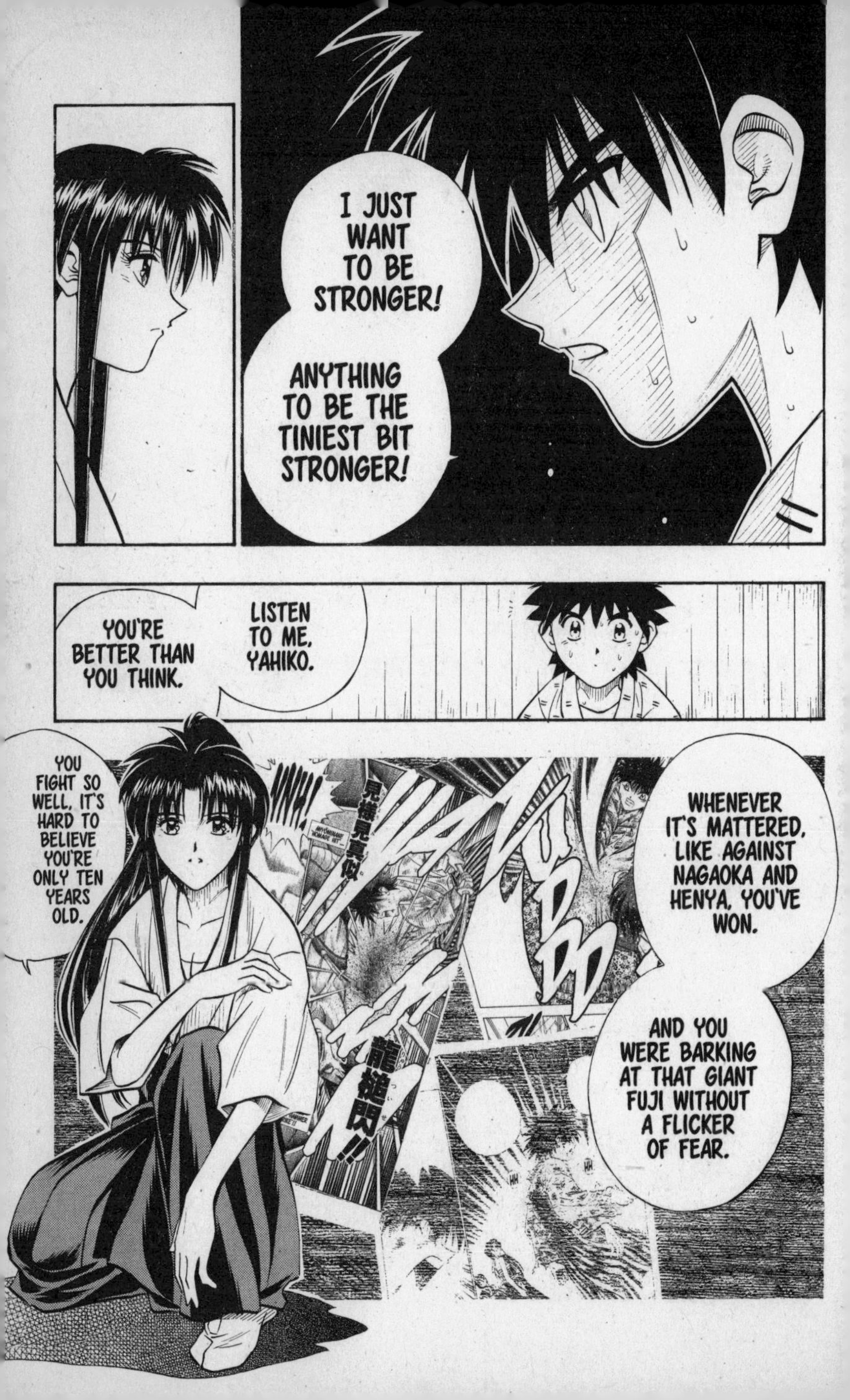
I JUST WANT TO BE STRONGER!
ANYTHING TO BE THE TINIEST BIT STRONGER!
LISTEN TO ME, YAHIKO.
YOU'RE BETTER THAN YOU THINK.
WHENEVER IT'S MATTERED, LIKE AGAINST NAGAOKA AND HENYA, YOU'VE WON.
AND YOU WERE BARKING AT THAT GIANT FUJI WITHOUT A FLICKER OF FEAR.
見様見真似
龍槌閃!!
YOU FIGHT SO WELL, IT'S HARD TO BELIEVE YOU'RE ONLY TEN YEARS OLD.

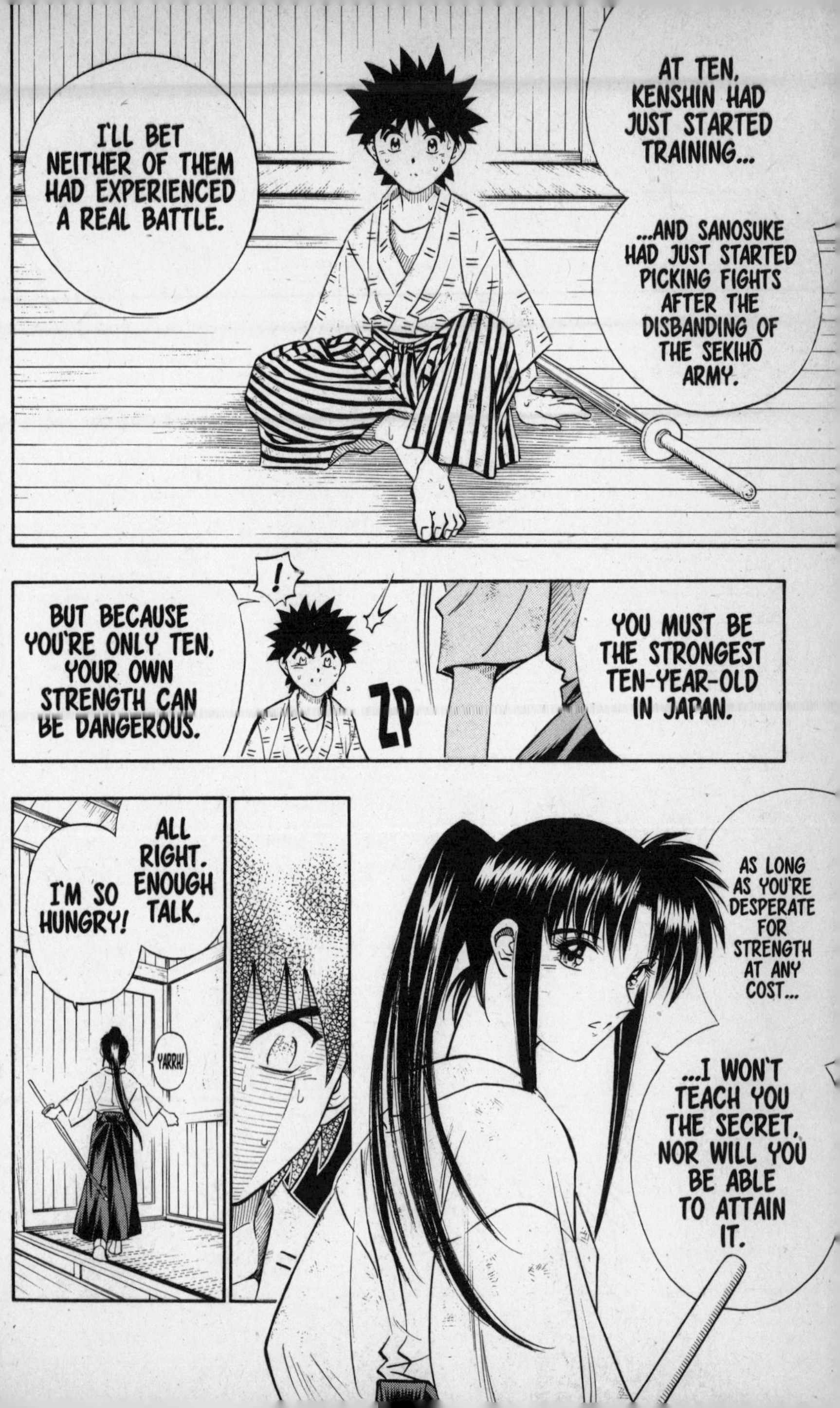
AT TEN, KENSHIN HAD JUST STARTED TRAINING...
...AND SANOSUKE HAD JUST STARTED PICKING FIGHTS AFTER THE DISBANDING OF THE SEKIHŌ ARMY.
I'LL BET NEITHER OF THEM HAD EXPERIENCED A REAL BATTLE.
YOU MUST BE THE STRONGEST TEN-YEAR-OLD IN JAPAN.
!
ZP
BUT BECAUSE YOU'RE ONLY TEN, YOUR OWN STRENGTH CAN BE DANGEROUS.
AS LONG AS YOU'RE DESPERATE FOR STRENGTH AT ANY COST...
...I WON'T TEACH YOU THE SECRET, NOR WILL YOU BE ABLE TO ATTAIN IT.
ALL RIGHT. ENOUGH TALK.
I'M SO HUNGRY!
YARRH!

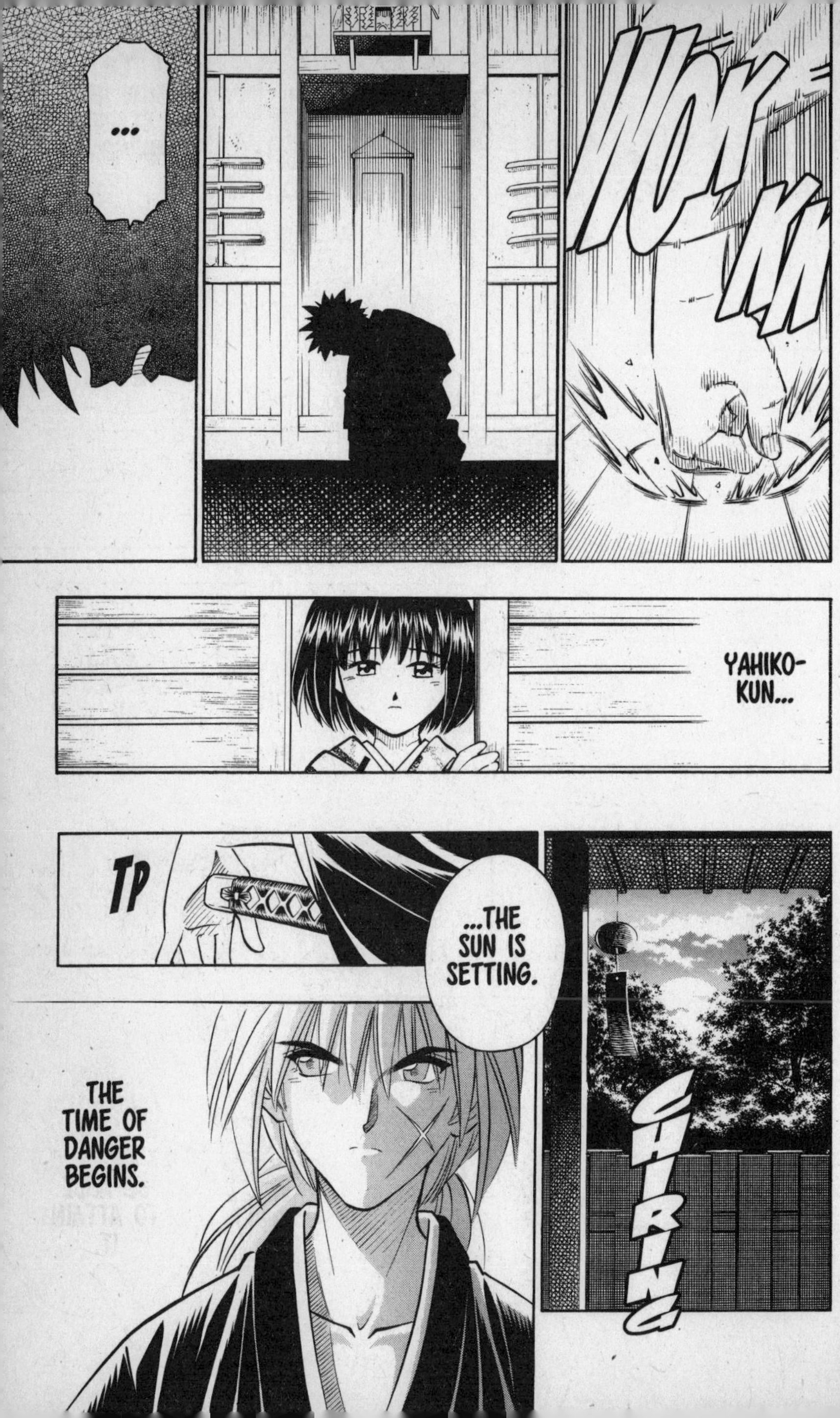
...
YAHIKO-KUN...
CHIRING
TP
...THE SUN IS SETTING.
THE TIME OF DANGER BEGINS.

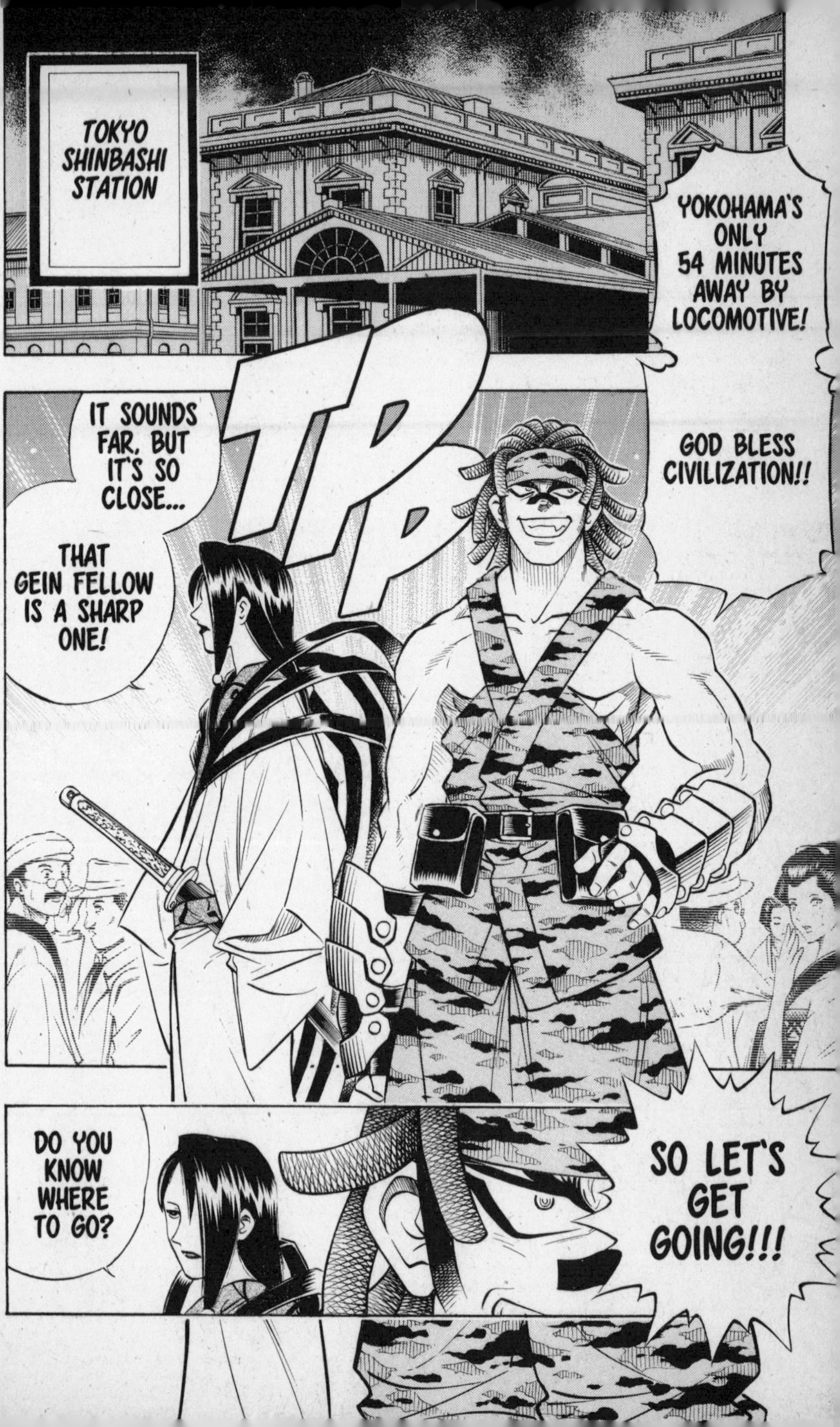

TOKYO SHINBASHI STATION
YOKOHAMA'S ONLY 54 MINUTES AWAY BY LOCOMOTIVE!
TP
GOD BLESS CIVILIZATION!!
IT SOUNDS FAR, BUT IT'S SO CLOSE...
THAT GEIN FELLOW IS A SHARP ONE!
SO LET'S GET GOING!!!
DO YOU KNOW WHERE TO GO?

READ THIS WAY

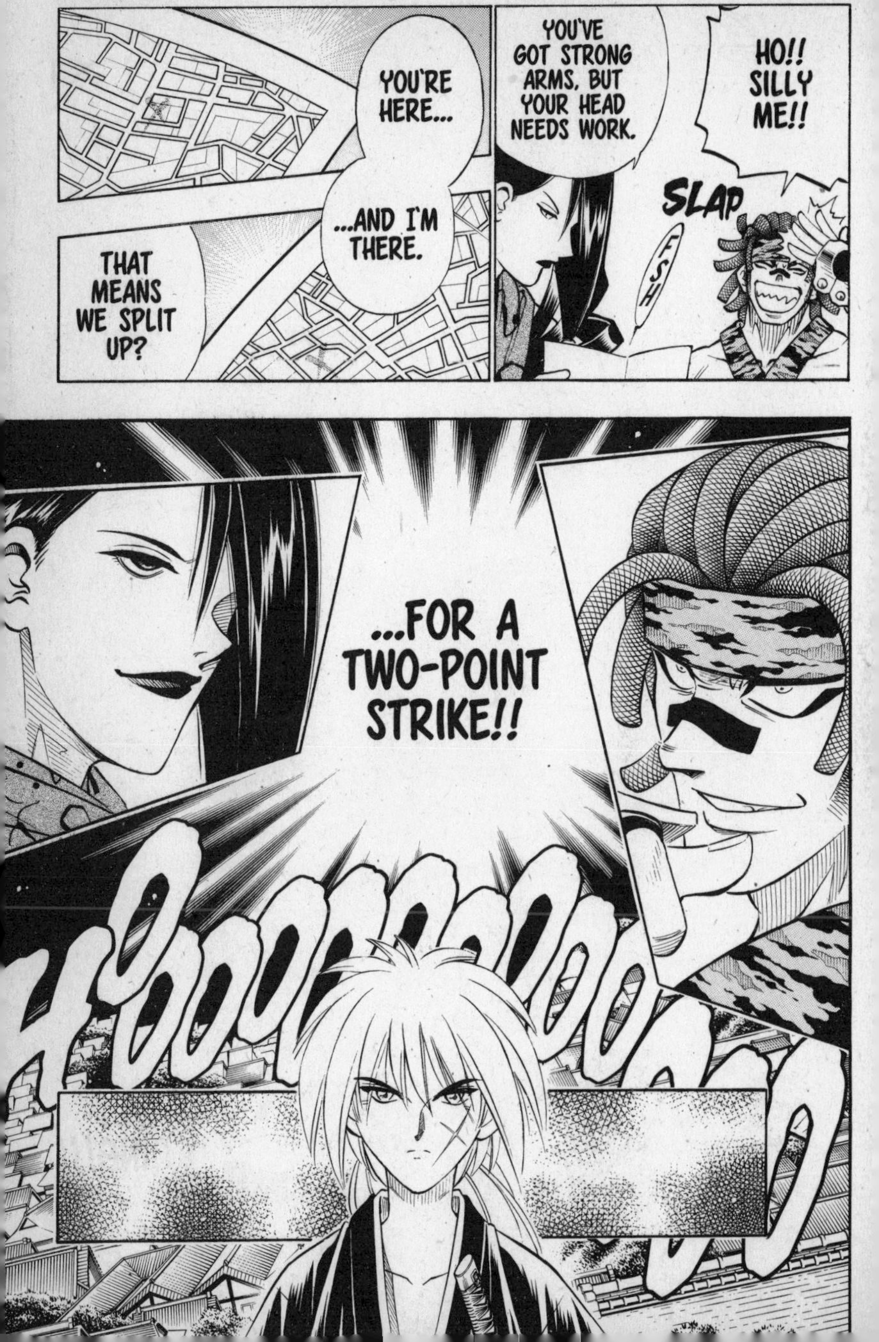
HO!! SILLY ME!!
SLAP
FSH
YOU'VE GOT STRONG ARMS, BUT YOUR HEAD NEEDS WORK.
YOU'RE HERE...
...AND I'M THERE.
THAT MEANS WE SPLIT UP?
...FOR A TWO-POINT STRIKE!!

Act 15—Twin Storms Blow!

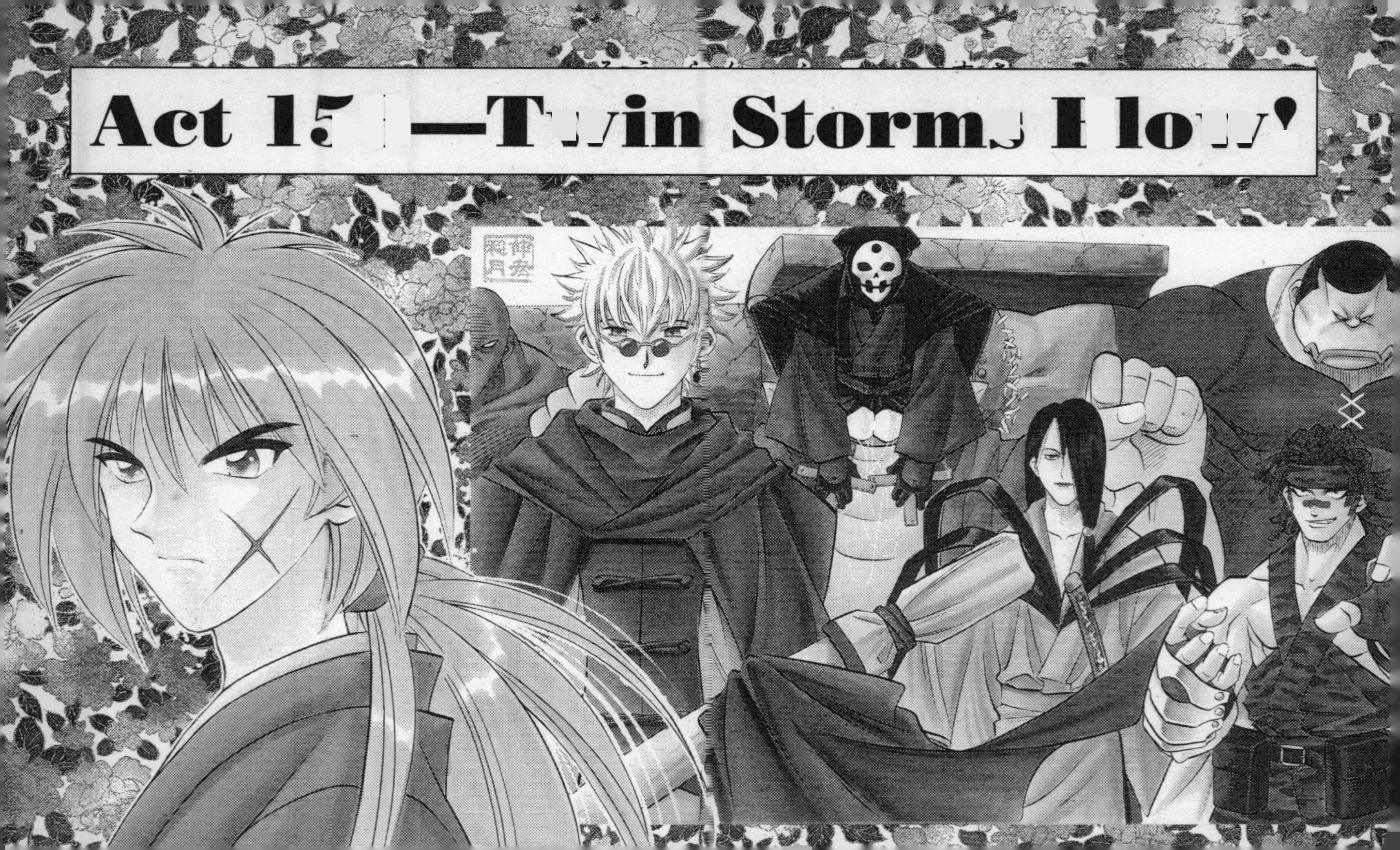

READ THIS WAY

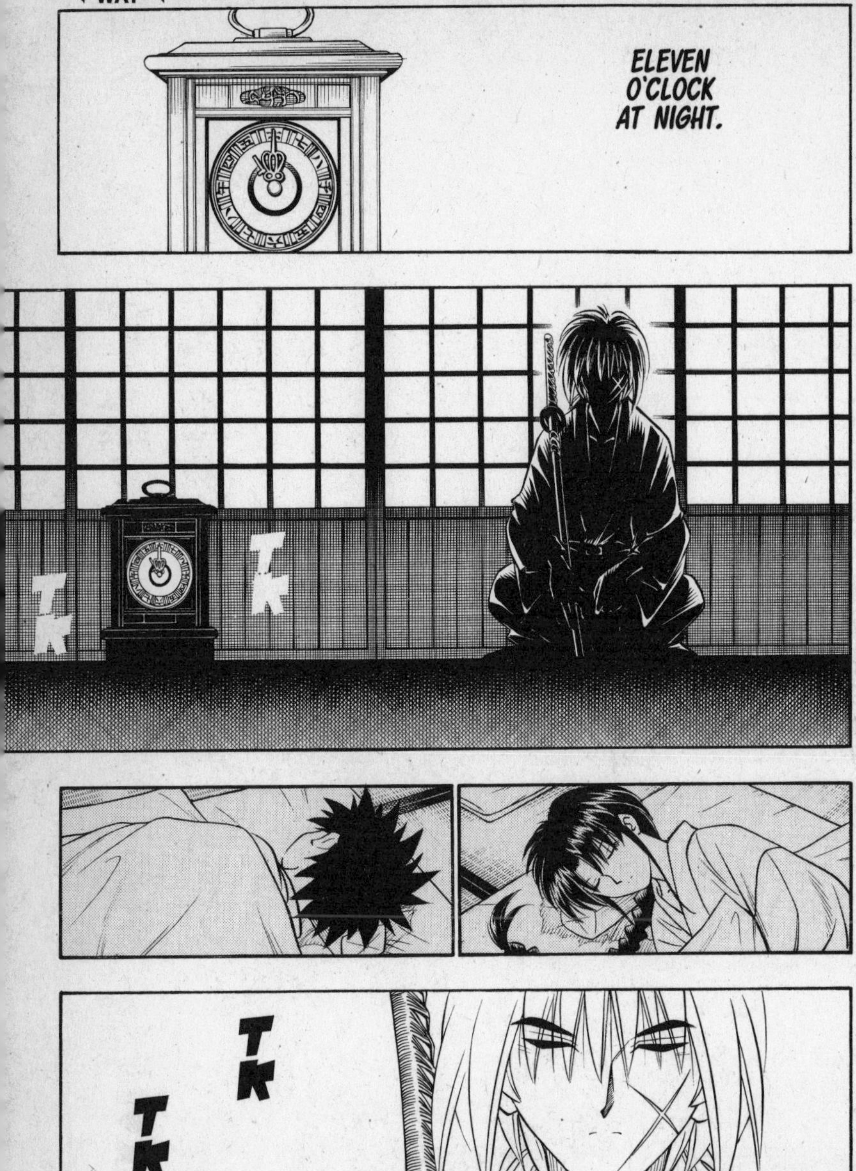
ELEVEN O'CLOCK AT NIGHT.
TK
TK
TK
TK

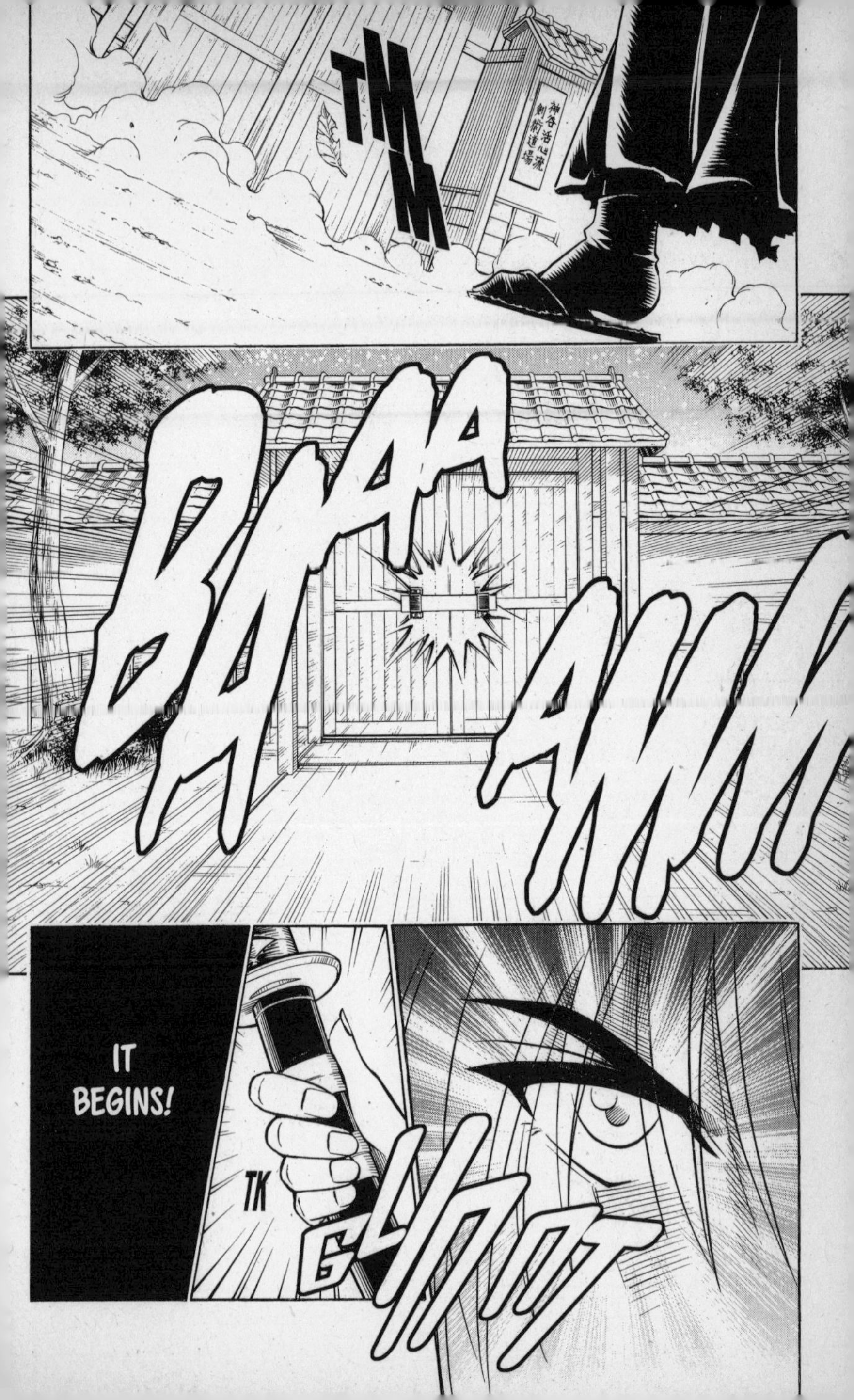
神谷活心流
剣術道場
TMM
BAAAAMM
IT BEGINS!
TK
GLINT

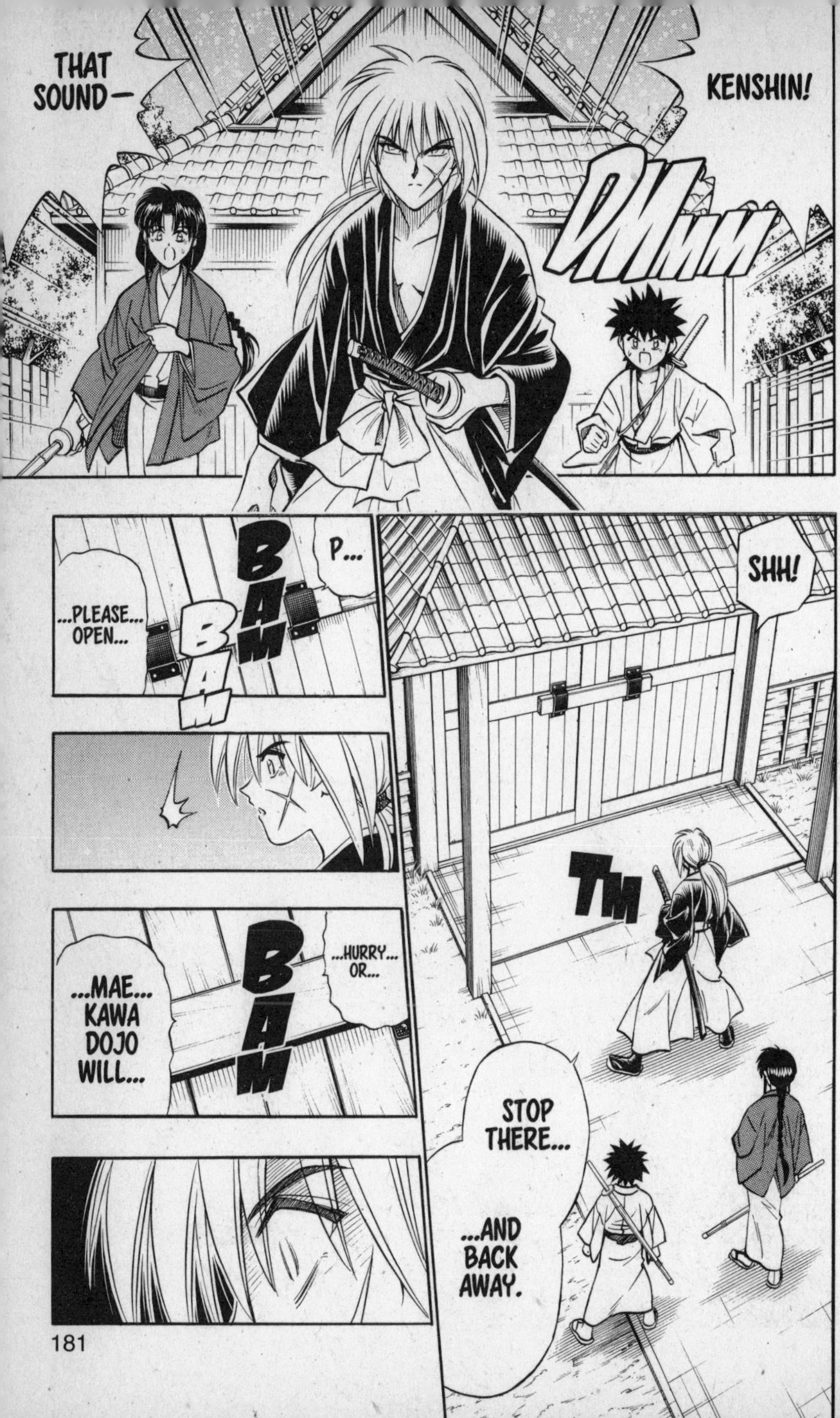
KENSHIN!
DMMMM
THAT SOUND—
SHH!
TM
STOP THERE...
...AND BACK AWAY.
P...
BAM
BAM
...PLEASE... OPEN...
...HURRY... OR...
BAM
...MAE... KAWA DOJO WILL...

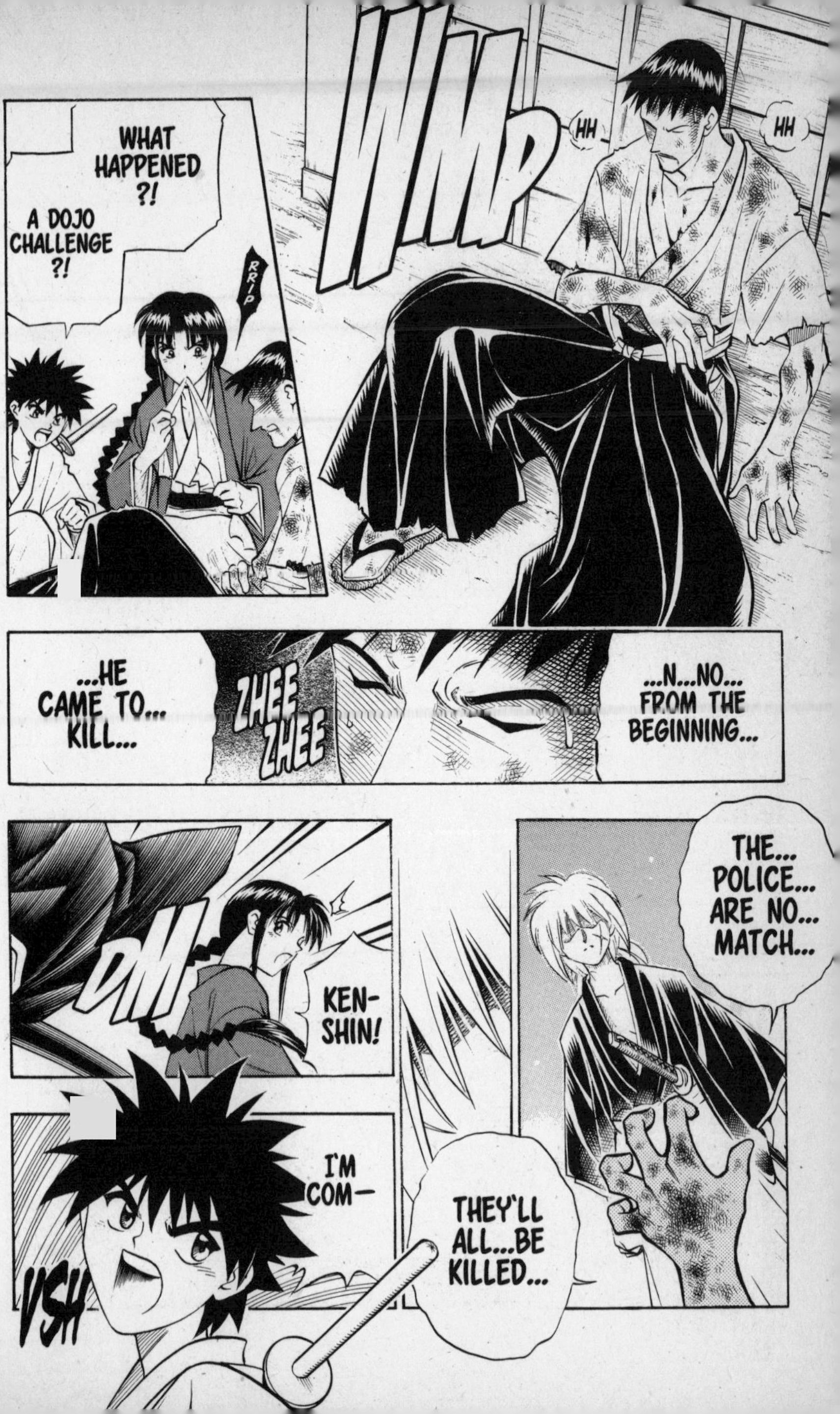
WHMP
HH
HH
WHAT HAPPENED?!
A DOJO CHALLENGE?!
RRIP
...N...NO... FROM THE BEGINNING...
ZHEE ZHEE
...HE CAME TO... KILL...
THE... POLICE... ARE NO... MATCH...
THEY'LL ALL...BE KILLED...
DM
KEN-SHIN!
I'M COM-
VSH

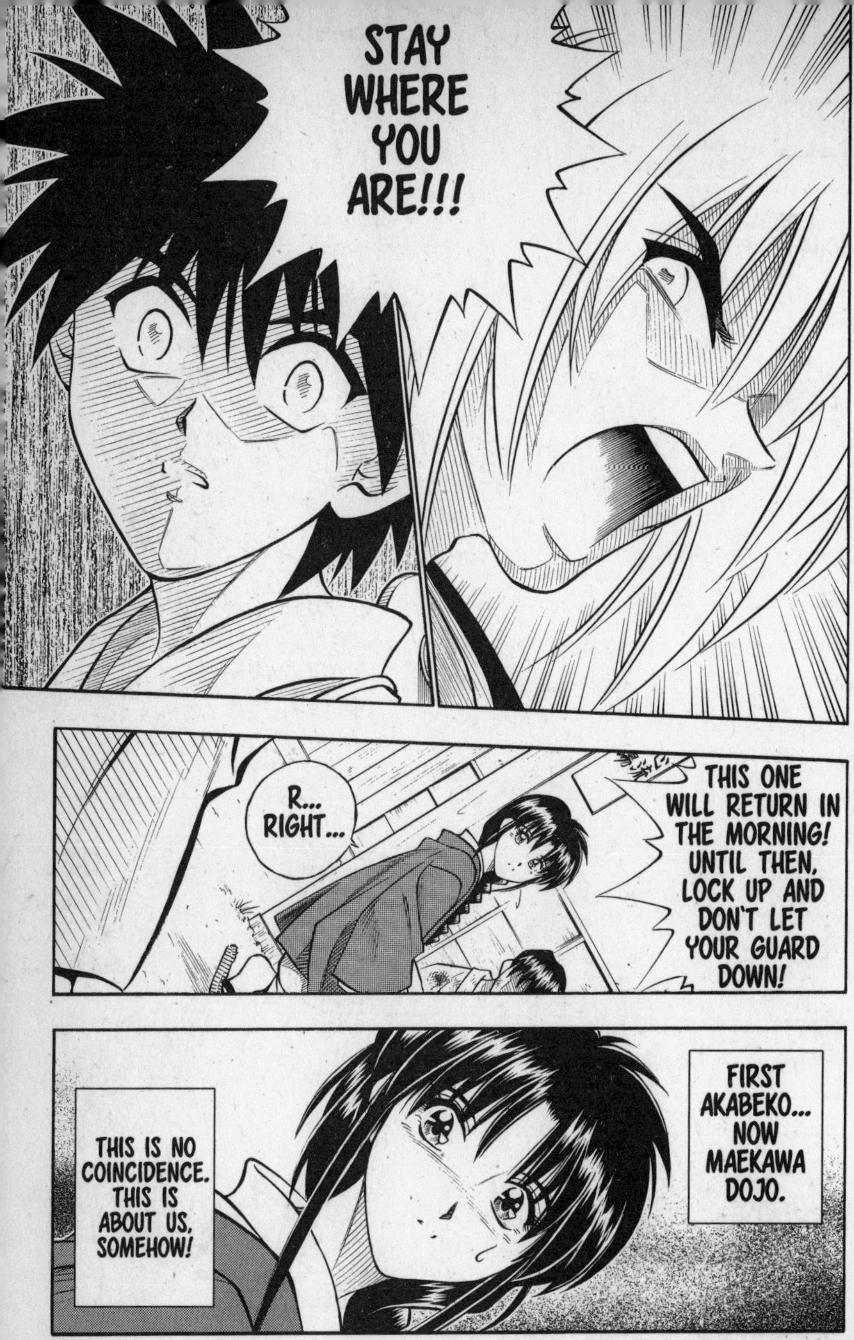
STAY WHERE YOU ARE!!!
THIS ONE WILL RETURN IN THE MORNING! UNTIL THEN, LOCK UP AND DON'T LET YOUR GUARD DOWN!
R... RIGHT...
FIRST AKABEKO... NOW MAEKAWA DOJO.
THIS IS NO COINCIDENCE. THIS IS ABOUT US, SOMEHOW!

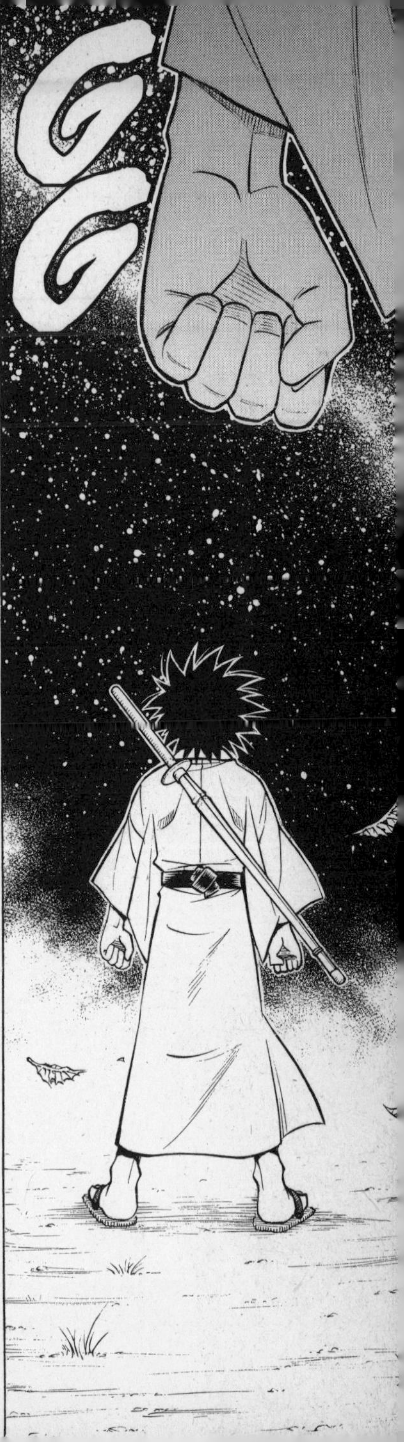
GGG

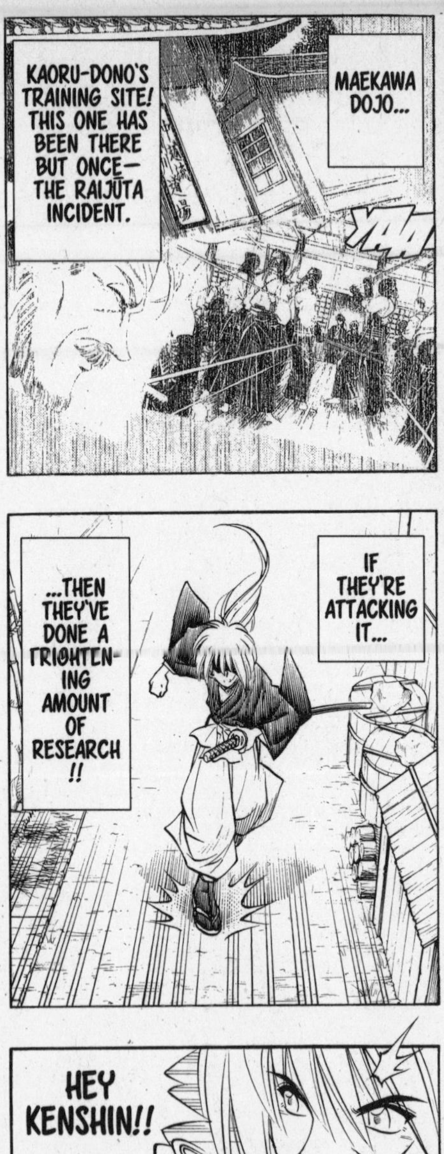
MAEKAWA DOJO...
KAORU-DONO'S TRAINING SITE! THIS ONE HAS BEEN THERE BUT ONCE— THE RAIJŪTA INCIDENT.
YAA
IF THEY'RE ATTACKING IT...
...THEN THEY'VE DONE A FRIGHTENING AMOUNT OF RESEARCH!!
HEY KENSHIN!!

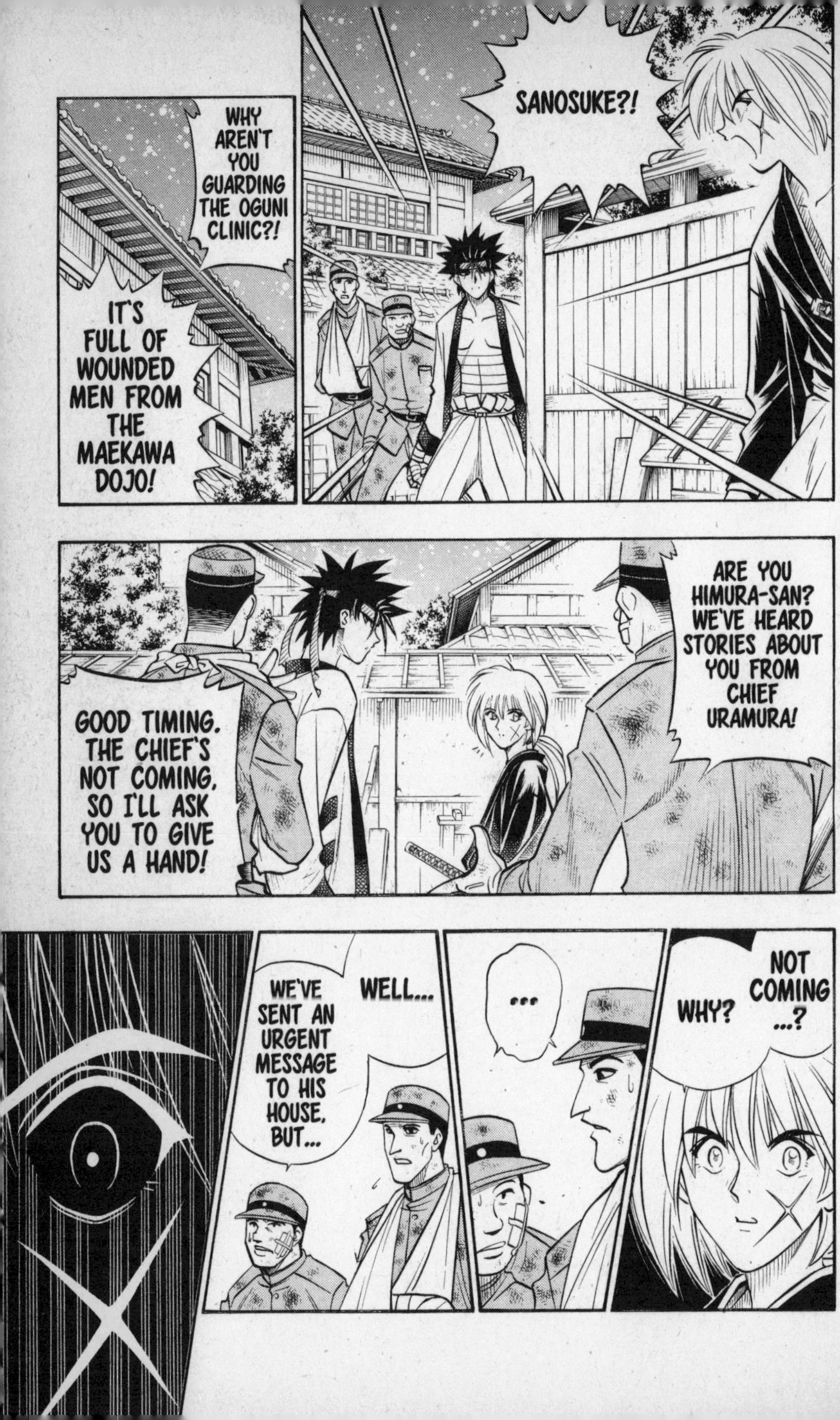
SANOSUKE?!
WHY AREN'T YOU GUARDING THE OGUNI CLINIC?!
IT'S FULL OF WOUNDED MEN FROM THE MAEKAWA DOJO!
ARE YOU HIMURA-SAN? WE'VE HEARD STORIES ABOUT YOU FROM CHIEF URAMURA!
GOOD TIMING. THE CHIEF'S NOT COMING, SO I'LL ASK YOU TO GIVE US A HAND!
NOT COMING ...?
WHY?
...
WELL...
WE'VE SENT AN URGENT MESSAGE TO HIS HOUSE, BUT...

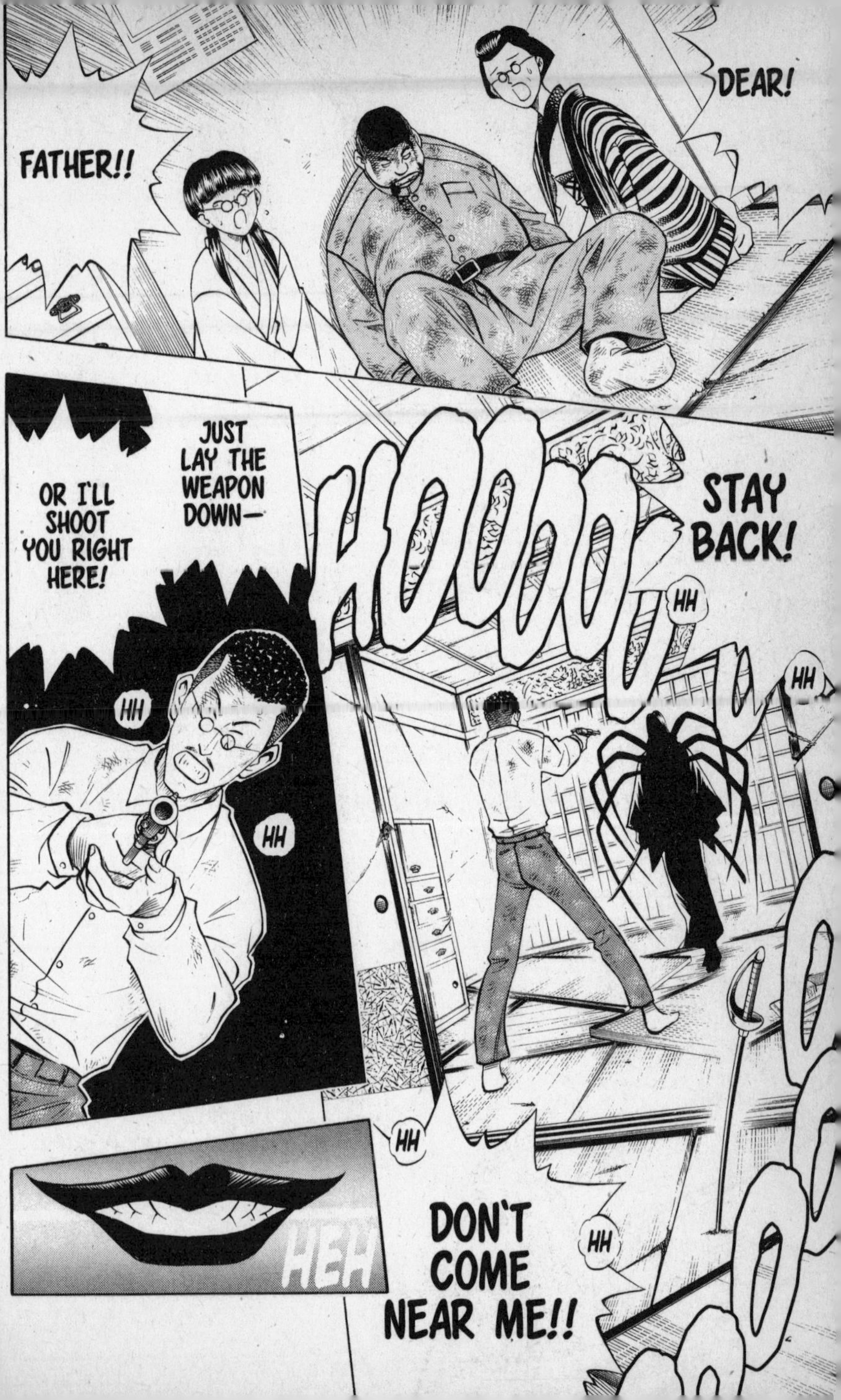
DEAR!
FATHER!!
HOOOOO
STAY BACK!
HH
HH
HH
DON'T COME NEAR ME!!
JUST LAY THE WEAPON DOWN—
OR I'LL SHOOT YOU RIGHT HERE!
HH
HH
HEH

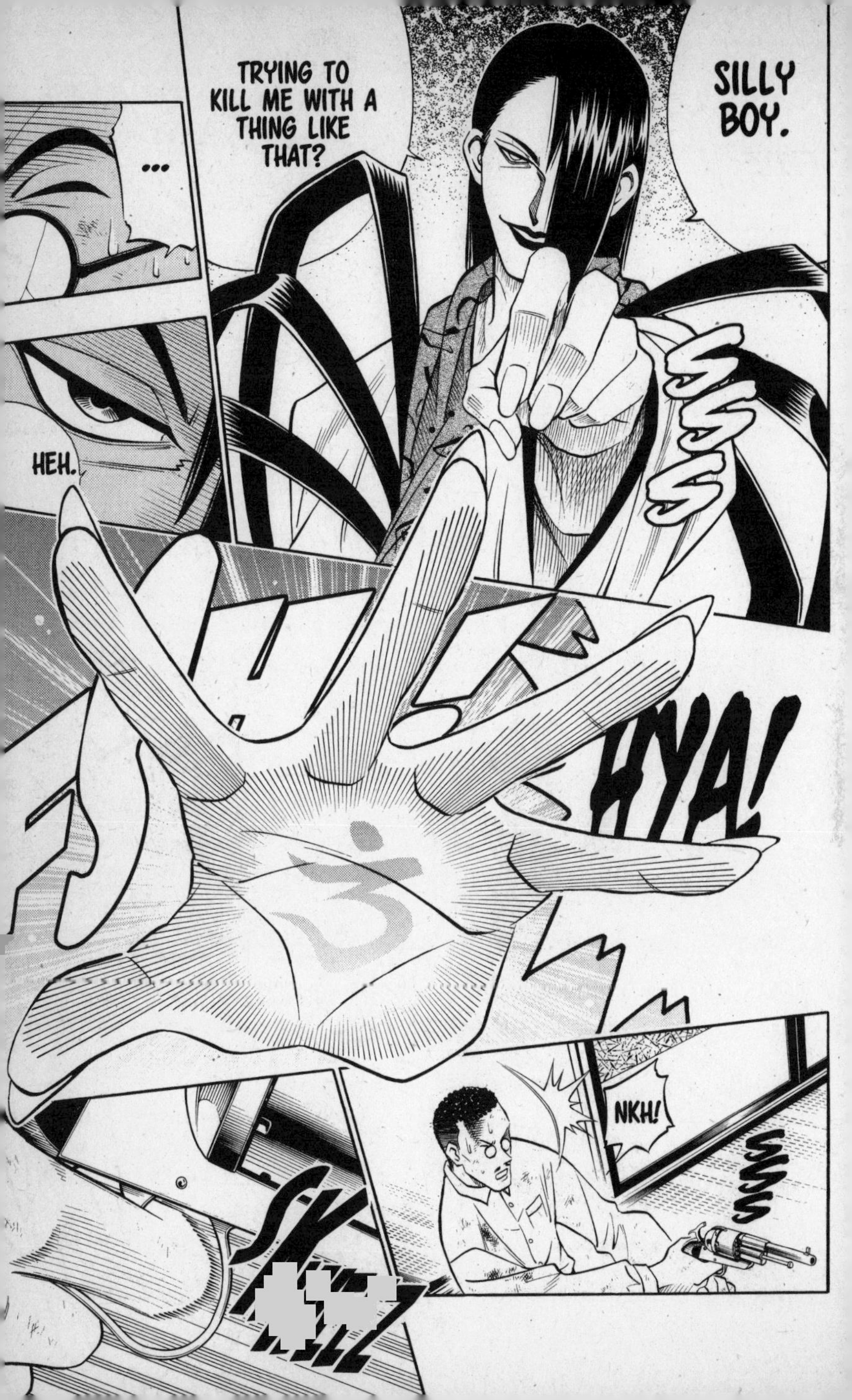
SILLY BOY.
TRYING TO KILL ME WITH A THING LIKE THAT?
SSSS
...
HEH.
HYA!
NKH!
SSSS

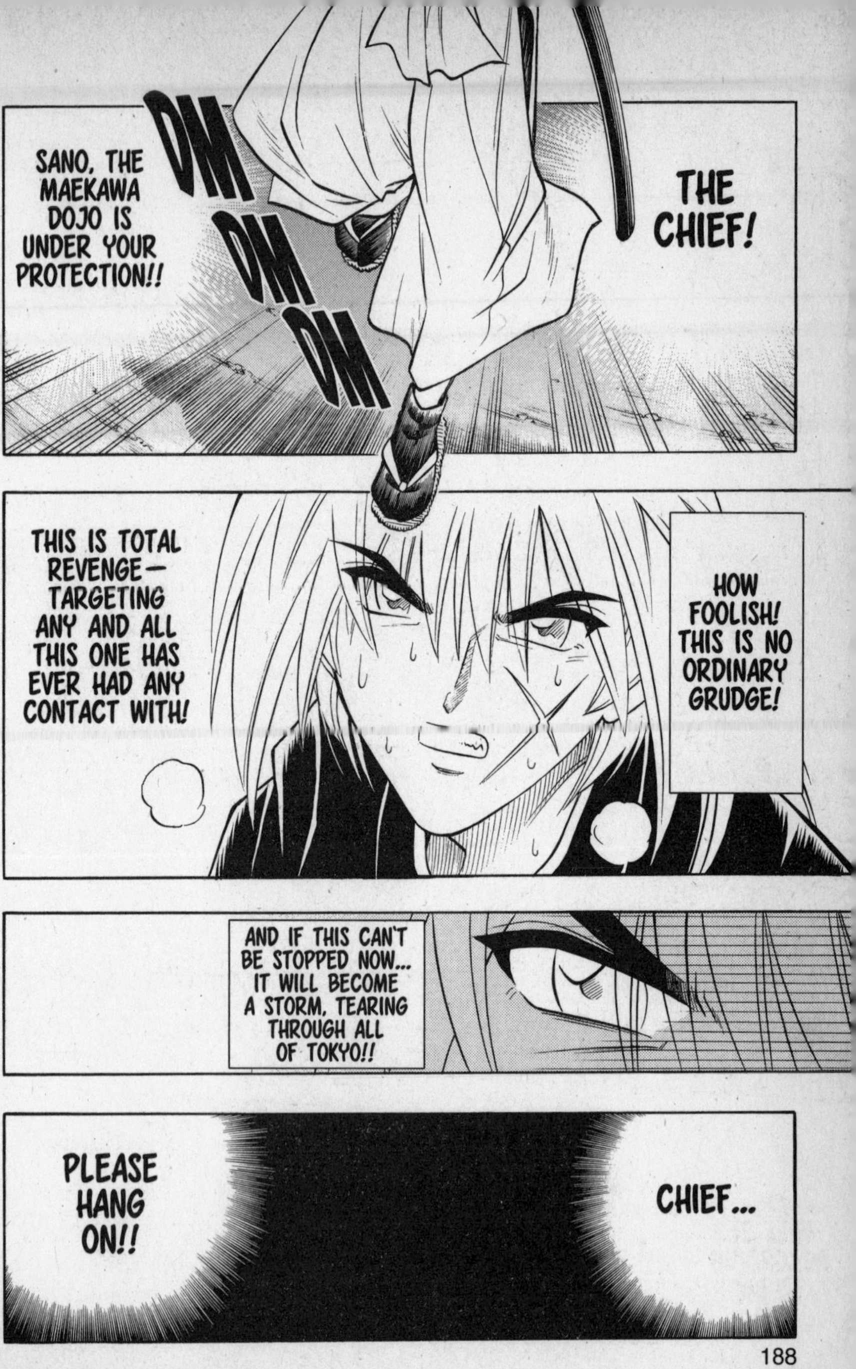
THE CHIEF!
DM DM DM
SANO, THE MAEKAWA DOJO IS UNDER YOUR PROTECTION!!
HOW FOOLISH! THIS IS NO ORDINARY GRUDGE!
THIS IS TOTAL REVENGE—TARGETING ANY AND ALL THIS ONE HAS EVER HAD ANY CONTACT WITH!
AND IF THIS CAN'T BE STOPPED NOW... IT WILL BECOME A STORM, TEARING THROUGH ALL OF TOKYO!!
CHIEF...
PLEASE HANG ON!!

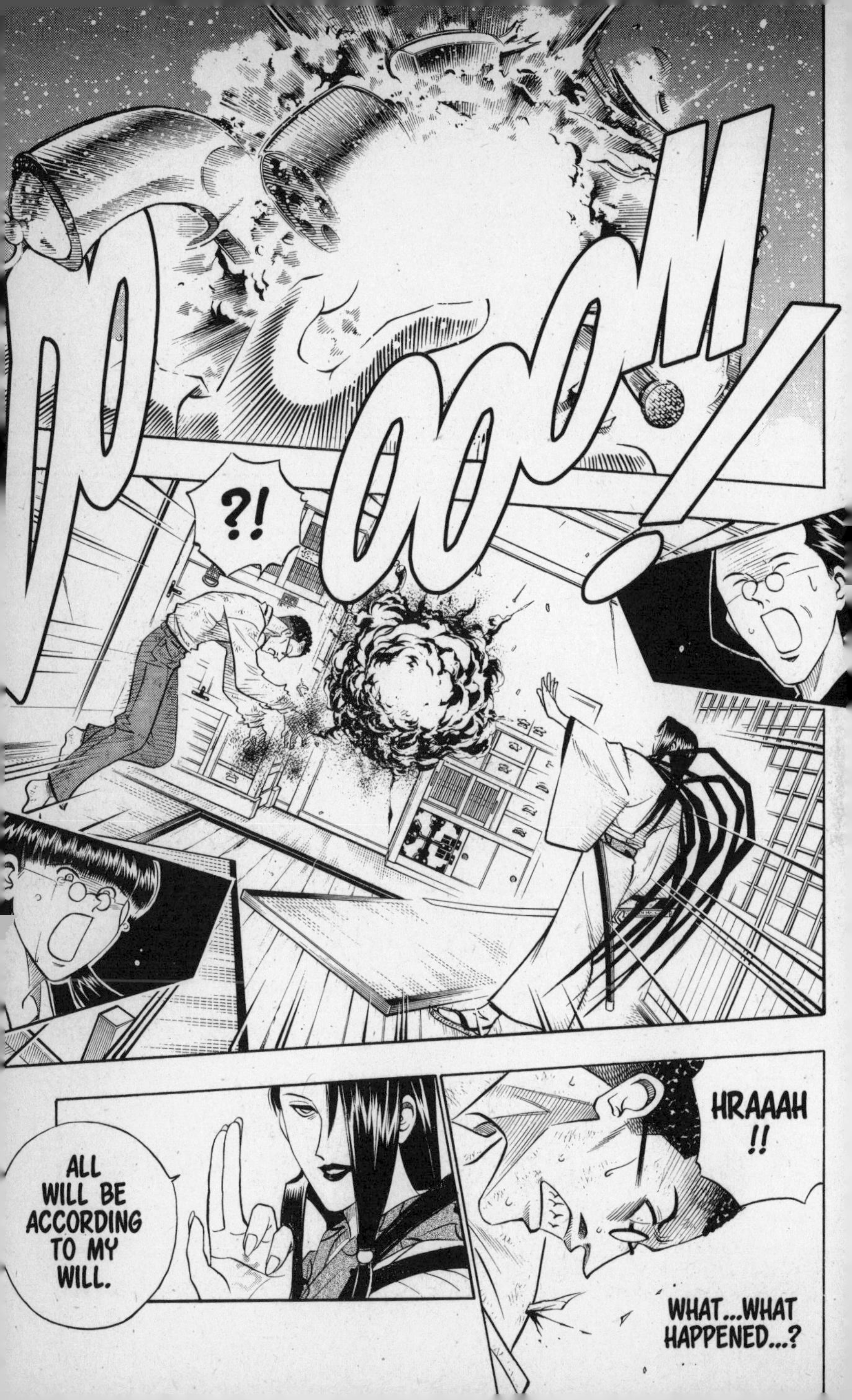
DOOOM!!
?!
HRAAAH!!
WHAT...WHAT HAPPENED...?
ALL WILL BE ACCORDING TO MY WILL.

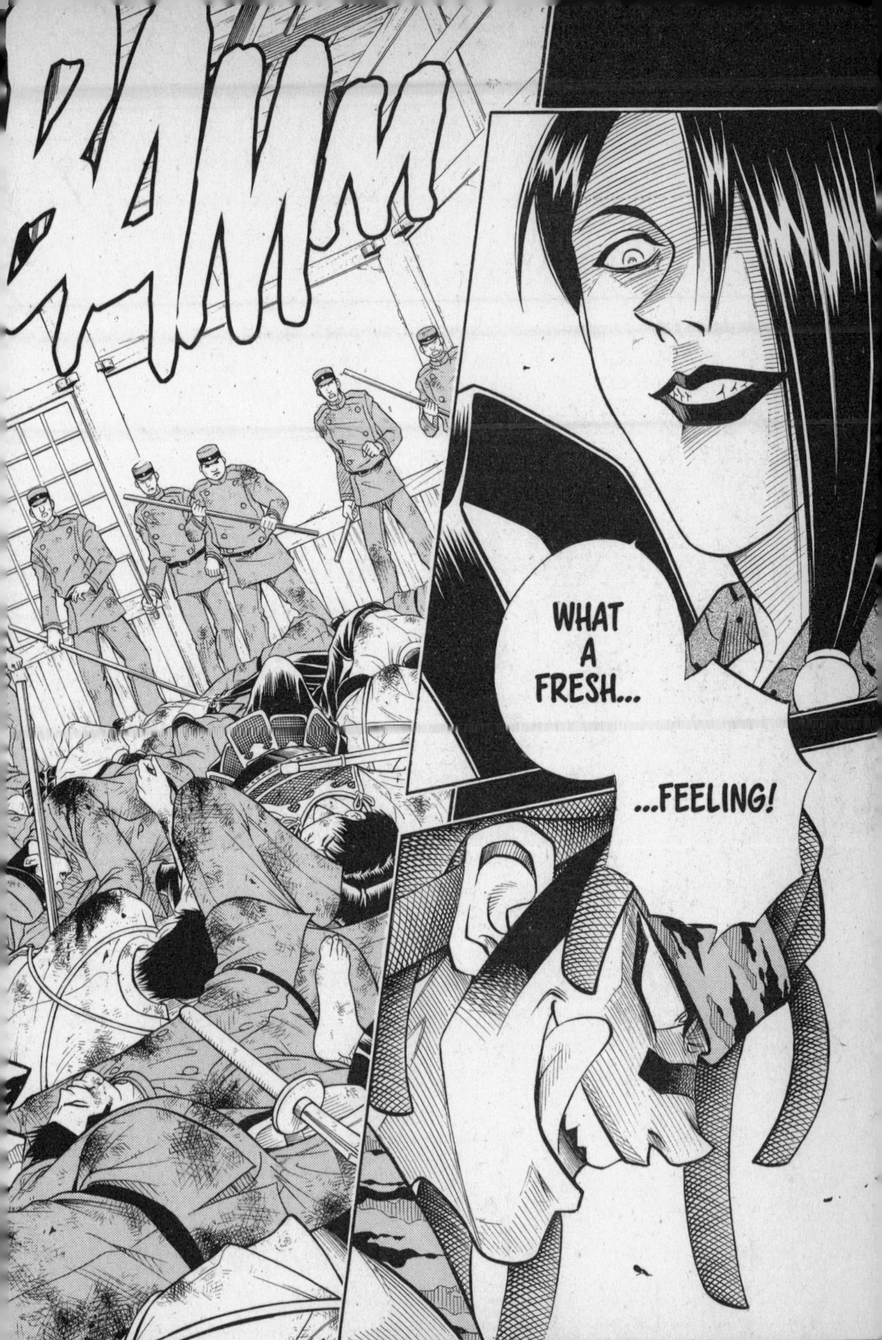
WHAT A FRESH...
...FEELING!

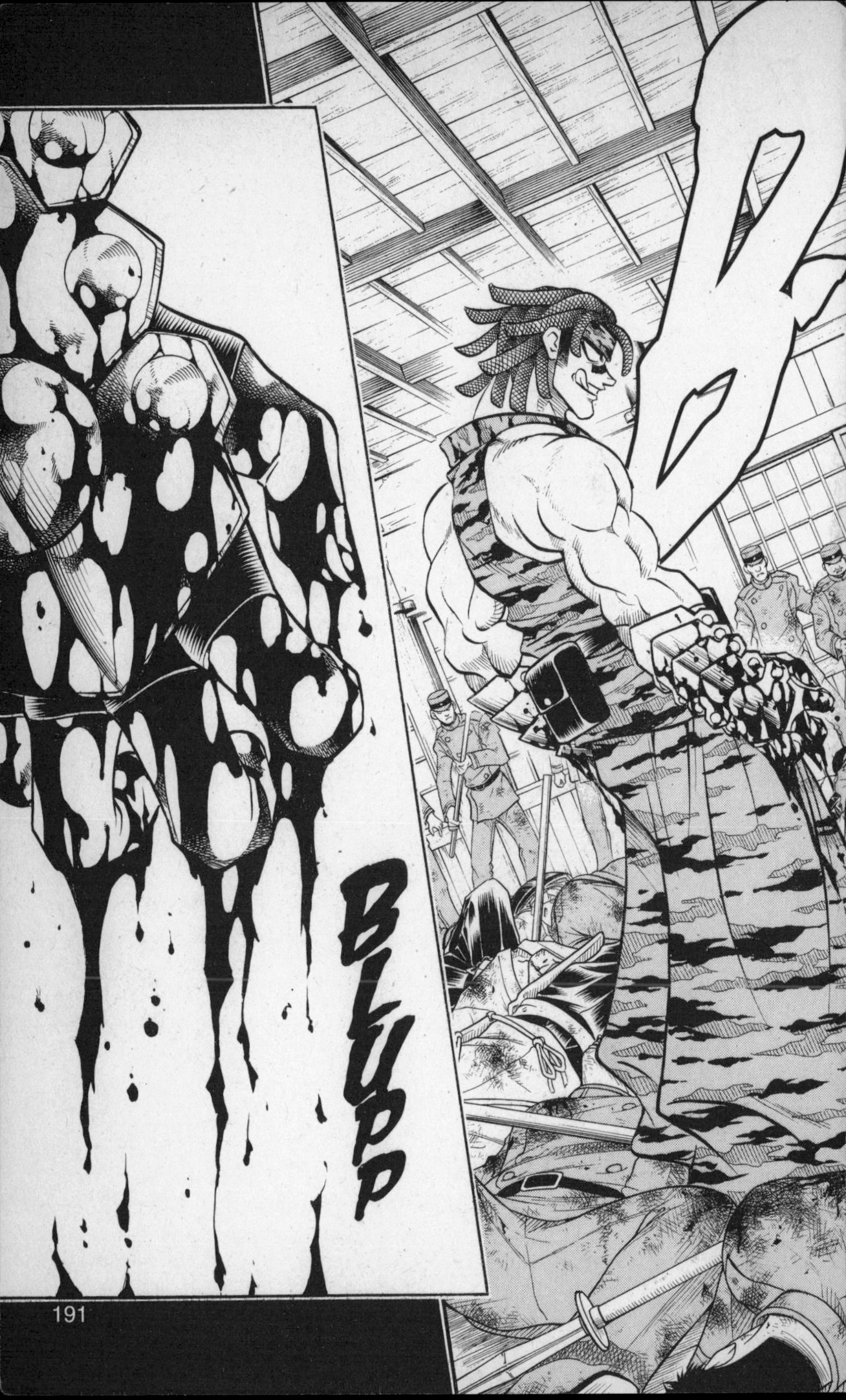
BLUPP

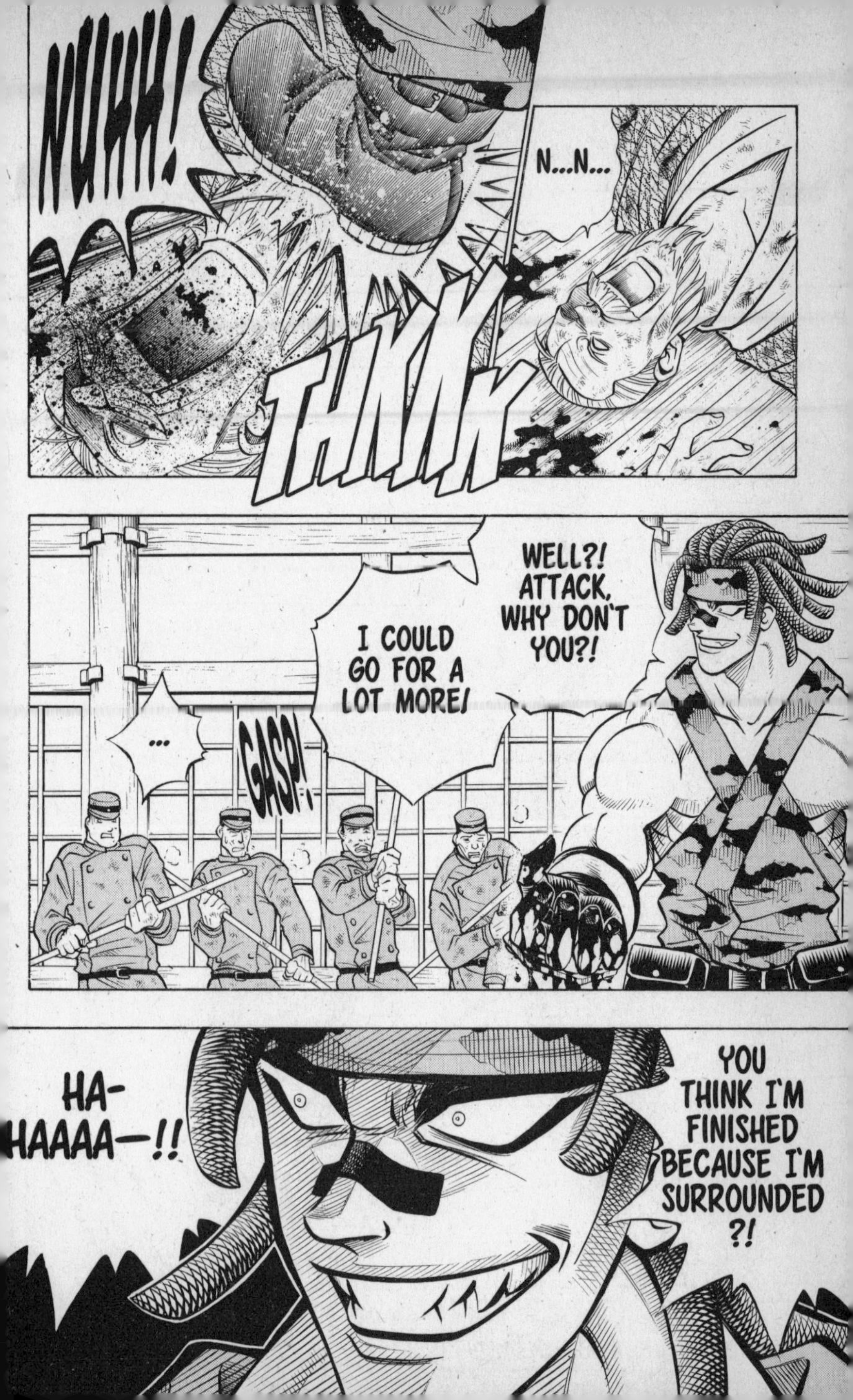
N...N...
NUHH!
THWAK
WELL?! ATTACK, WHY DON'T YOU?!
I COULD GO FOR A LOT MORE!
GASP!
...
YOU THINK I'M FINISHED BECAUSE I'M SURROUNDED?!
HA-HAAAA—!!

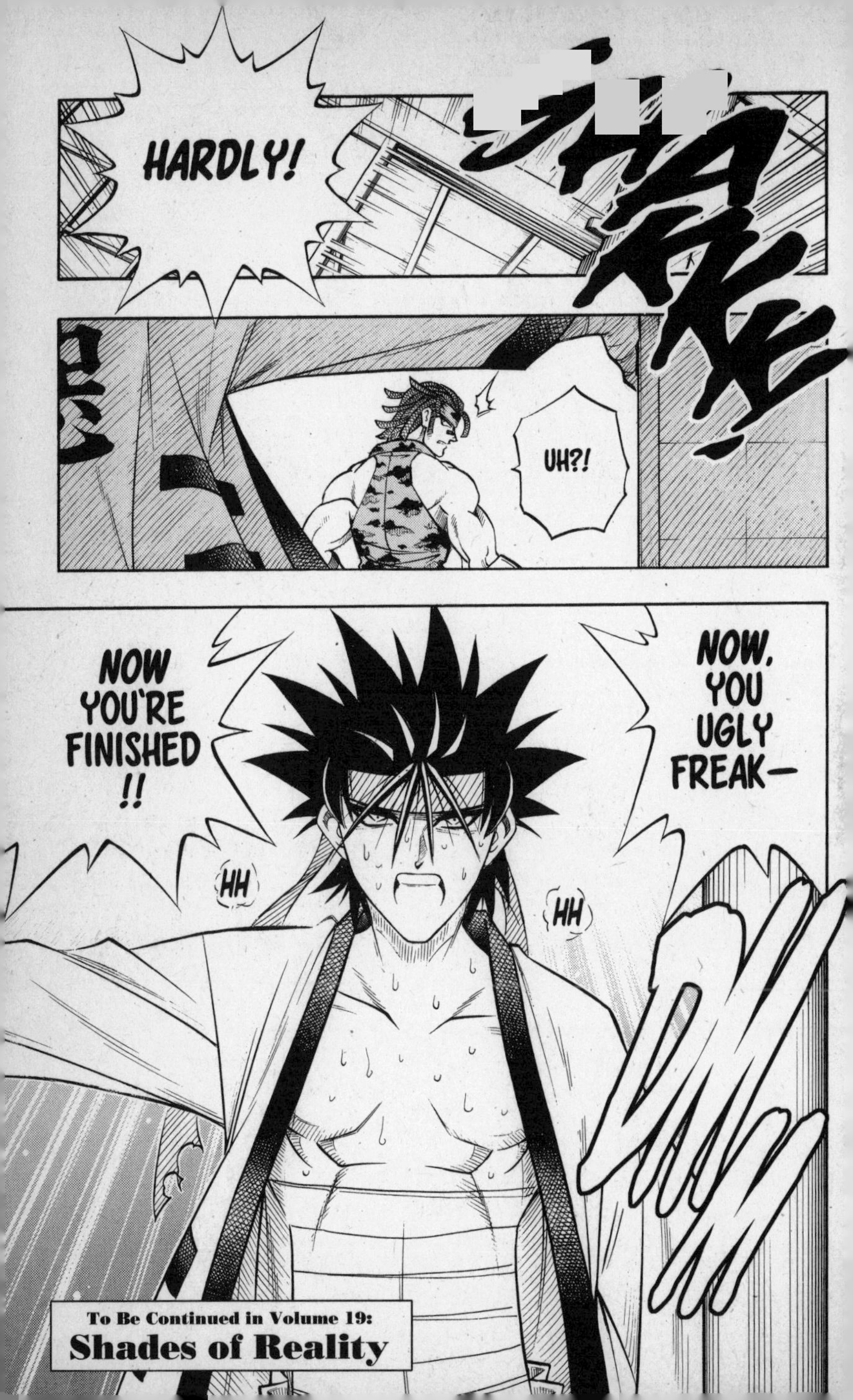
HARDLY!
UH?!
NOW, YOU UGLY FREAK—
NOW YOU'RE FINISHED !!
HH
HH
To Be Continued in Volume 19:
Shades of Reality

GLOSSARY of the RESTORATION

A brief guide to select Japanese terms used in **Rurouni Kenshin**. *Note that, both here and within the story itself, all names are Japanese style—i.e., last or "family" name first, with personal or "given" name following. This is both because* **Kenshin** *is a "period" story, as well as to decrease confusion—if we were to take the example of Kenshin's* sakabatô *and "reverse" the format of the historically established assassin-name "Hitokiri Battôsai," for example, it would make little sense to then call him "Battôsai Himura."*

hachimaki
Once worn as a charm against evil spirits (as in the series *Naruto*), **hachimaki**, or traditional Japanese headbands, are worn more contemporarily as mental stimulation—a way to express one's determination, or to put one's self "in the mood"

Himura Kenshin
Kenshin's "real" name, revealed to Kaoru only at her urging

Hiten Mitsurugi-ryû
Kenshin's sword technique, used more for defense than offense. An "ancient style that pits one against many," it requires exceptional speed and agility to master.

hitokiri
An assassin. Famous swordsmen of the period were sometimes thus known to adopt "professional" names—**Kawakami Gensai**, for example, was also known as "Hitokiri Gensai."

Ishin Shishi
Loyalist or pro-Imperialist **patriots** who fought to restore the Emperor to his ancient seat of power

Juppongatana
Written with the characters for "ten" and "swords," Shishio's **Juppongatana** are literally that—the ten generals or "swords" he plans to use in his over-throw of Japan

Kawakami Gensai
Real-life, historical inspiration for the character of **Himura Kenshin**

Bakumatsu
Final, chaotic days of the Tokugawa regime

Boshin War
Civil war of 1868-69 between the new government and the **Tokugawa Bakufu**. The anti-*Bakufu*, pro-Imperial side (the Imperial Army) won, easily defeating the Tokugawa supporters.

-chan
Honorific. Can be used either as a diminutive (e.g., with a small child—"Little Hanako or Kentarô"), or with those who are grown, to indicate affection ("My dear...").

"Day of the Dead"
An annual Buddhist event set aside for remembrance of the dead, the Japanese festival of Obon (sometimes known as the *"Day of the Dead"*) is currently one of the country's three major holiday seasons and takes place either in the middle of July or August, depending on the part of the country

-dono
Honorific. Even more respectful than *-san*; the effect in modern-day Japanese conversation would be along the lines of "Milord So-and-So." As used by Kenshin, it indicates both respect and humility.

Edo
Capital city of the **Tokugawa Bakufu**; renamed **Tokyo** ("Eastern Capital") after the Meiji Restoration

patriots
Another term for *Ishin Shishi*...and, when used by Sano, not a flattering one

rurouni
Wanderer, vagabond

sakabatô
Reversed-edge sword (the dull edge on the side the sharp should be, and vice versa); carried by Kenshin as a symbol of his resolution never to kill again

-sama
Honorific. The respectful equivalent of *-san*, *-sama* is used primarily in addressing persons of much higher rank than one's self...or, in a romantic sense, in addressing those upon whom one is crushing, wicked hard.

-san
Honorific. Carries the meaning of "Mr.," "Ms.," "Miss," etc., but used more extensively in Japanese than its English equivalent (note that even an enemy may be addressed as "*-san*").

shôgun
Feudal military ruler of Japan

shôgunate
See *Tokugawa Bakufu*

Toba Fushimi, Battle at
Battle near *Kyoto* between the forces of the new, imperial government and the fallen *shôgunate*. Ending with an imperial victory, it was the first battle of the *Boshin War*.

Tokugawa Bakufu
Military feudal government which dominated Japan from 1603 to 1867

Tokyo
The renaming of "*Edo*" to "*Tokyo*" is a marker of the start of the *Meiji Restoration*

Kinkaku/Ginkaku Temples
Subject of the famous novel by Yukio Mishima, the *Kinkaku-ji* or "Temple of the Golden Pavilion" was founded as a retirement home for a former *shôgun* and later converted to a Zen temple. *Ginkaku Temple*, which was founded by another member of the retired *shôgun*'s family, was built in the late 15th century and incorporates variations of designs from the *Kinkaku Temple*.

kodachi
Medium-length sword, shorter than the *katana* but longer than the *wakizashi*. Its easy maneuverability also makes for higher defensive capability.

-kun
Honorific. Used in the modern day among male students, or those who grew up together, but another usage—the one you're more likely to find in *Rurouni Kenshin*—is the "superior-to-inferior" form, intended as a way to emphasize a difference in status or rank, as well as to indicate familiarity or affection.

Kyoto
Home of the Emperor and imperial court from A.D. 794 until shortly after the *Meiji Restoration* in 1868

loyalists
Those who supported the return of the Emperor to power; *Ishin Shishi*

Meiji Restoration
1853-1868; culminated in the collapse of the *Tokugawa Bakufu* and the restoration of imperial rule. So called after Emperor Meiji, whose chosen name was written with the characters for "culture and enlightenment."

Mt. Hiei
Founded more than 1,200 years ago, the temple atop Mt. Hiei or *Hieizan* was built to protect Kyoto from evil spirits. Because police were barred from entering temple grounds, criminals began to gather in the name of "religious enlightenment." It is no coincidence, therefore, that Watsuki decided to set madman Shishio Makoto's lair there....

Oniwabanshû
Elite group of *onmitsu* or "spies" of the *Edo* period, also known as *ninja* or *shinobi*

IN THE NEXT VOLUME...

It began with a sin, committed by Kenshin, back during his bloody days as *hitokiri* or a government-sanctioned slayer of men. Although stopping most of the assassins who still come seeking revenge should be easy enough, what of the innocent? For once there was *another* love in Kenshin's life, one which—given his nature—must by definition have been tragic. Can Kenshin escape the shades of his past, and find the will to fight for the real world—for the living—for reality?!

Available in October 2005

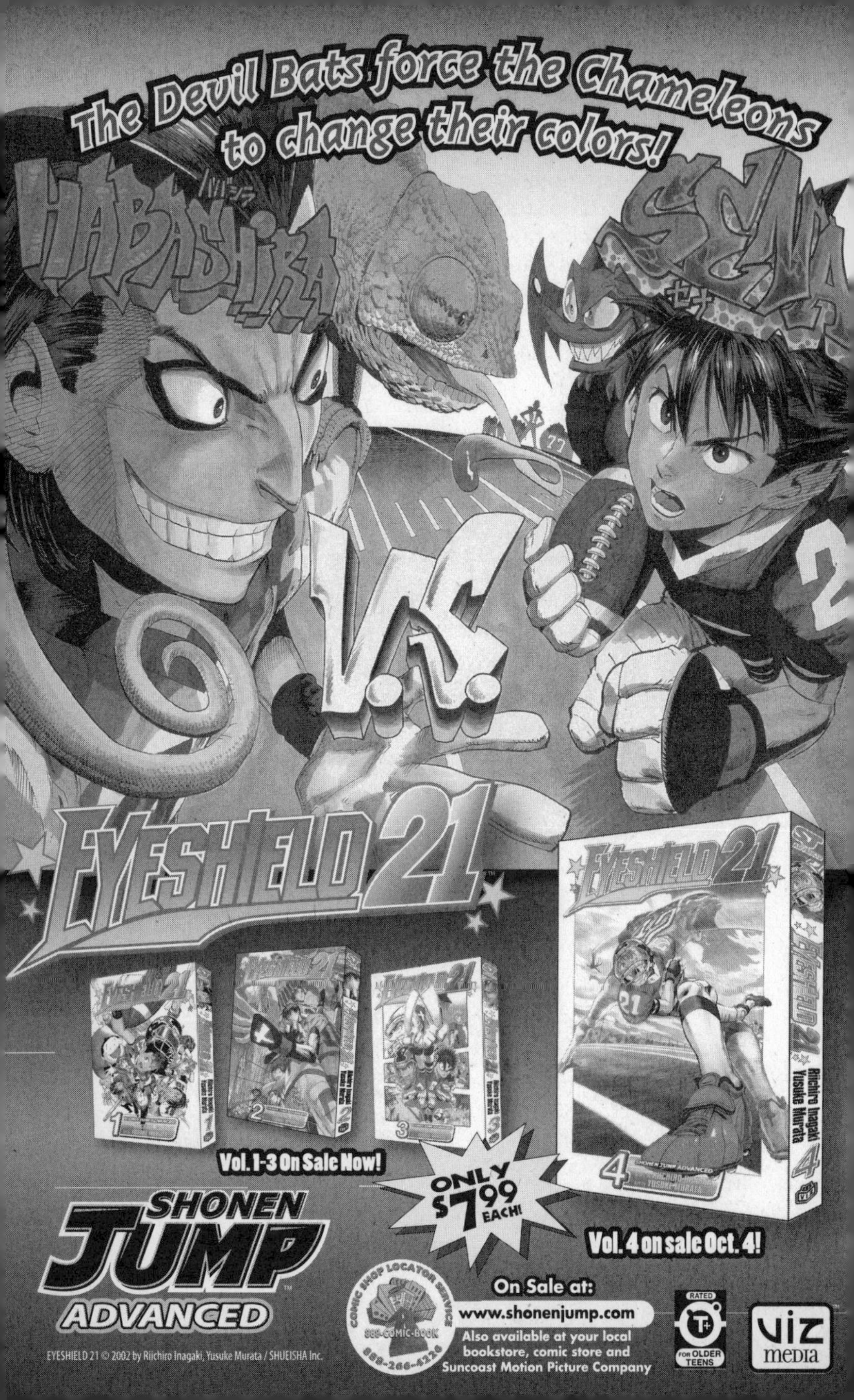
The Devil Bats force the Chameleons to change their colors!
HABASHIRA
SENA
V.S.
EYESHIELD 21™
Vol. 1-3 On Sale Now!
ONLY $7.99 EACH!
Vol. 4 on sale Oct. 4!
SHONEN JUMP™ ADVANCED
COMIC SHOP LOCATOR SERVICE
888-COMIC-BOOK
888-266-4226
On Sale at:
www.shonenjump.com
Also available at your local bookstore, comic store and Suncoast Motion Picture Company
RATED T+ FOR OLDER TEENS
VIZ media
EYESHIELD 21 © 2002 by Riichiro Inagaki, Yusuke Murata / SHUEISHA Inc.

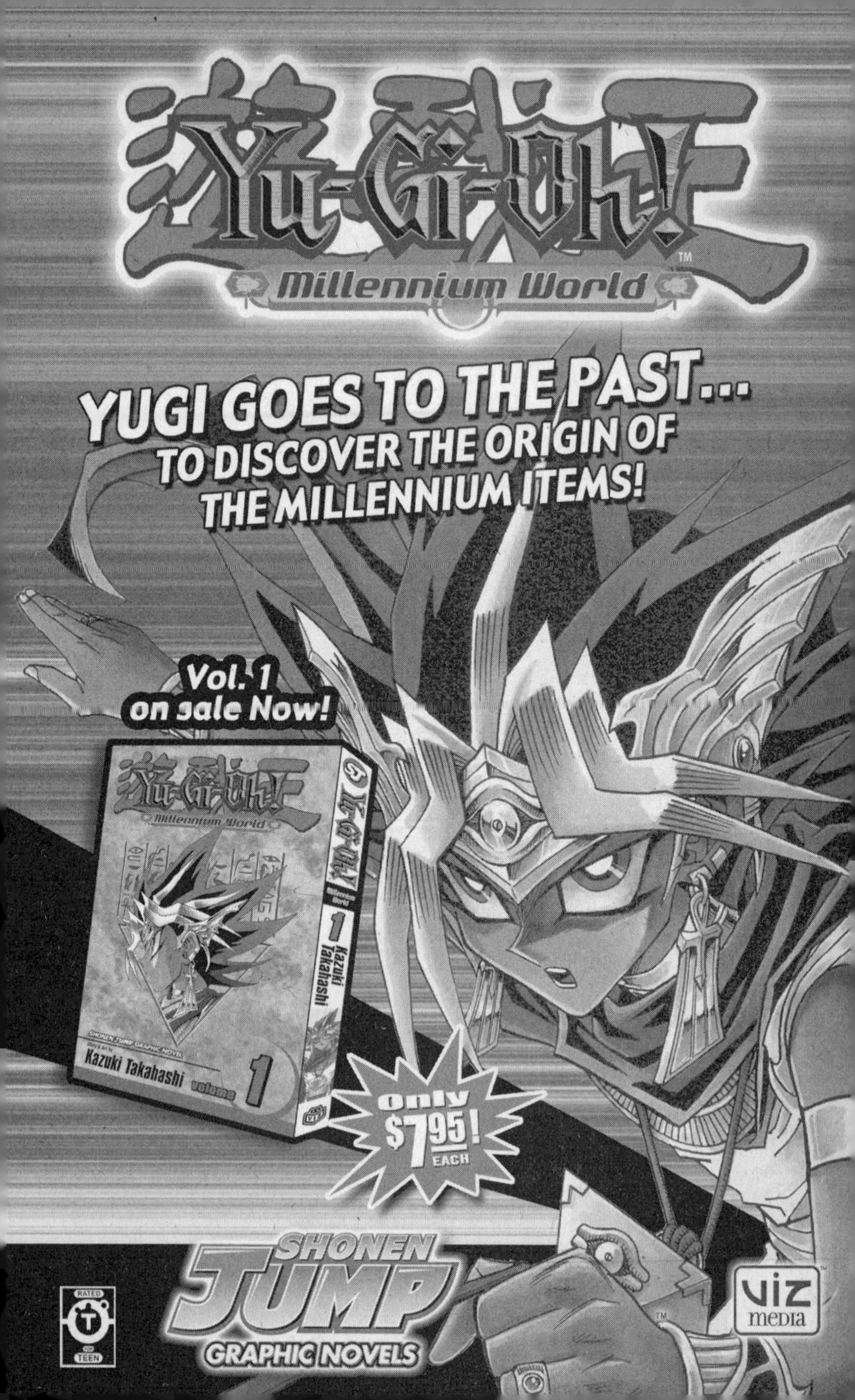

YU-GI-OH!
Millennium World
YUGI GOES TO THE PAST...
TO DISCOVER THE ORIGIN OF THE MILLENNIUM ITEMS!
Vol. 1 on sale Now!
Kazuki Takahashi
volume 1
Only $7.95! EACH
SHONEN JUMP GRAPHIC NOVELS
RATED T TEEN
viz media

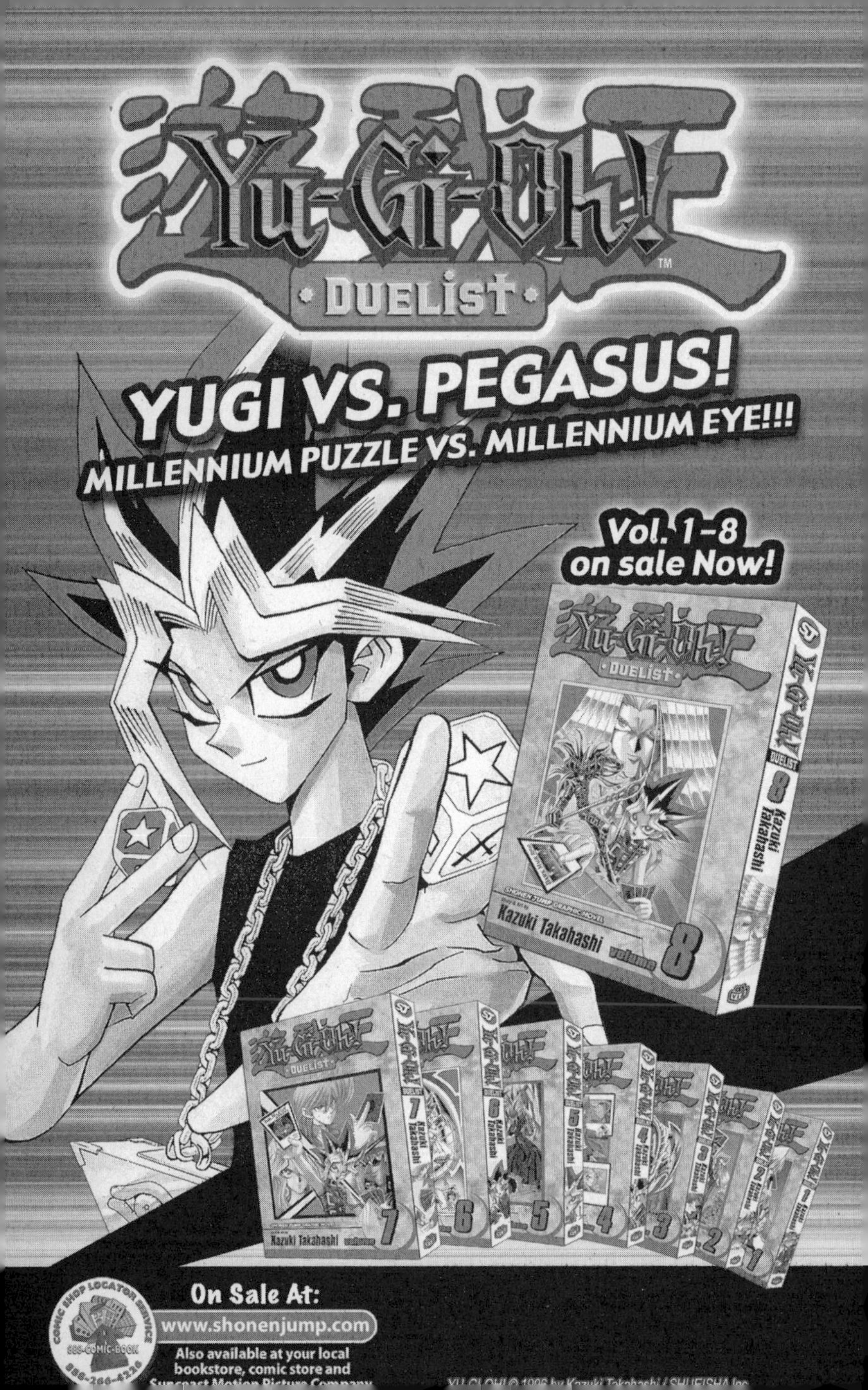
YU-GI-OH!™
DUELIST
YUGI VS. PEGASUS!
MILLENNIUM PUZZLE VS. MILLENNIUM EYE!!!
Vol. 1-8
on sale Now!
Kazuki Takahashi
volume 8
On Sale At:
www.shonenjump.com
Also available at your local bookstore, comic store and
COMIC SHOP LOCATOR SERVICE
888-COMIC-BOOK

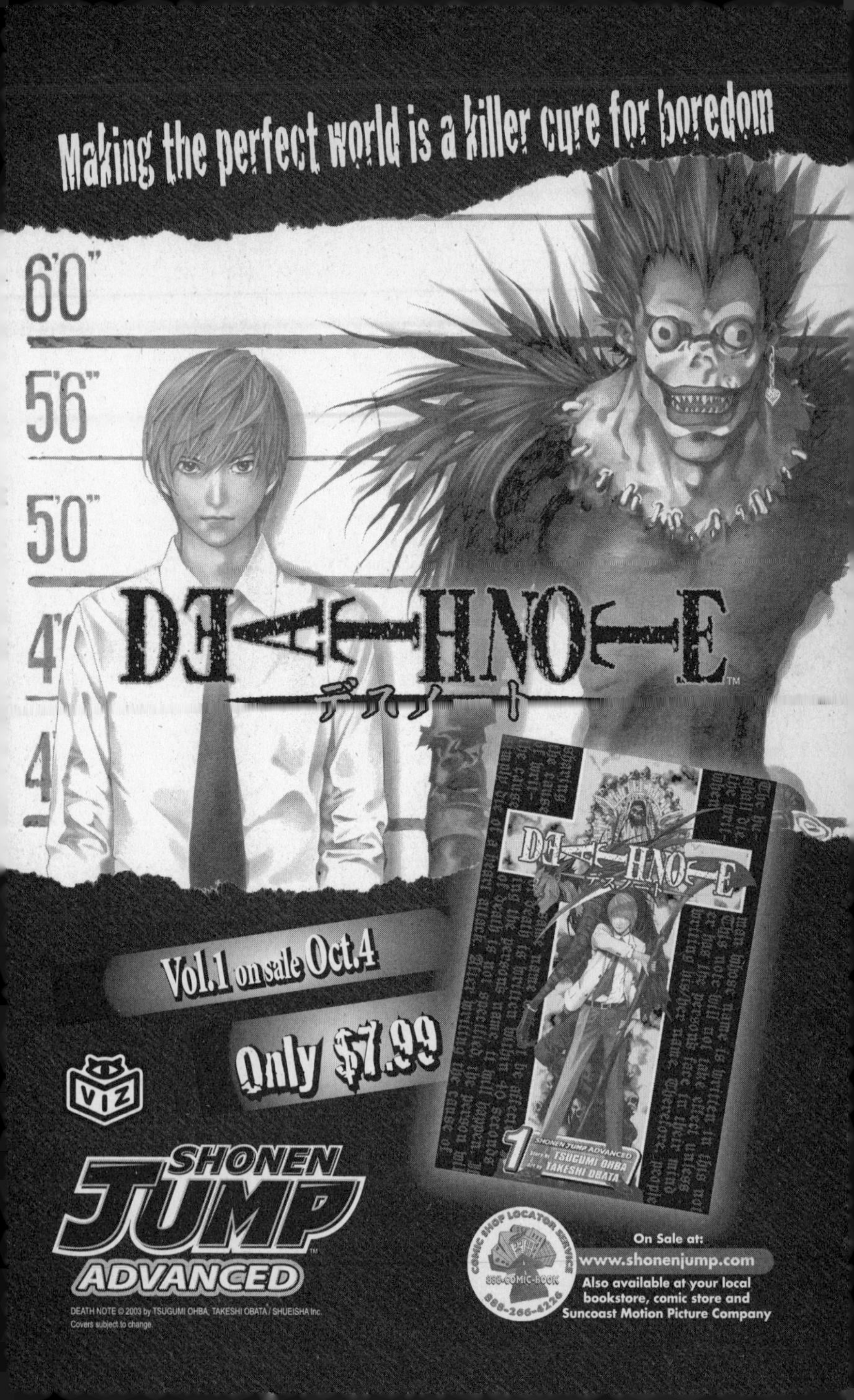

Making the perfect world is a killer cure for boredom
6'0"
5'6"
5'0"
DEATH NOTE™
デスノート
Vol.1 on sale Oct.4
Only $7.99
VIZ
SHONEN JUMP ADVANCED
DEATH NOTE © 2003 by TSUGUMI OHBA, TAKESHI OBATA / SHUEISHA Inc.
Covers subject to change.
COMIC SHOP LOCATOR SERVICE
888-COMIC-BOOK
888-266-4226
On Sale at:
www.shonenjump.com
Also available at your local bookstore, comic store and Suncoast Motion Picture Company

Check us out on the web!

www.shonenjump.com

SHONEN JUMP
THE WORLD'S MOST POPULAR MANGA

COMPLETE OUR SURVEY AND LET US KNOW WHAT YOU THINK!

☐ Please do NOT send me information about VIZ and SHONEN JUMP products, news and events, special offers, or other information.

☐ Please do NOT send me information from VIZ's trusted business partners.

Name: ______________________________

Address: ______________________________

City: ______________ **State:** ________ **Zip:** ______________

E-mail: ______________________________

☐ **Male** ☐ **Female** **Date of Birth (mm/dd/yyyy):** ____/____/________ (**Under 13? Parental consent required**)

1 Do you purchase SHONEN JUMP Magazine?

☐ Yes ☐ No **(if no, skip the next two questions)**

If **YES**, do you subscribe?

☐ Yes ☐ No

If **NO**, how often do you purchase SHONEN JUMP Magazine?

☐ 1-3 issues a year

☐ 4-6 issues a year

☐ more than 7 issues a year

2 Which SHONEN JUMP Graphic Novel did you purchase? (please check one)

☐ Beet the Vandel Buster ☐ Bleach ☐ Dragon Ball

☐ Dragon Ball Z ☐ Dr. Slump ☐ Eyeshield 21

☐ Hikaru no Go ☐ Hunter x Hunter ☐ I"s

☐ Knights of the Zodiac ☐ Legendz ☐ Naruto

☐ One Piece ☐ Rurouni Kenshin ☐ Shaman King

☐ The Prince of Tennis ☐ Ultimate Muscle ☐ Whistle!

☐ Yu-Gi-Oh! ☐ Yu-Gi-Oh!: Duelist ☐ YuYu Hakusho

☐ Other ______________________________

Will you purchase subsequent volumes?

☐ Yes ☐ No

3 How did you learn about this title? (check all that apply)

☐ Favorite title ☐ Advertisement ☐ Article

☐ Gift ☐ Read excerpt in SHONEN JUMP Magazine

☐ Recommendation ☐ Special offer ☐ Through TV animation

☐ Website ☐ Other ______________________________

4 Of the titles that are serialized in SHONEN JUMP Magazine, have you purchased the Graphic Novels?

☐ Yes ☐ No

If **YES**, which ones have you purchased? (check all that apply)

☐ Dragon Ball Z ☐ Hikaru no Go ☐ Naruto ☐ One Piece
☐ Shaman King ☐ Yu-Gi-Oh! ☐ YuYu Hakusho

If **YES**, what were your reasons for purchasing? (please pick up to 3)

☐ A favorite title ☐ A favorite creator/artist ☐ I want to read it in one go
☐ I want to read it over and over again ☐ There are extras that aren't in the magazine
☐ The quality of printing is better than the magazine ☐ Recommendation
☐ Special offer ☐ Other

If **NO**, why did/would you not purchase it?

☐ I'm happy just reading it in the magazine ☐ It's not worth buying the graphic novel
☐ All the manga pages are in black and white unlike the magazine
☐ There are other graphic novels that I prefer ☐ There are too many to collect for each title
☐ It's too small ☐ Other ______________________

5 Of the titles NOT serialized in the Magazine, which ones have you purchased?
(check all that apply)

☐ Beet the Vandel Buster ☐ Bleach ☐ Dragon Ball ☐ Dr. Slump
☐ Eyeshield 21 ☐ Hunter x Hunter ☐ I"s ☐ Knights of the Zodiac
☐ Legendz ☐ The Prince of Tennis ☐ Rurouni Kenshin ☐ Whistle!
☐ Yu-Gi-Oh!: Duelist ☐ None ☐ Other ______________

If you did purchase any of the above, what were your reasons for purchase?

☐ A favorite title ☐ A favorite creator/artist
☐ Read a preview in SHONEN JUMP Magazine and wanted to read the rest of the story
☐ Recommendation ☐ Other

Will you purchase subsequent volumes?

☐ Yes ☐ No

6 What race/ethnicity do you consider yourself? (please check one)

☐ Asian/Pacific Islander ☐ Black/African American ☐ Hispanic/Latino
☐ Native American/Alaskan Native ☐ White/Caucasian ☐ Other

THANK YOU! Please send the completed form to:

VIZ Survey
42 Catharine St.
Poughkeepsie, NY 12601

All information provided will be used for internal purposes only. We promise not to sell or otherwise divulge your information.